On the History and Transmission of Lacanian Psychoanalysis

I0131058

On the History and Transmission of Lacanian Psychoanalysis addresses key questions about the history and transmission of Jacques Lacan's work in North America through discussions with experienced psychoanalysts (who are also trained psychiatrists, psychologists, and psychotherapists).

Chris Vanderwees presents conversations with clinicians about their psychoanalytic formation and about the development of Lacanian psychoanalysis in North America over the past several decades. With oral narrative brought out through the technique of free association, then transcribed and annotated, each discussion is a trace of Vanderwees' encounter with each clinician and the result of collaborative efforts involving speech, writing, translation, and transmission. The conversational tone makes these discussions accessible not only for those already well-versed in Lacan's thinking, but also for anyone discovering his work for the first time. The range of contributions spans both French and English-speaking Canada, the United States, and Mexico.

Complemented by *On the Theory and Clinic of Lacanian Psychoanalysis*, this book of conversations conveys the diversity of historical and pedagogical perspectives on theory and practice as inspired by Lacan's system of thought. It will be of great interest to all psychoanalytic practitioners as well as academics and scholars of psychoanalysis.

Chris Vanderwees, PhD, RP, is a psychoanalyst, registered psychotherapist, and clinical supervisor at St. John the Compassionate Mission in Toronto, Canada.

The Lines of the Symbolic in Psychoanalysis Series

Series Editor:
Ian Parker, *Manchester Psychoanalytic Matrix*

Psychoanalytic clinical and theoretical work is always embedded in specific linguistic and cultural contexts and carries their traces, traces which this series attends to in its focus on multiple contradictory and antagonistic 'lines of the Symbolic'. This series takes its cue from Jacques Lacan's psychoanalytic work on three registers of human experience, the Symbolic, the Imaginary and the Real, and employs this distinctive understanding of cultural, communication and embodiment to link with other traditions of cultural, clinical and theoretical practice beyond the Lacanian symbolic universe. The Lines of the Symbolic in Psychoanalysis Series provides a reflexive reworking of theoretical and practical issues, translating psychoanalytic writing from different contexts, grounding that work in the specific histories and politics that provide the conditions of possibility for its descriptions and interventions to function. The series makes connections between different cultural and disciplinary sites in which psychoanalysis operates, questioning the idea that there could be one single correct reading and application of Lacan. Its authors trace their own path, their own line through the Symbolic, situating psychoanalysis in relation to debates which intersect with Lacanian work, explicating it, extending it and challenging it.

A Lacanian Conception of Populism
Society Does Not Exist
Timothy Appleton

On the History and Transmission of Lacanian Psychoanalysis
Speaking of Lacan
Chris Vanderwees

For more information about the series, please visit https://www.routledge.com/The-Lines-of-the-Symbolic-in-Psychoanalysis-Series/book-series/KARNLOS

"*On the History and Transmission of Lacanian Psychoanalysis* reminds us of what is most revolutionary and subversive about Lacan's psychoanalytic undertaking. Vanderwees traces multiple exploratory routes, mapping Lacanian discourse and practice as it has been utilized and revitalized at diverse institutional, global and historical sites. What emerges, in this careful and collaborative book, is a rich and textured overview, one which reminds us that there is no one Lacan, and that the Lacanian psychoanalytic adventure – like desire itself – necessarily resists domestication, uniformity, or a reduction to any one discourse of mastery."

Derek Hook, PhD, *Associate Professor of Psychology, Duquesne University; author*, Six Moments in Lacan

"In this book, Chris Vanderwees converses with significant figures in Lacanian psychoanalysis whose deeply personal relationships to psychoanalysis are interwoven with a tapestry of Lacanian movements they inspired in North America, Mexico, and Europe. The result is a vibrant collection beautifully rendered in conversations that exceed dialogics at every turn by contextually transmitting the desire of the analyst and the logic of Lacan's formulations against scientific empiricism, the post-Freudian 'institutionalisation' of psychoanalysis, and dogmas of neoliberally inspired therapies. This book serves as an important beacon of alterity, openness, and inspiration – literally the power of interlocution."

Eve Watson, PhD, *psychoanalyst; co-editor of* Critical Essays on the Drive: Lacanian Theory and Practice *(Routledge, 2023)*

"*On the History and Transmission of Lacanian Psychoanalysis*, Chris Vanderwees' masterful collection of interviews with Lacanians is like an all-access, backstage pass to the Coachella of psychoanalysis. They're all here, the most important practitioners in the field today: from the Willy Apollon, Danielle Bergeron, and Lucie Cantin cohort in Québec to the Cormac Gallagher coterie in Ireland, from the Après-Coup New Yorkers to crucial Lacan translator Dan Collins, from knots with Ellie Ragland to welcome appendices on François Peraldi and William Richardson. Certain themes emerge that will engage – or perhaps enrage, or enrapture – readers: the usefulness of interpretation and clinical orthodoxies, the marginal status of Lacan in the Americas, on whether we should read Melanie Klein (or Jung!), and perhaps the most important question: is psychoanalysis dialectics? Only a reading of these dialogues will answer that question, and we are to thank Vanderwees for being a generous, and also rigorous, guide to the psychoanalytic scene today."

Clint Burnham, PhD, *Professor of English, Simon Fraser University*

"What would it mean to transmit our knowledge of psychoanalytic practice? Is this even possible? These questions, which are already questions of theory, of practice, of coherence, of ethics…of the very possibility of psychoanalysis itself, urgently require some response. This marvelous book gathers some such responses and opens up a vital conversation which is essential to the future of the discipline. It is essential reading for anyone and everyone interested in the field, whether as an analyst, a theorist or an analysand."

Calum Neill, PhD, *Associate Professor of Psychoanalysis & Cultural Theory, Edinburgh Napier University*

On the History and Transmission of Lacanian Psychoanalysis

Speaking of Lacan

Chris Vanderwees

R Routledge
Taylor & Francis Group

LONDON AND NEW YORK

Cover image © Getty Images

First published 2024
by Routledge
4 Park Square, Milton Park, Abingdon, Oxon OX14 4RN

and by Routledge
605 Third Avenue, New York, NY 10158

Routledge is an imprint of the Taylor & Francis Group, an informa business.

British Library Cataloguing-in-Publication Data
A catalogue record for this book is available from the British Library.

Library of Congress Cataloging-in-Publication Data
Names: Vanderwees, Chris, author.
Title: On the history and transmission of Lacanian psychoanalysis : speaking of Lacan / Chris Vanderwees.
Description: Abingdon, Oxon ; New York, NY : Routledge, 2024. | Includes bibliographical references and index.
Identifiers: LCCN 2023018309 (print) | LCCN 2023018310 (ebook) | ISBN 9781032346373 (hardback) | ISBN 9781032346366 (paperback) | ISBN 9781003323136 (ebook)
Subjects: LCSH: Lacan, Jacques, 1901-1981. | Psychoanalysis.
Classification: LCC BF109.L23 V36 2024 (print) | LCC BF109.L23 (ebook) | DDC 150.19/5--dc23/eng/20230623
LC record available at https://lccn.loc.gov/2023018309
LC ebook record available at https://lccn.loc.gov/2023018310

ISBN: 978-1-032-34637-3 (hbk)
ISBN: 978-1-032-34636-6 (pbk)
ISBN: 978-1-003-32313-6 (ebk)

DOI: 10.4324/9781003323136

Typeset in Times New Roman
by SPi Technologies India Pvt Ltd (Straive)

Contents

About the Author

Chris Vanderwees, PhD, RP is a psychoanalyst, registered psychotherapist, and clinical supervisor at St. John the Compassionate Mission in Toronto, Canada. He is an affiliate of the Toronto Psychoanalytic Society and a member of the Lacanian School of Psychoanalysis. He is also co-editor (with Kristen Hennessy) of *Psychoanalysis, Politics, Oppression and Resistance* (Routledge, 2022), co-author (with Daniel Adleman) of *Psychoanalysis and the New Rhetoric* (Routledge, 2023), and translator of Betty Milan's *Analyzed by Lacan* (Bloomsbury, 2023).

Series Preface

This is a book to pace carefully in the reading of it, to engage with, and to question and think about in order to do justice to the incredibly wide sweep of arguments that you will find in it. It does justice, in its form and content, to the importance that is accorded history in psychoanalysis, and to the way that psychoanalysis conceptualizes the looping back of the present into the past, both at the level of the individual and at the level of the institutions and traditions that carry psychoanalysis forward. And it does justice to the very specific conceptualization of 'transmission' through historical time and from experienced readers and teachers of Sigmund Freud and Jacques Lacan to the many different kinds of researchers and students who make use of psychoanalytic ideas. Transmission in psychoanalysis, as editor Chris Vanderwees explains in his introduction to the collection he has assembled for us, requires and brings with it a host of other technical concepts. Indeed, these are themselves 'transmitted' along with the manifest material that is spoken of and written about.

The lovingly curated contributions in this book speak to us of their love of psychoanalysis, and they cannot but evoke the concept of 'transference' as a correlate of much transmission in the history of Freud and Lacan's lifework and legacy. That transference, which comes alive in a singular way for each subject engaging in psychoanalysis in the clinic, operates here not as an imaginary dialogical communication of underlying truths but as a symbolic frame in which we can contest what we are being told. In that way, the 'dialogues' that are gifted to us here in *On the History and Transmission of Lacanian Psychoanalysis: Speaking of Lacan* are not so much imaginary as allowing us to grasp the contours of what psychoanalysis revolves around but cannot ever itself finally capture or pin down, the real. That real must, of course, be factored through the imaginary and symbolic registers that make any dialogue and transmission possible, and interpreted, now also by the readers of this book.

What we find in this absorbing and innovative series of conversations on history and transmission in psychoanalysis are many competing and overlapping reflections on the subject matter that also enable us to be in a position to effectively transmit the core ideas to others. This is through a timely transmission of our work that crosses continents and languages in such a way as to encourage us to explore the nature of language as the medium of psychoanalysis itself.

Psychoanalytic clinical and theoretical work circulates through multiple intersecting antagonistic symbolic universes. This series opens connections between different cultural sites in which Lacanian work has developed in distinctive ways, in forms of work that question the idea that there could be a single correct reading and application. The Lines of the Symbolic in Psychoanalysis series provides a reflexive reworking of psychoanalysis that transmits Lacanian writing from around the world, steering a course between the temptations of a metalanguage and imaginary reduction, between the claim to provide a god's-eye view of psychoanalysis and the idea that psychoanalysis must everywhere be the same. And the elaboration of psychoanalysis in the symbolic here grounds its theory and practice in the history and politics of the work in a variety of interventions that touch the real.

Ian Parker
Manchester Psychoanalytic Matrix

Acknowledgements

This project was made possible only through the patience, persistence, and support of all of the clinicians who kindly and generously gave their time for the conversations now available in this book. The inclusion of some conversations could not have been possible without Daniel Wilson, Alireza Taheri, and Marie Hazan, who all helped me with French to English translations. Many thanks go to Ian Parker for his support of this book. Thanks also goes to Susannah Frearson at Routledge for all of her help with this project. I am also grateful to Derek Hook, Eve Watson, Clint Burnham, and Calum Neill, who took time to review this work and provide feedback.

This project was partially completed with the support of the Social Sciences and Humanities Research Council of Canada (SSHRC) while I was a Postdoctoral Fellow under Sharon Sliwinski's supervision in the Faculty of Media and Information Studies at Western University (FIMS). I am grateful to Sharon as well as Susan Knabe at FIMS for their support of my research and teaching during that time.

Before this book could be published, Dr. William (Moe) Robinson passed away in April 2023. I was lucky to be able to have several encouraging meetings and phone conversations with him over the years and hope that the interview included in this book will help us to remember his significant contributions to the psychoanalytic community in Toronto.

I would also like to express my gratitude to MCL for all of her support over the years. I am especially grateful to JH for her kindness and encouragement and also to HJV, who is our *dritë*.

Two conversations are reprinted here with permissions and additional notes, but original references can be found here:

- Vanderwees, Chris. "Free Association, Presence, and Patience: A Conversation with William (Moe) Robinson." *Psychoanalytic Discourse*. 5.1 (2020): 51–70.
- Vanderwees, Chris. "Treating Psychosis in Québec: A Conversation with the Founders of GIFRIC and the 388 [Willy Apollon, Danielle Bergeron, and Lucie Cantin]." *Museum of Dreams*. Ed. Sharon Sliwinski. Trans. Daniel Wilson. 2019. Web.

I am also very fortunate to include three important texts, which are reprinted in the appendix with the support and permissions of Marie Hazan, Mario L. Biera, Sara E. Hassan, and the editors of *The Letter: Irish Journal for Lacanian Psychoanalysis*. Here are the original source citations of these texts:

- Hazan, Marie. "Transmission, filiation et institution psychanalytique: recontre avec François Peraldi." *Filigrane*. 3 (1994): 135–161.
- Muller, John. "In Memory of William J. Richardson, S.J. Notes Toward a Semiotics of Address." *The Letter: Irish Journal for Psychoanalysis*. 65 (2017): 73–87.
- Richardson, William J. "On Heidegger to Lacan – An Interview with William J. Richardson with the participation of Mario L Beira PhD and Sara E Hassan MD." (June 21, 2005; Dublin, Ireland), *Acheronta*, 22 (2005): n. pag. Web.

Introduction

On the Question of Transmission

What do we mean when we speak about the transmission of psychoanalysis or, more specifically, Lacanian psychoanalysis? There are surprisingly few dedicated texts that attempt to wrestle with this question, let alone very much consensus as to what it might actually mean to "transmit" psychoanalytic practice. Literally, "transmission" is defined as an act of communicating information from one person or place to another across an intervening space and through a form of mediation. The prefix "trans" comes from Latin and connotes the sense of a person, place, or thing going across (whether through or beyond) from one state or condition to another, and "mission" literally indicates the act of sending or dispatching. Any transmission is therefore something sent or conveyed somewhere and usually to someone. Transmission has become a common term in Lacanian psychoanalytic discourse, where it refers to the issues at stake in transferring knowledge from teachers to students in psychoanalytic institutions and where it is linked to questions of transference, authority, and identification.

To become a practitioner, formal education in most psychoanalytic institutions (whether Lacanian or otherwise) generally follows Max Etingon's tripartite arrangement, which consists of a personal training analysis, treatment of analysands under supervision, and a didactic, theoretical curriculum.[1] It is a platitude to suggest that psychoanalysis cannot be taught or fully understood from books or supervisors but rather must be experienced directly through a confrontation with one's own subjectivity in a personal analysis. And yet referring to the tripartite educational model, Herbert J. Schlesinger suggests that

> [a]nyone who knows the system intimately…would observe that unlike a stool, the three legs are not of equal size or importance. Whatever the actual contribution of each leg is to the personal and professional growth of the candidate toward becoming a competent psychoanalyst, analytic educators tend to give most weight to the training analysis, next to the supervision, and least to the didactic curriculum.
>
> (135)

DOI: 10.4324/9781003323136-1

If the practice of psychoanalytic treatment is transmitted, the emphasis is not on the didactic curriculum or university discourse but through the analytic discourse that emerges in one's own analytic treatment. As Sigmund Freud stated in his "New Introductory Lectures": "when all is said and done, it is impossible to assimilate analysis without experiencing it personally" (150).

It was Jacques Lacan's assertion regarding the analytic discourse, the analyst's facilitation of the analysand's experience of free association, that "it teaches nothing" since "[t]here is nothing universal about it, which is precisely why it cannot be taught" ("There are Four" 3). In this sense, there is no truth about psychoanalysis that can necessarily be generalized or tailored to suit each person. If we accept that psychoanalysis can be grasped only through the subject's singular and idiosyncratic experience as an analysand, this premise is what led Lacan to conclude that psychoanalysis is therefore "intransmissible" ("Conclusions" 219). Yet transmission quite literally also refers to the hereditary conveyance of particular characteristics or qualities of one organism to its descendants. Here, transmission would be the act of handing down or passing on some inheritance or tradition to one's descendants. Transmission would then become linked to the notion of a lineage of thought and practice. Despite Lacan's insistence that psychoanalysis is not transmissible, surely there remains a kind of knowledge, a set of characteristics, a way of thinking and theorizing, or perhaps even a repeated traumatic kernel that must have been conveyed from one generation to the next so as to maintain at least some consensus or social imaginary regarding what it is that one can identify as "Lacanian." Certainly, Lacanian practitioners continue to undergo their own analyses, lecture in institutions, hold study groups, write in conversation with others, and provide supervision or control analysis to those undergoing psychoanalytic formation. As a result, some ethical traces of this practice must nevertheless be transmitted to another generation despite Lacan's own assertions to the contrary.

This book began with the intention of exploring the transmission of Lacanian psychoanalysis and the history of this transmission through dialogue. I sought to discuss what continues to be relevant about Lacanian psychoanalysis and what radically distinguishes it from other approaches to clinical practice. I also wanted to create conversations about how Lacan's revisionist return to Freud with attention to linguistics evolved in diverse North American contexts. I wanted to know more about what happened to clinical teachings that were so rooted in the French language when they were translated for Anglophones. Further, I wished to shed light on why Lacan's *corpus* continues to capture the attention of academics and clinicians so many years after his death. Engaged in my own clinical practice of listening to unconscious manifestations in discourse, listening alongside patients who are suffering, I wanted to engage in discussions with other clinicians about how such theory could be brought into contemporary conversations about mental health. Given that Lacanian thinking in North America is employed predominantly as a form of university discourse on critical theory (in ways that often seem antithetical to Lacan's teaching), I specifically undertook this project to investigate the importance and diversity of Lacanian psychoanalysis in clinical contexts. I especially wanted to examine how the ethics of this particular psychoanalytic practice has been historically transmitted and redeveloped from the Parisian milieu to various North American cultural scenes.

I envisioned a book of conversations that might emerge from travelling from city to city speaking with psychoanalysts about their clinical backgrounds, their thoughts about Lacanian practice, and their notions about the future of psychoanalysis.[2] I travelled to meet psychoanalytic colleagues and entered into dialogues about how they had previously undertaken projects to transmit something about the Lacanian clinic for another generation in another culture. It began this way until the coronavirus pandemic made travelling and meeting in person rather challenging, if not impractical or impossible. I decided to continue despite limitations, which means that the reader will find that a significant portion of the conversations in this book were conducted at a distance during government lockdowns and stay-at-home orders whether via telephone or virtual platform.

In an attempt to follow the notion of free association as much as possible, I endeavored to initiate each discussion with only a few simple questions but without a defined or predetermined path since I hoped to discover how and what a spontaneous interchange of discourse might reveal directly or indirectly about psychoanalytic transmission. In this sense, I have attempted to present an impression of free association as part of this book's form. For several years, I recorded, transcribed, and edited dozens of conversations with experienced psychoanalysts, who are also trained respectively as psychiatrists, psychologists, and psychotherapists, about their formations, their research interests, their clinical experience, and their understanding of the history and development of Lacanian psychoanalysis in North America over the past several decades.

This book appropriately opens with a conversation about free association with psychiatrist and psychoanalyst William (Moe) Robinson, who was a member of the Stockbridge Lacanian Clinical Forum (a group formed by clinicians at the Austen Riggs Center in Massachusetts) and who taught and trained psychoanalysts in Toronto, Canada for many years. The book then explores the emergence of Lacanian psychoanalysis with experienced clinicians who practice and teach in various regions, including Québec, Toronto, Boston, New York, California, Missouri, and Mexico. I have also included a conversation with Barry O'Donnell about Cormac Gallagher's contributions to psychoanalytic teaching in Ireland since Gallagher's translations enabled many clinicians and academics in the Anglophone world far beyond the Irish context to encounter Lacan's seminars for the first time. This book closes with appendices that include three important texts from members of the Stockbridge Lacanian Clinical Forum: an interview with François Peraldi conducted by Marie Hazan, an interview with William Richardson conducted by Mario Beira and Sara Hassan, and a text written by John Muller in tribute to Richardson's philosophical and psychoanalytic work. Each of these texts speaks to the complexity and challenges of psychoanalytic transmission.

Despite some inevitable circumscription through the editing process, the conversations convey the impression of free-floating and circular discourse to a great extent, but readers will also notice that my questions reflect my own curiosities and continuously evolving interests about particular aspects of psychoanalytic theory and practice. These transcribed and annotated exchanges remain as traces of my encounter with each clinician, each clinician's encounter with me, but are also the result of collaborative efforts involving speech, writing, and translation. The conversations reprinted here have been recreated elaboratively with each analyst for a more readable result but emerged originally through the primary technique of psychoanalysis (that is, freely associated speech with all its limitations). The text's conversational tone hopefully allows these discussions to be accessible not only for those already well versed in Lacan's thinking but also for students or laypersons encountering psychoanalysis for the first time. I hope that collectively these discussions will speak to questions of history, transmission, and the importance of Lacanian psychoanalysis for the myriad challenges that clinicians might face with their patients in the twenty-first century. The supplementary interviews in the appendix have been conducted by others but, I believe, are crucial to understanding the Lacanian movement in this context. I have attempted to revive something of the past in the present so that we might arrive at some *après-coup* when reading these conversations as one monograph. What will have ultimately been said here about the history and transmission of Lacanian psychoanalysis? I will now let the conversations that follow speak for themselves.

Notes

1 Max Etingon (1881–1943) was a Lithuanian-German medical doctor and psychoanalyst who was devoted to Freud and worked to create a structure for formal regulations and parameters related to psychoanalytic education, training, and practice. He was a co-founder of the important Berlin Psychoanalytic Polyclinic and was its president from 1920 to 1933 until the rise of Nazism. Etingon was a strong proponent of the notion that psychoanalysts must first be analyzed in order to practice. For more about the Etingon family, see Wilmers, Mary-Kay (2010).

2 Certainly, there are already excellent books of interviews with psychoanalysts that have been published in the past. Virginia Hunter, for instance, has an excellent book, *Psychoanalysts Talk*, where she presents the same case to many psychoanalysts from divergent schools of thought to explore the differences in clinical approaches. Laurie W. Raymond and Susan Rosbrow-Reich's *The Inward Eye* and Peter L. Rudnytsky's *Psychoanalytic Conversations* cumulatively account for more than two dozen interviews with analysts about their lives, careers, and thoughts about the culture and clinic of psychoanalysis. Sergio Benvenuto and Anthony Molino have also further interviewed an array of analysts for the *European Journal*

of Psychoanalysis and gathered these talks in a collection, *In Freud's Tracks*. While each of these books is an incredible achievement in its own right, none focuses directly on the history or development on Lacanian theory and practice.

Bibliography and Further Reading

Benvenuto, Sergio and Anthony Molino (eds.). *In Freud's Tracks*. Plymouth: Jason Aronson, 2009.

Freud, Sigmund. "New Introductory Lectures on Psycho-Analysis." *The Standard Edition of the Complete Psychological Works of Sigmund Freud*. Ed. James Strachey. London: Vintage and Hogarth, 2001, 1933. 1–182.

Hunter, Virginia. *Psychoanalysts Talk*. New York: Guilford Press, 1994.

Lacan, Jacques. "Conclusions." *Lettres de l'Ecole Freudienne de Paris*. 25 (1979): 219–220, 1978.

Lacan, Jacques. "There Are Four Discourses." *Culture/Clinic*. 1 (2013): 3–4.

Raymond, Laurie W. and Susan Rosbrow-Reich (eds.). *The Inward Eye*. Hillsdale, NJ: Analytic Press, 1997.

Rudnytsky, Peter. *Psychoanalytic Conversations*. Hillsdale, NJ: Analytic Press, 2000.

Schlesinger, Herbert J. "Supervision and the Training Analysis: Repetition or Collaboration?" *Tradition and Innovation in Psychoanalytic Education: Clark Conference on Psychoanalytic Training for Psychologists*. Eds. Murray Meisels and Ester R. Shapiro. New York: Routledge, 1990.

Wilmers, Mary-Kay. *The Etingons: A Twentieth-Century Story*. New York: Verso, 2010.

Chapter 1

Free Association, Presence, and Patience with William (Moe) Robinson

William (Moe) Robinson (1930–2023) was a psychiatrist and a training and supervising analyst of the Toronto Psychoanalytic Society & Institute. He graduated from the Queen's Faculty of Medicine in 1960, received his accreditation as a psychiatrist in 1966 from the College of Physicians and Surgeons of Ontario, and completed psychoanalytic training at the Canadian Psychoanalytic Society in Montreal. Robinson practiced as a psychoanalyst in Toronto for more than forty years. He trained and worked with Robin Hunter, who in 1969 was a psychiatrist appointed as the Director of the Clarke Institute of Psychiatry (later the Canadian Association of Mental Health). Later, he served as Director of the Toronto Institute of Psychoanalysis between 1991 and 1993. Robinson was responsible for training and supervising many psychoanalysts of the International Psychoanalytic Association in Toronto throughout his career but retired from practice in 2014. For many years in Toronto, he and Richard (Rick) Simpson led a reading group (later directed by Mavis Himes), "Speaking of Lacan," which was supported by their connections with the Stockbridge Lacanian Clinical Forum (led by John Muller and William Richardson), with Après-Coup in New York City (led by Paola Mieli), and with Cormac Gallagher in Dublin, Ireland, who was an early translator of many of Jacques Lacan's Seminars to English. I spoke with Dr. Robinson at the Toronto Psychoanalytic Society & Institute on March 12, 2019.

Chris Vanderwees: What are your thoughts about free association?
Moe Robinson: Well, we would have to think about the "free" in free association. What is free? What does it mean to be free? I remain very dedicated to Freud, Lacan, free association, and the unconscious. Have you read Freud's paper on [Luca] Signorelli? This is one of the first examples of parapraxis that Freud presents. He can't recall the name of Signorelli, the painter, but substitutes other names in trying to remember. Freud writes down all of his

DOI: 10.4324/9781003323136-2

associations and it produces a lot of material. It is the kind of exercise you can get lost in and maybe it turns up something, but maybe it doesn't turn up anything at all. Then what good is it? We'd have to try it in order to find out.[1]

I am very grateful for my own analyst. I don't think I would have ever survived without him. It was a remarkable experience because my analyst was a very patient guy. I will say that one of the most important interpretations my analyst made in six years was that he said, "Oh, is it?" and then bang. It changed everything in my life simply because he said, "Oh, is it?" He said it at the right time. He was intruding in my own narcissistic structure. I was saying, "Oh boy, this is really important," and all he said was, "Oh, is it?" I knew he was saying, "who the hell do you think you are?" It has always stuck with me. Keep in mind that interpretation can be something that you don't expect to happen.

There is an important paper on transference by Juan-David Nasio. He is a very straightforward guy. He says that the transference is something that goes on in the unconscious between the patient and the analyst. It is unconscious in both participants.[2] Most people do not think of it in this way. Many analysts are listening to the patient, think they hear the transference, and deal with it, but Nasio did not think of it this way. He was cautioning us to be careful because it is more than that. The transference is in you and the patient at the same time. Sometimes it will click. There is a case about a patient in analysis who wanted to leave early in one session. So, she left. Afterwards, the analyst walked out into the hallway. The patient was standing there waiting for the elevator. The analyst saw her eyes and couldn't believe it. Why in the world did he see her eyes? What emerged later in this analysis was that she had a picture of her mother over the top of her bed, looking down at her. For the analyst to see her eyes at the elevator told him something, but he had no idea about it. He just knew it was important. It emerged over the course of the analytic work that the patient was always under the mother's look when she went to bed every night. It is that kind of surprise that matters. It is not that someone tells you how to act as an analyst. It is the waiting that matters a great deal. It is a moment of change that neither he nor the patient had thought about consciously. It happened.

I had a patient who was a very bright, successful, and intelligent woman in the world. She and her husband were on vacation in Algonquin Park in a little cabin on an island. She was looking out at the marsh in front of them. There was a bird, an egret, standing on one leg there. She thought, "Oh, that's Dr. Robinson." This appeared to her in a dream that resulted from seeing the bird in the marsh. She had the thought that I was the bird. This said something that she hadn't been able to say before, but she said it in an associative moment after looking at a bird in a marsh. She dreamt about this bird, but she didn't think of me as the bird at the time. It's that kind of thing that I think matters so much in the work you do as an analyst. This is why you sit back and wait because you have no idea what is going to come or how it's going to come. This means everything under the sun to me.

When my wife died, I said to myself, "Now, what am I going to do?" I said, "Well, I'll just go back to work." Mostly, what you are told in analysis is that when death occurs you have to back off someplace. I said, "I'm not going to back off. I'm just going to go to work and they can say what they like." Every patient felt so relieved that I didn't pretend I was some big guy who could just go look after himself. I was hurt by what happened to me, and I could bring it there and let them say something. Every one of them had felt a tremendous relief. They told me their thoughts about my loss. That is where this point with my patient came up when she said, "I want to tell you that you were the bird." She sent me notes. All of my patients sent me notes and things like that. I've still got them. In the note, she said to me, "I know you were the bird." It would have never come out if I hadn't gone back to work and allowed my patients to say what they had to say about my loss. This might be very controversial in terms of some of the training you get. You're not supposed to bring things like that into your patient's life. Whereas sometimes it is important for your patients to see you as a human being, not as some distant creature who isn't there as a person or as some smart guy who knows it all. You are there as a person, an ordinary person. This means a great deal to me.

As I have gotten older, I think of everybody as just a person on the street, including the analyst and the patient. You're not a big shot. You're just a person like they are. Much of the teaching tends to push you to some specialty in your mind when, in fact, no matter what you know, you are just a person. I used to have a fantasy about my analyst. My office was downtown on at the corner of Bloor Street and Bedford Road. There was a subway shop where I used to have a sandwich. I always had the fantasy that I would walk around the corner one day and see my analyst crouching down begging. I thought, "No, that's not an insult." It said to me somehow, "He's everything. He is a guy who knows something and could be helpful, but he could also be a beggar." These kinds of thoughts allow you to open your mind up to see where you're going. Somebody else can't tell you what that is. You have to let it float up in you somehow. This is partly what the free associative world is really all about. It includes you as well as everything else you do. It takes you back to some simple reality that is very important.

CV: The beggar is often asking for change…

MR: Well, that's why patients are there, but something in them doesn't necessarily want to change, which is why we have to listen. You look like this on the outside, but you feel all sorts of stuff that you wouldn't dare let yourself think even though you might want to. It is everyday thinking about the work that is so important. It isn't written in a book someplace. It's just you. Your patient is just herself, you are just yourself, and you both let the thoughts go back and forth. I don't think the teaching says that enough to students. You're just somebody. There is a sense in training programs that you are really learning all this important stuff to be really good analysts. You can know all the world of things, but if you can't experience yourself as fragile and as nobody like your patients, I don't think you'll do the work properly. What about your own experience? Do you think about that?

CV: I think so. Some of my work at a local mission in Toronto may fall into this line of thinking. The sessions I have with people are analytic, but I also try to sit and eat with people, to just be with the people who are there.

MR: Couldn't that be part of an analysis, that is, to sit and eat with someone? It is in the depths of complexity, but it creates something in you that lets you be the listener. Be patient with yourself. When the analyst went out to the elevator, he didn't expect to see the patient's eyes. He just did. It told him something. You're interested in Lacan? Have you paid any attention to the signifier? What are you getting from that?

CV: I try to make use of the signifier especially when I hear the patient's repetition of a particular or peculiar word. It may be a word that is a little out of place or stands out. I might ask about that word or phrase and what it brings to mind.

MR: It will be something that is odd that is there, but it is more than that. The signifier that is a chain of signifiers is nothing, except it is part of a chain. You may have no idea where it is coming from, but it is there. It speaks. It gets you. It's there. It is important to let something be not an intellectual exercise but an event. What you have just said isn't not right, but it is that you are trying to think about something, which isn't the same as when the signifier goes bang.

I have written a paper, "Sticking with Lacan," which touches on [Ernest] Hemingway's "The Snows of Kilimanjaro." At the beginning of this story, something is going on at the peak of Kilimanjaro in the snow. It emerges in the story. As it finishes, you get to know what it is. There is a dead, frozen leopard in the snow at the top of this mountain in Africa. What is that dead leopard doing there? Hemingway must have lived with some horrible idea of not knowing what death was. His father committed suicide, his brother did, and Hemingway was sure he was going to kill himself. In our work, death is a crucial piece of business. We have to let ourselves think about it, not to think we know what death is, but to get a sense of something showing up.

CV: It usually takes a significant amount preparatory of work to help someone get to a place of free association. In most contemporary mental health clinics, free association is not even really practiced or encouraged. How do you imagine creating a space where someone would feel comfortable enough to say anything that comes to mind?

MR: The notion of free association is so exceedingly complex, so necessary, and yet so simple. It is also impossible for most people. Even when you are talking, I can hear there is something intellectual that you are looking at and thinking about. Free association is a happening. Nobody knows where it is coming from. It just happens. It is this happening that matters. It is hard work to lie down on the couch or sit there and talk, letting things just happen. The waiting and the silence of the analyst [are] part of this. Free association has to speak to you as something that will happen. You can't make it happen. You also never know where it is going.

In Freud's paper on Signorelli, you see the associative things that he talking about. He is going all over the place. He does all of this historical work, but this still doesn't help him to remember the artist's name. The important thing is to feel that there is something going on in here. None of us really know[s] about it. We have to just let it happen. It's not easy, as you were saying, but it is important for you to see if you can let it happen. When it is happening, you do not know where it is going to go. You don't know. It will take you somewhere, but you don't know where in advance. You have to give in to it. Can you give in? You'll have to try because you won't want to. Nobody wants to free-associate. People want to make a decision because they think they know, but this is not analysis.

CV: You mentioned the "free" of free association. Could you say more about this?

MR: Well, what do you think about it?

CV: There can be something liberating about the experience of free-associating during an analysis. Free association certainly allows me to feel that I am getting somewhere or that I am revealing something to myself, a bit that I didn't know was there. As you have described, there can be a surprise, an event, a happening. Free association also may allow for a moment to occur where it leaves me thinking about what happened, but I do not know what happened exactly.

MR: It is also "Who are you?" This is crucial because this is really what we want to know. We really want to know who we are. We think we're some recognizable creatures who know who they are, but if you free-associate you'd be surprised....Lacan says that desire is the desire of the Other, which means that the other is functional in the desire....You may forget something and try so hard to remember it. The only way it appears again is if you say, "Okay, to hell with it. I'll forget it and do something else." It shows up when you give up on it. Your desire to remember is struggling with something deep down inside you that says, "Okay, I want to remember, too, but I'm not going to do it when you want me to. I'll go ahead and do it by myself." There is something in us that wants to remember but can't remember. We all do this all the time. We forget and yet we know perfectly well what we are forgetting. That which we have forgotten may show up later all by itself because it wants to show up. It wants its want to be matched as much as your conscious wants for it to happen. There is a battle going on. There is no sense talking about the desire as being in the desirer. It is also in the desired. We don't like to know things like that.

There is need, demand, and desire. These are very different things, but desire is the desire of the Other. It is functioning at a verbal, mental, discursive, linguistic level someplace. It isn't that I want something or I am something, but I would like something. There is a delicacy in saying that there is something I like.

If you are interested in becoming an analyst to engage with this kind of thinking and listening, you have to let these things fiddle around within you. Lacan said that desire is the desire of the Other. He said it a long time ago, but I think everyone should ask questions about this. What is he really talking about? What does he mean when he says desire is the desire of the Other? Well, that's a good question and it isn't theoretical. Even though there is all of this Lacanian theory, it is more than that. Going deeper into a therapeutic world might be more complicated than you think.

Whenever I have conversations that I love with friends, I always apologize to them. Once these thoughts start moving in me, I think it is important to struggle with them on both sides. Maybe you are saying to yourself, "What the hell is he talking about?" What do you think? What are your associations?

CV: In terms of desire being the desire of the Other, this is the crucial position that the analyst must take up in order to be the cause of desire for the analysand. The analyst must primarily occupy the position of the question to open things up.

MR: How does he or she do that?

CV: The analyst might do this by not fulfilling the analysand's demand or by not answering the patient's questions all the time. Perhaps it is always better to ask the analysand where the question is coming from.

MR: I have another thought about this. I think about it all the time. I think about my analyst and how he saved my soul. There is something in the analytic process that is presence. It is the presence of the analyst. The patient knows perfectly well that he or she is there with you. You feel his or her presence with you. You can't do analytic work as a patient unless you have some good sense that your analyst is there. We would have to wonder what is "there" and what is "presence"? Does anybody know what presence is?

CV: How do you think of presence?

MR: It is a feeling that you know perfectly well. It is the feeling that whoever is with you is with you. It is to acknowledge the being-with. This is crucial, but it is something that isn't stated. It is just there. Presence is a word that has to be given some thought within yourself to know when you feel it and when you don't. Presence is beyond the appearance of being present. This is crucial for anyone's analysis for both the analyst and the patient. Your analyst is there with you.

CV: This sounds different from attachment concepts like containment or holding. Is there something distinct about presence?

MR: Isn't there? I think there is. You can feel it with people and not feel it with people. You know perfectly well something is going on. This is a very important part of psychoanalysis. I don't think you can free-associate unless the presence of your analyst lets you feel you can let go. This presence allows you to literally disappear into a free association. You have got to be able to let that happen in an analysis because most of the world we live within ourselves is not free association. Thoughts are usually stuck together more consciously. In this regard, free association could be thought of as dangerous because you have no idea where it is going. Yet to do free association in an analysis, you have to feel it's okay and that its safe, but you don't always feel that way. It is an experience. There is this odd presence in yourself that is trying to get somewhere. You can't do it by yourself. A good analyst is always there with you.

I am thinking of a person with very early trauma. People with very early trauma can be almost impossible to treat, but it is absolutely necessary to try. In the simplest sense, early trauma does not have any language. Psychoanalysis is about trying to put it to language. Another version of analysis is what you haven't said yet. This is the truth. You haven't said it yet. If you are in analysis, it is to say it someday. Lacan is all about language – the unconscious is structured like a language. This is why people get preoccupied with him in the first place. Language is so essential. The trouble is that if you can read Lacan and only read every tenth word, you will be a lot better off. You have to toss aside his monumental narcissism and just get down to reading what he is saying, which is not easy.

To be free is in itself only a kind of notion. If you get free, where are you going? Are you going somewhere or nowhere? Is it freedom to do what? There is freedom in God and nature. I would listen to my patients and hope that they could find that freedom through talking. It is there someplace. If you can listen to nothing else that I say, just let the utter complexity of this process speak to you. The complexity is crucial and will never go away. People will teach you that you make an interpretation and the patient will respond, but it doesn't work that way. We talk about the signifier. It just pops up. Suddenly, it is there somehow.

I'm no philosopher, but one of the things I have read is [Martin] Heidegger's *What is Called Thinking?*[3] It is a fascinating piece, but what really interests me is the word "calls." It is as if thinking happens because something is calling it to think. In the Heideggerian notion, perhaps the signifier shows up, but then something speaks inside you. The thinking starts to move in the process because something is calling for it to happen, asking it to think. The analytic work calls for something. The word "calls" has a depth because the call wants something but for a multitude of different reasons. It wants something from you but also recognition that it is there.

There is also the notion of the letter, which intrigues me, too. Of course, the letter carries the signifier. The letter itself is a serious notion.

CV: How do you understand the distinction between the letter and the signifier?

MR: The letter is always carrying something that is behind something else. It has some sense of being there and causing some necessity, but the signifier that the letter carries actually does something. The letter is not just a letter like X, Y, Z, but rather the letter is a carrier of a whole process in language. There is something present that isn't speaking for itself but gives the ability of other things to speak. Psychoanalysis is also being there while allowing something else to happen. It is in the transference, which is here and there and also not there. The letter is right there before anything ever happened, carrying the signifier.

CV: How do you make sense of the idea of the letter always arriving at its destination?

MR: Well, there is a lot written about that. Does the letter always arrive at its destination? Does it or doesn't it? Some people say yes and others say no. You must have studied the letter. What did you think while studying?

CV: I am recalling Lacan's discussion of the purloined letter in the Edgar Allan Poe story.[4] If we are thinking of analysis, perhaps the analysand speaks a word that repeats over the course of treatment. Maybe the analyst highlights this particular word, or the analysand hears something they have spoken out loud differently than when it was previously just a thought in the mind. It will be a word or a phrase from somewhere, but perhaps the analysand doesn't know what it means. It has been sent to them from somewhere, but the analysand may not be sure how to place it or how to open up the letter to see what is inside. It requires more talking and thinking to get to the bottom of it. In a sense, all speech in analysis might be understood as a being addressed not only to the analyst but also and especially to oneself where this speech will be heard differently on arrival, if it ever arrives or gets there.

MR: Does it always get there? It is a bit like Freud trying to find Signorelli's name. The associations spread out, but it is a matter of always working with the associative connection in its inordinate historical complexities. The letter is there, carrying the signifier. Why do ships cross the ocean? Well, because the ocean is there. The analyst is not doing some specific thing but is there in a very necessary and present way.

CV: The concept of the letter has a wonderful polyvalence to it. There is the letter that we mail or post but also the letter as the character of the alphabet.

MR: You have to ask yourself why is it the same word for both cases. Doesn't the letter carry something? You don't get a letter that hasn't got something in it.

CV: One example comes to mind of an analysand who told me, "I was a banker who had some success, but I am tired of the bank and all of the banking." Now, over the course of treatment, what he really desired to do was to bake, to become a baker, and carry on with baking. I couldn't help but hear the one letter difference between baker and banker. I asked him about it, but we did not get very far since it wasn't his wish to explore it further. Perhaps I asked the question too early or provided an interpretation that did not resonate with him. I am assuming, but this person may have felt I trivialized something.

MR: He may have run away from that one, but what you said mattered. It always depends on what you said at the time you said it. Sometimes, our constructions or interpretations can just run up some defensive operation the minute we say them to the analysand. Of course, this is why we wait. We have to wait for the analysand to bring it to the session through talking and associating. You have to let it float and free-associate. You might not get the answer. The letter did not yet arrive at its destination in your example.

CV: What brought you to a Lacanian way of working in psychoanalysis?

MR: I was connected with a woman who knew a Training Analyst in Buffalo, New York. They were both presenting at the University at Buffalo some version of Lacan. We had never heard of Lacan. We had no idea who he was. So, I went to Buffalo. What struck me was that there were lots of professors at this presentation. There were two lovely women who suddenly got together and started singing in the middle of the meeting. It wasn't part of the presentation. They just did it. They were singing in a beautiful way, a classical music. I started to wonder and ask questions about this whole Lacan thing. Something about psychoanalysis was stuck in me. I was becoming a Training Analyst at that point. Lacan opened up the whole notion of language, the study of language. He made it a big theory. Something began to emerge that I had never experienced before, which pushed me.

If you ask a question, it begins to move something. You start to follow it along. I started my university work in Western Ontario. I took a business administration course. I sat in the course and didn't know what they were talking about. I couldn't stay in that, so I got out of there. I left Western. I thought, "maybe I'll become a doctor." I didn't think I could be a doctor to save my soul, but I thought I'd try. I went to Queen's University, but I had to create the possibilities of applying. First, I had to go back and take high school science courses because I hadn't taken them before. When I was finally in the undergraduate program, one of the big surprises was a course that I took on philosophy. I got so anxious in that course because I never knew people thought things like that. I got so anxious that I couldn't stay in the course. It had never occurred to me that people would think like philosophers do. I also took an American literature course, where I discovered Hemingway. I fell in love with Hemingway. It really grabbed me, sparked something. I also took an experimental psychology course. It was amazing to me. A professor of mine, Walter Cohen, would sit at the front of the class on the table. I used to think, "How can this brilliant guy with a PhD in the university sit on the table like this at the front of the class?" This moved me. I thought maybe I could move into a world like education and philosophy where ordinary people can do things. I was lucky to get into Queen's University.

By the time I got to Queen's, I knew that I wanted to become a doctor, a psychiatrist. I knew it was what I wanted to do because I suddenly became aware that talking was something that people did to feel better. Back then, we had psychiatrists who were all very interested in talking and the talking cure. There was something in my interactions with them, little moments that meant so much to me. We were speaking of the letter. There must have been some letter that I carried for years, but I didn't know what to do with it. I began to think about it more through reading Hemingway and Poe. It really fascinated me that words could do something. This was an amazing discovery for me. People could talk about what was wrong with them and get better. It's still in me. It amazes me. We learn all these Freudian and Lacanian theories, but all of these theories are all trying to describe the struggle that is going on inside. Psychoanalysis is about the struggle of trying to find a way to speak.

CV: I am attracted to psychoanalysis as a counterintuitive way of thinking, but I always had trouble with the notion of interpretation. Interpretations pin things down and can close discussions. Susan Sontag has an essay, for instance, called "Against Interpretation," where she writes about interpretation as a kind of dissection, evisceration of the text or of speech. Interpretation can be aggressive.[5] Clinical Lacanian psychoanalysis seems different to me. It is more about a position of the question, of opening things up, of non-understanding, and of non-knowledge. It is perhaps a practice of following the letter or the thread.

MR: Thread is a word that sticks with the letter. You will have your own words that will tell you something. This is important.

CV: Since retirement, do you find that your way of thinking about the clinic has opened up to everyday kinds of life?

MR: I am very dedicated more and more to simplicity where theoretical thought and everyday life go side by side. I have been able to move towards simplicity, but it does not mean I have lost the theoretical foundation. When you pay attention to simplicity, you may begin to realize the massive expanse of the unconscious. You have to accept that it is more than anybody can understand. This is what is in all of us. The complexity of the spread of theory intrigues me. For instance, the only reason Freud begins free-associating is because he couldn't remember the name of the painter, Signorelli. So, Freud writes his associative world and he couldn't get far with it, but there it was. If you are an analyst, it is not about being a particular theorist. Psychoanalysis opens a world that you can never completely understand, but it is there. This is what is absolutely crucial.

    During my training as a psychiatrist, I had to be on call at nights in the hospital. I was a resident. One night, a woman came. She had to be admitted because she was having a psychotic episode. What has stuck with me ever since was that I can remember her because she told me that she ate a whole jar of olives the night before she came to the hospital. I think about this every time I make a martini with olives. I think, "Gee, what the hell did she do that for? Were the olives an attempt to make her feel better? Should I have done some olive tests on psychosis to see what was going on?" It always left me with some fascination.

    I am still fascinated that words can help people feel better. It is still unbelievable to me. One may believe the therapeutic structure of our inner world, but it is not like a cut on the arm or appendicitis. The words carry something that we could never have believed or thought before. This intrigue never goes away for me, but you also develop into a person who nobody believes. People couldn't care less about psychoanalysis. They will think you are trying to make something up because they don't want to know. Nevertheless, you stick with it. As I get older, I continue to analyze my dreams every night. Believe me, I have discovered somebody way back down inside me that I never knew existed, a fractured creature. I pay attention to my dreams and see how they move into everyday life. The analysis of my own dreams is about my everyday life but also about the depth of being that lives in my everyday life.

CV: I also wanted to speak more about the contemporary, short-term, quick-fix approaches to mental health in North America like CBT [cognitive behavioral therapy] or mindfulness, where there seems to be no place for dreaming or the dream. Jacques-Alain Miller has actually referred to CBT as a form of auto-coercion since this form of psychotherapy frequently requires that the patient conform to a particular program and the language of that program.[6] Therapy is programmed, manualized, reduced to life coaching, psychoeducation, and other cognitive approaches to conscious thought. There is little or no acknowledgement of the unconscious in these treatments. A supposed expert assigns worksheets and tells a person how to manage their symptoms. An approach that encourages the patient to speak about a dream or whatever comes to mind seems so antithetical to assigning homework and symptom-tracking sheets to a patient. Asking about a dream is so subjective, so personal, and potentially full of meaningfulness. Despite the theoretical complexity, what remains so important about psychoanalysis is the simplicity involved in listening very attentively, which can allow for patients to speak their inner world and to experience some surprise in what has been said. The person hears something that comes from himself or herself that they did not know they knew. In Lacanianism, it is not the clinician who knows. If anyone knows, it is the patient who knows. Patients are the experts on their own experience. We have to allow the person to speak what they know to help unravel or restore something very personal that cannot be generalized or programmed. Many of the people that initially begin to see me in the clinic for consultations do not even know what to do with the openness to speech, Freud's fundamental rule of whatever comes to mind. People who have been in the system for a while have gotten so used to diagnoses, pharmaceuticals, goal-setting, and short-term and cognitively driven work that they are not even used to being listened to. What do you think the future will be for psychoanalysis?

MR: Well, it may go down the drain, but that does not mean our experience is irrelevant. Our cultural world is totally different now. Everything is about money. People think explanations and practicality are all that matter. As a psychoanalyst, you have to stick with your thoughts. The thoughts are there and they speak. It will always keep speaking to you as long as you let it open up in a way that it will not stop opening up. You'll go through endless therapeutic versions of what life is about.

I'm thinking about my wife and I when we lived up north. We were having this big fight. We were frustrated with each other. It was nighttime. I went out on the porch and looked at the sky. I thought it was a beautiful night with stars everywhere. I thought, "Who the hell do we think we are? We are just a piece of dust in the universe." I went and told my wife, "We need to stop all this fighting. We are just a piece of dust in the universe." We got it together. It really meant something to me that I could be a piece of dust. The stars spoke to me. Every time I look at them now, they say the same thing. Every night, the stars are out. Analysis is about investigating some of these kinds of strange associations inside. It is worth far more than people know. Analysis can be about all the theoretical complexity, but it can also be very simple.

CV: What about simplicity between the analyst and the analysand?

MR: Every now and then, something goes click. A decent interpretation will be said at the right time in the right way. It's got to be straightforward and simple. An interpretation is not a piece of education to the patient. The interpretation occurs when something goes click for the analysand. Even though there is so much theoretical complexity, it may help very much to be straightforward and listen. We are not taught often enough in our training to just sit back, listen, and be patient. We must have patience with patients. You have no idea what is coming. You might have some little idea, but you'll have to wait for it to speak. You'll hear it. You'll know what it is when it speaks. It is about letting it open up until something clicks.

Notes

1 Readers can find Freud's example of forgetting the name of Luca Signorelli (c. 1450–1523), the Italian renaissance painter, in his 1898 paper, "The Psychical Mechanisms of Forgetfulness," as well as his expansion on this paper, which may be found in his 1901 publication of *The Psychopathology of Everyday Life*.

2 Nasio suggests that "*the analytic transference is equivalent to the unconscious*, they are homeomorphic in the same way that two systems correspond with each other in every point. Which is a way of saying that *the unconscious and the transference relationship are one and the same thing at the moment of the event*. There is transference between analyst and analysand only when the unconscious arises, unique, as a conjunction of the two partners, as well inside as outside the analyst's office, and in another time. The unconscious and transference exist only in the rareness of an hour when one of them speaks without knowing" (410–411).

3 Heidegger, Martin. *What is Called Thinking*. Trans. J. Glenn Gray. New York: Harper & Row, 1968.

4 Lacan, Jacques. "Seminar on 'The Purloined Letter.'" 1966. *Écrits*. Trans. Bruce Fink. New York: W.W. Norton & Company, 2006. 6–51.

5 Sontag, Susan. "Against Interpretation." *Against Interpretation and Other Essays*. New York: Picador, 1961. 3–15.

6 Jacques-Alain Miller writes in a "Note" on Lacan's Seminar XXIII that "the renewed interest in Lacanian studies…has effectively been sparked by the latter-day promotion of various methods, as harmful as they are brisk and simple-minded, of induced mental auto-coercion (CBT)" (138).

Bibliography and Further Reading

Freud, Sigmund. "The Psychical Mechanism of Forgetfulness." *The Standard Edition of the Complete Psychological Works of Sigmund Freud, Volume III (1893–1899): Early Psychoanalytic Publications*. Ed. and Trans. James Stachey. London: Vintage & The Hogarth Press, 2001a. 287–297.

Freud, Sigmund. *The Standard Edition of the Complete Psychological Works of Sigmund Freud, Volume VI: The Psychopathology of Everyday Life (1901)*. Ed. and Trans. James Stachey. London: Vintage & The Hogarth Press, 2001b.

Miller, Jacques-Alain. "Note." *The Sinthome: The Seminar of Jacques Lacan, Book XXIII*. 2005. Ed. Jacques Lacan, Trans. A.R. Price. New York: Polity Press, 2016. 137–138.

Nasio, Juan-David. "The unconscious, the transference, and the psychoanalyst's interpretation: A Lacanian view." *Psychoanalytic Inquiry: A Topical Journal for Mental Health Professionals*. 4.3 (1984): 401–411.

Sontag, Susan. "Against Interpretation." *Against Interpretation: And Other Essays*. New York: Picador, 1961. 3–15.

Chapter 2

On Cormac Gallagher's Translation of Lacanian Psychoanalysis in Ireland with Barry O'Donnell

Barry O'Donnell, PhD, is Director of Psychotherapy Programs in the School of Medicine at University College Dublin (UCD). He is also Director of the School of Psychotherapy at St. Vincent's University Hospital (SVUH). He practices psychoanalysis, provides clinical supervision, and publishes regularly in the psychoanalytic field. He is a member of the Psychological Society of Ireland (PSI) and the British Psychological Society (BPS, Chartered Psychologist status). He is a founding member of the Irish School for Lacanian Psychoanalysis (ISLP). O'Donnell has been in analysis with Cormac Gallagher over more than two decades.[1] Gallagher co-founded and was the first Director of the School of Psychotherapy at SVUH (1984–2006). He is a Lacanian psychoanalyst. This conversation was recorded on October 19, 2019.

Barry O'Donnell:	So, you're working on a project?
Chris Vanderwees:	I am trying to gather something of the history that has not yet been written about the transmission and translation of Lacanian psychoanalysis from France to Canada and the United States but also more broadly to the English-speaking world. When I first began reading [Jacques] Lacan years ago, Cormac Gallagher's translations were some of the first I had encountered. Could you describe something about Cormac Gallagher's influence on psychoanalysis in Ireland?
BOD:	You had originally written to Cormac Gallagher, who asked me to speak with you. There is no question but that his work and his action led to the development of Lacanian psychoanalysis in Ireland. Before Cormac Gallagher's work here in Ireland, the Irish Psycho-Analytic Association (IPAA) had been set up by Jonathan Hanaghan in the early 1940s.[2] There is no question but that Cormac Gallagher introduced something very new to psychoanalysis in Ireland, such as it was. Through his

DOI: 10.4324/9781003323136-3

work, psychoanalysis found its way into a major teaching hospital, a psychiatric service and university degree programs in UCD and the independent LSB College [now Dublin Business School (DBS) School of Arts]. Therefore, any discussion of psychoanalysis in Ireland needs to accord a central place to the work of Cormac Gallagher.

There have been other practitioners who have brought psychoanalysis back to Ireland after training elsewhere. One such practitioner was Tom McGrath, an impressive and important psychoanalyst who trained in Vienna and died far too young.[3] Another significant figure was Gallagher's co-founder of the School of Psychotherapy, UCD Professor of Psychiatry, Noel Walsh. Also to be considered would be the work of TCD [Trinity College, Dublin] Professor of Psychiatry Michael Fitzgerald. However, if you want to identify someone who really galvanized and got people interested and engaged in encountering psychoanalysis in Ireland so that we can say that there is a psychoanalytic 'scene' in Ireland, one has to identify Cormac Gallagher as that person.

We are actually in the final stages of producing the 68th issue of our journal, *The Letter Irish Journal for Lacanian Psychoanalysis*. It gathers the proceedings of a conference from last November [2018] that paid tribute to the work of Cormac Gallagher.[4] Not by chance, the topic was the question of the transmission of psychoanalysis and the symptom of the psychoanalytic group. What is it about the psychoanalytic group that makes it so difficult to work together to cultivate the effective transmission of this field? People attended from far and wide.[5] One consensus that emerged was that in order to address and handle the question of the psychoanalytic group, you must have in mind Lacan's teaching of the non-existence of the sexual relationship. In the editorial for the issue, I write about Gallagher and his work, about what he achieved in launching a psychoanalytic group that has had its difficulties and differences. It is as a result of his efforts that there is psychoanalytic work active in Ireland. One major tangible form of Gallagher's work are his translations, which are available on his website.[6] He has translated 19 of the 27 years of Lacan's seminars.

We also have a number of psychotherapy programs at UCD. Cormac Gallagher and psychiatrists Noel Walsh and Mary Darby founded the School of Psychotherapy at SVUH in 1984. UCD awards a master's degree in psychoanalytic psychotherapy for those who go through the program. It started off as a psychoanalytic program and it continues to be based on the work of Freud and Lacan. We tell prospective students when they contact us with an interest in the program that whether they know it or not they are expressing an interest in choosing to enter their own analysis and in reading the work of Freud and Lacan. We work on the principle that you cannot grasp psychoanalysis unless you are in analysis. Therefore, in order to have any chance of getting some sense of what Freud and Lacan were saying, students are required to be in their own analysis. This requirement was there from the beginning with Gallagher, Darby, and Walsh. It is not because we expect a student "learns" anything in an analysis – in the academic sense. Arguably, the opposite: an analysis is an encounter with the limits of one's own subjectivity and with its division, with our fundamental position as subjects who do not want to know the foundations of our singular subjective being. Without this component of an analysis, the program would become too easily caught in the university discourse or the master's discourse of erudition and interesting ideas. We very much privilege and emphasize the importance of the analysis.

In the 1990s, some graduates of the School of Psychotherapy (TSOP), with a push from Cormac and others, were able to set up programs on psychoanalysis and psychotherapy at LSB College, which is now part of the DBS School of Arts. We work closely with their program director, Terry Ball, and we continue to have a very close link with their students. The DBS students in the MA in Psychoanalytic Psychotherapy program join our students in the MSc in Psychoanalytic Psychotherapy for a Thursday morning Psychiatric Case Conference. It is a very rich weekly encounter between psychoanalysis and psychiatry in the Department of Psychiatry of a major Dublin public hospital. The School of Psychotherapy, from its launch, has offered a post-master's period of training – recognition that the two-year period of the MSc is only the beginning of a long engagement with one's own analysis and with the question of what it is to practice psychoanalytically. In more recent years, this post-master's period of study, supervised practice, and ongoing analysis has been formalized so that students can also satisfy recently developed requirements set out by professional bodies in Ireland occupied with the recognition and regulation of psychoanalytic practitioners – in particular, the TSOP training combining the master's and post-master's periods is recognized as a Specific Modality Training in Psychoanalytic Psychotherapy by the Association for Psychoanalysis and Psychotherapy in Ireland (APPI), a constituent member of the Psychoanalytic Section of the Irish Council for Psychotherapy (ICP).

I mentioned *The Letter*.[7] This is a journal first launched in 1994. As with any psychoanalytic journal, much work is required for it to continue. I remember Cormac Gallagher saying that we were doing very well given that most of the Lacanian journals from the groups in Paris do not often make it to a tenth issue. It has been a fundamental resource for us and for many in the English-speaking world. Its archive contains many papers by Cormac Gallagher, which provide very effective entry points in to Lacan's seminars – papers based on his translation of the same seminars. We also have papers by many who have contributed significantly to Lacanian psychoanalysis in Ireland – both Irish and international. *The Letter* has published papers by Charles Melman, Jean Allouch, Christian Fierens, and Guy Le Gaufey.[8] Much of the reading material for our teaching programs now comes from *The Letter*. There is so much work there that can help students into the work of Freud and Lacan. For us, it has been an achievement in publication and an invaluable resource. Anyone approaching the reading of a seminar would do well to read Cormac Gallagher's paper on that seminar.

Cormac retired from his position as Director of the School of Psychotherapy in 2006. Dr. Patricia McCarthy, a major figure in Irish Lacanian psychoanalysis, took on the mantle and continued to run the School in accordance with the principles established by Gallagher, Darby, and Walsh. Cormac himself has continued with his work in translation and in his practice. In more recent years, he has produced translations of Christian Fierens, who published not one but two readings of Lacan's *L'étourdit*,[9] the famously challenging text by Lacan from 1972.[10] Since he cannot be translating everything, Cormac has tried to select what will be valuable contributions and felt that each of these readings would be helpful to have in the English-speaking world.

Cormac Gallagher comes from Cork, in the south of Ireland. He entered the Jesuits and undertook a Jesuit formation. He also studied mathematics but moved into psychology studies and ended up in Paris in 1970. He had heard of the psychoanalytic field from a fellow Jesuit Jim Christie from Scotland and he then met with Louis Beirnaert, SJ, who was following the work of Lacan and psychoanalysis.[11] Beirnaert recommended that Cormac go and listen to Lacan. He did. This is the remarkable thing. When you read the seminars, if you imagine arriving from Ireland to Paris, with a background in mathematics, there to study psychology, and you have the openness of mind and steadiness of spirt to hear something in Lacan's seminar which captured a crucial aspect of our subjective being. He paid attention and began his own analysis while following the work of Lacan. Cormac Gallagher chose to follow the work of Lacan. *Vous suivez* were Lacan's words to him in an exchange some years later.

In these years, Cormac also continued to have a role here in Ireland. As well as within the Jesuit Order, he was appointed as a psychologist in the Department of Psychiatry in St. Vincent's Hospital (now SVUH), an old Dublin hospital that had just relocated to a new campus and new buildings. In 1974, Cormac went to work with a new professor of psychiatry, Noel Walsh, who was psychoanalytically trained. Trainee psychiatrists (some of whom are approaching retirement now) arrived to train in the hospital, young and green-horned, and found themselves in a Department of Psychiatry in a major public hospital, which had the courage to approach mental illness from a psychoanalytic position. These young psychiatrists were reading the case histories of Freud with Cormac Gallagher. I have heard that some of these psychiatrists thought this was happening everywhere until they realized that what was happening in St. Vincent's was quite unique. Many of these psychiatrists have since paid tribute to the impact of this encounter with psychoanalysis on their psychiatric practice, an impact that stayed with them. This is what eventually led to Noel Walsh, Cormac Gallagher, and Mary Darby forming the School of Psychotherapy in 1984. An integral part of the students' experience in the School was attending the Wednesday (now Thursday) morning Psychiatric Case Conference. This weekly event had usually Prof. Walsh engage a patient in a conversation in front of an audience of trainees – psychiatric and psychoanalytic – nursing staff, social workers, chaplains, and others. Prof. Walsh has been described by Cormac Gallagher as having "the ear of a trained analyst, the clinical experience of a consultant psychiatrist and the dramatic instinct of a David Frost."[12] This weekly event has been – it continues – a fundamental formative component of the psychoanalytic teaching in the School of Psychotherapy. Although inspired and guided by Lacan's teaching, the students on the program read the work of Freud – in accordance with Lacan's instruction for anyone in the psychoanalytic field to ground their understanding of the field in the work of Freud – I have always understood that only when a practice and a theory are grounded in the reading of the work of Sigmund Freud can they be correctly described as *psychoanalytic*. I have this understanding from Cormac.

CV: When did Cormac begin to translate Lacan's seminars?

BOD: I don't know. I suspect he must have been translating for himself from the early 1970s, when he arrived in Paris. One of his earliest translations he drafted for circulation was, I believe, Lacan's *Family Complexes in the Formation of the Individual*. I understand that he was translating to bring this work to the attention of students in the School. It was a necessity for him to translate. He wanted to teach the work of Jacques Lacan, and without translations nobody would be able to do their own reading of this work. Apart from that, Cormac is a capable and honest translator and seems to enjoy the work of translation. He would also translate as a way of working with people. He would compose a draft for a group that met regularly, and he would invite comments from the group. Each year, he would translate a seminar with the group, and by the end of the year with their help he would have a final draft of what he regularly referred to as a work in progress. For a number of years in the mid-1990s to mid-2000s, the translated seminar would be the theme of an annual conference in

Dublin. His practice as a translator of Lacan's seminars – which were spoken, originally – has always been to include the comments and interjections, the slips, the broken-off sentences, the "Can you hear me? No, we can't hear you." All of that exchange between Lacan and his audience – all of Lacan's speech in the room – would be included. Jacques-Alain Miller's editions tend to edit this content out and 'tidy up' passages – involving stepping over from editing to interpreting, arguably. I learnt from Cormac that each has to take her or his own responsibility in their encounter with the work and teaching of Jacques Lacan, Sigmund Freud too. Each of us is responsible for our own interpretation. Hence the importance of representing the content as completely as possible – what people heard in the room. Lacan made sure everything was recorded, too. A good example of this is when Lacan makes the slip when trying to say the name of André Lalande, the author of *Vocabulaire technique et critique de la philosophie* [*Technical and critical vocabulary of philosophy*] (1960) and produces a neologism, *lalangue* from Lalande, which he then holds onto.[13] In a number of his papers, Cormac reflects on the impossible task of translation in his introduction to Guy le Gaufey's article on sexuation.[14] He also invokes Freud's reference to the Italian play on words *Traduttore / Traditore* in his book on the joke as a formation of the unconscious.[15]

CV: How did Gallagher have access to Lacan's archive and all of this content to be able to translate?

BOD: Again, I do not know, except from what I have gathered. There are various transcripts and recordings that have circulated from people who attended Lacan's seminars. They would have been using recording devices. Lacan also had a stenographer in the room to make transcripts of the seminars. I know Cormac always kept in close contact with Charles Melman, a founding member of the *Association lacanienne international*, who would have provided reliable transcripts or recordings. Guy Le Gaufey has also been a source of material.

CV: As I understood, Cormac Gallagher's translations of Lacan were some of the earliest that were available and in circulation in English and were helpful to clinicians and academics studying in places like Boston, California, New York, and Toronto.

BOD: Yes, absolutely. I recently [July 2018] met David Lichtenstein and some other analysts from New York at a conference.[16] When I told them that I was from Dublin, they lit up and exclaimed, "Cormac Gallagher!" For many American analysts and academics, Cormac was their sole and primary way into Lacan's work. Cormac did not use the Miller editions for translation. Often there was a translation by Cormac Gallagher available in English that was not yet published or available in French. Jacques-Alain Miller announced, in the 1970s, that he would publish Lacan's seminars, but it is really only in the last 10 or 15 years that many have been published in French. Long before this, remarkably, Cormac had these available in English translations. Worth noting in this regard is his paper from the Spring 2004 issue of *The Letter* entitled 'Re-Englishing *Encore*'.[17]

In thinking about a way to set up a psychoanalytic School for the purpose of advancing Lacanian psychoanalysis – in particular, an arrangement for work on the texts – in 2007 Cormac reread and translated Lacan's 1964 texts on the question of a School. Central to these is 'The Founding Act', which founded the *École freudienne de Paris*. On the basis of these texts, guided by Cormac, a number of us established the Irish School for Lacanian Psychoanalysis in 2007 – the acronym is ISLP, so it has from day one been enjoyably known as 'I SLIP', which is most appropriate. It is a cartel-based arrangement. There are no committees, secretariats, or presidents. It involves participants making a commitment each year to work in a cartel and to produce something out of studying a psychoanalytic text – a psychoanalytic question.

CV: What do you think it is about Lacanianism that was able to flourish in Ireland more than other psychoanalytic orientations? Is there a cultural aspect here?

BOD: A very important psychoanalyst here in Ireland, Helen Sheehan, published a paper in *The Letter* called, "The Follower," which was written for a conference on Cormac Gallagher's work, held in 1998.[18] Helen Sheehan is asking this same question about how it could have happened that Freudian psychoanalysis as represented in the work of Lacan could land and find some soil to grow in the culture of Ireland in the 1970s and since. While Cormac Gallagher's achievement has been remarkable in its effects in the lives of so many, it is also the case that Freudian psychoanalysis is largely refused in Ireland – often by self-proclaiming 'psychoanalysts', which is problematic and concerning. We have a small group here with a serious (and that is not, therefore, humorless – far from it) commitment to psychoanalysis. The broader Irish society and culture may know the name of Freud but not much beyond that. Irish intellectuals and writers sometimes refer to not knowing what they were writing until it has been written, to unconscious processes. But they do not articulate this with reference to the Freudian unconscious.

CV: Many of the students in your programs are in their own analysis, but what are some of the aspects about analysis that you try to emphasize in your teaching?

BOD: There is a quotation attributed to the Danish physicist, Niels Bohr, who said "if quantum physics has not profoundly shocked you, you haven't understood it yet." Central to any encounter with the psychoanalytic field is engagement in one's own analysis. Only in that context might it be possible to come up against the division in one's subjectivity, the fact of being a subject of the unconscious, and, as if that were not shocking enough, to have to come to realize how much work each of us puts into not knowing it. There is no cure for this. The product of a psychoanalysis is not a position of self-mastery or mastery over any domain or object. The object causes the subject, we might say. The object, cause of desire, as Lacan articulates it – his introduction of the *objet a* – the o-object as Cormac chose to translate it to capture the English object and other – this o-object Lacan describes as 'lacan's invention'. The o-object is central to Lacan's work. We can get quite sentimental and soft about the word, "desire," as if it were some beautiful, ideal thing, but look at what Lacan is saying about it. The terrifying, heartless figure of Antigone is invoked to represent the tragedy of desire. In opposition to Aristotle's ethics of the good, Lacan bases his ethics on the Real. It is an unconscious desire because I do not want to know.

A major challenge is to differentiate between psychoanalysis and a psychotherapy. Freud struggled with this differentiation. He has difficulty forming and formulating psychoanalysis as psychotherapy. He is also clear that analysis and therapy are distinct. In the *New Introductory Lectures on Psycho-Analysis*, for instance, Freud says, "I have never been a therapeutic enthusiast."[19] Freud would not have produced analysis as distinct if he had only wanted to be "therapeutic." I am reminded that in his poem, *Memory to Sigmund Freud*, W.H. Auden writes about Freud's own "technique of unsettlement." This is not to be taken lightly. It can be difficult when you are a practitioner and someone is there in distress. It is difficult to wait, to maintain a psychoanalytic position. Each will want to jump to calm people down. This objective can drive an intervention that may be very helpful therapeutically. It may be required in some situations where there is serious risk of harm. It is not the direction of the psychoanalytic position. Other practice positions take charge of this kind of intervention, which, as I say, may be necessary and which can be carried out in a way that may allow a path to psychoanalytic work for the distressed, perplexed subject.

Lacan was not working to calm patients down and have them feeling well, or at least better. At least, I do not understand that to have been his primary project. His work goes in another direction. This work is to allow people the possibility of some contact with their desire, which is unsettling. For some people, there is not much choice. They need to work to find a way to live with something of their desire. It can be a matter of being able to tolerate and manage something of one's own desire. The alternative is being left with nothing more precise in response to the question – what is happening to me? – than the portmanteau generalizations: anxiety / depression.

Notes

1 Cormac Gallagher has translated 19 of the 27 seminars by Jacques Lacan along with other seminal texts by Charles Melman, Guy Le Gaufey, Jean Allouch, and Christian Fierens. He has also written many papers. Gallagher attended Lacan's seminars and case presentations during the 1970s. He underwent an analysis with Christian Simatos (1930–2020) and supervision with Claude Dumézil (1929–2013). Both were Parisian neuropsychiatrists and psychoanalysts who had been in analysis with Lacan. Gallagher would later complete a doctorate at Paris VII with psychoanalyst Jean Laplanche (1924–2012) of the International Psychoanalytic Association. Through his practice, teaching, writing and translating, Gallagher brought hundreds into contact with the psychoanalytic field.

2 Jonathan (also known as Jonty) Hanaghan (1887–1967). To date, there is no definitive published account of the influence of Hanaghan's work on the development of psychoanalysis in Ireland. I will note that the International Psychoanalytic Association (IPA) decided in 1949 not to recognize the Irish group (along with four other groups around the world) stating: "*Ireland*. An Irish Psycho-Analytical Society was founded in 1945. It appears to be doing some good work, but since none of its members have been analyzed, let alone trained, we did not feel justified in recognizing them." Ernest Jones was chairing the meeting and edited the Report (*Bulletin of the International Psychoanalytical Association*. 30 (1949): 178–209). Interestingly on the schedule at this first IPA congress since before the Second World War held in Zurich in August 1949 was Dr. Jacques Lacan, Paris, to deliver (again) his paper "*Le Stade du Miroir comme Formateur de la Fonction du Je dans l'Experience Psychanalytique*." See Ross Skelton's 1983 article, "Jonathan Hanaghan: The Founder of Psychoanalysis in Ireland." There is no indication that Hanaghan's work and group had any influence on Cormac Gallagher's first encountering psychoanalysis in Paris in 1970.

3 Several of Tom McGrath's papers can be found in archives of *The Letter: Irish Journal for Lacanian Psychoanalysis*.

4 The proceedings of the conference in 2018 paying tribute to the work of Cormac Gallagher can be found in Issue 68 of *The Letter Irish Journal for Lacanian Psychoanalysis* on www.theletter.com or by emailing info@tsop.ie

5 Toward the end of the two-day conference, Dr. Charles Melman in an exchange with Jean Allouch commented that the two of them had not been in the same room for 40 years, and he found, on the basis of their respective papers at the conference, that they had been working on the same questions. Dublin can be a venue for meetings between psychoanalysts that may not happen elsewhere. Cormac Gallagher maintained contact with psychoanalysts from a range of different groups over many decades.

6 http://www.lacaninireland.com/web/

7 http://theletter.ie/

8 Charles Melman (1931–) is a French psychiatrist and psychoanalyst who began following Lacan in the 1950s.

9 Lacan wrote *L'étourdit* in 1972 following Seminar XIX. *L'étourdit* is a notoriously difficult text to read, and the title plays on the French *l'étourdit* [dizzy or stunned], *le tour dit* [the said turn], and *dire* [saying].

10 The anecdote is that Lacan gave this text to Charles Melman who was the editor of *Scilicet*, the journal of the *École freudienne de Paris*. Melman handed it back to Lacan and told him it was incomprehensible. About thirty years later, Fierens produced his first reading of *L'étourdit*, which is a line-by-line commentary. Melman read Fierens' work and said that it was an excellent book. Fierens obviously felt his work was incomplete as ten years later he produced a second reading.

11 Father Louis Beirnaert (1906–1985) was a Jesuit and French psychoanalyst who worked to promote a better understanding of psychoanalysis within the Catholic church.

12 Gallagher, C., 'Psychological Object or Speaking Subject: from Diagnosis to Case Re-presentation', *The Letter Irish Journal for Lacanian Psychoanalysis*, Issue 46, Spring 2011 [www.theletter.com; also available on www.lacaninireland.com: http://www.lacaninireland.com/web/wp-content/uploads/2010/06/Psychological-Object-or-Speaking-Subject.pdf].

13 Lacan stumbled upon his condensation of article and noun *lalangue* on November 4, 1971, the opening week of his series of talks back in the Hôpital Sainte Anne entitled *The Knowledge of the Psychoanalyst*. He had begun the talk remarking on the passion for ignorance. He went on to refer to the work of Laplanche and Pontalis, a work well known to students of psychoanalysis. He first slips on the title of the book: "*Vocabulaire de la Philosophie*. What am I saying, *Vocabulaire de la Psychanalyse*. You see the slip, huh? Anyway it's as good as Lalande. *Lalangue*, as I write it now – I have no blackboard – well, write *lalangue* in one word: that is how I will write it from now on." Lacan, J., *The Seminar of Jacques Lacan: The Knowledge of the Psychoanalyst 1971–1972*. Translated by Cormac Gallagher. www.lacaninireland.com. Week of November 4, 1971, page 4. From this moment, *lalangue* enters Lacan's vocabulary and then, inevitably, the vocabulary of Lacanians. This concept first appeared as a slip, a formation of the unconscious of Jacques Lacan. For Lacan, *lalangue* refers to speech prior to grammatical, syntactical, or lexicographical organization. *Lalangue* can also refer to speech in its dimensions of stumbling, homophony, limits, ambiguity, and desire.

14 See *The Letter Irish Journal for Lacanian Psychoanalysis*, Issue 39, Autumn 2008.

15 Freud's translator James Strachey comments on the same phrase that it "might be emblazoned on the title-page of the present volume [Editor's Preface to Volume VI of *The Standard Edition of the Complete Psychological Works of Sigmund Freud*, p. 6]."

16 David Lichtenstein is a psychoanalyst and co-founder of Après-Coup Psychoanalytic Association in New York.

17 See www.theletter.com and http://www.lacaninireland.com/web/wp-content/uploads/2010/06/RE-Englishing-Encore.pdf

18 Sheehan, Helen. "The Follower." *The Letter: Irish Journal for Lacanian Psychoanalysis*. 14 (1998): 39–61.

19 Freud says, "you are perhaps aware that I have never been a therapeutic enthusiast" (151).

Bibliography and Further Reading

Freud, Sigmund. "New Introductory Lectures On Psycho-Analysis." *The Standard Edition of the Complete Psychological Works of Sigmund Freud, Volume XXII (1932–1936): New Introductory Lectures on Psycho-Analysis and Other Works*. Ed. James Stachey. London: Hogarth Press, 1955. 1–182.

Gallagher, Cormac. *Jacques Lacan in Ireland: Collected Translations and Papers by Cormac Gallagher*. Web. lacaninireland.com. Accessed 14 Jan. 2020. In particular.

Gallagher, Cormac. "Psychological Object or Speaking Subject: from Diagnosis to Case Re-presentation." *The Letter Irish Journal for Lacanian Psychoanalysis*. 46 (2011): 21–38.

Gallagher, Cormac. "Re-Englishing Encore." n.d. at http://www.lacaninireland.com/web/wp-content/uploads/2010/06/RE-Englishing-Encore.pdf; also available on www.theletter.com

O'Donnell, Barry. "What is Anxiety?" *The Letter: Irish Journal for Lacanian Psychoanalysis.* 64 (2017): 1–13.

Sheehan, Helen. "The Follower." *The Letter: Irish Journal for Lacanian Psychoanalysis.* 14 (1998): 39–61.

Skelton, Ross. "Jonathan Hanaghan: The Founder of Psychoanalysis in Ireland." *The Crane Bag.* 7.2 (1983): 183–190.

Chapter 3

Treating Psychosis in Québec with the Founders of GIFRIC and The 388 with Willy Apollon, Danielle Bergeron, and Lucie Cantin (Translation by Daniel Wilson)*

Willy Apollon, PhD, is a senior psychoanalyst at GIFRIC and philosopher (Paris, Sorbonne). He is supervising analyst and consultant analyst at the Psychoanalytic Treatment Center for Psychotics Adults, the "388." He is past president and founder of GIFRIC and director of the Psychoanalytic Center for the Family and has been responsible of a control seminar for the training of analysts and of a seminar on globalization and psychoanalysis in Montreal and Québec City. He has published widely on topics such as psychosis, the formation of analysts, the psychoanalytic clinic, perversion, aesthetics, family, and the analysis of cultural, social, and political practices. He is the author of *Voodoo, A Space for the Voices* (Éditions Galilée, Paris, 1976) [*Le Vaudou, un espace pour les Voix*] and *Psychosis: The Offer of the Analyst* (1999) [*Psychoses: l'offre de l'analyste*], *Sexual Difference at the Risk of Kinship* [*La différence sexuelle au risque de la parenté*] (1997), and *The Universal, Psychoanalytic Perspectives* [*L'Universel, perspectives psychanalytiques*] (1997), all published by Éditions du GIFRIC, Québec.

Danielle Bergeron, MD, is senior psychoanalyst and psychiatrist. She is medical chief for the Psychoanalytic Treatment Center for Psychotics Adults, the "388". At GIFRIC, she is supervising analyst and responsible for training; she also conducts a control seminar of the analytic act with clinicians analysts and teaches a seminar in short-term analytic treatment. Associate professor for psychiatry at Laval University, she teaches psychoanalytic concepts and is supervisor of a fellowship program for psychiatrist at the "388." She is now a Distinguished Life Fellow of the American Psychiatric Association. She has published on psychoanalytic treatment of psychosis and neuroses, ethical questions, the analyst-facing aesthetics and the Thing, femininity, science, and psychoanalysis.

* Daniel Wilson, PhD, lives in Montreal, where he teaches English language classes. He is interested in the relationship between the history of psychoanalysis and the contemporary clinic. He received a PhD in English from Cornell University.

DOI: 10.4324/9781003323136-4

Lucie Cantin, MPs, is senior psychoanalyst and psychologist. She is psycho-analyst at the Psychoanalytic Treatment Center for Psychotics Adults, the "388". She is a supervising analyst and is co-responsible for teaching at GI-FRIC. She is also responsible for a control seminar for the training of analysts and a seminar on Psychoanalysis and Clinical Psychology. She is vice-president of GIFRIC, where she is the editor of *Savoir*, a journal of psychoanalysis and cultural analysis. Further, she is the supervisor for the doctorate program in psychology at Laval University and supervisor in the master's program in Psychology at the University of Ghent (Belgium) and at the Université Libre of Bruxelles. She is additionally responsible for the Orientation Council of the Freudian School of Québec. She has published on the psychoanalytic treatment of psychosis, the clinic of neurosis, mysticism, femininity, masculinity, and perversion.

Apollon, Bergeron, and Cantin are the founders of the Psychoanalytic Treatment Center for Adults Psychotics, the "388". They are co-authors of three books in French: *On the Treatment of Psychosis, On the Stakes and Strat-egies for the Psychoanalysis of Psychotics*, and *On the Future for the Psychotic* [*Traiter la psychose* (1990), *La cure analytique du psychotique: enjeux et stratégies* (2008), and *Un avenir pour le psychotique: Le dispositif du traitement psychanalytique* (2013)], all published by GIFRIC. In English, they published the volume *After Lacan: Clinical Practice and the Subject of the Unconscious* (SUNY Press, 2002).

Introduction: A New Psychoanalytic Treatment for Psychotics

> With the '388,' for the first time, a group of psychoanalysts created a psycho-analytic treatment center for which they had thought through all of the clini-cal services, the organization and the style of management, by beginning from a psychoanalytic conception of psychosis and its treatment.
>
> (Cantin 2009, 293)

Willy Apollon, Danielle Bergeron, and Lucie Cantin are, with other colleagues, the founders of the Interdisciplinary Group of Freudian Research and Clinical and Cultural Intervention [*Groupe Interdisciplinaire Freudien de Recherche et d'Intervention Cliniques et Culturelles*, or GIFRIC], and they are the co-found-ers of the "388," a Psychoanalytic Treatment Center for Young Adult Psychot-ics in Québec City. There, about 100 people (who are between the ages of 18 and 35 when admitted) who experience schizophrenia and psychosis are pro-vided treatment and services, which includes treatment of the crisis. The Center was founded in 1982 in collaboration with the Robert-Giffard Psychiatric Hos-pital. The 388 (this number refers to the street number of the center) provides

an alternative to hospitalization in the form of an intensive program that includes social, cultural, and artistic activities along with psychiatric and psychoanalytic treatment.

Psychiatrists or other mental health professionals may refer an individual to
the center, but each person who attends the center must ultimately call the
center himself or herself, independently, to express their own request for treatment. The 388 also has five beds for the intensive treatment of those who are
experiencing a psychotic crisis. Available to users of the center 24 hours a day,
seven days per week, these temporary beds help prevent hospitalizations. On
the premises of The 388, unlike many hospitals, there are no restraints or
locked rooms.

Each patient in the program has access to a clinical team consisting of a
"clinical *intervenant*," a social worker, a psychiatrist, and a psychoanalyst.[1]
Patients are involved in some of the day-to-day operations and are able to use
the kitchen to cook for themselves and the living rooms to sit with others.
Throughout treatment, each patient works with a team of professionals who
approach them as a person who must have a specific understanding and relationship to the events that have occurred in his or her own life. Part of this
work helps the person articulate their experience not only through speech but
also through other creative forms of expression. The center provides daily activities, including workshops in painting, ceramics, and music, as well as so-
cio-cultural activities, cooking activities, and a walking club for exercise. Each
patient usually meets with his or her psychoanalyst once or twice every week.

Lucie Cantin writes that

Willy Apollon has opened up a set of new perspectives within Freudian
metapsychology and operated a number of major displacements in the approach to psychosis, which have allowed for the thinking of the conditions
necessary for the treatment and psychoanalytic cure of the psychotic.
Among these decisive contributions, let us note the redefinition of transference and of the position of the analyst; an approach to psychosis whose
logic is rethought from the structure of the subject's experience, from the
'spontaneous work' of psychosis, and from the enterprise in which the psychotic is engaged; a conception of the psychotic crisis and its treatment
within the framework supported by transference; and lastly, the work of the
dream and the logic of the analytic cure. At the same time, a daily practice
with psychotics – linked with this work for 37 years through weekly discussions and seminars – has permitted Danielle Bergeron and Lucie Cantin to
establish, develop, and put into practice the means, strategies, and procedures of this psychoanalytic clinic of psychosis. Cantin refers most notably
to what concerns the installation and handling of transference, the interpel-
lation of the psychotic subject and the support of his speech at different
stages of the analytic cure, the utilization of the dream in the calling into
question of the delusion and the psychotic enterprise, the management of

the crisis within transference, and the ethical constraint that arises when confronted with the new knowledge (*savoir*) produced in the analytic cure.

(cf Cantin, 2008, 87–120)

Since its creation, we have wanted to offer a *treatment* to the psychotic by proposing an analytic work to him wherein he is engaged, guided by the psychoanalyst, in reconsidering his entire psychic life. The objectives of this treatment are the profound reorganization of the mental universe, the reappropriation of speech and subjectivity, the disappearance of the psychotic symptomology, the resolution of the stakes governing the triggering of the crises, the restoration of an autonomy in personal and social functioning, and the return to an active life of civic participation (work, studies, volunteer work, artistic work, familial responsibilities). The analytic treatment – which is at the heart of the work undertaken by the psychotic at The 388 – is at the center of a *treatment's structure*, which receives, frames, and treats the effects of this work through a set of services, all of which are determined by the logic of the analytic experience and the ethics it commands. These services include a personalized psychiatric follow up, articulated and adapted to the evolutionary stages of the analytic treatment; the in-house accompaniment and treatment of the crisis – the center has beds available for this end; daily clinical supervision and support by *clinical intervenants* who are trained to ensure a 'long-term psychoanalytic follow-up'; art workshops run by artists who come in order to practice their art with the patients of the center; and finally, an activities program that aims at the restoration of the social link and the preparation for a return to an active life.

(Cantin, 2009, 286–287)

Aside from the novelty of the psychoanalytic treatment offered, the originality and success of The 388 lie in a management structure whose connection with the clinic is guaranteed by the active presence and authority of psychoanalysts in strategic decision-making roles. Thus, by being heavily implicated in maintaining the conditions that have proven to be essential for obtaining clinical results, the psychoanalysts frame the set of clinical practices and guarantee their connection to psychoanalytic ethics.

(Cantin, 2008, 87–120)

"One of the first surprises for the psychotic who comes to The 388," writes Willy Apollon, "is doubtless discovering for the first time someone who is prepared to listen to him, instead of being only interested in his symptoms, his behavior, and his reaction to medication" ("The Treatment" 212). In the past, psychiatrists and psychoanalysts used to suggest that the psychotic or schizophrenic person was incapable of dreaming or could not dream in relation to the psychoanalytic treatment as the person's imaginary was supposedly ab-sorbed in delusion or hallucination. For GIFRIC and The 388, dreams are particularly important for psychoanalytic treatment of psychosis as dream content can be a valuable way to gain access to the analysand's history but also may significantly help the analyst and analysand work around the delusion. The dream also importantly allows for the analyst and analysand to occupy a position of questioning without directly challenging the certainty in the struc-ture of psychosis. Images and events recounted from dreams may help the pa-tient piece together the past to better understand symptoms and behavior in the present, helping to manage and contain the onset of a crisis. "[I]n contrast to the delusion to whose certainty the psychotic clings for survival against the void," writes Bergeron, "the dream is a sort of neutral territory" (74). Addi-tionally, Bergeron writes that the retelling of a dream will produce "signifiers which recall events that marked the psychotic's life because they operated a rupture in that life by remaining non represented, unassimilable, and unspeak-able" and the "memories derived from dream-work, then, uncover the gaps, loose[n] threads in the fabric of the delusion, and thereby put the delusion into question" (74). Ultimately, the aim of the dream-work in the treatment of psy-chosis is to enable doubt to gradually weaken the delusion and for certitude to fall away. Therefore, the patient's delusion is never confronted directly, but rather the person is provided with a different way of working on the delusion with a supportive team that listens and helps the patient to speak. Further, when the person experiences moments of crisis during the dissipation of the delusion, the clinical team is present to provide the necessary support. With the assistance of The 388, many patients have been able to restore their relation to the social link, return to school and work, and live independent lives.

Separate from the activities from The 388, GIFRIC provides courses and training programs in Lacanian psychoanalysis for clinicians who come to study from across North America. GIFRIC also conducts research on the outcome data of The 388, which conveys highly successful results as many patients who attend treatment go on to lead generative and self-sufficient lives. Here in this interview, Apollon, Bergeron, and Cantin discuss their clinical backgrounds, the direction of treatment at The 388, and the challenges in maintaining the center despite dominant approaches to psychosis in psychiatry. This conversa-tion was recorded at GIFRIC in Québec on 15 December 2018 and made pos-sible with support from the Museum of Dreams at Western University and the Social Sciences & Humanities Research Council of Canada (SSHRC).

Chris Vanderwees:	How did each of you discover [Jacques] Lacan? Also, how did you discover each other?
Willy Apollon:	I studied philosophy in Paris. Michel de Certeau, who knew that I was in analysis with Louis Beirnaert, sug-gested that I should go to the seminars that Lacan was

giving.[2] I also had a friend who insisted that I meet Lacan. So, I went to the seminars. I met Lacan. It all happened very quickly. Over the years, I greatly appreciated the work that Lacan was doing at the school. During my internship at the hospital, I had the occasion to participate in the presentation of cases given at the Sainte-Anne, under Dr. [Georges] Daumezon.[3] These were generally psychotic cases. It was there that I became interested in psychosis. Michel de Certeau wanted to organize a working group on psychoanalysis and history in Paris. It was proposed that I would do the psychoanalysis component for the working group.

When I left Haiti, which was under François Duvalier, to go to France, I wanted to see Québec. What happened in October 1970 reminded me of what I had experienced in Paris in May 1968. I visited Laval University, and a chance encounter with two people changed things for me. One of these people, [whom] I did not know before, was the dean of the theology school. A few days later, he proposed to me that I stay in Québec to do what I had tried to do in Paris. I explained to him that psychoanalysis and theology were not exactly operating on the same level. The theology professor explained that what he really wanted was a place that the students from psychology as well as theology could learn more and take a course in psychoanalysis. The chair of the psychology department had already accepted to help with this. In the first six months, some friends in psychology, anthropology, and philosophy began to work together. This is how I stayed in Québec.

At the same time that I was giving a course on psychoanalysis in the psychology department, I was also teaching philosophy at College Garneau, and I participated in a research group at Laval University in the Institute of Human Science, directed by Fernand Dumont. With some colleagues, we decided that it would be good to have a space for research that was not governed by the rules of the university, because these are rules linked to subsidies and funding and not for research itself. This is how I created GIFRIC with some colleagues and students. I met Lucie Cantin in my philosophy class, and I met Danielle Bergeron in the class I gave in psychoanalysis in the Department of Psychiatry at Laval University. I taught philosophy at College Garneau and psychoanalysis at the university to students in psychology, philosophy, anthropology, and psychiatry. This is how it started.

Danielle Bergeron: After studying medicine, I specialized in psychiatry. In my first year of specialization, I became very interested in psychoanalysis with psychotics when, during my internship, I encountered a very smart psychiatrist who was using a Kleinian [after Melanie Klein] approach to treat psychotics at the mental hospital in Québec. During my second year of studies in psychiatry, the program offered us a course on psychoanalysis that was given by Willy Apollon. It was great! I was interested in this new approach to the human being that went outside what Freud proposed as Oedipus – beyond the triangle of the child, mommy, and daddy – and also beyond the Kleinian approach, which stays far too much in the imaginary. The Kleinian approach was perhaps useful to understand mental processes in young children, but in fact, with the adults on whom it was beginning to be applied, I realized that its efficacy was limited because it evacuated the dimensions of the real and of the symbolic. What interested me in the courses that Willy Apollon was giving was the concept of the Other, not the little other as in Oedipus but the big Other, which comes from Lacan. What was new coming from Willy Apollon was this concept of the human being as promoted by a culture, a society, and a civilization. This was a new idea for psychoanalysis. During my four years studying psychiatry, there was a moment where Willy Apollon invited me to participate in a group discussion about psychoanalysis and connected disciplines, such as ethnopsychiatry, philosophy, sociology, etc. This was the beginning of GIFRIC without it yet being called GIFRIC. I also went to Paris for my final year where I worked with a renowned researcher and professor of psychiatry, Pierre Deniker, who developed the use of chlorpromazine as a treatment for psychosis. With Jean Delay, Deniker was the first to use this drug for the treatment of psychotics, which had been previously used as an anesthetic.[4] While it was psychoanalysis that captured my interest, I also wanted to be up-to-date with advances in neuropsychiatric research in order to be better armed to defend the psychoanalytic approach in the psychiatric clinic.

At the very beginning of my year in France, I remember having had the opportunity to meet with Jacques-Alain

Miller, who welcomed me very warmly. It was he who offered me the opportunity to participate in the clinical section of psychoanalysis at the Freudian School of Paris. During the activities of the clinical section, Lacan came two or three times to meet us and to speak to us. This was for me a very enriching experience. Once, Lacan presented a mathematician to us, Michel Thomé, with whom he was collaborating at the time. Thomé gave us a presentation on the mathematic theory of knots. This was in 1977 and 1978.

I also took advantage of my year in Paris to participate in classes on psychoanalysis at the University of Vincennes, in the department founded and directed by Lacanians. I went there to take classes when I was not working at the hospital. I also want to mention that I had the chance to participate in Francoise Dolto's seminars on the psychoanalysis of children at the *Institut Océanographique*.[5] I had already read her books, which I had very much appreciated. I was able to discover that she was an important clinician. At that time, I felt the Lacanian approach was what we needed.

During this year, I also went to visit La Borde, which is an institution in the French countryside dedicated to the treatment of psychotics, within institutional psychotherapy. It was founded by Jean Oury, a psychoanalyst and psychiatrist.[6] Visiting La Borde gave me the idea of doing something like that for psychotics here in Québec City but, rather than in the country, in the heart of the city and not within the institution of a hospital but in an open center integrated into the urban community network.

I had the pleasure of meeting Lucie Cantin when we founded GIFRIC, formally signing the paperwork. This was in summer of 1978. Since then, we have become diligent collaborators and partners for the advancement of psychoanalysis.

Lucie Cantin: We were the students Willy Apollon was talking about earlier. I first knew Willy Apollon as a professor of philosophy at the Cégep. He was a professor of philosophy who left no one indifferent. We had the impression that he was not just talking about theory, and we all recognized something in his teaching that touched our own experience. I had read Freud in secondary school, which had particularly interested me. When I went to university to study psychology, I took the courses that Willy Apollon was giving in psychoanalysis in the anthropology department. When I did my master's in psychology, I completed my internship at the psychiatric hospital here in Québec. I was already particularly interested in everything that concerned psychosis. At the same time, we started to work towards GIFRIC, and I knew that what I was passionate about, above all, was psychoanalysis. These two things were happening at the same time. I wrote my master's thesis on a Québécois poet, Émile Nelligan, who was psychotic, and Willy was one of the readers. At this time, we were starting to work together. GIFRIC was founded in 1978, and The 388 was opened in 1982.

CV: What was it that interested you about Lacanian psychoanalysis?

WA: I was preoccupied with the relationship between voodoo, African civilization, Haitian civilization, and Francophone civilization. I first looked in anthropology and history but went towards psychoanalysis because they spoke of voodoo. Haitian psychiatrists explained voodoo through the idea of mental illness. Carried forward by the ideas of philosophy and science, I thought rather that there was something operating at the level of civilization. I went toward psychoanalysis to better understand it. When I became interested in psychoanalysis, I went to do a psychoanalytic cure with Louis Beirnaert, who was in the Lacanian direction. It seemed like a pertinent approach.

LC: From the very beginning of GIFRIC, there was a Tuesday seminar directed by Willy Apollon that was in the Lacanian direction of things. At the university, psychoanalysis was taught in a Freudian manner, but it was a vulgar Freudianism. It was really centered on interpretation in the sense that the analyst was the person who knew, interpreted, and gave meaning to what the patient said. At the same time, I had the experience of being in an analysis with a Lacanian, taking the clinical seminar with Willy Apollon, and taking psychoanalysis courses at the university. The psychoanalysis that they taught us at the university was a kind of explanation of Freudian concepts presented through a post-Freudian reading centered on the Ego, defense mechanisms, etc. and which became a kind of guide for interpretation applied to the clinic by the analyst. It was a psychoanalysis detached from the experience of the analysand. Nothing of this resonated for me with respect to my own analytic experience, nor with respect to the clinic and the theory of the clinic as developed in the seminar that Willy Apollon directed at GIFRIC. These were two separate and irreconcilable universes.

DB: During my studies in psychiatry, I was disappointed with how basic the treatment was for psychotics. People were basically inactive.[7] There was no engagement. There was a little bit of art, but the activities were like macramé and artisanal kinds of things. On the one hand, there was my experience in the hospitals, but on the other hand, there were the seminars with Lacan and the seminars given by Willy Apollon, which were very much centered on practical experience. It was very theoretical but very attached to experience. From my second year, I knew I wanted to do something else for psychotics. I wanted to find another way to work with people other than the way that was being done in hospitals.

To treat the problem of psychosis, you do not find what you need in Freud. There are not references or ways to orient yourself in Freud in order to treat psychosis. Lacan, like Freud, makes suggestions and proposes ideas, but none of them [offers] a global frame of treatment for psychosis. In the IPA [International Psychoanalytical Association], analysts talked about identifying with the psychoanalyst in order to become as normal as possible. But we know that the psychotic contests that which is presented as normality, as what is normal. He or she is pushed by something inside that leads him or her to develop a world that would have no defect. What Willy Apollon brought was a proposition for, and an application of, a clinic to effectively treat psychotics. What we wanted to do with psychotics was to find a way that they could develop their own subjectivity and their own interiority so that they could rearticulate themselves to the social. In fact, what we proposed was the first theoretical and clinical framework for a logic of the treatment of psychosis, and this has proven itself, and has offered results, for more than 35 years.

LC: What was developed in psychoanalysis in the hospitals, in work like art therapy, always had to do with interpreting what the psychotic was doing and of giving an interpretation that came from the therapist or analyst. When Lacan took up the original question of the foreclosure of the name of the Father, he made advances with respect to psychosis that Freud could not have made. But this was done by placing the accent on something that was defective, something that was missing for the psychotic, the signifier of the name of the Father. What Willy Apollon brought was the idea of not beginning from what is missing in the psychotic but rather beginning from the experience of the psychotic. What is the experience of the psychotic? And starting from this experience, how can we conceive of a clinic for psychosis?

CV: Many psychiatrists and psychoanalysts once believed, and maybe many still believe, that psychosis is unanalyzable. In Ontario, for instance, the primary health care approach to psychosis continues to be medications as has been the approach in North America since the 1980s. In opposition to this, you were able to create a center that provides a much more humanistic approach to treatment, including psychoanalysis. How did you begin to introduce this program in Québec? What were some of the obstacles in creating GIFRIC and The 388?

WA: There are two things that are distinct here. There is the possibility of treatment and then there is the fight. The most important, of course, is the possibility of treatment, which we have established. They are right to say that the psychotic cannot be analyzed. Psychiatry does not have a treatment for psychosis. If psychiatry had a treatment for psychosis, we would have results. Psychoanalysis, as psychoanalysts practice it, is generally a practice for the neurotic. It is a psychoanalysis conceived within the field of neurosis and within Western civilization. In the process, all the mechanics of the cure rests upon on the idea of a relationship between two people. One person speaks and the other person interprets. The central concept is the concept of the transference. Freud and Lacan never went beyond this.

What we have done is to say that psychoanalysis conceived for the neurotic will not work for the psychotic, nor will it work with the perverse person. We had to go to the very heart of psychoanalysis to the question of the transference. We had to subvert the question of the transference. Lacan says that the question of transference with the psychotic necessarily tends towards erotomania.[8] Lacanians remain within this perspective. Obviously, from this perspective, you cannot have a psychoanalysis of the psychotic. This idea of the transference as a relationship between the analyst and the analysand had to be dealt with. In this conception of the transference, the psychotic will think that the analyst is a person who is persecuting or who is complicit with the person against whom the psychotic is fighting. The psychotic transcends the you–me relationship. And he or she is correct.

LC: To continue in this line of thought, we can take the idea of transference as "the subject supposed to know" as not applying to the psychotic person. It would be he or she who would be supposed to know. For example, the person you just met a little while ago, when you were visiting the Center before the interview, spent all night writing a new conception of the world. It is he who knows. The psychotic does not think that you know. This is why at The 388, in the analytic cure with the psychotic, we don't use a couch. The psychotic does not enter into a you–me relationship and does not assume that the analyst knows. It is not necessary, as with the neurotic, for the analyst to efface him or herself, to subtract him or herself from the visual field of the patient in order to provoke a speech that is not an address to the other who is there and from whom the patient would expect a response.

DB: If I take a break for a holiday, sometimes some analysands will go see Lucie Cantin to ask if it is possible for them to continue the work with her. Sometimes this is because it is not important at the beginning to the analysand, who the person is who is there. The most important thing is to speak. It is asking to be said itself. I wanted to add also that at the beginning of our work in treating psychotics, other psychoanalysts said "psychotics don't dream, there is no subject as subject of the unconscious, and they will develop erotomania." They made these three affirmations. We decided not to ask them to identify with social and cultural ideals and prohibitions, concerning what it is to be a man, a woman, a husband, etc., but rather put the emphasis on what they were experiencing in themselves, this push to do something for the world. They started dreaming. So, if they were dreaming, there was a subject of the unconscious! The dream is one of the formations of the unconscious, and we discovered that it was not right to say that the person cannot dream and that there is no subject. Psychoanalysts were saying that psychotic people did not dream and that what they call dreams were just the transposition of the delusion into the form of the dream. At the beginning of the analytic cure, the psychotic often brings a long, long dream that is a reconstruction of the world, but then there is a moment where the dreams that surge up are dreams that surprise the psychotic, because they are no longer linked to the delusion. This happens when the analyst does not take him or herself for the Other, does not act like the big Other who knows.

LC: Given that the analyst is not in a position of knowing or interpreting for the psychotic, we do not directly confront the logic of the delusion. At the moment when the psychotic takes the risk of speaking in the cure, real dreams surge up. What we call real dreams are those that allow the analysands to have access to experiences, memories, and mental representations that are fundamental to their subjectivity. These have to do with experiences that they never talked about before, because they were impossible to speak about or were non-receivable in the social link. What the person discovers works against the logic constructed in the delusion in order to explain and give a meaning to these intimate and unspeakable experiences that they lived through in solitude. They discover, little by little, the profound roots of what cut them from others and from common sense. And this does not come from an interpretation given by the analyst, but from something their unconscious produces in a dream.

WA: In other words, we have modified the concept of the transference, which also changed our approach to the unconscious. What is important for us is that this gave results. Out of more than 600 psychotics over 35 years, we have only had four or five cases of erotomania. The modification we made in the concept of the transference was correct. It is the result that confirms for us that our position is correct. If we change the concept of the transference, you also have to change the logic of the cure, not only for the psychotic but also for the neurotic or the perverse person. We arrive at results in the cure that are different from the results that other analysts arrive at, and this includes the analysts in Paris. We are Lacanian because we begin from the perspective of Lacan, but we have profoundly modified the logic of the cure. What is important for us are the results.

LC: To give the broad strokes of the logic of the cure, we begin from the logic of experience. We realized that the psychotic is working, is occupied in the work of constructing a new world, a new conception of the human, a new social link. What people call their delusion is actually a personal "theory," a justification, a meaning elaborated to account for their experience.

We have divided the cure into three parts. First, there is the establishment of transference, which allows the psychotic to take the risk of a true speech, saying something that he or she had never said before. Second, there is the challenging of the delusion, the falling away of the delusional certainty provoked by the new "savoir" elaborated in the analytic process. Third, there is a challenging of this "project" of constructing a new language, a new social link, a labor in which the psychotic was wholly invested and for which the psychotic believed that he or she was solely responsible.

Speaking of the installation of the transference and this question of true speech, we are waiting for the psychotic to speak of that which he or she could never have been spoken about before, to refind (as we have said) experiences that have remained outside of language, and to speak of all of the unmotivated acts and of what happens during the crisis when he or she acts. In other words, what we call true speech is a speech about what has never before been able to find signifiers and which could not come through except through acts and symptoms.

```
TRANSFERENCE → DELUSION → ENTERPRISE → TOWARD THE SOCIAL LINK
       CRISIS      CRISIS       CRISIS
```

DB: What Willy Apollon has just written on the board shows the consequences of treatment that everyone at the center can recognize in terms of the progression of the analytic cure. The progression of the cure has consequences for the way the user presents him or herself, and on the activities of the user, that everyone can observe who is in the center. When he or she learns to speak truly, when he accepts to speak of events, of experiences that have happened, of acts that he has never spoken of and could never have spoken of before, the consequence that this true speech will have is that it will allow the psychotic to experience the crisis at The 388 without being hospitalized or doing acts that will have potentially damaging consequences. Once the crisis can be linked to the possibility of having faith in the analyst and, after, of having faith in all of the staff, there is the possibility of going through a crisis at the center.

During a crisis, the staff members can hear what the psychotic says, see what the psychotic does, and return to this after the crisis, with the patient. After the first crisis, the *intervenant* who is in charge fills out a crisis form with the user. The next time, the patient will be able to be vigilant about a future crisis. The patient will be able to know what the symptoms are that suggest a crisis is coming because there are witnesses who can help the patient to speak of the crisis and about the signs that announce the psychotic crisis. When he or she speaks of these experiences in true speech that brings something that goes against or goes beyond the delusion, or when he or she notices that what is going on in the delusion is linked to certain experiences in childhood or that they have the same form, then he or she can question the delusion until the delusion falls. This is when there will be another crisis, which we call the second crisis. But it will not be the same type of crisis as was the first.

WA: There is too much for him or her to lose.

DB: Yes, too much to lose. This crisis, the second crisis, is where he or she is involved in an inner world, is delusional, and has hallucinations, but at the same time he is also an observer of the crisis.

LC: For example, a patient came to his cure and talked about how for the last week he has been doing very badly and had been very disorganized. Normally, when this happened, he became a resident, but this time, for the first time, he was able to live through this experience alone, at his house. So, I asked him if he noticed a difference. He said, "Yes, I am doing badly, but I am exterior to this anguish." The subjective position appears in the first step. It is as if the subject remains not overwhelmed by what is at stake in the unconscious. It is like a first internal division.

DB: Their mission or enterprise is to change what they see as a defect of the world; it could be prostitution, jealousy, killing, famine in the world...

WA: In the enterprise, what is at stake is what they want to do for humanity.

DB: When they enter this last phase of the treatment, they are able to go through the crisis just with the analyst. They have moments where they are destabilized. It is difficult. They can have a hard time sleeping, but they come to their analytic treatment. Sometimes they ask to come more often, but they go through the third crisis with only the support of the analyst.

LC: It is difficult.

WA: Very, very difficult.

LC: It is very difficult because they have to renounce their great project to be the one who will change something for all of humanity. They will have to find a way to do something within society and culture. They see this as just something banal. At that time, some patients will say that they have to distinguish between psychotic ideas and what, within those ideas, are their ethical values that they want to keep and to do something with. It is a difficult moment because they have to find a way to be with others, to be one among others, and to create, from their singular subjectivity and sensibility, a mode of articulation to the social link. This is a crucial time. Some of them have a lot to lose. It is much more difficult for patients who have been sick since their adolescence and who were not able to finish their degree in school. They don't have a profession; but, more importantly, they have never been able to articulate themselves to the social link through any mode of participation.

DB: Sometimes, after two or three years of treatment, they can recommence with society, get a job, return to their studies, move into an apartment. Sometimes it doesn't work out and they have to try again. All of this is possible because of the treatment team and the training in psychoanalysis with the psychotic that the treatment team gets every week from Willy Apollon. There is a unity of the treatment team that comes from a shared recognition that each human is a subject who has the capacity to create his or her own life.

LC: The unity of this approach also implies that the psychiatrists who work at the center do not think that psychosis is the result of a defect in the brain. The psychiatrist is sensible to the fact that the analytic treatment has specific effects in the psychotic's life, in the psychotic's body, and that they must help the psychotic by treating these effects. This is very important. I would add that all of this work done with psychotics has profoundly modified our work with neurotics and with perversion.

DB: For example, an emphasis is put on what is out of language and what acts in the unconscious. The psychoanalysis with the neurotic is no longer centered upon the discourse or the interpretation of the language of the patient, but rather the attention is focused on what is out of language and which acts in the life and body of the patient and has to be spoken about. One of the difficulties is that the psychotic person is out of language, everything happens in his or her body in terms of behaviors and acts and this takes priority during the session. Therefore, if the analyst is not "active", nothing happens. To be "active" supposes that the analyst encourages the analysand to speak of what he or she has done and not only to expound about grandiose ideas or about persecution. The analyst is then attentive to the logic of acts and to their consequences. The analyst questions them to allow the psychotic to speak of the goals of acts and behaviors and to reveal the mission that the psychotic has given him or herself. In other words, we cannot, as some people say about the neurotic, wait until "it" speaks or until "the thing" speaks. With the psychotic person, you must support the speech as opposed to wait for it.

LC: This is an active work. And that supposes a specific position and an act of the analyst provokes a speech in the psychotic, without the analyst implicating him or herself personally.

WA: There have been many obstacles. From the second year of the center, they demanded to evaluate the center in order to close it.

LC: After giving us patients who had been treated for years at the hospital, they demanded that we treat and cure these patients in six months.

WA: In 2002, the fight became very strong. I asked the minister to do an evaluation of The 388 compared to the hospital. The minister said, "Yes." They sent three independent evaluators to evaluate the center. The evaluators were people that came from Montreal and Hull. They were not psychoanalysts. Two were psychiatrists and one was a director of a psychiatric hospital. They came to Québec. They met and discussed with a group of 42 patients. They met with the relatives and some professionals in the city. They analyzed the files of the patients. They spoke to the *intervenants* and the psychiatrists at the center. They met us to discuss our way of working with the psychotics. The report was that this was the best. Each of the evaluators came from a different psychiatric hospital, but the minister never evaluated the hospitals of the people who wanted to close The 388.

LC: What we fought and are still fighting comes from a certain group of psychiatrists who are generally involved with research for pharmaceutical companies, or they are people who think psychosis is a lifetime condition that has to be managed with medication or cognitive behavioral therapy and that people should be controlled in the community and lead lives that are not engaged and do not stress them out.

WA: Right now, there are a lot of young psychiatric residents who come to training, here, at GIFRIC, and this irritates and makes angry those in Québec who want to get rid of psychoanalysis in the treatment of psychosis.

DB: In Montreal, there is very well-known and respected psychiatrist, Dr. Alain Lesage, a researcher in social psychiatry, who is very invested and interested in the idea of what he calls the psychodynamic approach for psychotics. He proposed that I, as well as others who use a psychoanalytic approach with psychotics, along with residents in psychiatry who follow GIFRIC training, present symposia and workshops as part of the annual Congress of the Association of Psychiatrists of Québec this June. He says that, in the coming years, he wants people to know more and more about the psychoanalytic approach with psychotics.

LC: There is also a group of psychiatrists in Sherbrooke, a university town. A group of four psychiatrists, who followed the training here in GIFRIC, are now professors and supervisors and work with residents in psychiatry. They tell their residents to come for the training. Now, there is a group of them that wants to open a center like The 388 in Sherbrooke. We have worked with them on this project. It has been difficult to continue this work with them after the changes made by the former government in Québec, but they are continuing this work in Sherbrooke.

WA: In the next two or three years, it will be difficult for the people who are against psychoanalysis for psychotics because there is a group of relatives of users of The 388 who wrote directly to the minister to talk about how there is no comparison between the services of The 388 and the services offered in the hospital. The patients who proceed through the four steps of the treatment – which is to say, 65 percent – return to the social link. They have jobs, they pay taxes as any other citizen, and they don't come back to the center anymore. Some of them have become workers in public administration or architects, lawyers, or university professors.[9]

CV: What do you think about the state's resistance to your approach? Is it an overinvestment in drugs?

WA: It's not the government that is opposed to this, not the state. It is two or three groups of psychiatrists in Québec and Montreal who don't like what's going on and who criticize The 388 to government bureaucrats.

DB: It's psychoanalysis that bothers them, and the psychoanalysis that we practice here in particular. The thing they don't like is that the psychoanalysis that we sustain here is critical of a psychiatry that only sustains itself through the neurosciences, and that evacuates the importance of the speech of the subject who is sick, by putting forward from the beginning that psychosis is an illness of the brain. According to the guidelines of psychiatry, psychoanalysis is not considered as a recommended treatment for psychotics! But it is also recommended in the guidelines that the psychiatrist must find the best way to treat his or her patient. The antipsychotic medication helps to diminish the *passages à l'acte* which have adverse repercussions for the patient or for others. It helps to preserve vital functions. In this sense, it is useful. But antipsychotic medication also makes the patient shut up about delusional ideas and his or her mission when the patient knows that this is what psychiatry aims to do with the medicine. Indeed, the medication does not stop the patient from preserving his or her ideas: we know now, from experience, that despite the strong doses of medicine, the psychotic patient maintains his or her enterprise to reconstruct the world and that it is better to give the patient a space for speech and reorient his or her actions that are both achievable and useful for society rather than to try to stop the patient from thinking.

LC: When the government evaluates what is going on here, they are not interested in the clinical orientation, but in the clinical results. It is really the psychiatric milieu that is fighting against psychoanalysis. Perhaps this is because what we are doing challenges what they are doing as clinical practice.

DB: When the evaluating team came in 2002, they wrote a piercing phrase in their report. They wrote that to see something like 42 schizophrenics stand up and speak by themselves was extremely impressive.

WA: When they came, we put them in a room with 42 patients. It was the first time in their lives that they had been in a room with 42 psychotics.

LC: [Reads and translates the excerpt from the report] "We acknowledge that these are people with severe mental health problems and yet they make contributions to the interpersonal and social world. They are able to give their opinions about anything that concerns them as well as about the programs at The 388. During our two-hour meeting, there were no problems. Everyone raised their hands, took their turns to speak, and the person running the meeting had no problems controlling the event."

Before the evaluators came, the patients had written letters to the minister of health. People said, "Oh, it was not the patients that wrote this. It was probably the *intervenants*. It is too well written or maybe these patients are not actually sick." This is why the evaluators make a specific point in the report by saying that the patients were well behaved, that they participated, and that they had no suspicion that it was not these people who wrote the letters. This is also why they add that these are people who have illnesses that are serious and persistent. Many other critical comments have come over the years. For example, they accuse the psychiatrist of not giving medication, which is not true. They have also accused us of choosing patients who are not really sick or of having good "Lacanian patients."

CV: You spoke about the preparation of the individual who goes through the program. How does someone arrive at the center? How does the process begin?

LC: From the beginning, we have always required that the person, him or herself, call to ask for a meeting, even if it is a psychiatrist or another professional who spoke to the patient about The 388. When he or she arrives, we give them a meeting, which we call the intake interview. We are two who meet the patient. I am always present along with one of the three psychiatrists. We do not ask for a previous file before meeting the patient. We take an hour and fifteen minutes, or an hour and a half, and sometimes even two meetings to let the person speak about their experience from *their* point of view. At what moment, according to them, did the difficulties begin? What happened in their lives at this moment? What ideas did they have during the crises? What are the acts they posed? What can they say of their childhood, adolescence – in other words, of their subjective history and their own interpretation of what they have lived through?

WA: When a person meets a psychiatrist, they are usually required to do it. So, the psychiatrist has a power over this person. We do not want this.

DB: During the first interview, we also try to mobilize the patient to speak about something true. We help the patient to say something that is important for him or her. We try to know if he or she really wants to come to The 388 and if the person is ready to do what they will have to do. I remember an admission committee where we met with a patient who had been hospitalized many times. This man was always very aggressive before and during his hospitalizations. He frightened those around him as well as the staff of the hospital. He said that his psychiatrist told him that if he was admitted at The 388 he could go through his crises there rather than going to the hospital. In his report, the psychiatrist wrote that this patient usually arrived at the hospital with the police.

So, we told him, "This is not entirely true, not entirely correct. You can pass your crises at The 388, but this is on the condition that, with the support of the team, you change your way of managing your crisis. We can't treat someone here who is violent, aggressive, who is speaking loudly, who is breaking things. Look around, here. Everything is fragile, there are valuable stained glass windows in the living room, there are other users who you have to respect, and there are *intervenants* who can support you as long as you don't frighten them! We don't accept that people yell here. You will have to talk about what is going on, and you will have to learn to recognize the signs that precede a crisis in order to find a way for things to happen in a different way."

Eight months later, the psychiatrist from the hospital called us about this patient. He had been hospitalized in the psychiatric ward for a few days. He had not slept in two days, and after a heated discussion with his father, he had started to drink again, and he felt that he was losing control. So, he had called the police during the night to ask them to drive him to The 388. But the police took him to the hospital. The psychiatrist at the hospital said: "We had never seen him like this. He was quiet right from the beginning, he collaborated with us, and tried to understand what was happening to him." He was absolutely not aggressive nor threatening, as he had been before. He was able to come to The 388 to finish the treatment of this crisis. Everything went well and was calm. There was collaboration, and the discovery that being sensitive to the predictors of his psychotic decompensations allowed him to look for help in time and that being able to speak of what disorganized him rather than acting aggressively was beneficial.

LC: In this first meeting, we want to engage the subject, and his or her responsibility, in the treatment. Often the person says that this is the first time that they have had this kind of interview. When they arrive, the people are welcomed by an *intervenant* who explains the various services to them. During the intake meeting, we explain what the psychoanalytic cure is. We explain that the cure is confidential and that they will also have a team composed of an *intervenant*, a social worker, and a psychiatrist. After this first interview, we ask for the patient's previous file in order to integrate it with our data about both previous hospitalizations and [...] the psychiatric services that they received before their admission to The 388. When we think the person is going to be accepted, we tell them to call back in five or six days, which gives us time to discuss the admission interview with our colleagues. If we don't think the person will be accepted, we call them back and refer them to a service that will be more appropriate for them.

DB: After this, the patient has a first meeting with the psychiatrist and with the *intervenant* who will be responsible for the patient and who will be the patient's point of reference in his or her everyday life. This first meeting proceeds in the following manner: The psychiatrist describes, to the *intervenant*, what was at the heart of the patient's admission interview and asks the patient to fill in details or add nuances, if necessary. From this, we make a first plan of intervention for the next six months based on what the patient says during the first meeting about his or her difficulties and about what he wants to fix in his life. We also talk about which art workshops the person will participate in and in which activities he or she will register, to make sure that the activities are beneficial. Usually, we want them to participate in at least one art workshop. It is important that the person develop capacities that are not just in speech, but that are also aesthetic, because there are some life experience that cannot pass through words. That's how it starts.

CV: Does the person prepare for their analysis?

LC: Sometimes we let the team get to know the patient better before the beginning of the analysis. It can be difficult at the beginning of the treatment because often the patient who starts an analytic cure will not talk a lot outside of the analysis. This can be very hard on the team because the *intervenants*, psychiatrists, and social workers need to know what is going on to sustain the person during a crisis.

DB: Normally, the person will start the analytic cure eight to ten months after their admission. There are some logistical concerns, but sometimes a person will start an analysis immediately when they begin to come to The 388 because without the analytic cure they would be at risk of rapidly disorganizing.

LC: The patients will talk amongst themselves when someone new arrives, explaining what the analytic cure is and what you need, like a little dream notebook.

DB: The users help each other. This is an important point.

LC: There is solidarity.

CV: How is the frame of the analysis structured in terms of frequency?

DB: It depends. We discuss it with the patient. It depends on how available they are. Some people are working and do not have a lot of time. Usually, it is one or two times per week. During a crisis, the person may ask to be seen more often at a frequency of three or four times per week. The sessions last 25 or 30 minutes, sometimes less, sometimes more. It is usually the analyst who decides when to end the session, but sometimes it is the patient who says, "I have said enough for today." A person may say, "I have just said a big piece of something, so, I'm going to stop for now." We have to respect that.

LC: During the first meeting of the cure, I say to them that this is a confidential place. I will not say anything to the psychiatrists, the *intervenants*, and I will not write anything in their official file. I tell them that this means that they have the responsibility to speak to the other members of the treatment team and to tell them if they need more support at a certain moment. I explain to them that the analytic cure is a space of free speech and that that they can say everything that they have never been able to say elsewhere. I explain to them also how, and from what basis, we will work: from dreams, thoughts, preoccupations, the context and playing out of psychotic episodes, acts that they pose, memories and important events in their lives, the moment that their first psychotic crisis was triggered, etc.

DB: Confidentiality is the necessary condition in order for the cure to function. This is the condition through which we can hear everything so long as they go for support when they need it.

LC: The patients respect this framework very well. Even when they are speaking about something like suicidal ideas, for instance, sometimes we can ask them, "Did you speak of this with the psychiatrist?" We may tell them they have to speak with the psychiatrist and they always do.

DB: I remember a patient who came to a session and said, "Why do you want to know me?" I asked him, "Why are you asking this question today?" There was probably a reason. He said, "Everyone I speak to uses what I say against me. The people who I talk to about my experiences use it against me afterwards. The people who want to know who I am, what my history is, use it against me when I respond." I said, "I don't want to know you. I want to help you to know something of yourself so that you can manage to have a better life. I don't need to know you." This calmed him.

CV: There is a new category that Jacques-Alain Miller speaks about, "ordinary psychosis". It is an expansion of the way we think of psychosis. Is this category useful to your thinking or your clinical work?

LC: For now, it is not very useful for us. I have read many things about this. They describe the category of psychosis where there are no elementary phenomena: no delusion, no triggering, and no hallucinations. It's interesting but for us, in our clinical practice, this is not very useful. Maybe this is because we also have patients who are not presenting a true delusion or hallucination, but when we listen to them in the analytic cure, we are able to see that there is a kind of psychotic work, an enterprise, someplace.

WA: Either we think that psychosis is an illness in a medical perspective or we think psychosis is what a psychoanalyst calls a structure. Maybe people who think that psychosis is an illness find this idea of ordinary psychosis useful because they are usually treating neurotics. For us, psychosis is not an illness. It is a structure. The psychotic may be sick and he may not be sick. Jean-Jacques Rousseau was a psychotic. Auguste Comte was a psychotic. Mackenzie King was a psychotic. President [Woodrow] Wilson was a psychotic. The psychotic can be sick, but it is a structure.

LC: Psychosis is a certain way for a subject to be in relation to both *jouissance* and the believable, having been directly confronted too early with the defect in language through fundamental experiences of his or her subjectivity.

DB: There are patients who take months or years before they talk about their projects, the experiences they are currently living through or that they previously experienced in their bodies, or about what we call "the internal object," which they refer to as the little things that have been installed in the backs of their necks, the little things in their bodies that connect them to certain beings in the universe or to influential, and often imaginary, people at the level of global socio-politics. I think that if you start from the position of thinking that psychosis is a disease, then you are the one who knows and the psychotic has to speak to the one who knows! In such a situation, the person is not going to speak about what is true for them.

On the subject of the concept of ordinary psychosis, it may be true that this is a useful concept for the French and maybe even a good thing for them, but we don't use this category.

WA: It is the sign that these are not people who treat psychotics.

LC: I think that this concept was developed from a group of clinicians, Lacanians, who were meeting to present cases. They presented cases where it was difficult to know if the person was psychotic or neurotic. They had three big "conversations" over 10 or 15 years. It was in this context that they collaborated on cases to develop the category of "ordinary psychosis".

DB: I remember a man. We met him some years ago. He was a 35-year-old teacher, who was still working. He did not have a delusion, but he was following a movement in physics that said that electromagnetic waves can act on your body and give you many kinds of health problems. What we learned from him was that, in order to preserve his health, he slept at home every night in a tent that protected him from those waves.

LC: He was not able to come to The 388, because, if he needed to be a resident, he could not install his tent.

DB: Was he delusional? Some scientists say that it is true, that there are waves that can have effects like this. What we would say is that his life was becoming more and more difficult for him because of all the restrictions that he gave himself because of his conviction that there were waves that were destroying his organism.

LC: All of his life became centered on this.

DB: He showed us paintings that he had done on the interior walls of his house. The entire home was painted. It was magnificent, extraordinary, a true artist's work. But he was no longer functioning with others. People were finding him to be bizarre. The French psychoanalysts might have said that he was an "ordinary psychotic".

WA: For us, this is a psychotic person.

DB: This man had found a transitory solution to go through life, but now he had hit a rock. He had too much of a hard time with the functioning of his organism and with his vital functions, and it was disturbing him too much. What he had elaborated was at the limit of delusion. Now, contrary to what we thought 30 years ago, when someone asks us if we think that there are extraterrestrials, we might say, "Maybe!" Now we know that before his death, Stephen Hawking, the well-known astrophysicist, was not working to find out if there were extraterrestrials in the universe, but rather where they were in the universe!

LC: Someone may tell us that someone is watching them through the computer. A patient once said that, because of the things that he bought on the internet, he had a visit from the provincial police. Later, the police actually told him that they had been watching him for six months. The delusion is not a criterion for determining if the person is psychotic. The criteria of ordinary psychosis are finally criteria that are close to the criteria of psychiatry.

DB: It is when we say that the person is having a hard time in his or her life because he or she, alone, is in charge of some kind of enterprise to improve all of humanity, that we say that this is a structure of psychosis.

LC: This work is at the heart of psychosis, and the delusion is a theory that the person has elaborated to explain this work.

CV: At the center, the community, which includes the programs for art, music, cooking, literature classes, and the walking club, seems to be crucial for the treatment. How do you see the relationship between psychoanalysis and therapeutic communities?

DB: A patient once said, "Knowing that I can call anytime, day or night, knowing that there is someone there who will listen to me, who I can talk to, this helps me. It helps to know that it is there even though it won't solve my problem." The mutual aid and support [are] important, but there also needs to be a work on experiences. The community side of treatment does not suffice in itself.

LC: The patients don't think of it as a social place, but rather as a real place of work where they come to do a certain kind of work. Often, as the work progresses, they will stop coming, because they want to be out in the world, not in this place of treatment. Even if it is true that there is a scene of mutual support and solidarity in the center, these are things the patients will begin to develop outside of the center. It is important for them to articulate themselves to the social link.

DB: For several years, for instance, the *intervenants* prepared Christmas baskets for users who live alone, or people who live with a family member, but live in difficult financial conditions and do not have the means to offer themselves any little treats for Christmas. The GIFRIC foundation takes care of this. Before bringing the Christmas baskets, which are brought by the *intervenants* and a user, we decide who the users are who will most benefit from a basket. Right now, we are looking at the information we have collected over the past two years. One of my patients works very hard, he does not make a lot of money, his family lives out-side of the province, and he was on the list this year. When they offered him a basket, he said, "Thanks very much, but I work now. I do not need it." He is taking steps to be in the social rather than staying in a position that he identifies as being someone who would be sick or unable to do things for himself.

CV: Thank you for having me. I admire your care, compassion, and serious-ness with this work. It is an inspiration. You've created something of a dream, here.

DB: One for the museum!

Notes

1 We choose to keep the French term "*intervenants*" (or clinical *intervenant*) to desig-nate the professionals trained by GIFRIC to ensure the long-term psychoanalytic follow-up, on a daily, weekly, or monthly basis depending upon the evolution and stages of the treatment. The clinical *intervenants* have different backgrounds (psy-chology, anthropology, nursing, philosophy, etc.) previous to the psychoanalytic training given by GIFRIC.

2 Louis Beirnaert (1906–1985) was a French Jesuit and psychoanalyst. In 1953, Beir-naert, Father Charles Durand, Charles Nodet, and Father Bruno de Jésus-Maries established the International Association of Medico-Psychological and Religious Studies. Beirnaert was also a member of the Société Française de Psychanalyse and the *École freudienne de Paris*, where he undertook a supervisory analysis with Lacan (Roudinesco 198). Michel de Certeau (1925–1986) was a French Jesuit and aca-demic known for his philosophy of everyday life.

3 Saint-Anne Hospital Center is located in Paris and specializes in psychiatry and neurology. Lacan was also an intern at Sainte-Anne from 1927 to 1928 and a con-sultant psychiatrist there during the 1950s and held his seminars there until 1963.

4 French psychiatrists Jean Delay (1907–1987) and his assistant Pierre Deniker (1917–1998) drew from Henri Laborit's (1914–1995) work experimenting with chlorpromazine. Laborit published a paper on chlorpromazine in a 1952 issue of *La Presse Médicale* entitled, "A new vegetative stabilizer," where he commented that the drug produced effects of uninterest, apathy, and drowsiness. In the same year, Deniker and Delay published multiple papers detailing their experiments adminis-tering chlorpromazine to 38 male patients who were being treated for various sorts of excited states at Sainte-Anne Hospital. By the end of 1955, chlorpromazine be-came widely available for prescription in France and spread to be part of psychiat-ric treatments of psychosis throughout the world (Ban 496).

5 Françoise Dolto (1908–1988) was a French pediatrician and psychoanalyst known for her theories on child development and the unconscious body image. She was a close friend of Jacques Lacan and a member of his school.

6 Jean Oury (1924–2014) was a French psychiatrist and psychoanalyst as well as a member of the Freudian School of Paris. He founded La Borde clinic in 1953, em-phasizing principles of therapeutic community and institutional psychotherapy. Psychotherapist and philosopher Félix Guattari (1930–1992) also worked for much of his life at La Borde under Oury's direction. For an interview with Guattari on La Borde, see "La Borde: A Clinic Unlike Any Other" in *Chaosophy: Texts and Inter-views, 1972–1977*. Belinda S. Mackie also has written an excellent work, *Treating*

People with Psychosis in Institutions: A Psychoanalytic Perspective, which provides an overview of both the La Borde clinic in France and The 388 in Canada.

7 In a 1952 article outlining the use of chlorpromazine for the treatment of psychosis, Deniker and Delay wrote a detailed description of the effects of the drug on a patient: "Seated or lying down, the patient is motionless on his bed, often pale and with lowered eyelids. He remains silent most of the time. If questioned, he responds after the delay, slowly, in an indifferent monotone, expressing himself with a few words and quickly becoming mute. Without exception, the response is generally valid and pertinent, showing the subject is capable of attention and of reflection. But he rarely takes the initiative of asking a question; he does not express his preoccupations, desires, or preference. He is usually conscious of the amelioration brought on by treatment, but he does not express euphoria. The apparent indifference, or delay in response to external stimuli, the emotional effect of neutrality, the decrease in both initiative and preoccupation with an alteration of conscious awareness or in intellectual faculties constitute the psychic syndrome due to treatment" (qtd. in Moncrieff 32). Since the early uses of chlorpromazine, a second generation of antipsychotic medications, which are more preferable given the lower risk of side effects, has been produced. Chlorpromazine, however, remains on the list of the World Health Organization's List of Essential Medicines and continues to be prescribed throughout the world as a generic drug for treatment of psychosis.

8 Erotomania is frequently understood as a delusion where a person (usually more common in women) believes that another person (frequently of elevated class or public social status) is in love with them despite clear evidence to the contrary. Psychiatrist Gaëtan Gatian de Clérambault (1872–1934) influenced Lacan's thoughts on psychoanalysis and erotomania, which is sometimes called "de Clérambault's syndrome." It is understood as a kind of sexual obsession that transcends the barriers of financial or social class. For a brief overview of de Clérambault's theory of erotomania and its influence on Lacan's thinking, see relevant chapters in Élisabeth Roudinesco's *Jacques Lacan*, including "Psychiatry Teachers" and "The Story of Marguerite."

9 See Apollon, Bergeron, and Cantin's chapter, "Problems of Femininity in the Psychoanalytical Treatment of Psychotic Women" in *Lacan on Psychosis: From Theory to Praxis*, where they present evidence-based outcome data from a sample of 69 patients (men and women) with psychosis and schizophrenia whose frequency of hospitalization was reduced by more than 60% after receiving treatment from The 388.

Bibliography and Further Reading

Apollon, Willy, Bergeron, Danielle, and Lucie Cantin. *After Lacan: Clinical Practice and the Subject of the Unconscious*. Ed. Robert Hughes and Kareen Ror Malone. New York: State University of New York, 2002.

Apollon, Willy, Bergeron, Danielle, and Lucie Cantin. *La Cure Psychanalytique du Psychotique: Enjeux et Stratégies*. Québec: Collection Nœud and GIFRIC, 2008.

Apollon, Willy, Bergeron, Danielle, and Lucie Cantin. "Problems of Femininity in the Psychoanalytical Treatment of Psychotic Women." *Lacan on Psychosis: From Theory to Praxis*. Ed. Jon Mills and David L. Downing. New York: Routsledge, 2019.

Apollon, Willy, Bergeron, Danielle, and Lucie Cantin. *The Subject of Lacan: A Lacanian Reader for Psychologists*. Ed. Kareen Ror Malone and Stephen R. Friedlander. "The Treatment of Psychosis." New York: State University of New York, 2000. 209–229.

Apollon, Willy, Bergeron, Danielle, and Lucie Cantin. *Un Avenir Pour le Psychotique: Le Dispositif du Traitement Psychoanalytique*. Québec: Collection Nœud and GIFRIC, 2013.

Apollon, Willy and Feldstein, Richard, eds. *Lacan, Politics, Aesthetics*. New York: State University of New York, 1996.

Ban, Thomas A. "Fifty Years Chlorpromazine: A Historical Perspective." *Neuropsychiatric Diseases and Treatment*. 3.4 (2007): 295–500.

Cantin, Lucie. "An Effective Treatment of Psychosis with Psychoanalysis in Québec City, Since 1982." *Annual Review of Critical Psychology*. 7 (2009): 286–319. http://www.discourseunit.com/arcp/7.htm

Cantin, Lucie. "Comment penser l'évaluation du traitement psychanalytique des psychose." *La cure psychanalytique du psychotique: Enjeux et Stratégies*. Ed. Willy Apollon, Danielle Bergeron, and Lucie Cantin. Québec: Collection Nœud and GIFRIC, 2008. 87–120.

Guattari, Félix. "La Borde: A Clinic Unlike Any Other." *Chaosophy: Texts and Interviews, 1972–1977*. Ed. Sylvère Lotringer. Los Angeles: Semiotext(e), 2009. 176–194.

Mackie, Belinda. *Treating People with Psychosis in Institutions: A Psychoanalytic Perspective*. London: Karnac, 2016.

Moncrieff, Joanna. *The Bitterest Pills: The Troubling Story of Antipsychotic Drugs*. New York: Palgrave Macmillan, 2013.

Roudinesco, Élisabeth. *Jacques Lacan*. Trans. Barbara Bray. New York: Columbia University Press, 1997.

Chapter 4

Speaking of François Peraldi in Québec in Four Parts

Part 1 with Michel Peterson (Translation by Alireza Taheri)

Michel Peterson, PhD, is a psychoanalyst, social worker, and professor of literature. Peterson works as a clinician for asylum seekers who have been victims of organized violence. He is the author of *L'instant du danger: Réflexions d'un psychanalyste et témoignages sur l'exil force* [The Moment of Danger: Reflections of a Psychoanalyst and Testimonies on Forced Exile] (Montréal, éditons du passage, 2012) among other books. He has also published Portuguese translations of Jacques Derrida, Francis Ponge, and Réjean Ducharme. He is the founder and director of the collection "Voix Psychanalytiques" ["Psychoanalytic Voices"], published by Liber editions. Peterson is the editor and publisher of the seminars of François Peraldi (1938–1993), who was the first person to bring clinical Lacanian psychoanalysis to Québec, QC. This conversation was recorded on September 27, 2019.

Chris Vanderwees: As I was researching for this project, I came across the work of François Peraldi, who was very influential in Québec but who I had not heard about before. Had you attended his seminars?

Michel Peterson: It is actually a strange situation. Peraldi was teaching at the University of Montréal in translation studies between 1980 and 1993. At this time, I was a student and Peraldi was "teaching psychoanalysis" in the translation department. I knew him and all of his work, but I never attended his seminars. And, yet, I am the one who has published Peraldi's seminars.

DOI: 10.4324/9781003323136-5

CV: Perhaps we could begin with another question. What was your first en-
        counter with psychoanalysis?

MP: It was in 1980. I was studying philosophy and literature at the University
        of Montréal. I met Claude Lévesque, a professor there who was teaching
        philosophy, including [Georges] Bataille, Derrida, [Maurice] Blanchot,
        and Lacan. He was a very close friend of Peraldi. This was my first con-
        tact. I wrote a paper in his seminar, and he told me it might be a good idea
        to meet with the psychoanalysts. This was almost 40 years ago.

CV: When did you discover Peraldi?

MP: It was in 1982 or 1983. Peraldi was on the floor above in translation
        studies. There was a lot of back-and-forth between the two floors. I be-
        came a translator prior to becoming a psychoanalyst. I was translating
        from Polish and Portuguese to French. Eventually, I became a psycho-
        analyst. I was never a student of Peraldi's. Although I never went to his
        seminars, I had access to his archive, all of the documentation, all of the
        papers, and seminars. I know almost everyone who went to his seminars,
        but I never went to the seminar myself, which was good for me in a way.
        This made it easier to publish Peraldi's work since I was not as involved
        in the games or headaches of transference, whether it might have been
        infatuation or hate or love or jealousy. I did not have to deal with the
        rivalry between the peers.

CV: What was it in Peraldi's works that you saw as being particularly valua-
        ble? Is there something about his work that significantly influenced your
        own practice?

MP: There are two or three important things here. Peraldi was really the first
        person to bring Lacanian psychoanalysis to Québec. What Peraldi was
        doing was very interesting, not just because of his interest in Lacan but
        because his work represented a fundamental rupture from what psycho-
        analysis had previously been in Québec. Peraldi is a turning point in
        Québec's psychoanalytic history. Prior to Peraldi's arrival, psychoanaly-
        sis was mainly brought to Québec and maintained by Catholic religious
        groups. The main person of the early psychoanalytic groups in Québec
        was Noël Mailloux, a French-Canadian priest and psychologist who
        also taught at the University of Montréal.[1] He separated the depart-
        ment of psychology from philosophy. He used the psychology depart-
        ment as the vehicle for teaching psychoanalysis. Mailloux was never
        analyzed, but he was immersed in psychoanalysis and had an intricate
        epistolary correspondence with Anna Freud. There was another gentle-
        man, Miguel Prados, who was a refugee from Spain and was also instru-
        mental in the dissemination of psychoanalysis in Québec.[2] Prados left
        Spain because of Francisco Franco and immigrated to the province,
        here.[3] Before Peraldi, there was also another person who was influential,
        Gregory Zilboorg, a Ukrainian psychoanalyst who studied in the Soviet
        Union.[4] This was a very interesting configuration because, on the one

hand, there was a kind of Soviet psychoanalytic presence and, on the other hand, there was a religious kind of psychoanalysis coming from Mailloux. This created a unique and interesting combination.

Mailloux and Prados, along with Theo Chentrier, Erik Wittkower, Alastair McLeod, and Georges Zavitzianos, played a key role in the introduction of psychoanalysis in Québec. Mailloux and Prados together founded *Le Cercle Psychanalytique de Montréal* [the Psychoanalytical Circle of Montréal] in 1946. Mailloux actually mainly founded the group but could never fully participate, because he was never analyzed. Paradoxically, Mailloux was a "founder" but also was not really part of it. The society was split into two parts: one part Francophone (the Société Psychanalytique de Montréal) and the other Anglophone (the Québec-English branch). The actual training curriculums and styles between the French and the Anglo were radically different. The Anglo side was academic, bookish, and more of the International Psychoanalytic Association, whereas the French was starting to go in a more free direction but all within the same institute. The libraries between the Anglo and French parts were kept separate but in the same room, and somewhere in there is Freud in German.

In 1975, Peraldi leaves France and comes to Québec at a time when he is wrapping up his PhD thesis with Roland Barthes on translation, symptoms, and dreamwork in Freud.[5] Peraldi was teaching psychoanalysis in the university in the translation departments at the University of Montréal and at McGill University but outside of the Psychoanalytic Institute. This is all during the rise of poststructuralism with thinkers such as Derrida, [Julia] Kristeva, and [Michel] Foucault among others. The people attending Peraldi's seminars were not initially clinicians. Those in attendance were not psychiatrists or psychologists but rather sociologists, anthropologists, philosophers, and literary people. These seminars were conducted outside the Institute but created a whole generation of people interested in psychoanalysis who would then go on to train and become the first generation of Québécois psychoanalysts of a Lacanian orientation. I am of the analysts of this generation.

Peraldi founded the Lacanian Clinical Forum with William Richardson, John Muller, Ess White, and Donna Bentolila, which was set up in New York, but the seminars continue to be held twice per year with a meeting in Stockbridge [Massachusetts] and a meeting in Montréal. Therefore, Peraldi is someone who not only brought the Lacanian orientation to Québec but created links in Boston, New York, and Toronto. He disseminated Lacanian teaching beyond the province.

What is interesting is that the Francophone Lacanian psychoanalysts of Montréal have almost no relation (with few exceptions) with the Anglophone Lacanian psychoanalysts within the city, but they create strong links with Anglophone psychoanalysts, for instance, in the United States and Toronto.

Alireza Taheri:	This is Freud's notion of the narcissism of small differences.[6]
MP:	Exactly. There were also three analysts who were very good friends of Peraldi. These analysts – two women and a man – taught Lacan within the Montréal institute for some years, but at some point, representatives of the International Psychoanalytical Association [IPA] said that these teachings had to stop or the Institute would go so far as to lose accreditation. Lacan has never again been taught at the Institute.

I completed training at the Lacanian school in Montréal, but I also did an IPA training at the Montréal Psychoanalytic Institute. Despite the fact that the Training Institute accredited my course, having done all of the clinical hours, supervisions, analysis, and other requirements,

I was not allowed by the General Assembly to become a member of the society or with the IPA, mainly because of my previous formation at the Lacanian school. There was a massive hate and demonization of Lacan within the Society, which is still sensitive today. Many of the active Lacanian analysts in Québec trained under Peraldi and hence the Institute has a hidden, but rather obvious, disdain for this whole group of analysts who have been working in the field for 25 years.

Ever since Peraldi passed away, Lacanian psychoanalysis in Québec has three faces. There is *Le Pont Freudien* [The Freudian Bridge] associated with Jacques-Alain Miller's group in France. There is the group of the *École Lacanienne de Montréal* [Lacanian School of Montréal] founded by Jean-Paul Gilson, a Belgian gentleman. Gilson's group was created after the dissolution of the Cercle lacanien d'Études freudiennes [Lacanian Circle of Freudian Studies]. There is also *Groupe interdisciplinaire freudien de recherche et intervention cliniques et culturelles* (GIFRIC) [Freudian Interdisciplinary Research Group of Clinical and Cultural Intervention] founded by Willy Apollon, Danielle Bergeron, and Lucie Cantin in Québec City. None of these Lacanian groups [has] any affiliation to the International Psychoanalytic Association in Montréal.

In the early 1970s, prior to the arrival of Peraldi, psychoanalysis in Québec circulated and functioned within the university in a very religious way with the influence and maintenance of Mailloux and Prados. Peraldi enters the scene in the mid-'70s with this whole baggage of post-Freudian theory, poststructuralism, Bataille, Lacan, Nietzsche, [Martin] Heidegger and was also gay (and would later pass away from AIDS). He had certain philosophical ideas that were shocking to what psychoanalysis was prior to his arrival. Peraldi was a massive rupture on many levels. He was originally invited to come to Québec by a poet, Daniel Sloate, who was then based in Montréal.[7] Peraldi was a colorful personality, a person who frequented clubs in New York City. There are many shocks with Peraldi and his thinking but also in his "life".

Peraldi put much effort into linking linguistics, philosophy, anthropology and psychoanalysis. This was not at all done in Québec before him. He was particularly interested in India and Mexico. With Mexico, Peraldi was interested in the notions of sacrifice. With India, he was interested in the study of the Gods. He worked with Anglophone anthropologists who were studying both Mexico and India at the time. All of this would inform his psychoanalytic study and understanding of the drives. For example, Peraldi was trying to understand the death drive through Indian ideas about the Hindu goddess Kali or through the nirvana principle to help enrich psychoanalysis.

CV: From what I have heard, Peraldi would not have claimed to be Lacanian but preferred to say that he was "Lacanizing." How do you make sense of his preference for this descriptor?

MP: Thankfully, Peraldi was not a Lacanian. He was able to think independently of Lacan and was critical of Lacan. He did not belong to the high bourgeoisie of the Lacanian world. Despite using and engaging with Lacan's thoughts, unlike many of the cliché Lacanians, Peraldi did not participate in this mimicry or mimesis of Lacan. He retained his own voice despite the influence. Even when William Richardson and Peraldi, for instance, called it the Stockbridge Lacanian Clinical Forum, they did not mean to imply exclusive Lacanianism. "Lacan" or "Lacanian" was a kind of unifying signifier but not one that was meant to exclude anything. For Peraldi, Lacan was really just a starting point, something to bounce ideas from, but not a point that is meant to fetishize, reify, or idealize concepts. Peraldi's intention was certainly not to rigidify the concepts of Lacan. I have a similar approach to Lacan. I recognize the importance in Lacan's work, but there are questionable moments just like in the work of anyone. As a clinician, I do not limit myself to this one approach.

CV: Did Peraldi also work with children in the clinic?

MP: He did not particularly work with children, except early in his career, but the question of the infantile was part of his interests. In earlier years, he did work collaboratively with Françoise Dolto, who was a pioneering, original Lacanian who worked with children as a pediatrician and psychoanalyst, but he did not really work with children in his practice.[8]

CV: What would you say are the core concerns about psychoanalysis in his work?

MP: Peraldi's first seminar is *Le Sujet* [The Subject], the second seminar is called *L'Autre, Le Temps* [*The Other, Time*], and the third seminar is *La mort* [*Death*]. His last seminar is *L'enseignement de Lacan* [*Lacan's Teaching*], which is not yet published. He was not interested in psychosis in any exclusive way. What really interested Peraldi was the question of time and temporality in relation to unconscious memory and the stratification of memories. For Peraldi, time is the vector through which we can think of the drive. The question of being appears in Peraldi's work through Heidegger's influence, but he is not thinking of it in an ontological way since he might have stated that it is being where it is lacking. Peraldi is also interested in comparing these notions as they appear within a Western philosophical and psychoanalytic tradition and how they are worked with in a different, occidental context. In relation to Peraldi's studies in temporality, he spent three years on death in his seminar and was engaged in working on Lacan and Heidegger and their interstices. He also worked with William Richardson on the overlaps between Lacan, Heidegger, and their understandings of death.

   For Peraldi, death is not just another thing he is thinking about psychoanalytically. He actually almost prioritizes the question of death over psychoanalysis. Death provides access to situate and understand psychoanalysis altogether. In all of these Freudian case studies, including the Wolfman and [Daniel Paul] Schreber, Peraldi is most attentive to what is happening with the anxiety of death and this is the focus of his thinking. At almost every generation of the Peraldi family, there was a suicide. Obviously, this contributed to his fascination with death. How is death transmitted from generation to generation? Peraldi was preoccupied with this question. He was so interested in Heidegger that he even had the dream of creating an institute of higher Heideggerian studies. He was in correspondence for years with Catherine Duncan, an artist and filmmaker, where they discussed the works of Heidegger. This correspondence, which consists of over 500 pages, also served as a continuation of his self-analysis.[9]

   Peraldi was never so preoccupied with questions of institutions and prestige or the conflicts, rivalries, and other petty aspects between groups. He was focused on psychoanalysis as a form of thinking for the social and political. He did not dirty his hands much with the institutions that might say, "You can do this" or "You cannot do that." For him, psychoanalysis was a mode of thought. In the last sentence of his correspondence with Catherine Duncan, he writes that "*La psychanalyse çe n'est pas grand' chose.*"[10]

CV: What was it that caught your attention about Peraldi's work? How has Peraldi been important for you?

MP: His students confirmed my interest in his work because many of them became such interesting psychoanalysts through his influence.

Peraldi's fascination with other cultures and anthropology was also of much interest to me. I am very interested in anthropology. Of my three children, I have two daughters who are anthropologists, one who lives in Mexico. I recently got back from studying in India. I founded a collection, "Voix Psychanalytiques" ["Psychoanalytic Voices"], which has a threefold objective. The first objective is to provide a history of psychoanalysis in Québec. Peraldi is obviously a big part of this collection. The second objective is to make links between psychoanalysis in Québec and psychoanalysis elsewhere (for instance, Portugal, Brazil, Tunisia, and India). Thirdly, I wanted to make links between psychoanalysis and other traditions such as yoga and Buddhism. What was mostly interesting to me about Peraldi is that he tried to pull psychoanalysis out of its Western cage. When I discovered that Peraldi was working with Indian culture, it was fantastic. I am so interested in how Indian culture conceives of the unconscious. It is not as though people do not conceive of the unconscious in India, but the psychical apparatus is comprehended in a totally different way. Peraldi was thinking about this relation.

CV: Did Peraldi have an interest in society in the sense of a social imaginary?

MP: Whether it is yoga, Hinduism, or Buddhism, Peraldi was concerned with making encounters with the non-Western. He was trying to make use of non-Western concepts to put into question our Western psychoanalytic tradition. Peraldi examined destructiveness and the drive alongside different notions, which can be found in Patañjali, who was a fourteenth-century Indian yogi and wrote the yoga sutras. Peraldi also asked questions about what we take for granted in sequential stages of development when in India there is a different conceptualization. Through encounters with other cultures, Peraldi wanted to raise questions and not become so rigidified.

Peraldi was concerned with the tripartite notions of woman, the feminine, and the maternal and the distinction, nuances, or radical differences between these three levels. He was also close to Luce Irigaray and Marguerite Duras.[11] He sought ways in these non-Western traditions to highlight different perspectives between woman, the feminine, and the maternal while drawing upon the yoga sutra or the Sanskrit epics of the Mahābhārata and the Rāmāyaṇa. Ultimately, a lot of Peraldi's work is guided by the question, what does a woman want? Of course, this was also a central question for Freud.

Peraldi was also thinking about the idea of pulsatility and pulsion. For him, it was not only about the Freudian or Lacanian drive but also about how the drive moves and the way it pushes subjects in and out of structures onto other ones. One of Peraldi's points of departure from Lacan is that he does not reify neurosis, perversion, or psychosis so stringently. He was interested, for instance, in how a neurosis could touch elements of perversion. He is not wedded to the idea that neurosis is repression, perversion is disavowal, and psychosis is foreclosure. Peraldi thought there could be movement between these structures.

Peraldi's last seminar, *L'enseignement de Lacan*, precedes the work that Élisabeth Roudinesco did, providing a systematic, pedagogical reading of Lacan. He ends his seminars with work that is really attributed to Lacan. I would suggest for anyone who has an interest in reading Peraldi to read his pedagogical work in *L'enseignement de Lacan* before reading the earlier seminars.

AT: You have this interest in pre-modern Indian philosophies, and Peraldi also had an interest in texts like the yoga sutras, the Mahābhārata, and the Rāmāyaṇa. Most psychoanalysis today is utterly uninterested in these topics. If pre-modern philosophy is ever mentioned, it is to make the separation. Most notably, it is the Ljubljana Lacanian School or the Slovenian School that insists on yin and yang, for instance, as being of the pre-modern imaginary while suggesting that what they are interested in is the scientific Real. Lacan said that psychoanalysis is a discourse that is born from modern science.[12] He talks a lot, for example, about Galileo or medicine, etc.[13] In Peraldi's work and your own, these pre-modern philosophies are brought together with psychoanalysis rather than making a separation. One field feeds the other. The Jungians have done something of the job that you and Peraldi seem to have been working on. The Lacanians look down upon the Jungians as if they were engaged in some phantasmatic kind of thinking that is stuck in the imaginary. How might you respond to this difference between yourself and Peraldi and other Lacanians who are way too snobby for this sort of exploration in these fields?

MP: Jean-Michel Vappereau once told me in a conversation that Lacan had never really come to a final conclusion about how he felt about Jung.[14] Lacan had the complete works of Jung in his library and was engaged with Jungian thinking but did not speak much about Jung in his work. Lacan never came to a final verdict about Jung's work. Certainly, Lacan never came to such a verdict on Jung as Slavoj Žižek or other members of the Ljubljana School have in their writings. As soon as the Ljubljana School mentions Jung, it is usually to toss it out. Lacan was interested in Buddhism; he learned Chinese and worked with scholars at the School of Oriental Languages in Paris. There are many seminars where Lacan begins working with Chinese characters. Although I respect what Žižek has done in all sincerity, I feel Žižek has closed everything off to focus on the Western tradition, notably the German philosophical and psychoanalytical traditions.

AT: For Žižek, it is not even "the West" but rather a post-Kantian West and Christianity.

MP: If we go back to the paper that Lacan wrote on "Variations on the Standard Treatment" published in 1955 or "The Situation of Psychoanalysis and the Training of Psychoanalysts in 1956," he mentions Jung and Wilhelm Reich as two people who opened up the work of psychoanalysis to asymptomatic pathologies. These pathologies do not have to do with the transference neurosis proper, and Lacan gives Jung and Reich credit for this. Žižek and the Ljubljana School often make the Freudo-Marxists an object of attack because they are infatuated with Saint Paul, which raises questions around the law. Psychoanalysts are the ones doing the most harm to psychoanalysis precisely when they want to retain a purity of psychoanalysis.

AT: The notion of a pure something is so anti-Hegelian. I have always found this to be a very curious thing about Žižek insofar as he is an advocate of purity but is also a Hegelian. Hegel was an anti-purity thinker, which was his brilliance. Hegel is not interested in anything pure, because things flip to their opposites; everything is tainted by its Other.

MP: I am recalling a cartel group in Montréal who focused on Jung's work and presented their research recently. The work was ridiculed and mocked.

AT: Jung does provide us with some fascinating nuggets. He once said that people suffer more from the way they avoid illness than from the illness itself.[15] This is both psychoanalytic and a good point. I am surprised to hear that Peraldi rejects, or at least does not accept, the stringent separation of the structures. Most Lacanian orientations really adhere to a separation of the structures as in neurosis, perversion, and psychosis. There is some discussion of the mobility between neurosis and perversion even in Lacan's work, but very little. Certainly, psychosis is cast as separate. How is this legitimized? What is the argument here?

MP: For Peraldi, the mobility of structures was very important. He came to Québec at a time when he was almost the only Lacanian. He was able to bring the Lacan of his own making here because he had nobody opposing him with the orthodoxy of Lacan, which now exists. In this way, Peraldi had some freedom at the time. Part of how he constructed his own version of Lacan was to wed it to poststructuralism rather than to structuralism. Important figures for Peraldi were also Jacques Derrida, Luce Irigaray, and Michèle Montrelay, but specifically their reluctance to accept the phallus as this principal structuring signifier. Of course, Derrida provides a famous critique of phallogocentrism in philosophy and language throughout his own work. Peraldi aligned himself with this. The fact of his own homosexuality also played a part in this. He saw Freud as a person who radically challenged phallogocentrism but also founded psychoanalysis on phallogocentrism. Peraldi thought, if we removed phallogocentrism, we could rethink sexual difference along different lines. These lines of thought are still pursued today by Judith Butler.

If we rethink the phallic signifier as a central one, we have to rethink all of the structures as well. Sexual difference and the structures as in neurosis, perversion, and psychosis all really hinge on what the subject is doing with this phallic signifier. Is he or she repressing it? Is he or she disavowing it? Is he or she foreclosing it? If he or she is repressing it, is he or she identifying with it, having it, being it? It becomes a matter or having it or not. For Peraldi, this is a bit funny. He goes back to Freud and Josef Breuer's *Studies in Hysteria*, where psychoanalysis begins precisely with sexual ambiguity.

Freud has an assumption of the link between psychosis and homosexuality, which forms the central part of his argument around Schreber that the whole madness was a denial of being gay. Of course, Lacan throws this out. Lacan suggests that this is a bit much. We obviously don't need that. Nonetheless, we can compare what Peraldi does to Lacan as much to what Lacan does to Freud. Peraldi considers Lacan's thinking to be not as phallocentric or stuck as Freud's was but yet as still caught up with the phallus as a central signifier, which is an idea that leads to stringent separations between masculinity and femininity as well as neurosis, perversion, and psychosis. Peraldi was not just battling Freud and Lacan but battling a kind of Freudianism that was more archaic than Freud himself. Ultimately, Freud was an atheist whereas Mailloux and the Ernest Jones generation of psychoanalysts in Québec, for instance, were "religious". I have the transcripts of Peraldi's teachings, and it is fascinating to see someone teaching concepts like *jouissance* or Freud's "Beyond the Pleasure Principle" to a group of religious people in those days.

Bibliography and Further Reading

Chagnon, Gilles, Hazan, Marie and Peterson, Michel. *Penser la Clinique psychanalytique. Le Lacanian Clinical Forum*. Montréal: Liber, 2010.

Harari, Roberto. *Lacan's Seminar on 'Anxiety': An Introduction*. Trans. Jane C. Lamb-Ruiz. New York: Other Press.

Jung, Carl. "Psychology and Religion." 1938. *Collected Works of C. G. Jung, Volume 11, Psychology and Religion: West and East*. Ed. and Trans. Gerhard Adler and R.F.C. Hull. Princeton: Princeton University Press, 1969.

Peck, M. Scott. *The Road Less Travelled: A New Psychology of Love, Traditional Values and Spiritual Growth*. New York: Simon & Schuster, 1978.

Peraldi, François. *L'Autre; Le temps: séminaire 1982–1985*. Ed. Michel Peterson. Montréal, 2007.

Peraldi, François. *La mort: séminaire 1985–1988*. Ed. Michel Peterson. Montréal: Liber, 2010.

Peraldi, François. *La sémiotique de C.S. Peirce: Au-delà de la sémiolinguistique*. Paris: Larousse, 1980.

Peraldi, François. *Le sujet: séminaire 1981–1982.* Ed. Michel Peterson. Montréal: Liber, 2006.

Peraldi, François. *Lettre à Catherine Duncan, 1967–1993.* Ed. Michel Peterson. Montréal: TAMAM, 2017.

Peraldi, François (ed). *Polysexuality.* New York: SemiotextI, 1995.

Peraldi, François. *Psychanalyse et traduction.* Montréal: Presses d' l'Université de Montréal, 1982.

Peraldi, François. *Traduire: application de quelques concepts de la sémanalyse' l'operation traduisante.* Diss. Sorbonne Université, 1975.

Peterson, Michel. "La Pensée-Peraldi". *L'analyste à l'œuvre. Relire François Peraldi,* Eds. Louise Grenier et Marie Hazan, Montréal: Liber, 2008. 13–50.

Peterson, Michel. "Le Mythe de Kâlî Et La Jouissance Féminine Chez François Peraldi". *Québec-Asie Récits et.figures de l'altérité,* Ed. Janusz Przychodzen. Québec: Presses de l'Université Laval, 2009, p. 79–104.

Peterson, Michel. "Un Cadavre De La Psychanalyse Québécoise: Réflexions Sur l'effacement Du Père Noël Mailloux." *Interfaces Brasil/Canadá.* 17.1 (2017): 179–194.

Peterson, Michel, *La dépasse.* Montréal: Tamam, 2017.

Vigneault, Jacques. "Peraldi, François (1938–1993)." *The International Dictionary of Psychoanalysis.* Ed. Alain de Mijolla. New York: Thomson, 2005. 1247.

Part 2 with Louise Grenier (Translation by Alireza Taheri)

Louise Grenier, MA Psych, is a psychologist and psychoanalyst in private practice. She was a lecturer in the Department of Psychology at the University of Québec in Montréal (UQAM) until 2010. She is a member of the Order of Psychologists of Québec, founder and head of the Psychoanalytic Animation Circle, and Coordinator of the Group of Interdisciplinary Psychoanalytical Studies at UQAM. Grenier is the author of several books and articles on psychology and psychoanalysis. Her most recent work is an edited collection, *Lettres du Divan: Écrire à son psychanalyste* [Letters from the Couch: Write to Your Psychoanalyst] (Liber, 2017). She was supervised by François Peraldi (1938–1993), who was the first person to bring clinical Lacanian psychoanalysis to Québec. She attended Peraldi's seminars from 1979 to 1991. This conversation was recorded on September 29, 2019.

Chris Vanderwees: What was your first encounter with psychoanalysis?

Louise Grenier: I began reading Freud at the age of 18. The theory and clinical cases fascinated me. Eventually, I studied psychology and during this time I began my own personal analysis. I did my analysis for two reasons, obviously for the training and formation and for the necessity to fulfill this requirement but most importantly for personal reasons. Every analysis deals with your personal suffering.

CV: What about your discovery of Lacan or Peraldi or this branch of clinical theory, this way of working with people in the clinic?

LG: At the University of Québec in Montréal, I got more involved with Lacan and psychoanalysis as a student of "dynamic" or "psychodynamic" psychology. This is a euphemism of psychoanalysis given that psychoanalysis is a taboo term in universities in North America. My teacher was Mireille Lafortune, who was a student of Françoise Dolto.[16] Through the guidance of Lafortune, I decided to attend Peraldi's lectures at the University of Montréal around the years 1979 and 1980. Specifically, these were lectures on semiology and Lacan.

Peraldi held a subversive and revolutionary lecture series because the International Psychoanalytic Association (IPA) in Montréal was stringently opposed to Lacan. The IPA held an orthodox idea of what "real" psychoanalysis is, and the Lacanian variant was considered unimportant. At that time, the reigning IPA institute in Montréal considered Lacan to be talking nonsense, to be saying incomprehensible and ridiculous things. To them, Lacan spoke a whole other language. Lacan was berated for this.

For Peraldi to come and teach Lacan really disturbed the whole psychoanalytic milieu in Québec. Peraldi was not a member of the IPA. He was a complete outsider of the Québécois psychoanalytic scene. He gave lectures for two hours, every two weeks. The lectures were free and were entirely separate from his function at the University of Montréal. The seminars were not part of his regular teaching curriculum but were something he did on the side. Peraldi's seminars attracted many different types of people, including psychiatrists, philosophers, psychologists, and literary people, and some of the psychoanalysts from the IPA did attend. He was sometimes invited to the society, here and there. This is how I came to read Lacan. It was through Peraldi's influence.

Peraldi also invited psychoanalysts to come speak as guest lecturers from all over the world, including Françoise Dolto, Gérard Miller, Chantel Maillet, and Philippe Julien.[17] Jacques-Alain Miller never came, because it seemed that Peraldi was not particularly warm with him. Peraldi also invited analysts from the Stockbridge Lacanian Forum to speak, including William Richardson and John Muller. What was great about Peraldi is that he made Lacan accessible. He got rid of the impenetrable aspects. This made his contribution very important for clinical work. Peraldi emphasized that this is not just high theory but that Lacan's work has practical clinical implications. Specifically, Peraldi brought Lacanian psychoanalysis forward not as the adaptation of the ego to society but rather as the unfolding of desire and the way that desire affects a given subject.

Peraldi was a highly cultured intellectual who was interested in philosophy, literature, mythology, and theatre. He was also a very travelled human being and went throughout the world. At this time in Québec, psychoanalysis basically meant psychiatry. Peraldi was dislodging this link between psychiatry and psychoanalysis in his lectures. He suffered a lot of rejections. He was kicked out of hospitals and places that he tried to work. He subverted psychiatric environments in order to introduce outlooks that were philosophical, literary, linguistic, or semiological. Peraldi also had a very solid, strong character. He was comfortable with conflict and contradiction. He really made use of his pugnacious, conflictual character, which is rather French. At the time and still today, Québec was rather the opposite. People were much more diplomatic. And so this character had the effect that Peraldi wanted, but he did suffer the consequences in some ways, sometimes making enemies for himself.

CV: In some of your own writing about Peraldi, you have highlighted his work on psychosis, masochism, and femininity. How do you see that Peraldi extended or went beyond Lacan?

LG: As I understand your question, you are asking if and to what extent Peraldi went beyond Lacan. I am thinking about it a bit differently, not so much as whether he went beyond Lacan or not but rather what is significant is the particular use and reading that he made of Lacan. Peraldi was very interested in the three registers of the symbolic, the imaginary, and the Real. What he really specifically sought to teach was the notion of the signifier and how as clinicians we can sharpen our ear to hear it in the clinical session. First and foremost, he used Lacan to think clinically but also to understand theatre and literature, most notably the works of Racine or Duras.[18] He was interested in psychosis and did some work on Schreber.[19] He also did a lot of work on autism and on children. Peraldi was fascinated by language, of course.

Peraldi put forward a distinction between knowledge and thinking or thought. Whereas knowledge [savoir] is transmitted, thought is very individual and specific to the subject and marks the moment of a subject's emancipation from the knowledge that is transmitted. He called it le saut de la pensée [the leap of thought], as in the way that thought hoists you above what you receive. In this sense, he had a thought based on a knowledge that was transmitted to him. Peraldi believed that this leap of thought is what allowed the subject to exist, no less than that.

Alireza Taheri: In regard to the Schreber case, Lacan speaks about the death of the subject. Lacan also talks about psychosis in terms of a subject who does not speak but rather is spoken. Can these ideas such as thinking, not speaking, and the dying of the subject be linked with Peraldi's definition of thought as that which allows the subject to exist?

LG: One of Peraldi's great strengths as a teacher is that he was not simply trying to receive or transmit Lacanian knowledge, but he made a point to think with it. He tried to go beyond it and tried to do something with it. He also tried to make sure that this is what his own students would also do. He tried to have his students think beyond the knowledge that was given to them. Peraldi was not a blind follower of Lacan. He was not thinking in the mold of the cliché Lacanian who throws the jargon around. He emphasized clinical cases, which were a good way to help the audience who were not initiated with Lacan at the time. The audience lacked Lacan's erudition but also his knowledge of psychoanalysis. Peraldi was able to get the audience to slowly catch up. He was able to get those who attended the seminars to put their own clinical work into question as well as their own analysis. Peraldi was interested in questions of masochism, questions of femininity, questions of autism, questions of psychosis all while being preoccupied with enabling thinking to be emancipated from inert knowledge.

Peraldi was also interested in foreclosure and the name-of-the-Father. For me, these notions and the way Peraldi taught them have a lot of clinical resonance. At the moment, I am working with a patient who is not psychotic, but she is a person who has a strong, well-formed ego, is a professional, meets the standards, ideals, injunctions, and imperatives of society rather well. This person functions very well, but I sense an absence of the subject somewhere. There is a kind of a hole somewhere. This hole is what Lacan calls the Real, an unsymbolized kernel, which I would liken to the unconscious in the originary sense of primary repression, not the secondary repressions. This is the struggle this particular woman is having. As a child, she was overwhelmed by and taken in with the mother's discourse in a kind of symbiotic fusion, but without the words to express that fusional, primary Real. Without the words, she has trouble separating, which is why the clinical work is important. She has a constant anxiety of falling back into this abyss. How does one listen to a person in this context? The source of the listening has to come from that suffering, from that fusion, from that Real, rather than from the notion of adaptation. At the level of adaptation, there is no problem. She is doing very well in this respect. The suffering is clearly somewhere else. Suffering is always the motor of the analysis. This woman also writes poetry, which gives her access to the archaic, the primordial, or what Lacan called *das Ding* [the Thing]. She has a defense where she tries to keep the analysis at the level of a Sunday afternoon conversation or at the level of something mundane. It can be difficult to loosen the resistance so that the analytic work can take place. If it was not for Freud, for Lacan, and for Peraldi and this radical shift away from adaptation and towards suffering, I would have been, like many other clinicians, captivated by the results, which are stellar in this case. What would have been missed in this case, however, would have been precisely this kernel of pain, which is what we should be interested in as clinicians.

CV: It seems Peraldi was also interested in excess and polysexuality. His interest in culture, anthropology, and sexuality, for instance, remind me of Georges Bataille or Deleuze and Guattari.[20] Where do you see the influence of this notion of excess on Peraldi's work?

LG: The themes of polysexuality and excess are central to Peraldi's thinking and perhaps in his private life as well. He would cause a little shock in the classroom when he would pass around images of masochism, images of people choking each other, images of extreme *jouissance* and danger. He was really interested in tension, excess, and *jouissance* at its limits. These were theoretical and personal preoccupations. Peraldi was gay, but this was something that he hid. He would sometimes disappear and go to New York. Despite his bold personality, this element of his sexuality was private and censored. He never spoke about it in psychoanalytic circles. He was interested in the quest for *jouissance*. Perhaps Peraldi also went beyond Lacan in this preoccupation with perversions and this type of limit of *jouissance*, which ties him to the authors you have mentioned, such as Bataille or Deleuze and Guattari.

There is a case in Michel de M'Uzan's book, *De l'art à la mort: itinéraire psychanalytique* [*From Art to Death: Psychoanalytic Itinerary*], which really interested Peraldi.[21] The case is about a masochistic patient who reports his extreme *jouissance* to the analyst. In the case, there is a kind of knowledge that the patient has that the psychoanalyst does not. This allows the patient to hold a position of superiority but also allows Peraldi and de M'Uzan to think about the status of *jouissance* in relation to language. *Jouissance* is precisely that which can never really be said. As a result, the patient's *jouissance* in this case becomes enacted or staged in different ways. The subject stages something and then tells the analyst about it. Peraldi was very interested in questions like this. How can *jouissance* be said in some way? In other words, how can *jouissance* be brought in relation with the social Other? How can such *jouissance* leave the privacy of suffering and somehow touch the Other of language and society despite the fact that it is unspeakable in its essence. We are touching on Schreber in regard to the push to woman, his delusion of transformation into a woman, this massive amount of *jouissance*. What happens with Schreber is that the Other is enjoying the subject. In times of extreme *jouissance*, the subject is faded and lost. This is why Peraldi was also interested in mystics and Lacan's Seminar XX, *Encore*.[22]

Catherine Millot is the author of *La vie avec Lacan* [*My Life with Lacan*], which has won many literary awards. She was in love with Lacan. She followed him along everywhere despite the fact that he was married and had other mistresses in this extravagant life. Millot was in love with Lacan in a very sacrificing way. She is the one who introduced Peraldi to the mystical women who sacrifice for the Other in this glorified way. Peraldi's response to this was, 'No, no, they are just erotomaniacs who like to have sex.' I would argue that what is really at stake in *jouissance* and in the way it annihilates the ego or what puts it in suspension for some time is that return to the archaic, the primordial Real, the primordial unconscious. It is the return to the infantile. The baby can be the object of the mother's *jouissance* unless there is some separation. This touches on Schreber's *jouissance*, for instance, which becomes displaced onto a God figure in his delusions.

Peraldi was especially interested in the archaic, in *jouissance*, and in these extreme limit cases, which means that his work was specifically working on the link to the mother. Lacan was working on something else, that is, insofar as he refounded psychoanalysis on the question of the father. What Lacan does with Freud is that he brings the Oedipal right to the beginnings of life. The triangulation exists from the start since the mother's discourse carries some direct or indirect reference to the father all the time. There is no such thing as just a symbiotic mother–child relationship.

AT: Peraldi was interested in the excess, in Bataille, in polysexuality, in extreme cases of *jouissance*, etc. He's a gay man who goes to New York. He is interested in the archaic and the mother. And then we have Lacan, the name-of-the-father, the symbolic order, the patriarchy, and the phallus as primordial signifier. Along this line, there is a very famous and conservative Lacanian analyst in France, Pierre Legendre, who is also a historian of law.[23] He is a brilliant guy, but he also insists on this line that a man is a man, a woman is a woman. He insists this in the face of transgenderism. One could even say that Jacques-Alain Miller falls into this similar kind of discourse. Why could we also not say simply that Peraldi is anti-Lacanian?

CV: Peraldi might have said he was "Lacanizing" but resisted being called "Lacanian." He was also interested in Deleuze and Guattari, who were anti-psychiatric and could be called anti-Lacanian despite being heavily influenced by Lacan's ideas and seminars.

LG: I think there may be something to Peraldi's problematic relation with Lacan. He was not particularly interested, as some Lacanians are, in these stringent differentiations and distinctions. He was not interested in differential diagnosis or labels like neurosis, perversion, or psychosis. He was really interested in human experience. He suffered because he could not situate himself socially that well. He was generally on the margins in his thinking and was sexually on the margins. He was neither an IPA analyst nor exactly a Lacanian analyst.

CV: Although he was ostracized, Peraldi was also an amazing organizer. He created a cartel network in Québec for the study of psychoanalysis. It seems to me that part of his way of being was not to belong to a group but to bring the group to himself.

LG: Yes, it's true. Yet a lot of his friends, his colleagues, the people whom he supported, whom he invited to give talks, whom he listened to and whom he collaborated with, just kind of forgot him after his death. Some people denied that they had any partnership with him. These are people that he recognized and supported in his own life. This contributed to Peraldi's vanishing from the scene. He is like a free electron, not bound to anything. He opened new windows for everybody at the time. A lot of people who were dissatisfied with their own analyses were attracted to him. I was also very attracted to this free electron aspect of him. I am also a little bit this way as well, but I would consider the extent to which he was this free electron requires a certain stamina and will that is quite rare in the way he was able to withstand so much rejection, so much resistance. He stood so apart and so against the grain. This made me and many other people question the form of analysis they were experiencing in terms of very formulaic, orthodox, or classical Freudianism. In this sort of Freudianism, interpretations can become very reified. Everything is laid out in a rigid structure.

AT: Did Peraldi practice scansion?

LG: He practiced scansion to the full Lacanian extent. I do not use scansion in my own practice. I am not strict about a session being 50 minutes long, but rather I work within a ten-minute margin of difference from the 50- or 45-minute mark.

AT: This is the more human way of doing scansion.

LG: The rationalization is that the scansion will leave the patient with the last thought and that this may enable the working through, but I am not sure if this is just an *a posteriori* rationalization or if there is some validity, so I do not practice scansion fully. I have a friend who is a Lacanian analyst in Strasbourg whom I correspond with who urges me to use scansion. I do not practice it, because the element of arbitrariness is too heavy to guarantee. Questions could be raised about scansion. Is the analyst stopping the session because he or she is bored? Or is the analyst stopping the session because there is actually some pregnancy in what was just said?

AT: Why did Peraldi leave France?

LG: It is a mystery. It is hard to say why. Maybe he was rejected from the training in Paris because of his homosexuality, but it would have been the same prejudice in Québec as well at that time. He would never have talked about his personal sexuality. He was a very sociable, affable, gentle, and generous person, but yet there was this split, this secret, and his AIDS. He had a great disappointment but also a huge hope for psychoanalysis. He got a lot from psychoanalysis, contributed a lot, but at this personal level there was a disappointment in a certain conservatism that could be found in Lacan, which may not be what Peraldi found in Lacan. I was surprised to hear that you were interested in Peraldi. How did that come about?

CV: With these interviews, I'm trying to learn more about how this Parisian phenomenon of Lacan's thinking about clinical work was transmitted to Canada and the United States. As I began to talk to psychoanalysts about their work or about translating Lacan to English, Peraldi's name was mentioned several times. How would you say Peraldi has influenced your own thinking and practice?

LG: What I take home most of all from Peraldi, his teaching, and the years I knew him is not so much a psychoanalytic concept but rather the freedom of thinking, the freedom of listening, an openness, and especially an attentiveness to the signifier. This means that we should try not to let interpreting and explaining block us from listening. Explaining and interpreting to the analysand open the way for the analyst's imaginary and this clouds one's ability to listen. What we have to avoid is blocking new signifiers. We have to be open to new signifiers whether they come from dreams, memory, or the transference. It is a question of displacing the ear so that you are focused not so much on the content or meaning and rather on the way things are said. This gives us a chance to slip into the unconscious material. It is the ear that needs to shift. When people want to make you hear something, when someone insists, 'Listen to me,' for instance, it is often because the person wants to hide something from you at the same time.

I was surprised to hear that anybody would be interested in Peraldi now. The mark that he left on the history of psychoanalysis in Québec was erased. Peraldi was not spoken about much. I wrote about him a little bit after he died, but since that time, there has not been much published on him. I feel there is a continuity between his living life and his posthumous life. Peraldi was someone who hid a lot, kept a lot secret. He made traces as he erased them. In this sense, his legacy has been replicated. Peraldi was free. He did not belong to any faction or to any school. He was ostracized by most of the psychoanalytic circles at the time. He did write a few papers in English. Despite Peraldi being able to speak English very fluently and giving speeches all over, there is a remnant of the way he was erased then and the way he is erased now.

Bibliography and Further Reading

Grenier, Louise. *Femme d'un seul home: Les séparations impossibles.* Montréal: Québecor 2006.

Grenier, Louise. *Filles sans père, L'attente du père dans l'imaginaire féminin.* Montréal: Québec Livres, 2015.

Grenier, Louise. *L'absence de la mere: Retrouver le lien perdu avec soi.* Québecor: Outremont, 2011.

Grenier, Louise. "La folie à corps perdu, À partir de lectures de son œuvre hommage à François Peraldi (1938–1993)." *Le Coq-héron* 169.2 (2002): 137–158.

Grenier, Louise. "Le sexe malentendu. Regards sur la sexualité féminine en psychoanalyse" *L'Autre, Le temps: Séminaire 1982–1985*, Ed. François Peraldi. Montréal: Liber, 2007. 229–246.

Grenier, Louise. "Le temps d'une halte sur les sentiers du silence. François Peraldi (1938–1993)." *Filigrane.* 9.1 (2000): 80–113.

Grenier, Louise. *Les violences de l'Autre: Faire parler les silences de son histoire.* 3rd edition. Montréal: Québecor, 2017.

Grenier, Louise (ed). *Lettres du divan: Écrire à son psychanalyst.* Montréal: Éditions Liber, 2017.

Grenier, Louise. "Qu'est-ce qu'être une femme? ou Réflexion sur la notion de sujet au féminin en psychoanalyse." François Peraldi, *Le Sujet. Séminaire 1981–1982.* Edi. Michel Peterson. Montréal: Liber, 2006. 179–194.

Grenier, Louise and Marie Hazan (eds). *L'analyste à l'œuvre: Relire François Peraldi.* Montréal: Liber, 2008.

Grenier, Louise and Isabelle Lasvergnas (eds). *Penser Freud avec Patrick Mahony*, (en co-direction), Montréal: Liber, 2004.

Grenier, Louise and Suzanne Tremblay (eds). *Le projet d'Antigone: Parcours vers la mort d'une fille d'Œdipe.* Montréal: Liber, 2005.

Part 3 with Gilles Chagnon

Gilles Chagnon is a psychiatrist, psychoanalyst, and assistant clinical professor at the University of Sherbrooke in Québec. He has published a novel, *Rupture* (Éditions du Désert, 1996); co-edited an essay collection with Danielle Monast, *François Peraldi: voix, legs, parcours d'un psychanalyste* (Liber, 2005); and written literary texts in various journals as well as articles on psychoanalysis. This conversation took place on July 7, 2020.

CV: What was your first encounter with psychoanalysis?

GC: I encountered psychoanalysis when I was studying French literature. Before I studied medicine, I spent two years in French literature. Freud and

Lacan were already popular in literary theory and the humanities. When I studied medicine, I was attracted to psychiatry. I began a residency in psychiatry at the Université de Montréal. There are many different university hospitals there, but the hospital I chose was Sacré-Coeur because there were a lot of analysts there. When I began my formation in psychiatry, there were many psychiatrists who were psychoanalysts directing the university department. I thought this would be a good place to do clinical psychoanalysis. During my residency, I was astonished at the dogmatic way they would teach psychoanalytic knowledge. It was not about trying to help us develop our own thinking as I was trained to do when I studied literature. It was a dogmatic transmission of psychoanalysis. I was bringing books of Lacan, but these analysts had never read his work. They only had many prefabricated thoughts about him. They were against his thoughts and against his way of practicing analysis.

When I read Peraldi's articles at that time, it was like finding a well after a long walk in the desert. Finally, there was someone who demonstrated freedom of thinking who could transmit psychoanalysis differently. He has articles on schizophrenia, including "L'élangage de la Folie" [The language of madness],[24] and there is a lot of transgression in terms of his conceptualization. At the time, I was completing my year in general psychiatry. I was confronting basic psychiatric material. This brought me to ask for an analysis with him when I was doing my residency.

CV: You mentioned the paper, "L'élangage de la Folie," which I have read. This paper is critical of several fields in relation to the treatment of psychosis. In the paper, he also seems to be criticizing anti-psychiatry as well. This particular paper has a polemical or political edge. How much was Peraldi on the side of anti-psychiatry?

GC: I think he inherited something from the anti-psychiatry movement. He also read a lot of Althusser's work.[25] Many of Peraldi's first articles are about the social and economic dimensions of psychiatry. When you follow his articles year after year until the end, you can see there is a displacement towards Heidegger's thoughts on the question of being and ethical theory. At the beginning, he was structuring something in the anti-Oedipal field. Later on, Peraldi really relies on Oedipal theory as the center of the Freudian discovery. He was in constant evolution with his own thinking.

CV: Peraldi was also skeptical or suspicious of institutions. Perhaps he saw institutions not being places for free thinking. I suppose I am also thinking about these questions in his gravitation towards Lacan and Lacan's own troubles with the IPA. Why did Peraldi resist any form of institutionalization of psychoanalysis? And how can we make sense of his thinking about the transmission of psychoanalysis – or, as he calls it in his paper, the "transaction" – without the institution?

GC: Peraldi was in a dialectic relationship with the psychoanalytic institutions in Montréal. He was a non-founder. Of course, he contributed a
lot in bringing Lacanian thinking into Québec. He did form a network
of psychoanalytic cartels.[26] Many analysts said that in his interview with
Marie Hazan, shortly before he died, he was very pessimistic. If you
follow his thoughts from the beginning about psychoanalytic transmission, he was always critical about what he called the "psychoanalytic
wall." This was also alive in his practice. He was not trying to transmit
something that we could reassure ourselves with about what we know
but rather was trying to transmit something that was really alive.

CV: As his analysand, you must have worked closely with him for some time.
Could you say more about his technique? And would he have practiced
something like scansion?

GC: He was extraordinarily silent in the analytic process. He explains clearly
this in the "Silent Father" paper:

> It is my opinion that the first phase of most psychoanalysis - what-
> ever its duration may be – is the building up of the Imaginary
> world of the patient (namely the world of his imagos). It is also the
> building up of the Imaginary transference within which a revealing
> or unveiling or unmasking (as Serge Leclaire would say) interpre-
> tation can eventually occur. During this phase one can see all the
> mechanisms of defense constitutive of the Ego at work. Most of
> the time it is useless to talk either to analyze the Imaginary trans-
> ference or to respond to the demands of the patients or to try to
> unlock his mechanisms of defense by denouncing them, although
> all this work has to be done by the analyst and most of the time in
> silence since it is not at the level of the Imaginary that the analyst's
> interpretation finds its effectiveness.

I think he was rigorous to follow this line of thinking and intervention.
He avoided psychoanalytic metalanguage when he spoke. In my article,
"*La petite tante aimée et la vampire*" ["The little beloved aunt and the
vampire"], which is a fragment of my analysis, I speak about an intervention that he made.[27] I had a dream where he made what he would
have called a "revealing" interpretation, but after the imaginary had already been built up. There was an effect.

I recall another article that Peraldi wrote, "*La castration sadique-anale de votre père*" ["The sadistic-anal castration of your father"], which
is an article with a lot of humor, [which] refers to the decision of Peraldi
to end his psychoanalytic work with his analyst. He was creative with his
work, so I do not know if the story is real or not, but this is not the
point. He talks about how, when he was in Paris, he had a pet snake in
his apartment, a boa. The snake broke its glass cage and was in the
apartment. When Peraldi had to go out, he put the snake in the

bathroom toilet. The snake escapes the toilet and reappears at the neighbor's downstairs. He tells the story to his psychoanalyst, S.D., a female analyst. She finally said, "You have accomplished without suffering the sadistic-anal castration of your father." He thought within himself, "Seven years of an analysis to end up with this bullshit." He decided to quit after a few weeks. This was the end of his analysis.[28] I think he was rigorous to not reproduce that in his own work.

CV: It sounds like he suddenly experienced a very reductive interpretation. It is a great example of how the analyst's own imaginary can shut down the production of new signifiers.

GC: Yes, something that closed what was at stake.

CV: Did you also attend his seminars?

GC: I did not attend the seminars. I was in analysis with him for five years, from 1985 until 1990. Although I was in analysis with him and read his work, I abstained from attending his seminars and conferences. I think it was the same for other people that I know who were in analysis with him. Peraldi was not at ease with his analysands being his students or his collaborators. He carefully separated his private life from his public life. Even if he was committed to a particular subject, for instance, his writing on sadomasochism, where he describes what is happening in the boroughs of New York in the dark rooms. He did not hide that, and it was obvious that he was there, but his reflections never implicate that he was there acting. We can suppose that was the case especially from his letters to his friend Catherine Duncan or considering the way he finally died. He was careful to not produce something that would show something of his ego.

   This was the same with his boyfriend. He wrote an article about him as a travel companion.[29] He explains the man is dying from AIDS, but he never mentions it was the man who was sharing his life. It is only through his letters to Catherine Duncan that we see that the two men were in a relationship for ten years. He was private but also trying to find a way not to hide behind theoretical elaborations, which is part of his originality.

CV: In his writing and seminars, Peraldi is interested in transgression, extreme forms of masochism, and psychosis. He was on the edge of something. What do you think this was about for him?

GC: I think this was his attempt to shake up the established psychoanalytic institutions and framework. He said, "An analyst who is not writing from his symptomatic realm is not writing a psychoanalytic paper." To hide behind theories and try to apply concepts was not interesting to him. He wrote so many articles but never wrote a book. I think he was in "perpetual exile." This was one of the signifiers that came up during the symposium we held ten years after his death. He said that "I am a traveller in perpetual exile and I tell [raconté] my travels." This motive of exile is central. When I read his letters to Catherine Duncan, it seems this was the trajectory of his life. He first moved from France to the

United States but later moved to Montréal because his friend Daniel Sloate was there teaching in the Department of Linguistics at the University of Montréal.[30] While he was in Montréal, he also had an apartment in New York. Throughout his correspondence, he writes that he is not really happy in Montréal. He does not demonstrate much warmth for Québecors or for the intellectual life in Québec. He was always in the thought or the desire of elsewhere. It was only after ten years that he decided to stay in Montréal and not go back to France. He writes that to return to France would have been for him to be annoyed with the pretension of Paris. He was in-between in all of his life.

CV: It seems as though he could not easily find a group or place of belonging.

GC: Of course, he did help with founding the Lacanian Clinical Forum with John Muller, William Richardson, Ess White, and Donna Bentolila. He was faithful to all the meetings of this group, which still meets twice a year for two days. It is a very open group. After Peraldi's death, John Muller led the group in Stockbridge and always kept an empty chair beside him in the memory of François.

CV: Is there something from your analysis with him that you would say continues to inform your work now with patients or analysands?

GC: The most important point is to try to maintain the psychoanalytic position of listening. It is to let go of the imaginary field of the patient. It is not about trying to deconstruct or point out defense mechanisms. This is not easy. It was easier when I practiced psychiatry in Montréal. I had a home office with a couch. When I moved to Sherbrooke in the country, I stopped practicing psychoanalysis for many years because I was overwhelmed working in a clinic for psychosis. Finally, I resumed my private practice two years ago. Now I work in a private clinic where I can practice psychoanalysis but without the couch. It is different when you have to maintain a direct presence and be in the sight of the person. The couch definitely helps facilitate the process, but I was also working with patients who did not want to be on the couch in Montréal. What is your practice in this regard?

CV: In my office, the person has the choice to use the chair or the couch. I have the opportunity to work within a community mental health organization where I encounter cases of psychosis fairly often. In such cases, I obviously would not encourage the use of the couch and I believe the face-to-face relation is much more helpful. There is an interesting question that could be raised about the couch in terms of the imaginary, as you have said, or in the context of the look [le regard].[31] I usually let the person decide when they are ready or not to use the couch. I have also had the experience where people sometimes go back and forth between using the chair or the couch depending on what has been happening for them. I imagine Peraldi would have only used the couch.

GC: For the preliminary sessions, I think a person would have used the chair, but after that, the person would use the couch. Of course, some patients avoid the couch and may feel completely abandoned without being able to see the analyst. Sometimes these feelings are overwhelming and it is not possible to do that kind of work with them.

CV: The person's reaction to being on the couch can be too distressing, or the person may simply benefit more from the face-to-face relation, which might be much more containing or help to hold something together during the appointment.

In thinking more about Peraldi, I appreciate the openness of his work. I also think he is such an important figure in the transmission of psychoanalysis in North America and seems not to get very much credit outside of Québec for his contributions.

GC: Unfortunately, this is also the case inside of Québec. So many years after his death, there are still a lot of resistances to what he thought and tried to teach. Michel Peterson has had to confront some of these resistances in editing his seminars and correspondences. He can tell you more about how things are in Québec.

CV: Michel did mention this resistance to me. After Peraldi's passing, he suggested there was a silence about his work. How do we account for this? Is this silence about his work a conservatism about his sexuality or a resistance to the material he is raising to think about?

GC: It is all of this. He was a free-thinker and this was also his approach to Lacan. Peraldi was very conscious that Lacan made a major contribution to psychoanalytic field, but he was never in adoration of Lacan. I have worked with the group of Charles Melman in France.[32] They do a lot of great work there, but the group does relate to Lacan as someone who has said everything. Peraldi was more critical of this sort of relation. His position was to promote freedom of thought. I read that you have a PhD in English literature. Is that correct?

CV: Yes, I do.

GC: This is a much different perspective when you come from literature or philosophy rather than psychology or psychiatry. The difference must come from a sense of the process of sublimation and of being.

CV: How would you describe your transition from psychiatric thinking towards a more psychoanalytic approach to mental health?

GC: When I finished my residency, I spent five years just practicing general psychiatry but also doing psychotherapy. At the beginning of my practice, it was possible for me to work in psychotherapy as part of my schedule. It was only five years after this that I authorized myself to practice psychoanalytic interventions in a different setup than that hospital. At that time, I began to work in a cartel with various colleagues. I also asked an analyst of the Société psychanalytique de Montréal (SPM) to be my supervisor. This is how I positioned my constant process of thinking about theory and my practice. The way we practice 20 years later is much different than the beginning. There is a constant evolution in the practice.

One of the first questions that I asked Peraldi in the preliminary sessions was "What would happen if I wanted to be part of the official society?" He said, "Well, you will have to find your own way." I think he meant that there is no definitive way to be a psychoanalyst.

This is true of transmission in general. It is important to have institutions, which are necessary to establish basic knowledge and research. Otherwise, psychoanalysis would just be something in the air or something mystical. This is not the way it should to be. Freud and Lacan founded many institutions. Freud founded the International Psychoanalytic Association (IPA). Lacan founded his own schools. Both of them excluded people. Freud broke up with Carl Jung and also decided to exclude Wilhelm Reich from the organization because he was unorthodox. Freud hugely contributed to the process of institutional foundation. Lacan founded his school but also dissolved it. As Lacan says in his last seminar, *l'école* [the school] should not be confused with *la colle* [the glue].[33] This speaks of the necessity of having also what Peraldi called the "psychoanalytic margin." It is necessary to have the institutions, but it is also necessary to have this counter-power, this margin to keep alive the essence of psychoanalysis, which is the question of the unconscious. You cannot catch this in a definitive way in a book or in a teaching. It can only be transmitted in the analytic process. Nancy McWilliams's work, for instance, *Psychoanalytic Diagnosis*, is very interesting.[34] It's okay. I also read books like this sometimes, but what I find most interesting is to keep alive this thinking about the margin. It is a dialectal relationship that is really necessary for the transmission of psychoanalysis.

CV: What it is like to work with Melman's group?

GC: I have studied there for three years. All of the cartels study the same seminar during the academic year from October to the summer, and at the annual August meeting there are many discussions and exchanges about the particular seminar. Marcel Czermak and Cyril Veken were trying to create a practice from the *presentation de malade* – that is, where a clinician speaks with a patient during a presentation in front of other clinicians, as Lacan did for many years at Sainte-Anne.[35] Following the hour-long clinical interview, those in attendance discuss the case, except the patient is not present for this discussion. From this work, Czermak and Veken published a book, *Les jardins de l'aisle*.[36] Cyril Veken came to conduct a *presentation de malade* with our group, which consisted of mainly psychologists in training and psychiatrists who were interested in psychodynamic work. We performed interviews with patients and continued this work in making a series of seminars, including the *presentation de malade*. The patients who were brought to our seminar were sometimes very difficult to understand or treat. Some clinicians were concerned about the *presentation de malade* being a spectacle or exploitative to the patient in some way, but the patient provides consent beforehand and this exercise is for the purpose of learning and working together with colleagues to discern the best care for the patient's own benefit. The seminars generated a lot of activity at the hospital in Montréal where I was working.

CV: What have you found helpful in your own practice about Lacan's approach to clinical ethics?

GC: I think it is to be centered on the signifier. This is very important. It is there. The unconscious is not hidden 100 miles underground but is in the signifier. You have to try to catch the signifier to extend what is at stake when the person is speaking. Why is this person saying what they are saying right now? I think Lacan is very useful to help us focus on this point. Of course, his three registers – the Real, the Imaginary, and the Symbolic – are also so important. These registers can help to think through ways of listening. We might hear something much different from what the patient is trying to tell us.

CV: What about the knot, the Real, the Imaginary, and the Symbolic? This is such a different way of conceptualizing psychology and the mind. Of course, Lacan also eventually develops this idea of the *sinthome* as the additional ring that might hold the others together. What are your thoughts about this knot theory and its application to the clinic? When we are listening, how might we discern the distinction between these registers in practice?

GC: At the beginning of treatment, we have to receive, as Peraldi says, the imaginary material – that is, however the patient has constructed his or her own narrative. The patient lives with this fixed narrative. We have to introduce the possibility to move within this narrative rather than to be the object of this narrative. We have to acknowledge and listen to this narrative in the process, but we have to keep in mind that we are there to produce new significations about what was withdrawn from the Real. There is something from the Real that probably contributed to this narrative of the patient with his imagos of father, mother, siblings, or abusers. In this level of significations, we have to maintain the position of someone who can help in a symbolic way. We have to help the patient to give themselves liberties and freedoms in relation to the primitive imago.

CV: Allowing the patient to build up the imaginary at the beginning allows the patient to really paint a picture or tell the story in order to hear something of the dynamics that might repeat. At some point, the analyst may then be able to make a more symbolic intervention to help reveal part of the patient's repetition compulsion. This might have an effect on the Real.

GC: This can only occur in the transference process. It is the *point de capiton* [quilting point] from which we can let something from the Real exist and be transformed.[37]

CV: In "La transaction" ["The Transaction"], Peraldi conveys a very different idea about transference.[38] He discusses unspoken communication between analyst and analysand and the idea of "thought transmission" in analysis. In the paper, he is trying to make sense of a phenomenon where communication appears to occur without words or maybe it is being communicated between the words. He takes this idea to the level of quantum theory and even draws upon questions of telepathy. He develops the idea of transference as transaction. It is an idea that troubles the binaristic distinction between transference and countertransference and moves us towards notions of transference as mutual exchange or distribution of thoughts.

GC: He is referring to a very primitive level of communication between patient and analyst. Maybe dreams are operating on this level when we are thinking of them as part of the transference process. The dream operates at a point where all the ego defenses are sleeping. This is what I mean in terms of primitive communication.

CV: This also speaks to the question of transmission. If transmission is the passing down of an experience of the unconscious for the analysand who is in training, for instance, what can we say is being transmitted?

GC: It is a similar process to art. We can learn some techniques for writing or painting or calligraphy or piano, but to share something with others from these techniques is to let something out from the Real, which is particular to the essence of the subject. In psychoanalysis, we have a respectful relation with someone in order to build the transference. If something from the Real is there and processing, we find ourselves different at the end of the treatment. This also happens in creative process, which is why we could say that the production of the artwork may transform the person. It can be like a vision or an unveiling. When I was a teenager, for instance, I read Marcel Proust and this opened up a whole field for me of consciousness. This also happens, for instance, when I am listening to [Franz] Schubert. It is part of our inner story to integrate works of art or to produce artworks ourselves. Such creative processes are very close to what we are trying to do in psychoanalysis.

When we accept someone in therapy, it is because we have a wish or desire to bring this person somewhere else. It is a wish to bring the patient out of the narrative prison that they have built. It can be so difficult to change psychical conditions, because we feel especially secure in our symptoms. We have to put the security in balance. Sometimes it works and sometimes we fall into the repetition. In fact, we cannot know. After all, it is only the patient who can say.

Bibliography and Further Reading

Chagnon, Gilles. *Elle arrive avec l'été*. Montréal: Éditions du Passage, 2009.
Chagnon, Gilles. "L'errance d'Oedipe aujourd'hui." *Filigrane*. 19.2 (2010): 21–31.
Chagnon, Gilles. "Psychanalyse et psychiatrie." *Filigrane*. 17.1 (2008): 29–43.
Chagnon, Gilles. *Rupture*. Westmount: Éditions du Désert, 1996.
Chagnon, Gilles, Marie Hazan, and Michel Peterson. *Penser La Clinique Psychanalyt-ique*. Montréal: Liber, 2010.
Monast, Danielle and Gilles Chagnon. *François Peraldi: Voix, Legs, Parcours D'un Psy-chanalyste*. Montréal: Liber, 2005.

Part 4 with Marie Hazan

Marie Hazan, PhD, is a psychologist, psychoanalyst, and professor in the De-partment of Psychology, Université du Québec à Montréal (UQAM). She con-ducts research on psychoanalysis and has written several books and articles. She previously attended the seminars of François Peraldi (1979–1992). This conversation took place on May 5, 2020.

CV: When did you discover psychoanalysis?

MH: I come from Lebanon. When I was studying philosophy in Beirut, my encounter with psychoanalysis was with reading Freud's work about dreams. This was a big discovery. My first year at university was in Bei-rut, and the year after, I went to Lyon, where I also studied philosophy. While I was there, my friends were in psychology. I realized that I did not like philosophy at all after three years. It is not for me. I very much like reading Freud. I would say Freud is a "hero" in a kind of adolescent transference. For me, he is a kind of grandfather. It is like a family link, but it is not an unconditional love. I do find that he is a genius discov-erer, and I got very interested in his life and the complex notion of trans-mission of psychoanalysis. I have written about Anna Freud as well and Freud's complex relationship with his daughter.[39]

CV: Can you tell me about the circumstances of where you would have met Peraldi?

MH: After getting my master's in Lyon, I went back home to Beirut, but when the civil war started, I returned to Lyon and did the first year of a PhD in psychology. When I went to university in France in the 1970s, the education was in between something very old, traditional, rigid, and closed-minded and something emerging that was new. After this, I came to Montréal because I was not able to work in Lyon as this was a very unfriendly place to be Lebanese at this time. Cultur-ally, I had links in Montréal, where my family immigrated before me. I arrived in Montréal during the summer of 1978. From the begin-ning, I had friends who went to Peraldi's seminars. In January 1979, I attended his seminar. This place belongs to my first encounter with my professional life, my Québecer life, and my Canadian life. It was a very rich time for me.

When I went to Peraldi's seminar, it was like a bridge between my academic life in Lyon and here in Montréal. It was ten years after May 1968. In May 1968, I was still in Lebanon and too young to be part of the movement. It was a big event, a turmoil, and a huge change in French society. Peraldi, who was born in 1938, was 30 years old then. On the other hand, French society was still conservative, especially in the academic field. As a gay person, which he never said he was, he was not included in the psychoanalytic world. He was not allowed in the International Psychoanalytic Association (IPA), but I did not know back then that it could have been an issue. He did not talk about this. It was like a wall. There were many closed avenues for him in France. In Québec, perhaps Peraldi was able to have the fantasy of coming to a place where he would have more space or where nobody had come before him. He would say, "I was alone. Nothing was happening." Of course, it is a fantasy, an omnipotence fantasy.

CV: From reading some of the writing about his work, I gather Peraldi could also be shocking or unsettling. What was the atmosphere like at his seminars, and what was his style of presentation like at this time?

MH: It depends on the years. I attended the seminar many years in a row. In the beginning, it was in a small classroom (of the literature department of University of Montréal) and a friendly atmosphere. The attendants, students and young professionals, analysts, or professors were from different fields. Peraldi focused a lot on pluridisciplinarity. It was important for him to have dialogues with intellectuals from various fields like philosophy, linguistics, anthropology, history, and politics. At a certain point, he was interested in East Indian religions. Many of the attendees were not officially students of the department. Later, the seminar was in a bigger, square room in another building of the University of Montréal, with more persons. Even though it seemed very friendly and people became friends – we often would go to have supper together afterwards – it was intimidating, in my opinion. If you cared to ask a question, you did not know what sort of response you might get. You could get silence or something unpleasant or perhaps something very nice. I guess he was a bit daunting. There were also colleagues of his generation and even older in attendance, analysts from the society of psychoanalysis [Canadian Psychoanalytic Society] on the French side (*Société psychanalytique de Montréal*). Peraldi had friends on the English side of the society (Québec English branch), but I did not know them at the time.

On one hand, he was very open, unformal, and nice, inviting guests to his home and cooking for them. On the other hand, he could be patronizing and serious, but maybe it was also the time period.

Teachers were supposed to be like this. Peraldi was a professor of linguistics and gave his seminar, but he was not part of the psychoanalytic institutions. I guess that he would not know how people would react to him. He was quite provocative. For instance, he was invited to present papers at conferences where he would attack psychiatric institutions. This was the times. He was also searching for recognition but not denying his own ways. He had prestigious persons coming from Paris to attend and to present papers at his seminar. It was a place to be.

CV: How did you find his style of teaching? Would he deliver a lecture?

MH: He would deliver a well-prepared lecture. We were very good students, listening. Michel Peterson later edited these lectures for publication, he did a lot of minutious work. It was not an informal atmosphere. He would seek participation sometimes, but mostly to have people present papers. Some of the students in attendance were his analysands. There was a disruptive guy attending the lectures, and we found out later that this was one of his analysands. Some analysands were not allowed in the seminar. This added to the tension or strange atmosphere. I asked him, "Why do you allow your analysands in the seminar?" People beginning their analysis should not go to listen to their analyst like some guru. Peraldi was not a guru, but still. There is something that can't be worked out if the analysand is in admiration of the analyst. This is what happened with Lacan, but also anywhere, in psychoanalytical institutions and universities, lots of idealization, love and hate.

The seminar became a bit like a mythological place, people telling me, "Oh, you 'belong' to Peraldi's seminar." I did not feel I belonged to the seminar. I also do not describe myself as Lacanian. I like some ideas of Lacan, and he made big changes in psychoanalysis, but I also read the work of other analysts. For me, Lacan is amongst other authors except for the institutional point of view. I am more pluralist.

CV: It is clear from Peraldi's work that he is anti-establishment...

MH: Yes, he was an iconoclast. He would destroy the icons and Gods. He was not a believer or a Talmudic guy. Some of the Lacanian followers are Talmudic. They go into his papers and research to debate about how Lacan said this or that. I would say that Peraldi was not like this. Peraldi was more eclectic and also not as well known in the Lacanian world as we thought. He had some friends there but was not belonging to a church. He would have hated this.

CV: Did it ever come to light why he left France?

MH: I don't know what brought him to Montréal. It's a good question. I think he must have needed more space for breathing. Roudinesco has said that he was not accepted because he was gay.[40] This had not occurred to me, but it is very possible. It could be one of the reasons. Maybe he could not easily exist in some contexts with his personality being the way he was.

CV: People have said he was an outsider who maintained a distance from institutions. Peraldi's writing suggests that some of the anti-psychiatrists influenced him (for instance, Deleuze and Guattari) perhaps as much as he was influenced by Lacan.[41]

MH: Deleuze was also a special personality. I'm not sure that I would compare him to Peraldi. I don't remember him citing Deleuze and Guattari so much. Peraldi was certainly an outsider and not a classical sort of Lacanian. He did not want to belong to anything, but he wanted to be part of the world and to be known and accepted. He was phobic of the institution. In this way, he fit in well with the Montréal landscape. Maybe people here do not like to be put in boxes. What Peraldi did was special, but it belongs very much to this time period. People wanted to explore new things, things that were unusual and unclassified.

CV: Of course, Peraldi was also quite interested in the notion of the death drive, one of his seminars revolving around this idea from 1985 to 1988, *La Mort* [*Death*]. How do you understand his work in this context?

MH: He was preoccupied with the death drive. Afterwards, we thought maybe this was because he was ill. He was emphasizing that the death drive was different from aggressivity and that it must be understood as linked with the *pulsions de vie* [*Eros*] and that disunification [*désintrication*] between the two can cause damage. Peraldi would differentiate the death drive from sadism, and all of this was linked to sexuality, but it was not explicit in his seminar except through some articles.

There was a day that he presented a picture of a person who died while trying to achieve some sort of *jouissance*. I don't remember the circumstances except that the picture was awful. This picture was going around the classroom and people did not know what to say. There was silence. Finally, one person asked him about his choice of the theme, "Why would you do that?" He replied, "*Comme dirait Luce Irigaray, je ne donnerai pas ma carte d'identité sexuelle!*" [As Luce Irigaray would say, I will not give my sexual ID!"[42] Afterwards, someone had told me that he was active in sadomasochist sexuality and that he had pictures in his New York apartment. My friend had "accidentally seen the pictures, was choked-up, and wanted to share with me about it, but I was defensive and did not want to talk about "it" and I could not face this reality. I thought it was none of my or her business. In fact, Peraldi published papers on different sexualities, but I was not aware of it at this time.

New York was one place for him, but also the Lacanian Clinical Forum where he had a very positive link with John Muller of Austen Riggs, Bill Richardson from Boston College, and Donna Bentolila, who was an Argentinian psychoanalyst who lived in Florida but passed away two years ago. They founded the Lacanian Clinical Forum together. Peraldi had very good relations there, and the Forum was much more friendly. The Lacanian Clinical Forum is a nice and interesting place. I go there twice a year. In the fall, we meet at Austen Riggs. In the summer, we meet in the countryside in Québec. This year is the first year it was cancelled in 30 years, because of COVID19. Otherwise, the group meets regularly and there is no membership procedure except a small fee. There are clinical and theoretical presentations throughout the weekend gathering.

CV: How would you say the Lacanian approach or Peraldi's thinking alongside Lacan's has influenced your own clinical work?

MH: The important thing is the place of the signifier. Anecdotally, it is about being not so much in a place to interpret, but rather being open to the discourse and listen. It is not necessarily Lacanian, but it is important to be open to free association and the dreamwork. For me, what I remember of Peraldi's teaching is the link with the history of psychoanalysis and Freud's beginnings. Peraldi also emphasized the matter of the death of the father. My explanation is not very academic in the sense of pedagogy or having certain texts to follow, but this is a clinical approach towards an opening and listening. This is different from swallowing one seminar after the other. I try to be open to different authors and different approaches.

CV: I hear your emphasis on openness…

MH: Yes. This openness is the way Peraldi would work and present, and perhaps it is less specifically about what he would say.

CV: Despite drawing upon Lacan, Peraldi never seemed to identify with Lacanianism. He did not call himself a Lacanian.

MH: Exactly. He did emphasize the importance of the imaginary, the symbolic, and the real RSI as well as the death drive. Also, sexuality was important for him to discuss. Sexuality is often excluded from the thoughts of psychoanalysis today. The emphasis now is so much about the relationship with the archaic, the mother, or related to the attachment theory. There seems to be no more mention of free association, dreams, or sexuality. This is so different from what Freud (or Peraldi) would be interested in talking about. Louise Grenier has said that Peraldi was also concerned with femininity in his specific and original way, different from the usual Lacanian approach. Many students have benefitted from Peraldi's approach as an introduction into the Lacanian field.

With the Lacanian Clinical Forum, I forget that there is "Lacanian" in it because it is not necessarily so Lacanian. I am curious… what is it that Lacan means for you?

CV: I first discovered him in the English department, and his discussions of speech, language, and writing always fascinated me, along with the work of Derrida and deconstruction. The members of the French schools really intrigued me: Deleuze and Guattari, Michel Foucault, Jacques Rancière, Antonio Negri, Luce Irigaray, Hélène Cixous, René Girard, and Roland Barthes. Once I began training in therapy and analysis, I realized the complexity of the clinical Lacan. I learned that Lacan was not really analyzing literary and cultural texts so much as thinking about cultural texts in ways that might enrich our thinking about clinical work.

MH: Peraldi actually did not like Derrida and his theories; he would criticize him, saying that he was not analyzed. What you say is interesting because a few years ago we did some general research with Robert Letendre about psychoanalysis in universities and colleges.[43] In part, it is true that psychoanalysis will not usually be taught in psychology departments today, but rather in literature departments. Where I teach, at UQAM, psychoanalysis is stronger than it was when I began, but this is also a different psychoanalysis than Lacanianism.

CV: I have certainly found the work of other schools of psychoanalysis to be very helpful. As you were saying earlier, perhaps to revolve around the work of only one analyst or school could be very limiting. With the school of object relations, for instance, [Donald] Winnicott's work has been helpful to me, especially where he speaks of the transitional object or the use of an object. I also think that Didier Anzieu's work is brilliant where he attends to new ways of considering object relations through the skin-ego.

MH: Did you know that Didier Anzieu was the analysand of Lacan? And that his mother was working for Lacan as a housekeeper? She was still related with Lacan at the time of Anzieu's analysis. He did not know this story, later discovered, and ended his analysis with Lacan.

CV: Yes, this is a bizarre circumstance. Anzieu's mother was the case of "Aimee," who became the subject of Lacan's doctoral dissertation. When Anzieu learned of this connection, he ended his analysis with Lacan. He is also one of the most important critics of Lacan.[44]

MH: It is not the only bizarre thing. Catherine Millot also wrote a book about her romantic relationship with Lacan.[45] She was his analysand. This was a period of time where analysts were very patronizing and in the place of the master. You cannot remove this from Lacan's legacy. It is part of it. Lacan shows something of the *tache aveugle* [blind spot]. He did not see what we see now.

CV: This is an interesting question though, isn't it? Many people around the world declare themselves as Lacanians – and we speak of him because he was an incredible and fascinating thinker – but he was also undoubtedly quite a questionable or dubious figure. We have learned much more about him as time has passed. There is also the tragic book written by his daughter, Sibylle.[46] I once heard Patricia Gherovici present a lecture on psychoanalysis, and she offered a sort of double-edged critique within a joke – I paraphrase her now – that "it is curious that the biggest scandal for the IPA about Lacan is not that he took a patient as a lover or that he was a terrible father but that he shortened the length of the session."

MH: Yes, this is really why Lacan was removed from the IPA! I do not think Peraldi practiced short sessions. I do not really know anybody who practices the variable length as maybe Lacan did. Peraldi could have conducted 30-minute appointments or would cut five minutes before the end. As I said, the signifier, the death drive, as well as the imaginary, the symbolic, and the real were the most important for him to emphasize. We also worked a lot on the seminar, *on Identification*.[47] We tried to go through the formal logic, the question of identification, and the Other. These were very new things at the time and were not the classical point of view. This was not the family psychoanalysis oriented like mommy, daddy, me. Classical analysis approaches the Oedipal complex as the repetition of the same where the son would be like the father, as if they were the same person. Peraldi would say the transference is not the love you would imagine. The transference descends from the imaginary and is something much more strange and awkward, dark and harsh. He was also interested in psychosis and not being a conformist. He was not interested in trying to have people "fit" – that is, fit in the system or fit in the schema. This is not the purpose of psychoanalysis.

CV: Patients often say at the beginning of consultations that they are looking for a "good fit."

MH: Peraldi would teach that psychoanalysis is not a good fit. A patient would have told him, "I have told you all of what I had to tell about my life and past." Peraldi might have said, "Now your analysis is beginning."

CV: He's a very interesting person because he has a way of thinking that is not necessarily academic in a sense that attempts to get outside of established ways of thinking and writing. This thinking is different from certain kinds of structured analytical training where interpretations might come from repetitions of the same, as you have said. Peraldi seems to have had attentiveness to emerging signifiers...

MH: ...to something that erupts from the unconscious. This is precious for me from what I remember from his teaching. This is what I try to teach the students. Have you seen this recent television series on Netflix called *Freud*?[48] Even though it is really absurd and kind of outrageous, it may relate to Freud more than many of the other things that have been written about him that are so boring. The show gets into the transmission of ideas, dreams, and free association. These are the things that are important. The way that psychoanalysis is taught today is often so far from this, for instance, when we only speak about attachment or the fusion with the mother, the archaic... there is something missing. It can become more psychological than psychoanalytical. As you have said, work that only attends to the side of the signifier and discourse is also not psychoanalysis. There can be two ways of getting away from Freud. I could say that maybe one line of thinking goes too far on the side of discourse and the other line of thinking goes too far on the side of the mother.

CV: How can we begin to explain this distinction you've mentioned between psychology and psychoanalysis? Could we say that psychoanalysis is less focused on assessment or diagnosis and more upon a practice of listening?

MH: Psychoanalysis is about openness to the unconscious rather than evaluating and measuring. I do teach the structures as a frame even though I have reservations about putting people in boxes. You have to learn what is in the boxes but try not to be imprisoned by them.

CV: I get the impression from Peraldi's work that he was not even really so concerned or interested in the boxes or categories of neurosis, perversion, and psychosis.

MH: I was just remembering that I once had a presentation and I mentioned [Jacques] Laplanche and [Jean-Betrand] Pontalis.[49] He became angry and sarcastic. He was very much against any aspect of labelling.

CV: He was upset at Laplanche and Pontalis's dictionary-like categorization of psychoanalysis?

MH: He was upset that I had quoted something from them about structure or stages, but the very next day he would have said Laplanche and Pontalis are a good reference. This was his style, and people could be petrified at times. One day he might say, "Oh, that's very interesting – tell me more about that…", or he might say, "Laplanche and Pontalis are garbage!" He would say, "Derrida, yuck!" He would also insult André Green.[50] There were some incidents where Green came to Montréal and attacked "the Lacanians". I was not a Lacanian, but this was at a time when if you were a Lacanian, it might be seen as very bad. Peraldi was a person who would put all of the labels, boxes, and close-minded categories into the garbage.

CV: You had also interviewed him. What was that experience like?

MH: What was it like? It was a very sad experience. I wrote that I had lunch with him a few months before. I was visiting him at his home. I was with a close friend, and we had supper with him. It was a very nice house, and we had beautiful food and drinks. We laughed and had fun, but when I went to see him for the last time, he was not at all the same person. I interviewed him on February 24 and he died on March 23. He was not the same as before and was very sad, bitter, and angry. He was also not smiling and was very emaciated. He was previously *bon-vivant*, but he had lost a lot of weight.

I ran into problems afterwards from some of my friends because of what he had said in the interview. They said it was not like him and that I should not have published this, because he was critical of psychoanalysis and Lacan. He said that Lacan was a *faussaire* [forger] like somebody who would sell false paintings or counterfeit money. I asked him about transmission. I said to him that in the IPA groups transmission was very formal and scholastic. He said the Lacanian groups might be worse because the candidate does not even learn the rules. He was denigrating psychoanalysis and all of it. Was it related to his sickness? He was dying and only 53. He was in a period of life where he would have had many years of productive and good life. It was sad. AIDS was just beginning and he died in 1993. It is stupid, but at the time I was much younger and could not imagine that he would be so angry because he presented death during his seminars in sort of a romantic way. He was not accepting it, which is understandable now. I thought that I had to publish the interview, that he was himself in that interview, an angry and bitter part of himself, but I think it was really him. Maybe there were some exaggerations, but it was him. I do not know why I should have hidden or changed anything he told me.

CV: In much of psychoanalysis, we reduce things to the subject or the individual. Within Lacan, there is desire as desire of the Other, which could include social or cultural aspects, but with Peraldi, he was interested in anthropology and religion and the effects of the institution. He was partly very much concerned with what is external to the subject.

MH: May 1968 in France was an anti-authoritarian revolution. Peraldi was libertarian in this spirit. The groups that emerged in 1968 were queer and feminist groups, which were very much included in the discourse in his teaching. He talked about hysteria as a manifestation of forbidden and oppressed femininity.

CV: Peraldi is also not very well known. He wrote a few papers written in English and published an edited collection, *Polysexuality*, but does not seem to have gained much recognition outside of Québec.[51]

MH: He does not belong anywhere except maybe with his colleagues from the Lacanian Clinical Forum who had a lot of friendship for him. Even here in Québec, he has somehow disappeared, for now at least. It is strange. It is now 27 years since he died. He is not read so much. Maybe it is partly that he was not so scholastic or dogmatic. He did not have ready-made thoughts to transmit. It is good, however, to see some people remembering and revisiting his work from time to time.

Notes

1 See Peterson, Michel. "Un Cadavre De La Psychanalyse Québécoise: Reflexions Sur l'effacement Du Père Noël Mailloux." *Interfaces Brasil/Canadá*. 17.1 (2017): 179–194.
2 In the early 1940s, Noël Mailloux (1909–1997) formed the Institute of Psychology at the University of Montréal. Miguel Prados (1899–1970), a Spanish neuropathologist, founded the Montréal Psychoanalytic Club in 1946. In 1948, Mailloux joined Prados and brought many well-known psychoanalysts to give lectures in Québec. A Parisian psychologist, Théo Chentrier (1887–1965), also helped introduce Freudian

thought to Québec and was the first member of the IPA to live in Canada since Ernest Jones's (1879–1958) stay in Toronto between 1909 and 1913. Despite its success, the Montréal Psychoanalytic Club never provided clinicians with psychoanalytic formation or training.

3 Francisco Franco (1892–1975) was a Spanish general and politician who ruled as Spain's head-of-state and dictator from 1939 until his death.

4 Gregory Zilboorg (1890–1959) was a Ukrainian psychoanalyst and psychiatrist who studied in St. Petersburg, Russia. Zilboorg worked under Vladimir Bekhterev (1857–1927), who was a Russian neurologist and is considered the "father" of objective psychology.

5 See Peraldi, François. *Traduire: application de quelques concepts de la sémanalyse à l'opération traduisante*. Diss. Sorbonne Université, 1975.

6 The "narcissism of small differences" or "narcissism of minor differences" refers to the Freudian notion that communities with close relationships and territories may engage in disputes and mutual aggression as a result of hypersensitivity to details of difference. Freud coined this term in *Civilization and Its Discontents* to speak about cultural differences between nation-states, but for Lacanians the concept closely aligns with the field of the imaginary where envy becomes a decisive element in the narcissistic image and in the preservation of a lack (Harari 25).

7 Daniel Sloate (1931–2009) was a Canadian poet, translator, and playwright who earned a doctorate in French literature from the Sorbonne University in Paris. He was an associate professor in the Linguistics Department at the University of Montréal and the Director of the Translation Program at McGill University.

8 Françoise Dolto (1908–1988) was a pediatrician and psychoanalyst who was a close friend of Jacques Lacan and produced several major works on child psychoanalysis.

9 Peraldi, François. *Lettre à Catherine Duncan, 1967–1993*. Montréal: TAMAM, 2017.

10 Peraldi's last sentence of the correspondence with Duncan could be translated as "Psychoanalysis is not a big thing" or "Psychoanalysis is no big deal."

11 Luce Irigaray (1930–) is a Belgian-French feminist philosopher who has written many major works. Marguerite Duras (1914–1996) was a French novelist, playwright, and filmmaker.

12 "It is obvious that psychoanalysis was born from science. It is inconceivable that it could have arisen from another field" (Lacan, *Écrits*, "On the Subject" 192).

13 Galileo Galilei (1564–1642) was an Italian physicist and astronomer who is associated historically with the development of the scientific revolution.

14 Jean-Michel Vappereau is a French psychoanalyst and mathematician who studied topology and was close to Lacan.

15 In "Psychology and Religion," Jung writes that "Suppression may cause worry, conflict, or suffering, but it never causes a neurosis. Neurosis is always a substitute for legitimate suffering" (75). Among the many extensions to Jung's statement is this one from M. Scott Peck: "But the substitute itself ultimately becomes more painful than the legitimate suffering it was designed to avoid. The neurosis itself becomes the biggest problem. True to form, many will then attempt to avoid this pain in this problem intern, building layer upon layer of neurosis. Fortunately, however, some possess the courage to face their neuroses and begin – usually with the help of psychotherapy – to learn how to experience legitimate suffering" (17).

16 Mireille Lafortune (1935–1998) was a Québécois psychoanalyst. She began practicing psychoanalysis in the late 1960s, independently of the Canadian Psychoanalytic Society. She was also one of the first to teach psychoanalysis in Québec as a professor at University of Québec in Montréal from 1970 to 1991. French pediatrician

and psychoanalyst Françoise Dolto (1908–1988) wrote several major works on child psychoanalysis and was close to Jacques Lacan.

17 Philippe Julien (1926–1986) was a French psychoanalyst, professor, writer, and philosopher. Gérard Miller (1948–) is a French psychoanalyst, professor, filmmaker, and columnist.

18 Jean Racine (1639–1699) was a French playwright who wrote mainly tragedies. Marguerite Duras (1914–1996) was a prolific French novelist, playwright, screenwriter, and experimental filmmaker.

19 Daniel Paul Schreber (1842–1911) was a German judge who wrote the well-known book, *Memoirs of My Nervous Illness*. Schreber's account of his own illness has been understood by Freud and Lacan to be a case of psychosis or psychotic structure.

20 Georges Bataille (1897–1962) was a French intellectual, theoretician, and librarian who wrote essays, novels, and poetry that would be reappraised after his death by prominent thinkers, including Jacques Lacan, Michel Foucault, Jacques Derrida, Jean Baudrillard, and Julia Kristeva. Bataille theorizes the notion of excess and the accursed share throughout his works. Gilles Deleuze (1925–1995) was a French philosopher and Felix Guattari (1930–1992) was a French psychotherapist and activist who worked at La Borde clinic in France. Deleuze and Guattari wrote several major works together, most notably *Anti-Oedipus: Capitalism and Schizophrenia* (1972), in which the authors draw upon Bataille's ideas about excess.

21 Michel de M'Uzan (1921–2018) was a French neuropsychiatrist and psychoanalyst. His book *De l'art à la mort: itinéraire psychanalytique* was published in 1977 with Gallimard, Paris.

22 Lacan, Jacques. *The Seminar of Jacques Lacan, Book XX: On Feminine Sexuality, The Limits of Love and Knowledge*. 1975. Ed. Jacques-Alain Miller. Trans. Bruce Fink. New York: Norton, 1998.

23 Pierre Legendre (1930–) is a French psychoanalyst and Research Director at the École pratique des hautes etudes [Practical School of Advanced Studies] in Paris.

24 See Peraldi, François. "L'élangage de la Folie" [The language of madness]. *Santé mentale au Québec*. 3.1 (1978): 1–17.

25 Louis Althusser (1918–1990) was a French philosopher who extended the work of Karl Marx. Althusser is often said to have renewed Marx in a way that is loosely parallel to Lacan's renewal of Freud.

26 A "cartel" is a psychoanalytic study group often consisting of three to five people plus a supervisor who moderates the group work.

27 Chagnon, Gilles. "La petite tante aimée et la vampire." *François Peraldi: Voix, legs, parcours, d'un psychanalyste*. Eds. Gilles Chagnon and Danielle Monast. Montréal: Liber, 2005. 37–49.

28 Peraldi, François. "La castration sadique-anale de votre père…" *Interprétation*. 21 (1978): 87–100.

29 Peraldi writes of Francisco Ayala (1943–1989) in "Franco et sa mort." *TROIS*. 6.2–3 (1991): 212–215.

30 Daniel Sloate (1931–2009) was a translator, poet, and playwright.

31 This Lacanian concept is better known in English as "the gaze."

32 Charles Melman (1931–) is a French psychiatrist and psychoanalyst who began following Lacan in the 1950s.

33 During the final Seminar XXVII, *Dissolution*, on March 11, 1980, Lacan warns of his school becoming stuck: "*Comme le démontre qu'à y revenir on ne trouve qu'à s'engluer – où j'ai moins fait École… que colle…*" ["As the proof that to come back to it we find only to get stuck – where I liked to go to School…"]. Translated from unpublished manuscript.

34 McWilliams, Nancy. *Psychoanalytic Diagnosis: Understanding Personality Structure in the Clinical Process*. New York: Guilford Publications, 2011.

35 *Presentation de malade* refers to the clinical interview with a patient for the purpose of study or teaching clinical trainees. Lacan not only served as an intern at the Sainte-Anne in Paris from 1927 to 1931 but also held his seminars at the hospital from 1953 to 1963.

36 Czermak, Marcel and Cyril Veken. *Les jardins de l'asile: Questions de clinique usitée et inusitée*. Paris: Association freudienne/lacanienne, 2013.

37 Sometimes also translated as "anchoring point," the *point de capiton* (literally an "upholstery button") in Lacanianism denotes the point where the Saussurean signifier and signified become tied or knotted together for the subject in a relatively fixed meaning.

38 See Peraldi, François. "La transaction." *Filigrane*. 1 (1992): 37–52.

39 See Hazan, Marie (2019).

40 In *Our Dark Side: History of Perversions*, Élisabeth Roudinesco (2009) writes that "The great clinicians of perversion, for their part, have, from Masud Khan to Stoller and François Peraldi, always formed a separate community. It is as though there was always a danger that they would be accused of colluding with what fascinates them because they had signed a pact with the Devil" (158).

41 In 1975, Peraldi participated in the influential "Schizo-Culture" conference that took place at Columbia University, where participants included R.D. Laing, Gilles Deleuze, Félix Guattari, Michel Foucault, Jean-François Lyotard, and many other radical intellectuals of the time.

42 Hazan recounts many reflections on Peraldi's seminar, including this particular instance in "Le séminaire de François Peraldi: témoignage d'une rencontre paradoxale avec la transmission de la psychanalyse à Montréal" [François Peraldi's Seminar: Testimony of a Paradoxical Encounter with the Transmission of Psychoanalysis in Montreal]. *Filigrane*. 10.2 (2001): 74–91.

43 Robert Letendre (1946–2017) was a psychoanalyst and professor in the Department of Psychology at Université du Québec à Montréal from 1981 to 2006.

44 Anzieu had a complicated history as an analysand of Lacan's whereby he discovered that Lacan had also treated his mother as the well-known case of "Aimee." For an account of this, see Élisabeth Roudinesco's *Jacques Lacan & Co.: A History of Psychoanalysis in France, 1925–1985*. Chicago: Chicago University Press, 1990.

45 Millot, Catherine. *Life with Lacan*. Trans. Andrew Brown. Cambridge, UK: Polity Press, 2018.

46 Born on November 26, 1940, Sibylle Lacan, second daughter from Jacques Lacan's first marriage to Marie Louise Blondin (1906–1983), committed suicide in Paris on the night of November 7–8, 2013. See Lacan, Sibylle. *A Father: Puzzle*. Trans. Adrian Nathan West. London: The MIT Press, 2019.

47 Lacan's *Seminar IX* from 1961–1962 has not yet been officially translated into English.

48 *Freud* is an Austrian-Hungarian produced crime drama, which aired on Österreichischer Rundfunk (ORF) and was released on Netflix in 2020.

49 With his colleague Jean-Bertrand Pontalis (1924–2013), French psychoanalyst Jacques Laplanche (1924–2012) published *The Language of Psycho-Analysis* (1967), which remains a canonical encyclopedic book on psychoanalysis. It was translated into English in 1973 and has been updated with multiple following editions.

50 André Green (1927–2012) was an influential and prolific French psychoanalyst who was influenced by the theories of Lacan, Winnicott, and Wilfred Bion. Green was

also a prominent critic of Lacan and accused him of disregarding the importance of affects.

51 Peraldi, François (ed.). *Polysexuality*. New York: Semiotext(e), 1995.

Bibliography and Further Reading

Chagnon, Gilles, Hazan, Marie, and Michel Peterson. *Penser la clinique psychanalytique: Le Lacanian Clinical Forum*. Montréal: Éditions Liber, 2010.

Grenier, Louise and Marie Hazan. *L'analyste à l'œuvre: Relire François Peraldi*. Montréal: Éditions Liber, 2008.

Hazan, Marie. "La grossesse de l'analyste: Fantasme ou réalité? ou la réalité dépasse-t-elle la fiction?" *Santé mentale au Québec*. 15.2 (1990): 168–180.

Hazan, Marie. *Le couple: réussir l'impossible: Entre idéal et réalité*. Montréal: Les Éditions Québec-Livres, 2014.

Hazan, Marie. *Le masculin: Psychanalyse des représentations des hommes au Québec*. Montréal: Les Éditions Québec-Livres, 2010.

Hazan, Marie. "Le roman familial psychanalytique d'Anna Freud et le nôtre. Filiation et homosexualité." *Filigrane*. 28.1 (2019): 149–168.

Hazan, Marie. "Le séminaire de François Peraldi: témoignage d'une rencontre paradoxale avec la transmission de la psychanalyse à Montréal." *Filigrane*. 10.2 (2001): 74–91.

Roudinesco, Élisabeth. *Our Dark Side: A History of Perversion*. 2007. Trans. David Macey. Cambridge, UK: Polity Press, 2009.

Chapter 5

From Psychoanalysis with Lacan in Paris to California and Beyond with André Patsalides

André Patsalides, PhD, is a psychoanalyst and founding member of the Lacanian School of Psychoanalysis in Berkeley, California. He completed his psychoanalytic training in Belgium and with Jacques Lacan in Paris. He is Emeritus Professor at the University of Louvain (Belgium) and a member of the Belgian School of Psychoanalysis. He currently resides in Paris and continues to teach and practice. This conversation took place on 14 March 2021.

Chris Vanderwees: Can you tell me about your formation in psychoanalysis?

André Patsalides: The first time I learned about psychoanalysis was when I was 15 years old. It was in the library of my uncle Michael where I read Freud's *Introductory Lectures on Psycho-Analysis* as well as a book by Wilhelm Stekel.[1] At 15 or 16 years old, I was thinking about what I wanted to do in life. This was the late 1950s. I wanted to be a psychoanalyst, but I hesitated. I was also interested to be a musician. I tried many instruments, but once I got beyond my hesitation, I decided to become a psychoanalyst and a university professor. I was pretty young when I started my studies in chemistry, mathematics, and pure science at the university. I was interested in scientific topics, but I later changed my focus to psychoanalysis when I was 20 years old. When I left chemistry and mathematics, I pursued a degree in the humanities where I studied criminology, psychology, sociology, and anthropology. I started my analysis with Antoon Vergote, who was a professor at the Dutch University of Louvain.[2] During the mid-1960s, the Belgian School of Psychoanalysis was formed by Vergote and some of the members of Lacan's school. I became a member of this Belgian school, and I am now the oldest member. I completed a doctoral dissertation and also went through the habilitation process to qualify as a university professor. At that time, I studied Hebrew for two

DOI: 10.4324/9781003323136-6

years to read the Torrah with Albert Guigui. This was a long process and is almost like completing another PhD. Since my degree was in criminology and I was also a shrink, my first job was to be a deputy at the juvenile court of Brussels. I still have the card from the court with the picture of my face from that time. I wonder to myself, "Am I the same person?" This was more than 60 years ago. I am now 80 years old.

CV: What about your analysis with Lacan?

AP: I later continued my analysis with Lacan from 1971 to 1975. I was in analysis with him for four and a half years. Taking trains and buses, I would go from Brussels to Paris every week, sometimes twice per week to meet with him. At that time, it would take about five hours to get to Lacan's office. You would have to wait. There was a huge crowd of people there made up of highly intellectual Parisians who were jammed in his waiting room. Often there would be 12 or more people waiting for him at a time. He would come out to the waiting room and say, "You, come in." This would be regardless if you were waiting for hours or if you had just stepped in the door. When I stepped into the waiting room for one of my first sessions, he noticed that I was new and called me to come in. During one of these early sessions, I told him that I did not know what to say. He took my hand and was leading me to the door to tell me, "Goodbye." I began to stutter a bit, and he brought me back and said, "You wanted to say something?" Well, what I said at that moment was very important to me. As you know, he had this technique of the cut. You could have a session of three minutes, or if you were very lucky you might have a session that would last ten minutes or a quarter of an hour. That is all you could expect. This was standard. When I was in the room with him, sometimes he was drawing Borromean knots. He was a one-of-a-kind genius. He brought something absolutely new to the field of Freud. When I teach psychoanalysis, I always start with Freud and move to Lacan where he continues with the concept of the unconscious. I terminated my analysis with Lacan around 1975, but my analysis was not finished. I continued through many other stretches of analysis given that I had a very heavy clinical practice throughout my career.

CV: Did you attend Lacan's seminars as well?

AP: I attended many times. His way of speaking was very special. He would stop, start, sigh. He was incredibly bright. There is actually a video of the speech Lacan gave at Louvain in 1972. He gave an outstanding lecture at the Grote Aula, a huge auditorium at the university. A guy came to throw water on him and on the table. You can find this video on the Internet. You can see me in the video if you recognize me. I was in my early thirties then.

CV: I heard that you may have a story about Lacan's twisted cigars…

AP: Lacan used to like to smoke Culebras, which are cigars made of three other cigars braided and banded together. It was said that these cigars were rolled on feminine thighs. Lacan was fond of this story. In Brussels, I was able to find a brand of this cigar that was rare in Paris. I paid him once with a cigar box.

CV: You also mentioned you were interested in music...

AP: Yes, I was in Afghanistan in 1974. I went to meditate in front of the Buddhas of Bamiyan, which were carved into the rock of a huge cliff and have now been destroyed by the Taliban. I also wanted to go to Bukhara, which was part of the Soviet Union. I wanted to study a musical instrument there of which I was very fond. I had to get to Moscow and then take a plane to Bukhara, which was 50 miles from the border, but I was cornered by Soviets with machine guns. So, I gave up this pursuit. I also studied Arabic and Hebrew with a Rabbi, Albert Guigui. We studied the old Hebrew. It took me two years of studying to be able to read the Torah in the original text of the *Bereshit*, but now after 55 years or so, I have forgotten everything.

CV: What is the musical instrument called?

AP: It is called the *qanun* in Arabic. It is a horizontal sitar like the santoor or the Iranian santur. *Qanun* comes from the Greek, *kanon*, which is the rule, the scale, or the law. It is an instrument well known in Turkey as well as in the north of Iraq, Syria, throughout the Middle East, but also in Egypt. Around the time that I was in Afghanistan, I also visited the Kalash people. In approximately 350 BC[E], when Alexander the Great destroyed Persia and went to India, he was afraid because he saw elephants for the first time in his life. He came back from India and went to Persia, but many of his soldiers deserted him and went to an area that is very extreme and difficult to go where they encountered the Kalash. Some of the Kalash people are believed to be the descendants of Alexander the Great's soldiers. With an interest in anthropology, I lived with the Kalash people for several months just northeast of Kandahar and Kabul. It is a place called Kafiristan, which means the "land of the non-believer."

CV: When did you come to the United States?

AP: After these travels, I came to the United States in 1977. I was on exchange with a professor and psychologist from Sonoma State University in California, Bernd Jager.[3] Jager wanted to go my home university of Louvain, which has the archive of [Edmund] Husserl.[4] As you know, Husserl was a Jew and was persecuted by the Nazis. One of his assistants, [Herman] Van Breda, discovered a huge number of Husserl's manuscripts in Germany and smuggled them to Louvain.[5] Van Breda gave the documents to the university and this archive has now become a mecca for anyone who wants to study Husserl. Since Jager wanted to go to my university, I had the opportunity to go study at Sonoma State. I was 34 or 35 years old and had not yet set foot in America.

I arrived in California in 1977 at Sonoma State University, where I would teach for eight months. I taught a class about Lacan's Seminar XX, *Encore*, which includes the diagram of sexuation. The seminar had been published only for two years at that point. I found that the best way to study and master a topic was to teach it. By doing the work of preparation for teaching, you learn very well what you are teaching. I divided the class into two groups: men in one group and women in the other group. We studied the diagrams on sexuation together. I asked each group to speak about their orgasmic experience according to Lacan, if they wanted. A few years ago, I presented the responses from this course regarding what the women and men had said about their experiences. What the women had to say was so wonderful, but what the men had to say was so stupid and flat. I did this to try to explain what Lacan is saying about male and female sexuality through quantum logic. I also gave a seminar on Rudyard Kipling's *The Jungle Book* and Lacan's theories on sexuality. *The Jungle Book* is a masterpiece that can help to explain Lacan. I wanted to present this book as an example that could be understood as an illustration of Lacanian theory.

In 1977, I also initiated a cartel. The plus-one of the cartel was Jacques-Alain Miller. At this time, we had good relations, but absolutely not since. Miller wanted to take over what I had built in California, as he has done everywhere else. At this time, I wanted to institute the first cartel for my first Lacanian School of Psychoanalysis in California. I asked for the relief of my duties at Louvain. The chancellor of the university was my former professor of mathematics from when I was younger and studying chemistry. He gave me the authority to do my teaching at Louvain for three months each year and then to be in California for the rest of the year and to work there as a professor of Louvain. For many years, I went back and forth between Louvain and Sonoma State. In 1978, I asked Lacan to be a plus-one for a cartel at our school in California. This is the last time I wrote to him.

In 1982, I lived in India. I met the Dalai Lama and stayed with him at a Buddhist dialectic school where I was observing the learning of children under the age of ten. It was a remarkable experience. During this year, I was also invited to speak about cross-cultural topics in Kuwait at the Institute of Banking Studies. I was also invited to speak in Algeria. I was always invited to speak about Lacan, cross-cultural topics, and the connections between East and West, which was my forte. In 1983, I went to the Institute for Oriental Studies in Egypt. There was a top scholar there who befriended me, and I lived for many months in a monastery near Al-Azhar. There was a priest whose name was [Georges] Anawati, who wrote a very extensive book called *An Introduction to*

Islamic Theology. I worked there to study about psychoanalysis, Islamic studies, and perspectives of religion. I was especially interested in a period of time where there was peaceful coexistence between multi-religions, including Jews, Muslims, and Christians during the twelfth century under Muslim rulers in Spain.

I also taught many seminars, lectures, and case conferences at Sonoma State University throughout the 1980s and 1990s. I taught many seminars together with Bernd Jager. When you come to the campus as a visiting professor, you give a public lecture to the whole department of psychology once per year. One year, I gave a big lecture on Maimonides, who was a Jewish scholar living in the beginning of the twelfth century in Córdoba.[6] He wrote a book called *The Guide for the Perplexed* in Arabic. Maimonides is also known for a treatise called *The Treatise of Eight Chapters*, which is a masterpiece about psychology and ethics. I also gave a lecture on Ibn Tufail, who was a mathematician and philosopher who also lived during the twelfth century.[7] During the twelfth century, all knowledge was studied together from mathematics to grammar to psychology to theology to philosophy to medicine. Ibn Tufail wrote a book called *Alive, Son of Awake*, where he tells a story of a little boy born from chemistry on an island in the Indies. There is one antelope on the island that gives him his milk. The boy lives alone until he meets the first human being and they begin an extraordinary exchange. It is an incredible story that inspired Islamic thinkers and many philosophers of the Enlightenment period. I lectured and taught in Todmos-Rutte under the supervision of Karlfried Graf Dürckheim.[8]

CV: Did you eventually settle in California?

AP: The group that I had created in 1977, where we would think about Lacan, eventually became so important and so critical that I decided to give up Louvain. I decided to settle in California in 1990.[9] In 1992, we created the palimpsest for our Lacanian School of Psychoanalysis, which I borrowed from the Dutch School of Psychoanalysis. As a group, we were too small to create a committee that would oversee people who wanted to become psychoanalysts. So, I proposed the method of the palimpsest with my friend Nathan Adler as a way for people to be clear about why they wanted to study Lacan and to speak about their ideas.[10] I lived in California for two years straight, but after this period of establishing the school, I began to travel to Louvain for two or three months, then back to California for nine or ten months. The founding members of the school were people who were attending my seminars at the time. Some of the people who are on the program registered with me to create the school, but when it came time to go forward with the program, they never showed up.[11] The only remaining members of the school from the original founding of the school are Raul Moncayo and Marcelo Estrada.[12]

When we founded the school, I tried to cover all possible areas of psychoanalysis. I was especially interested in psychosomatic phenomena. I taught courses in the Lacanian School of Psychoanalysis for 15 years, from 1990 to 2005. All the years I was in California, I had a full practice. I trained many psychoanalysts in the Lacanian approach. In 2005, we had a conflict in the school. Someone wanted to create a program for group psychotherapy. I objected. We absolutely do not do group therapy from the Lacanian perspective. I moved to Paris in 2005, but I came every year to speak to a group that Raul Moncayo was leading on Mission Street in San Francisco. He saved the school with his teaching and commitment to psychoanalysis and it continues today.

CV: Can you tell me about your paper, "Butterflies Caught in the Network of Signifiers"?

AP: My friend Owen Renik was the editor of *Psychoanalytic Quarterly* and asked me to write a paper about the Lacanian approach to psychoanalysis. I co-authored this paper with Beatrice Patsalides. The title comes from Seminar XI, where Lacan speaks about Chuang Tzu, who dreams he is a butterfly. We elaborated all of Lacan's theory across 30 pages. It is the first paper ever published about Lacan in an IPA [International Psychoanalytical Association] journal to summarize his work in this way.

CV: You have travelled to many places for your research on religion and communities of faith. How do you bring together an understanding of psychoanalysis and religion?

AP: This is a very big question. I have had many interests throughout my life, which I studied for several months or several years. I study something and move onto something else, but Freud and Lacan have always been my compass. I consider religion as a fact. Am I a believer? I'm not sure. I call myself agnostic and an inquirer. I meditated in front of the Bamiyan Buddhas etched in the cliff in Afghanistan without being a Buddhist. I have been to mosques. I was in Damascus for a while where every Thursday evening there would be two hours of meditation and jumping in a collective *zikr*. After this exercise, you space out, my friend. I was interested in religious phenomena and the unconscious phenomena of humans. Religion was not a commitment for me. It was not a belief. For me, it was an inquiry, a curiosity.

Notes

1   See Freud, Sigmund. *Introductory Lectures on Psycho-Analysis. The Standard Edition of the Complete Psychological Works of Sigmund Freud, Volume XV (1915–1916): Introductory Lectures on Psycho-analysis (Parts I and II)*. 1916. New York: Vintage and Hogarth Press, 2001. 1–240. Also, see Freud, Sigmund. *Introductory Lectures on Psycho-Analysis. The Standard Edition of the Complete Psychological Works of Sigmund Freud, Volume XVI (1916–1917): Introductory Lectures on*

Psycho-Analysis (Part III). 1917. New York: Vintage and Hogarth Press, 2001. 241–463. Wilhelm Stekel (1868–1940) was an Austrian physician who became one of Freud's earliest followers and helped to form the first psychoanalytic society.

2 Antoine or Antoon Vergote (1921–2013) was a Belgian Roman Catholic priest, theologian, philosopher, and psychoanalyst. His major publications are written in French, but he also wrote in Dutch. A professor of psychology, Vergote was interested in the psychoanalysis and psychology of religion and lectured on these topics in the faculties of philosophy and theology. His Dutch publications on the psychology of religion have had great influence in this field in the Netherlands. See Westerink, Herman. *Controversy and Challenge: The Reception of Sigmund Freud's Psychoanalysis in German and Dutch-speaking Theology and Religious Studies*. Berlin: Lit Verlag, 2009.

3 For more on Bernd Jager (1931–2015), see Mook, Bertha. "A memorial dedication to Prof. Bernd Jager." *Journal of Phenomenological Psychology*. 46 (2015): 227–28.

4 Edmund Husserl (1859–1938) was a German philosopher who is known for establishing the school of phenomenological thought.

5 Herman Leo Van Breda (1911–1974) was born in Belgium. He became a Franciscan priest, philosopher, and founder of the Husserl Archives at the Higher Institute of Philosophy of the Catholic University of Leuven. Van Breda saved a significant amount of Husserl's manuscripts and writings from being destroyed by the Nazis.

6 Maimonides or Moses ben Maimon (1138–1204) was a medieval Sephardic Jewish philosopher, astronomer, and physician who was also one of the influential Torah scholars of the Middle Ages. He wrote *The Guide for the Perplexed* sometime around 1190 in Classical Arabic using the Hebrew alphabet.

7 Ibn Tufail (c. 1105–1185) was an Arab Andalusian Muslim polymath. Tufail was a writer, philosopher, theologian, physician, astronomer, and political advisor.

8 Karlfried Graf Dürckheim (1896–1988) was a German diplomat, Zen master, and psychotherapist. Following the completion of a doctorate in psychology, Dürckheim became an avid Nazi supporter. Following World War II, he went into hiding in Japan but was caught and imprisoned for 16 months and underwent a spiritual rebirth. He devoted the rest of his life to teaching meditation and spiritual change.

9 See Benveniste, Daniel. "The Early History of Psychoanalysis in San Francisco." *Psychoanalysis and History*. 8.2 (2006): 195–233.

10 Nathan Adler (1911–1994) was an American psychoanalyst and professor of clinical psychology who lectured for many years in California. He is known for the book *The Underground Stream: New Lifestyles and the Antinomian Personality*, which was published in 1972. At the time of Adler's passing, he was the vice president of the Lacanian School of Psychoanalysis (California) in 1994.

11 Founding members of the school listed on the 1994 program include Nathan Adler, Martine Aniel, Randy Badler, Murray Bilmes, Michael Brown, Yvette Chalom, Marcelo Estrada, Ann Haley, Mardy Ireland, Suzanne Miller, Raul Moncayo, André Patsalides, Nelly Russell, Anna Shane, Inez Souza Valois, Carrie Thaler, and Andrew Wilson.

12 See Vanderwees, Chris. "Reflections on Training Institutions and the San Francisco Bay Area Lacanian School of Psychoanalysis, An Interview with Raul Moncayo." *Lacunae: APPI International Journal for Lacanian Psychoanalysis*. 19 (2019): 8–37.

Bibliography and Further Reading

Patsalides, André. *Georges Spencer-Brown: Laws of Form*. Paris: Encyclopédie des Oeuvres Philosophiques, 1985.

Patsalides, André. "*Jouissance* in the Cure." *Anamorphosis*. 1 (1997): 3–12.

Patsalides, André. "L'homme et la Loi – Prolégomènes à une théorie de la criminology." *Criminologie et justice pénale*. (1990): 259–276.

Patsalides, André. "Le lent gage de l'autre - Psychanalyse et langage, Religion et Mystique." *Cahiers internationaux de symbolisme*. 40–41 (1980): 93–113.

Patsalides, André. *Seit, Raun und Initiation – Psychoanalytische Perspectiven*. Rütte: Opus Magnum, 1989. 1–7.

Patsalides, André and Axelle. "Le sujet et le paradoxe – Introduction à l'oeuvre de Spencer-Brown." *Litura*. 1981. 1–31.

Patsalides, André and Malone, Kareen Ror. "*Jouissance* in the Cure." *The Subject of Lacan: A Lacanian Reader for Psychologists*. Eds. Kareen Ror Malone and Stephen R. Friedlander. New York: State University of New York Press, 2000. 123–134.

Patsalides, Beatrice and Patsalides, André. "Butterflies Caught in the Network of Signifiers: The Goals of Psychoanalysis According to Jacques Lacan." *Psychoanalytic Quarterly*. 70.1 (2001): 201–230.

Chapter 6

Space, Logical Time, and *Après-Coup* Association in New York with Paola Mieli

Paola Mieli is a psychoanalyst in New York City. She holds a doctorate in philosophy (University of Milan) and a PhD in psychopathology and psychoanalytic research (University of Diderot, Paris VII). She is a founding member and president of Après-Coup Psychoanalytic Association (New York). She is a member at Le Cercle Freudien (Paris), at Espace Analytique (Paris), an honorary member of the European Federation of Psychoanalysis (Strasbourg), and an Associate Researcher at the Centre de Recherches en Psychanalyse, Medicine et Société at the University of Diderot – Paris VII. She is a contributing editor of the journal *Insistance: Art, psychanalyse et politique* (Paris). The author of numerous articles on psychoanalysis and on culture published in Europe and America, Mieli has written *Figures of Space: Subject, Body, Place* (2017); *Figuras do espaço: Sujeito, corpo, lugar* (2016); *A Silver Martian: Normality and Segregation in Primo Levi's Sleeping Beauty in the Fridge* (2014); *Sobre as manipulacaoes irreversiveis do corpo* (2002); and *Being Human: The Technological Extensions of the Body* (with co-editors Jacques Houis and Mark Stafford, 1999). She is also the publisher and director of the *Sea Horse Imprint* based in New York. This interview was recorded via Skype on 12 May 2019.

Chris Vanderwees: When did you first encounter psychoanalysis?
Paola Mieli: In my teens, in Milan, where I'm from. The north of Italy is a region that has been impacted by the French, Austrian, Spanish, and German culture. It is the child of the Enlightenment and the Middle European tradition. The '70s were a historically and politically intense period, probably the most fervent moment in Italy's history after the Second World War, when the cultural and economic changes of the '60s resulted in strong transformative movements – the workers, the women, the gay, the students' movements – which led to major social reforms and to a vigorous social environment. Unfortunately, the reaction to these openings came strong and harsh. In high

DOI: 10.4324/9781003323136-7

school, I was already involved in reading and working groups where we studied politics and psychoanalysis. I followed the activities of *La Pratica Freudiana*, an association based in Milan, founded by two Italian members of the *École freudienne de Paris*, which included seminars, international conferences, and interdisciplinary exchanges. Later, at the State University of Milan, I studied philosophy, particularly philosophy of language. I had the chance to go to Paris, where I met Pierre Klossowski, who became a main interlocutor in my studies. I attended some sessions of [Jacques] Lacan's latest seminars. Of course, I did not understand a word he was saying. Yet his teaching had a great and lasting impact on me. I was struck by his style and the ethics of his *einsegnement*. Surrounded by an enormous crowd of people, in awe and adoration (people who after his lessons were spending hours in discussing what they had just seen and heard, in the cafés nearby), he didn't mind showing his uncertainties and impasses, his vulnerability, his will to research. He wasn't speaking from the position of a master but that of an analysand, subverting any expectation for the transmission of an academic, pre-constituted knowledge. His teaching was an invitation for everyone to put themselves to work. This was relevant to me right away. Even though he was sick and older at that time, he definitely appeared as an extraordinary clinician and thinker.

I started my analysis in my teens with an excellent classical Freudian analyst from the *Società Psicoanalitica Italiana* (SPI), affiliated with the International [Psychoanalytical Association] (IPA). After a couple of years of intense work, this gentleman moved to a distant location where I could not follow him. Since I wanted to continue my analysis in my mother tongue, as at that time I thought it was imperative to do (an idea I questioned later on, as I explained in my paper "The Space of Transmission: An Act Between Languages"),[1] I selected an Italian analyst member of the *École freudienne* of Paris. Lacan appeared too old and busy to be approached anyway. The new *tranche* of my analysis lasted a few years. At its end, the idea of becoming an analyst had taken over. I had progressively shifted my interest from philosophy to psychoanalysis. My background in philosophy remained fundamental, but when I went to Berlin to do a postdoctoral fellowship in linguistics and German philosophy, I realized my vocation was analytical. It was the city itself, Berlin, divided by the wall – where one could still hear the voices of the lives buried by the war – that woke me up. Suddenly, I began to realize how many of my beloved philosophers had implicitly participated to the construction of an ideology that turned into Nazism and how much the Jewish question was also my question. I decided to continue my analysis for my formation but this time with the clinician I'd learned to appreciate and trust the most: Serge Leclaire.[2] We ended up working together for years. He was the analyst of my life, a magnificent clinician, particularly gifted in transmitting the ethics of the analytic position.

After the dissolution of the *École freudienne*, the scene in Paris was complex. I was an outsider, a student from a younger generation who was observing a tormented debate. I didn't appreciate, nor understood at the time, the tension created by the different groupings after the dissolution, nor the manners of the newly founded *École de la Cause freudienne* – a hierarchical structure of power, distant, in my experience, from the spirit of the psychoanalytic circles surrounding the *École freudienne*. I was stunned to learn of the *Delenda* tribunals initiated by [Jacques-Alain] Miller in the early '80s, where analysts were judged as good or bad, as right or wrong. Not my cup of tea. I preferred to follow the teaching and researches of some of the old guard members of the *École freudienne*, such as Moustafa Safouan, Jean Clavreul, Michèle Montrelay, Alain Dider-Weill, and Françoise Dolto.

CV: When did you first come to the United States?

PM: I visited New York for the first time in 1983 and fell in love with the city. At that time, I knew very little about the Unites States, except that I didn't like some aspects of its politics, though I've always been an admirer of its Constitution. The energy, the multiculturalism, the collection of diversities, the non-provincialism, the multifaceted relation of the city with the arts, deeply attracted me to New York. Trying to find ways to visit again, I proposed a project to Italian radio and television about American psychoanalysis. They accepted it and I was sponsored to travel, research, and interview local analysts. Once, after interviewing the head of a day clinic in Manhattan, he proposed to me to work there. He was looking for an analyst who could speak different languages and, being himself a German immigrant, he was interested in my continental background. I took the offer. It was in 1987. The choice was daring, as it implied a radical distancing from the familiar and the known. Of course, things turned out to be more difficult than anything I could expect.

Among other things, I progressively realized the implications of the distance between the local analytic environment and the one I was coming from. [Sigmund] Freud's teaching in the USA had a very different impact than in Europe; considered outdated in the analytic milieu (according to a belief in progress, that tends to consider everything that comes after better than what precedes it), his texts were either not studied or transmitted inaccurately, not philologically. Lacan had moved exactly in the opposite direction, contrasting the neo-Freudian orientations and calling for a return to Freud, a move that deeply influenced continental analysis. From its origins, psychoanalysis in the USA was integrated to the medical discourse, which fostered the idea of a new therapeutic practice devoted to assimilation, normativization, and adaptation. The analysts who had left Europe to flee the Nazi persecution had themselves a wish for recognition and integration, contributing to the distancing from the Freudian project. The symptom was – and still is – considered by many as a disorder to be eliminated in order to refind a lost psychic balance, a conception radically different from that of Freud, who understood symptoms as comprise formations, the fruit of a specific psychic causality. For Freud, there is no such thing as a "normal" state of things. In his paper *The Question of Lay Analysis*,[3] he distances himself from the American medical (and consumeristic) ideology and clearly differentiates the field of psychoanalysis from that of other disciplines, sustaining the interdisciplinary background necessary to a lay formation and denouncing the alleged necessity to get a degree in medicine to become an analyst as the most dangerous resistance to psychoanalysis itself – a resistance revived nowadays by the requirement, in many countries, to obtain a degree in psychology to enter the profession.

As soon as I moved to New York, I organized reading and clinical working groups in order to continue my formation and establish fruitful local exchanges. I met very knowledgeable colleagues, who had different backgrounds but also an interest in continental analysis, who became great interlocutors and friends: Alan Roland, Alan Bass, David Lichtenstein, Donald Moss, Berry Opatow, François Peraldi, and Ed Robins. In the fall of '87, a group of us organized a colloquium on "Time and Psychoanalysis," a topic chosen specifically for its significance in our field, differently conceptualized by diverse orientations. The colloquium was held at Columbia University; speakers included analysts from New York, Paris and Montreal.[4] It went well and showed that there was interest in these kinds of discussions. I thought that there was space for the creation of a new association. I proposed it to David Lichtenstein and Donald Moss, who participated in the founding of Après-Coup Psychoanalytic Association. After a short period, Donald Moss assumed other responsibilities and his cooperation came to an end. David Lichtenstein continued to be an active member of Après-Coup until 2015.

Originally, I thought to call the association "Nachträglichkeit", but nobody could really pronounce the word. "Après-Coup", the common French expression with which Lacan translated *nachträglichkeit*, was much better. It was an overdetermined choice: this name underscored a central theme of the Freudian discourse, that of the logical time proper to psychic causality, generally overlooked in the American analytic context and wrongly translated into English as "deferred action"; it indicated a central problematic in the unfolding of the analytic act; it identified the theme of translation as the central issue in the proper understanding of texts and the formations of the unconscious; it also referred to the time when the association was established, in the aftermath (*après-coup*) of the dissolution of the *École freudienne in Paris* and of the death of Lacan – in the aftermath, also, of the colloquium on time in New York; finally, it underscored a significant moment in the trajectory of our formation as analysts.

The association was not conceived as a school but a place to study and research, a meeting place for analysts motivated by the desire to establish an analytic community devoted to Freud's and Lacan's work and pursue their own permanent formation. I had as a model my experience in the circles of the *École freudienne* in Paris and of the *La pratica freudiana* in Milan, where one could study psychoanalytic and scientific texts closely but also exchange with scholars coming from different fields – science, philosophy, religion, linguistics, history, the arts, etc. – all these fields being essential for the understanding of the subject of language.[5]

Analytic formation is permanent. I don't think it's possible to practice as a psychoanalyst without a continued involvement in researching and studying, without the knotting together of what Lacan calls analysis *in intension* and analysis *in extension*, two faces of the same Möbius strip. The analyst, says Lacan, should be at least two: the analyst in his/her position as analysand (*in-tension*) and the analyst who reflects upon his/her practice, elaborating it with others (*ex-tension*).[6] Appropriate exchange with others and constant researching allows an ethical position to be maintained, which balances the solitude of one's own practice, the singularity of the analytic act.

At the beginning, the association was small. I started giving my regular seminars. People would attend in small numbers, but the spirit of the encounters and the level of the exchanges were challenging and inspiring. Colleagues and friends from Paris participated in this novel association, pleased to come to New York to work together. Serge Leclaire, Michele Montrelay, Jacques Hassoun, Claude Rabant, Jean Pierre Winter, Alain Didier-Weill, Marie Magdeleine Chatel-Lessana, and Jean Michel Vappereau came often, sometimes regularly, lecturing and supervising. This soon created a mixed faculty, both local and international, that progressively developed over the years, later including more analysts from Europe and from South and Central America: Isidoro Vegh, Roberto Harari, Pura Cancina, Nestor Braunstein, André Michels, Erik Porge, Catherine Vanier, Alain Vanier, Colette Soler, Betty Berardo Fuks, Marco Antonio Couthinio Jorge, and many others.

In a few years, in the aftermath of personal analysis, supervision, teaching, and researching, it became clear that some of the participants of our group had started forming themselves analytically, and the question was raised of the nature of our organization. Loyal to the name we had given to it, it was in the aftermath of our practice that we were reckoning with its effects. The Après-Coup program has always been *in progress*, the result of a shared growth. It has been modified over the years according to the needs encountered in the course of our work. People were forming themselves within our association and were looking for a recognition within the social bond. The question was raised of a formal recognition of the association on the part of the State. At first, I was skeptical about this possibility, as our program was structured differently than that of the existing institutes, traditionally modeled after academic course of studies. Our goal was to incorporate our association with respect to the ethics of psychoanalysis, which we had sustained for years, according to our Freudian–Lacanian tradition.

We applied to the state department of education. Of course, it was a long process, where we explained in detail the nature and the structure of our program and the history of the tradition we were coming from. The recognition came in 2002, a historic first registration of a Freudian–Lacanian association in the State of New York, a registration *après-coup* – afterward – of our psychoanalytic program and of the way in which it had operated and continues to operate. We wished to give to Après-Coup the title of "school", in line with the French spirit of the *École de psychanalyse*, but the term "school" could not be used, as it is allowed in the State only for academic studies. We then preferred to stay with the term "association", to differentiate ourselves from the existing institutes. In 2001, the vote was cast for the regulation of psychoanalysis in the State of New York; and, in 2006, the law was introduced establishing that in order to practice psychoanalysis, it is necessary to get a license from the State (as is the case with all other professions).[7] At that time, the members of [Après-Coup] unanimously voted against the transformation of the program of the association into a program leading to licensure, as this would imply conforming to standard regulations which would have deformed the spirit of our psychoanalytic program.

Après-Coup has always welcomed as members and participants not only analysts or people in analytic formation but also people coming from other fields – which encourages interest in psychoanalysis and fosters an intermingling of bodies of knowledge necessary to theory, the clinic, and the transmission itself. At the same time, it has developed a specific Formation Program, for those who want to engage in a psychoanalytic formation – people who acquire their State licensing independently. People who attend the activities of the association and decide at a certain point of their own trajectory to undertake an analytic formation can have their attendances credited as part of the Formation Program. The program was conceived in this manner in order to create an environment respectful to the subjective trajectory and to the temporality of one's own unique path toward analytic formation.

Psychoanalytic institutes are mostly viewed as organizations leading to a professional certification and a social inscription. One decides to become an analyst the way one decides to become a lawyer or a dentist; and, in fact, a person potentially becomes one the day s/he enrolls in an institute, following the rules and the timetables pre-established by the curriculum, together with the will of the instructors. The condition *sine qua non* for analytic formation, personal analysis, becomes a secondary matter, undermining the fact that the wish to become an analyst (a phantasmatic ideation among others) radically differs from the effect of the analytic act. The request of many institutes for people to enroll to be already practicing in the field of mental health is, in this sense, paradoxical.

The singularity of the time proper to an analytic formation is in no way comparable to the linearity of academic courses or of a technical apprenticeship. This is a major difference between training and analytic formation, between a career choice and a vocation resulting from the subjective experience of the formations of the unconscious. No wonder why at the end of their institutional trajectory, after the immediate gratification of their "diplomas", many people end up being at a loss and unhappy in their profession. We constantly see it in supervision.

Après-Coup introduced into the vocabulary of North American psychoanalysis the expression "psychoanalytic *formation*", which today has gained a foothold. *Training* suggests the idea of apprenticeship, the acquisition of a knowledge related to theoretical procedures and practices necessary for a certain technical *expertise* – as does occur in professional fields, including sports. The idea of acquiring a pre-constituted knowledge that can be applied *ad hoc* undermines the particularity of the function of knowledge in psychoanalysis. No doubt, acquiring a very extensive body of knowledge is necessary to our practice, but it's also imperative to be able to suspend such knowledge "in the act". Psychoanalysis is the experience of the subjective division, of the taking into account of unconscious knowledge and of a relation between knowing and truth that cannot be anticipated. The analyst's desire can only be the consequence of an analysis, not its condition. The entire articulation of the transference as a manifestation of the emergence of the *subject-supposed-to-know* implies a progressive deconstruction of any hypostatized notion of knowledge. The word "formation", from the Latin *formare* – to give form, to create – better conveys the uniqueness of analytic experience, its creative quality and its transforming effects, which lead to a new ethical position and the possibility of a *savoir faire* in the dealing with the symptoms. Nothing to do with the *conformity* required of candidates in reproducing the believes of their masters.

CV: How do you understand the psychoanalytic notion of time?

PM: I am not sure to what degree Freud's revolutionary notion of time is fully appreciated. He works with different aspects of time: chronological, which involves antecedence, progression, contemporaneity, and succession; historical, which accounts for the series of material events that occurred in reality; the time peculiar to psychic causality, which Freud defines with the term *Nachträglichkeit*, the absence of time that characterizes the drive. These aspects interact, producing the experience of subjectivity as well as the subjective experience of history. In particular, the logical character of *Nachträglichkeit* allows for a radically new conceptualization of the shaping of history, both individually and collectively. Woven into the fabric of signifiers that traverse the generations, this temporality invests a past inscription and reactivates it in the psychic formations of the present. The logical character of *Nachträglichkeit* was discovered by Freud early on in his studies of trauma. Clinical reflection showed to him that an event that is originally experienced in an anodyne fashion, therefore not traumatically, can acquire a traumatic signification when a new event evokes it, and attributes to it, in the present, a particular sexual connotation. What happens afterwards gives a novel connotation to what precedes it. The trauma is constituted therefore in a temporal scansion that occurs *Nachträglichkeit*, in the aftermath. But this scansion does not indicate a gap between stimulus and response or a pause between action and reaction; it's *not* a deferred action – as the concept has been wrongly introduced in the English psychoanalysis literature, generating all sorts of confusions. Rather, it indicates the efficacy of the present which invests a past inscription producing an unexpected effect of meaning. Psychic causality shows that what happens before does not necessarily determine what follows and what follows can have a determining impact on the reading of what precedes it. This is particularly significant clinically, where fantasy can produce *après-coup* the material with which the symptoms are woven. The logical structure of temporality has also a huge impact in the understanding of the transmission of trauma among generations; symptoms can express in the present effects of meaning that relate not only to the experience of the persons manifesting them but to that of the generations preceding them and in which their personal history is inscribed.

The temporality *Nachträglichkeit* is also that which informs the emergence of signification in the speech act. When one is speaking, it's only at the conclusion of the enunciation that the effect of meaning emerges, at the moment when speakers complete their saying – a temporality that underlines the difference between enunciation and statement, highlighting the function of pauses and punctuations in the speech act. It is what interrupts the sequence of the chain of signifiers in the articulation of a saying, that allows for the emergence of effect of meaning, independently from the intentions of the speaker. The nature of the speech act is what gives to the talking cure its power. The fundamental rule of free association that guides the analysand's speech, saying "whatever comes to mind", corresponds to a listening guided by what Freud defines as *gleichschewebende Aufmerksamkeit*, an equally suspended attention. A keen ear for unconscious processes, as Freud puts it, is oriented by the logical rigor of the signifying chain, by the capacity to listen to what produces sense and nonsense beyond the speaker's intentions. This implies a putting into parentheses, a suspension, of any predetermined knowledge. It is what speech lets emerge beyond what we think we say that allows for the encounter with a knowledge we did not know we had.

How can we define psychoanalysis? There are many tentative ways to do it. One way is to describe it as the subjective experience of the separation between truth and knowledge, as a practice which allows for the emergences of one's singularity and style. But this implies allowing for the transference to unfold to its end – what is possible only if the position of the "subject supposed to know" fades, both on the side of the analyst and on the side of the analysand. From this point of view, there is a major difference between Lacan's articulation of the cure and that of other schools. Lacan spent many years of his life studying the structure of transference and conceptualizing the end of analysis, in particular in view of the formation of the analyst; he indicated how the identification to the analyst, enhanced by the Neo-Freudian orientations, is very distant from an end. Distinguishing the wish to become an analyst from the desire of the analyst, he pointed out how at the moment in which analysands start practicing, they identify themselves to the subject of deception (*sujet de la tromperie*). This calls for a new stage in one's own analysis, a new logical step for an analysis to possibly reach its end.

CV: What about the relation of time to Lacan's notion of scansion or the cut?

PM: The question of scansion is related to the nature of the act of speech and to the structure of the signifying chain. As I mentioned before, this highlights a temporality *Nachträglichkeit*, which produces effect of meaning in the aftermath of the speech act and indicates the split existing between the saying and the said. In this split, something of the truth of the subject can emerge. This is particularly noticeable in the slip of the tongue, in the missing words, in the memory lapses, when unforeseen meaning or nonsense can appear, laden with a knowledge that expresses itself beyond the speaker's intentions. For Freud, the main entries to the unconscious are slips of the tongue, dreams, wit – those formations of the unconscious which emerge through the grid of the censorship. He thinks that the secondary process that informs rational thinking is always marked by censorship; it is never a reflection of the truth, but a manipulation of the truth. The question, then, is how to make people hear what they are actually saying, beyond what they believe they are saying. A punctuation, or a scansion in the appropriate timing, allows for the effect of meaning to resonate and for a subjective truth to manifest itself, a truth otherwise lost underneath the repetition of the signifying chain, in the blah-blah of one's own self reflections.

In this sense, scansions are related to the variations of the length of sessions. For instance, when something crucial has been said, a scansion may cause it to resonate in the aftermath of the analytic encounter. It's important to realize that each session, as much as it is part of a series, is also a unique opportunity. In it, the analyst has the chance to intervene at the right time, but this time is not going to return. Which is why each session should be treated with the same dignity as if it were the last one, since it is the last chance one has to intervene at that time. This requires a great degree of presence and (suspended) attention on the part of the analyst – definitely much more than sitting for 50 minutes letting a pre-established time run its course. Each session should function as an irreplaceable beat in the chain of sessions that constitute a treatment. Each of them weighs on what precedes and follows – and orients the direction of the treatment, provided that one intervenes at the right time and with the right scansion.

The practice of the so called "short session" – mostly a practice of systematic interruption – needs to be radically distinguished from that of the variation of the length of the sessions, which has a variable duration within the 45 minutes frame or more. Short sessions are a mannerism just as stereotypical as that of the fixed length of the session. Every systematic, mechanical technique empties the particularity of the unique timing of a discrete act of speech, which should dictate the unfolding of the analytic act. This may involve, for instance, occasionally adding an extra session. Time, frequency, and payments are essential tools of the frame of the cure, necessary tools that allow for the transferential grammar to unfold and for the symptoms to unknot. Such tools need to be related to the singularity of the case and are based on the respect and the attention devoted to each particular person. From this point of view, frequency imposed by external agencies or by institutional requirements contradicts the care that needs to be paid to the analysand. For someone with a phobic structure, for instance, intense frequency can be detrimental, as it can be for some cases of psychosis or post-traumatic stress.

CV: How do you see space and place as having an effect on analytic time?

PM: Time and space are knotted together. In the analytic literature, a lot has been said about time, in particular in the aftermath of Lacan's extraordinary paper on logical time, written in 1945.[8] And, of course, lots has been said and developed in the domain of topology. Not as much has been written about subjective space per se. There are plenty of philosophical books on space, but they do not take into account the libidinal reality of the subject. Psychoanalysis introduces a de-ontologized notion of the subject and a different conceptualization of the relation of the subject to the world, marked by the drives. The subject is an effect of the relation to the Other. Space is libidinized and affected by logical time.

CV: When we are speaking about space, is this a psychic space or a phenomenological space?

PM: The way we inhabit the world, our experience of it – of this room, of this environment, of our conversation, and so on – is mediated by the signifying relation through which we approach it. The idea of studying the world "as it is" is based on the belief that the world can be observed without mediation. Psychoanalysis (but not only: also, quantum physics, for instance) shows that our approach to the world is always mediated. Freud would say mediated by the psychic scene, Lacan by the laws of the signifier. People are implicated in the world that concerns them. Not only is the subject implicated in the object – the observer in the data s/he studies, the researcher in the object examined, the spectator in the spectacle – but the subject emerges as an effect of a transferential relationship with what is other. It emerges from the collective since "the collective is nothing, but the subject of the individual", as Lacan points out. The structural prematurity of infants imply they can only survive through the care of others, what supports the identifications with the others' fantasies and expectations. The primary affective environment is always organized by the exchange with the other, by the unfolding of the drives and the satisfaction they inscribed in the body. The drive objects situate the subject in its environment, draw the coordinates of its extension, and make the world intrinsically libidinal.

I call subjective "place" the particular space that belongs to a given subject, his, her, their singular spacial-temporal relation with the world. Clinical practice shows the significance of the subjective relation to place within the transference. The manner someone approaches the analyst's office or inhabits it, as well as the manner in which a person relation to space emerges in dreams, parapraxis, and so on, [is] always unique, intimate, and full of subjective implications.

I remember an interesting project made by an artist student of mine. He analyzed the daily trajectory of a series of people around him, their moving around the city in their everyday engagements and errancies. He realized that each of them always took the same path, traveling the same roads or walking the same track. Each person had created a specific route to reach some usual locations. Without even realizing it, they had carved their own place out of the city.

CV: Perhaps like a cognitive map?

PM: Yes, a cognitive map, but not only. A person might say, "I take this way because at that particular corner there is street that I like to see every morning." The street is not neutral. It has a signifying and affective connotation. There is a physical space and there is a phenomenological space; [Maurice] Merleau-Ponty had written extraordinary things about it. Psychoanalysis adds to it another dimension, that of the knotting together of the imaginary, the symbolic, and the real. Since the beginning, human beings have created spaces to impress, to organize, to elevate, to subjugate, to imprison. Architects know well that space and its organization have a great power on human psyche.

CV: Is there something of the uncanny that influences your thinking?

PM: In our relation to the world, to our place, suddenly may emerge what Lacan calls an "edge phenomenon", a phenomenon that shakes the recognition of our surroundings. The appearance of such edge implies a break, a suspension. An example of it could be the unexpected revelation, for instance, that the landscape I see out the window is no more than a painting leaning on the window, as [René] Magritte masterly illustrates. Suddenly, the place reveals the presence of a fault in the signifying network that organizes it, something that cannot be put immediately into words. The real that inhabits the place appears surreptitiously. The *Unheimliche*, the uncanny, belongs to this order of phenomena. Part of the second chapter of my book *Figures of Space* is dedicated to the it.[9] I introduced the question of the uncanny through Edgar Allan Poe's tale "William Wilson" and through Luis Buñuel's *The Exterminating Angel*.[10] Space has a profound relationship to it.

CV: What are your thoughts on working in an American context of regulations, the cognitivist approach, and the emphasis on empiricism that is concerned with reducing experience to what one can supposedly see and measure? How do you see the future of psychoanalysis as a practice or as a treatment in this contemporary situation?

PM: The cognitive model inscribes itself in the tradition I mentioned before, that of assimilation and normativization, which is characteristic of a certain approach to suffering conceived as "disorder". It is no accident that the pharmacological ideology and that of the neuroscience so much in fashion today have been so easily integrated into the dominant USA therapeutic conception, including psychoanalysis. This adaptive psycho-medical thinking reproduces the notion of the individual fostered by the society of efficiency and is fed by the neoliberal model. These are approaches informed by the ideal of the quick fix, where the aim is for symptoms to be kept under control or suppressed, not analyzed and resolved. Of course, these practices are at the service of the biopolitical power which regulates the life of citizens. Lots of financial resources are invested in them because they generate huge profits. These models claim to be scientific; in truth, they only refer to the "discourse" of science, in its mediatic nature. They promote the ideal of measurable and empirical data without accounting for how these data are mediated by the researchers and for the ideology that animates the research.

There is nothing more distant from psychoanalysis. Already in the late fifties, Lacan had pointed out that the subject of psychoanalysis is the same as the subject of science, except that, if this is case, it is precisely because psychoanalysis is concerned with the subject *foreclosed* by science, whose truth returns to the fore in the shape of symptoms. It is this foreclosed truth that reaches our offices. And, indeed, I sit in my everyday practice and often see people who go through all sorts of treatments – pharmacological, neurological, behavioral, and so on – and who, at the end of the day, keep feeling miserable and developing symptoms. So, they come to psychoanalysis. The more these pseudoscientific practices alienate and repress the subjective truth, the more symptoms proliferate. This could be good news for our practice. Psychoanalysis, however, in the media and in popular culture, is excluded from the equation – and given these premises, it may be a blessing. Yet, this says also something of the responsibility of psychoanalysts in the neoliberal ideology. I saw analysts emulating the discourse of science and presenting measurements and statistics on the evolution of treatments, based on the recording of patients' sessions (!). Outrageous. If so-called "psychoanalysts" are party of the biopolitical discourse, this is obviously a choice entailing all sorts of implications – even more so if they are not aware that, in so doing, they contribute to an exploitative and segregating system.

I do not think that psychoanalysis worthy of its name could ever be prevalent in this kind of society. But it will persist as the other face of the coin of the alienation of our time. It is probably going to remain marginal and in progress yet an essential practice to address suffering and restoring the possibilities of contributing constructively to the social link.[11] But for this to be, it's necessary to protect its transmission and its ethics – which is opposite to the ideology of the quick fix and the ready-made responses, to ready-made diagnoses, fed by our consumeristic society. There are a lot of things that can be done, but this implies for psychoanalysis to be transmitted properly and rigorously. Which is why I'm critical of certain institutional practices, as well as with the cavalier pastiche of training promoted by certain groupings, typical of the US tradition of eclecticism.

CV: What do you imply when you refer to the ethical position?

PM: Recently, a group of young analysts in New York asked me to republish a letter I wrote many years ago. It is called "Letter to Our American Colleagues" and deals with some of the issues we have been speaking about today. I was surprised they considered it still pertinent today.[12] Analytic treatment implies a modification of the libidinal economy, which involves resolving symptoms and inhibitions, but also an ethical transformation, toward an encounter with difference, with the relative, with the unknown, with the not-all. In deconstructing the mystifying function of individual and group identifications, in dissipating their violence, psychoanalysis restores to the individual the subjective responsibility for his and her own choices and own actions; it allows for the assumption of the causes of which one is the effect, including the assumption of one's own subjective responsibility in the social reality of which one is part. In this sense, the practice of singularity can contribute to the practice of social democracy.

In 1967, Lacan positioned on the horizon of psychoanalysis in extension – that is to say, in the social link – three perspectival vanishing points: a symbolic one, pertaining to the Oedipal myth; an imaginary one, related to the institution; and a real one, that of the concentration camps. Each of these paths traced the direction for a reflection on the responsibility of the analyst and his indispensable ethical commitment, be it an unmasking of the way in which the Oedipal ideology partakes in biopolitical logic, be it a deconstruction of the imaginary identifications that reinforce the institution's totalitarian structure, and be it a confrontation with the pervasive real of our social reality that strengthens segregation. In our days, the logic of the "state of exception" creates new camps and new persecutions (of refugees, of sick people, of old people, and so on). Clearly, this puts into question the analyst's role in the social link, and the relation between analytic discourse and other discourses, and all the more in a system in which "mental health" itself takes part in the machinery of segregation.

Becoming a psychoanalyst can be a tough undertaking. It is not easy. You have to have talent and a vocation for it, but, most importantly, you have to blaze your own trail. If appropriate conditions for formation and transmission do not exist, one has to create them.

Notes

1 P. Mieli "El espacio de la transmisión: un acto entre las lenguas", *La traducción en psicoanálisis*, Lapsus calami, Revista de Psicoanálisis, Buenos Aires, Otoño 2014.
2 Serge Leclaire (1924–1994) was a French psychiatrist and psychoanalyst who underwent a didactic analysis with Jacques Lacan as part of training at the *Société Psychoanalytique de Paris*. Leclaire followed Lacan through his conflicts with the International Psychoanalytic Association to the *Société Française de Psychanalyse* in the split from the *Société Psychoanalytique de Paris* in 1953 and again to the *École freudienne de Paris* during the second split in 1964. He is the author of influential works, including *Psychoanalyzing* (originally published in French in 1968) and *A Child is Being Killed* (originally published in French in 1975).
3 Freud, Sigmund. (1926). "The Question of Lay Analysis." *The Standard Edition of the Complete Psychological Works of Sigmund Freud, Volume XX (1925–1926): An Autobiographical Study, Inhibitions, Symptoms and Anxiety, The Question of Lay Analysis and Other Works*. New York: Vintage and Hogarth Press. 177–258.
4 Speakers included Jean-Gerard Burstein, Marie-Magdeleine Chatel, Catherine Millot, Gérard Pommier (Paris), François Peraldi (Montreal), Paola Mieli, Barry Opatow, David Lichtenstein, and Donald Moss (New York).
5 In "Questions," Mieli (2017) emphasizes Freud's remarks on psychoanalytic training and the need for the humanities: "analytic education cannot be limited to the

medical domain but must include several humanistic disciplines ... In addition to regular courses, seminars, workshops and working groups in psychoanalysis, an institute should offer – or request and supervise attendance in – courses not only in psychopathology, differential diagnosis, neurology, pharmacology, but also in linguistics, anthropology, philosophy, literature, art, epistemology, history of religion, law. And it should make sure that participants develop an active role and engage in forms of intellectual production, rather than merely play the passive part of students learning their teachers' words by rote. This broad field of differentiated disciplines will prepare the ground appropriately for the analyst's listening to the subject's discourse and its cultural diversity and become the base for a psychoanalyst's continuing education. The coming into being of an analyst as the result of an analysis can then be seen as only a first major step into a universe of learning that will accompany him/her throughout life" (20).

6 P. Mieli, "Revenir sur la formation", in *Essaim*, n. 45, Erès, Paris, 2020.

7 In New York State, practicing the profession requires a state license in one of the following sectors: medicine, psychology, clinical social work, or psychoanalysis.

8 See Lacan, Jacques. Logical Time and the Assertion of Anticipated Certainty. *Écrits*. 1966. Trans. Bruce Fink, in collaboration with Héloïse Fink and Russell Grigg. New York: W.W. Norton, 2006. 161–175.

9 See Mieli, Paola. (2017). *Figures of Space: Subject, Body, Place*. Trans. Jacques Houis. New York: Agincourt Press.

10 Poe, Edgar Allan. "William Wilson." (2011). *The Complete Tales and Poems of Edgar Allan Poe*. San Diego: Canterbury Classics. 271–283. This tale was first published in 1938 but was later translated into French and published in a Paris newspaper, *La Quotidienne*, in two installments. "William Wilson" is a notable publication in the Lacanian context since it was the first of Poe's works to be translated into a language other than English and also Poe's introduction to the French public. Luis Buñuel's "The Exterminating Angel" is a Spanish surrealist film produced in 1962.

11 In "Questions," Mieli (2017) nicely outlines the necessity of marginality for psychoanalysis: "In opposition to any idea of conformity, psychoanalysis is fundamentally an experience with and towards otherness, a practice of de-identification that enhances the relation to difference. It is the subject's practice of 'exile,' a leaving behind of mystifying individual and group identifications and of the guarantees provided by the already known. It is a journey towards what is unknown and foreign within the subject, as manifested, for example, in the formations of the unconscious" (19).

12 Mieli, Paola. (2017). Questions Raised by the Report on the Psychoanalytic Consortium on Analytical Training. Letter to Our American Colleagues. *The Candidate Journal*. 7: 15–21.

Bibliography and Further Reading

Freud, Sigmund. "The Question of Lay Analysis." *The Standard Edition of the Complete Psychological Works of Sigmund Freud, Volume XX (1925–1926): An Autobiographical Study, Inhibitions, Symptoms and Anxiety, The Question of Lay Analysis and Other Works*. Ed. James Strachey. New York: Vintage and Hogarth Press, 1926. 177–258.

Lacan, Jacques. "Logical Time and the Assertion of Anticipated Certainty." *Écrits*. 1966. Trans. Bruce Fink, in collaboration with Héloïse Fink and Russell Grigg. New York: W.W. Norton, 2006. 161–175.

Lacan, Jacques. *The Seminar of Jacques Lacan, Book XXII, RSI, (1974–1975)*. Trans. Cormac Gallagher. n.d. Unpublished. Retrieved from http://www.lacaninireland. com/web/wp-content/uploads/2010/06/RSI-Complete-With-Diagrams.pdf

Mieli, Paola. *A Silver Martian: Normality and Segregation in Primo Levi's Sleeping Beauty in the Fridge*. New York: CPL Editions, 2014a.

Mieli, Paola. "Acte analytique, acte juridique: Paradoxes, apories, contradictions." *Essaim*. 23.2 (2009): 69–87.

Mieli, Paola. "Du son qui guide l'image: Notes sur pulsion, corps et espace." *Insistance*. 1.1 (2005): 131–138.

Mieli, Paola. "Durer au titre de symptôme." *Insistance*. 3.1 (2007): 315–320.

Mieli, Paola. El espacio de la transmission: un acto entre las lenguas. *Lapsus calami. Revista de Psicoanálisi*. Otoño 2014: Buenos Aires, 2014b.

Mieli, Paola. "Femininity and the Limits of Theory." *Psychoanalysis and Contemporary Thought*. 16.3 (1993): 411–427.

Mieli, Paola. *Figures of Space: Subject, Body, Place*. Trans. Jacques Houis. New York: Agincourt Press, 2017c.

Mieli, Paola. "Jimmy, tout à coup." *Insistance*. 14.2 (2017b): 179–183.

Mieli, Paola. "Le temps du traumatisme." *Actualité de l'hystérie*. Ed. André Michels. Toulouse: ERES, 2001. 43–60.

Mieli, Paola. "Questions Raised by the Report on the Psychoanalytic Consortium on Analytical Training. Letter to Our American Colleagues." *The Candidate Journal*. 7 (2017a): 15–21.

Mieli, Paola. "Revenir sur la formation." *Essaim*, n. 45 Paris: Erès, 2020.

Mieli, Paola. "Secret Weapon." *Psychoanalytic Quarterly*. 68.1 (1999): 110–118.

Mieli, Paola. *Sobre as manipulacaoes irreversivels do corpo*. Rio de Janeiro: Contra Capa, 2002.

Mieli, Paola. "Tale-Telling and the Open." *Division/Review*. 1 (2011): 37.

Mieli, Paola, Stafford, Mark, and Jacques Houis (eds). *Being Human: The Technological Extensions of the Body*. New York: Agincourt/Marsilio, 1999.

Chapter 7

Topology, Knots, and Ordinary Psychosis with Ellie Ragland

Ellie Ragland (1941–) is a psychoanalyst in private practice in Columbia, Missouri. She is Professor Emerita of the Department of English at the University of Missouri, where she taught critical theory, psychoanalytic theory, and comparative literature and world literature. She is the author of over 100 articles and has lectured nationally and internationally at over 100 universities and colloquia. She has held an NEH [National Endowment for the Humanities] grant and a Humanities Fellowship at the University of Illinois. She has received honors including the Gold Chalk Award from the University of Missouri for excellence in teaching and the Gradiva Prize from the National Association for the Advancement of Psychoanalysis for an edited collection with Dragan Milavanovic, *Lacan: Topologically Speaking*. Ragland was also a lecturer in the Department of Psychoanalysis at the University of Paris VIII from 1994 to 1995. She was previously the editor of *Newsletter of the Freudian Field* (1987–1994) and is currently the editor of *(Re)-Turn: A Journal of Lacanian Studies*. This interview took place on 4 February 2020.

Chris Vanderwees: When did you first encounter psychoanalysis and Jacques Lacan? What about Lacan caught your attention?

Ellie Ragland: I was teaching at the University of Illinois in Chicago. I taught in the French department for 17 years, starting in 1972. One of my colleagues in the department went to France for a year on sabbatical. She came back and threw two volumes of the *Écrits* on my desk. The publisher, Seuil, printed this text in two volumes before they released one large volume. My colleague threw these volumes on my desk and said, "This man is unreadable and he's a mean person." She said, "I could not even get his attention during the seminar." I had done my dissertation on [François] Rabelais and reader response at the University of Michigan. She knew I had an interest and said, "You like this sort of thing, so, here, take it!"

DOI: 10.4324/9781003323136-8

I went home that day and I started reading the "Discourse of Rome" from 1953. This paper would be called "The Function and Field of Speech and Language in Psychoanalysis" in the *Écrits*. It was terrible. I couldn't stop. I was getting a headache, a stomachache. I was getting hungry, but I couldn't stop reading. I was completely mesmerized. I sat until I finished the whole thing, reading and reading. My first encounter changed me from one way of thinking to another in one fell swoop. I started studying Lacan, writing about him, and began being invited to give lectures in various places about him. The response to my work was that for about 15 years I was a superstar. Every weekend, I was going to a different university or a different analytic group. It really intensified when I published my book, *Jacques Lacan and the Philosophy of Psychoanalysis*. Many people in English or French departments became interested.

I moved from a French department to an English department because of my work on Lacan in English. Norman Holland hired me at the University of Florida, where he had a psychological institute for the study of the arts.[1] I have always had French as a great tool, which many people at the time did not have. Almost none of [Jacques-Alain] Miller's seminars, for instance, are available in English. Of course, these seminars are very important and important to my thinking of Lacan. I was able to write *Jacques Lacan and the Philosophy of Psychoanalysis* because I had French. I could read everything that was available in French, which put me about ten years ahead of the curve. This was my beginning with Lacan.

CV: Had you attended Lacan's seminars?

ER: My ex-husband, Henry Sullivan, and I went frequently to Paris for different reasons.[2] Henry had friends in Paris who went to Lacan's seminar. One friend said, "I'll take you to Lacan's seminar this week." I said, "No, I don't want to go. He's too important to me." I felt he was too important for me to go see him in front of a group of a thousand people and not have any contact with him at all. At the time, some of my friends who were living in Amsterdam said to me, "Since you cannot possibly get in touch with Lacan now that he is so famous and popular, what you should do is find somebody in the side group that are his disciples who surround him and get in touch with them."

Later, I was in New York to give a paper and was with Stuart Schneiderman in his apartment after the talk. He had gotten a telephone call from Jacques-Alain Miller. Stuart said, "You should invite him to Canada." We were living in Canada at the time. In my early publications, there would not be anything about Miller because I did not yet know about him. In my first book, for instance, there is not anything about Miller. This book was my reading of Lacan and some of the people who were his early disciples. After Stuart had suggested to contact Miller,

Henry organized a conference called "The Reception of Post-Structuralism in Anglophone and Francophone Canada" at the University of Ottawa. We invited Miller and he came to the conference in 1984.[3] This was Jacques-Alain Miller's first time in North America. After Ottawa, Miller went on to New York City. This began a period of Miller coming three or four times a year to the United States. Often he came even without pay. He just came and worked with us. He came to work with us at Kent State, in New York, and again in Canada. Miller was incredibly supportive of our work. This is when I formed my close relationship with him. I spent about ten days out at the country home of Jacques-Alain and Judith Miller. This very much charted the way I see Lacan.

CV: I am aware of the English translations and works of Alan Sheridan, Cormac Gallagher, Anthony Wilden, John Muller, and William Richardson as well as of Stuart Schneiderman's writing. With *Jacques Lacan and the Philosophy of Psychoanalysis*, however, you produced the first substantial overview of Lacan's system of thought, opening up the *Écrits* and the *Four Fundamental Concepts of Psychoanalysis* for an English academic readership to find a way into these texts. Not only does this book continue to provide a clarifying commentary on Lacan's major innovations, including the split subject, the signifier, the three registers (Symbolic, Imaginary, Real), and the question of gender, but you illuminated some of the consequences of his new psychoanalytic epistemology across the humanities and social sciences. How would you describe the reception of Lacanian ideas in the United States at the time of your early writings?

ER: People were totally mesmerized by Lacan. The first book I wrote on Lacan is still selling, which is amazing. It came out in 1986. At the time, the book seemed to open the door for so many people, including those who were members of psychoanalytic institutes. Members of the International Psychoanalytic Association, for instance, who were interested in Lacan found his work so difficult to access. Also, the clinical work was not nearly as available as it was now since Miller has really pushed hard to open up the Lacanian clinic. I was invited to speak to English departments and philosophy departments. I was speaking to people in psychology, sociology, French, and with psychoanalysts themselves. I was invited to speak all over the place after that book.

CV: In the North American context, Lacan's ideas were initially enthusiastically taken up in departments within the university setting, but the clinical reception of Lacan was quite different. North American psychiatry and psychoanalysis did not take up Lacanianism in the same way as the humanities in the university.

ER: The North American clinicians could not understand Lacan's ideas. If they did understand, they had no idea how to apply these ideas to the clinic or how they would use these ideas in psychoanalysis. This is why

Stuart Schneiderman's book, *Returning to Freud*, was so important for its inclusion of papers on clinical cases.[4] On the one hand, I can attest to the fact that there was a strong interest in the North American clinic about Lacan, but on the other hand, it seemed the more people were interested, the more there was also a strong resistance to his work.

I had one experience when I was living in Chicago. Miller created the only Paris psychoanalytic workshop in Chicago. There were several workshops in New York, which Schneiderman hosted. In Chicago, however, there was only one. Miller came to speak there in 1986. One of the analysts from the IPA [International Psychoanalytical Association] institute and his wife, who was a professor in humanities at the University of Chicago, had me over to their house and insisted that I call Jacques-Alain Miller and tell him, "He cannot come to Chicago. He's not welcome. We don't do Lacan." Of course, I refused to call him. Miller came anyway. He spoke in three different venues and made very strong headway in Chicago. In the internal political group at the institute, that is, the heavy-duty IPA people, they were really furious that Miller had come to Chicago. There were some nasty questions for Miller from the people at the institute during the talks. Once some people had a sense of the subject and of the imaginary, symbolic, and the Real, the general tone was that Lacan was crazy or an imposter or a charlatan. In contrast to this, some people were much more enthusiastic. I had a correspondence with an object relations psychoanalyst from California, for instance, who was very interested in Lacan. It was a mixed beginning for the clinic in North America, but mostly negative.

CV: Of course, there is the history of Lacan's excommunication from the IPA, but what was the resistance to Lacan? It almost seems as if his ideas were perceived as a threat.

ER: The excommunication had to do much more with the politics of Paris. I should say that Canada was always more receptive to Lacan. I went back and forth to Canada for years to work with analysts there. In North America more generally, analysts were intellectually threatened because they were intellectually challenged. Some analysts wanted to be able to take a book by Lacan, *Écrits*, for example, hulk over it and access it overnight or over a weekend. Such analysts were very challenged by this and would complain that Lacan does not talk about feelings.

CV: This is part of the experience of reading Lacan. One must stomach the non-understanding.

ER: Absolutely. Most people having the physical experiences that I first did when I was reading *Écrits* would have put down the book and blamed it on Lacan. Back then, many people encountering Lacan said, "He's unreadable, a psychotic, a crazy man." Most people could not access it, but I could not stop reading him despite the strong physical reaction I had to this incredible use of language.

CV: You have also written at length about Lacan's reformulation of the Freudian death drive in *Essays on the Pleasure of Death*. Lacan's persistence with developing his theorizations around the death drive is one of the major distinctions between his work and the work of other variants of psychoanalysis. In *Beyond the Pleasure Principle*, Freud moves through speculative, philosophical, biological, psychological, and behavioral premises surrounding the human compulsion to repeat harmful patterns, thoughts, behaviors, and dreams. How might we describe Lacan's extensions of the death drive as they might apply to *jouissance* in a clinical context?

ER: As you know, if we are to read Lacan's work, *jouissance* is one of the major things we must conceptualize, think about, and understand. When I first told a French person about the book I had written, *Essays on the Pleasures of Death*, she asked, "What is it about?" I said that it was about what Lacan did with *jouissance*. She said, "*Jouissance* is a good thing!" She was thinking about it in the French sense where it simply means orgasm. He took the concept of the excess in sexuality, the peak moment, and translated that into how it is that we really are subject to our symptoms. We serve our symptoms. We have *jouissance* invested in our symptoms to the point that we will kill ourselves with our symptoms rather than do anything to change them. It is a much deeper way of delving into symptoms.

Analysts have to work with the symptom. Lacan's understanding of the symptom is much different than the American emphasis on having the patient become a positive self and to be happy. When Miller gave his talk to the Paris workshop in Chicago, he held up a book by Heinz Kohut, who was on the back cover smiling. Miller made a joke. He said that in English you could combine the self-object and get an "SOB."[5] This made people mad in Chicago since they were very influenced by Kohut. People did not like the joke.

Lacan's reconceptualization of the death drive around the symptom as the fourth order that links three registers – the symbolic, the imaginary, and the Real – together along with the father's name is so important. From this, he develops what become differential diagnoses between neurosis, perversion, and psychosis. Lacan suggests that giving into our symptoms is actually what holds the other dimensions together, which then structures the way we think, speak, and behave.

Lacan speaks about James Joyce and the *sinthome* in Seminar XXIII. Joyce was psychotically structured, but he was not mad. Lacan emphasizes in this seminar that Joyce was able to take his symptoms in psychosis and do something creative. Joyce's way of working with language was creative. It was not a horrible thing. When we use the diagnosis of psychotic, sometimes people think of all the worst possible things. In reconceptualizing ordinary psychosis and emphasizing Seminar XXIII, Miller has tried to understand psychosis as being able to use one's symptom creatively. The person is still attached to the symptom, but it will make a difference whether or not the person uses this symptom creatively or destructively.

CV: As I understand it, ordinary psychosis is a diagnosis that does not include the phenomena that you might find in cases of psychosis where there may be hallucinations or delusions. How would we distinguish psychosis from ordinary psychosis?

ER: This is a really big move that Miller made when he put forward his seminar on ordinary psychosis in 1998.[6] There is a lot of conversation that goes on in the Freudian field about ordinary psychosis. Some people think ordinary psychosis can be triggered where a patient may have hallucinations or delusions that appear when met with the confrontation of something in the symbolic sphere where it is a challenge too great for one to meet. Others say ordinary psychosis is untriggered and that hallucinations and delusions do not appear. There is still a lot of work going on with this category. People usually think there is no transference with the psychotic patient, but this is not true. It is a matter of having to reconceptualize how transference works in psychosis as opposed to neurosis.

CV: The most significant difference would be that in psychosis the person will not see the analyst as the *sujet supposé savoir*, but rather it is the psychotic who is the one who knows.

ER: The psychotic patients are always the ones who know. Ordinary psychosis is not neurosis. In ordinary psychosis, the person may not have a break and may not have symptoms and delusions, but one of the several major signs of ordinary psychosis is the "push towards woman," the push to be one with the primordial mother or symbiotic mother.[7] This is very present in ordinary psychosis. The rigidity of speech is also very much part of this diagnosis. There is concreteness around language that is totally literal. The person could be incredibly brilliant but this highly literal quality will also emerge in the work.[8]

CV: I wanted to ask about your more recent work where you turn towards Lacan's emphasis on mathematics and topology. Of course, Freud provides us with two topographies with the conscious, preconscious, and unconscious as well as the ego, superego, and id. Lacan, however, moves towards topology, which is quite different, insisting that it is not simply a clinical guide for thinking about structure. For Lacan, topology is the structure itself, communicating a space without dimension or uncanny objects that resist our imaginary perceptivity with examples including the Möbius strip, the cross cap, the Klein bottle, and the torus. These objects that Lacan chooses for us to think about are very bodily. They are structures that convey something of an experience of the inside-outside of the body, which is hard to grasp. How do you see Lacan's insistence on topology as important for clinical psychoanalysis?

ER: I worked on this is my book, *The Logic of Structure*.[9] In the structuring of objects, there is always the importance of the cut. The cut provides separation and puts you in a position to relate to the object whether it is the gaze or the voice as well as how you relate to the object whether it is inside or outside. In his later seminars, Lacan is very preoccupied with topology.

One of the things I would say is that Lacan is the first person that I know in any field, certainly in the human sciences and humanities, to come up with the idea of a cause, which is not just an effect. With topology, Lacan is talking about what is sometimes called a "rubber geometry" or "rubber math." When we talk about language early in life, the child imitates the parent's speech through sounds until he or she can put enough of the sounds together to form words and sentences. Lacan emphasizes that the very earliest thing that happens with the baby is hearing the mother's voice in the womb. Noam Chomsky and his students have conducted empirical studies that prove the baby does hear before it is born.[10] Of course, the newborn is not yet putting together language, but if you put the infant in somebody else's arms other than the mother's, the infant will cry. These sorts of empirical experiments are the opposite of Lacanian studies, but Chomsky's work lets us know how important the symbiotic bond is to the infant even before birth. From birth onwards, the subject is being constituted all of the time as a Borromean knot.

In this knot, we have the Real, which is one of the three main dimensions. In the Real, we have the need to sleep, to eat, to defecate, to be dry. These kinds of needs structure the dimension of the Real, which is the dimension of trauma, that which is impossible to bear. The infant cries all of the time insofar as it is adjusting to being and becoming a person. The symbolic introduces language and the conventions of a given society, what Lacan calls the Other, which does not exist but exists in the way that one's community gives the possibilities and expectations of what one should say, do, think, or eat. The imaginary refers to the power of images that structure a part of mentality that is dependent on the body.

In the Borromean knot of the Real, the symbolic, and the imaginary, there are overlaps between each dimension, which constitute three different forms of *jouissance*. Between the symbolic and the imaginary, there is *sens*. Between the symbolic and the Real, there is the phallic signifier, capital phi [JΦ]. Between the Real and the imaginary, there is anxiety, the barred O, or the big Other as barred [JA]. In the center of the Borromean knot is the *objet petit a*, the little object a, the object of desire, which is causal in all of these reactions. Lacan refers to the partial objects of desire and the four main drives that come from them: the oral drive, the scopic drive, the anal drive, and the invocatory drive.

The objects would be the breast, the gaze, the voice, the feces, the urinary flow, the imaginary phallus, the phoneme, and the nothing. In "The Subversion of the Subject," Lacan speaks about these eight objects that initially cause desire, which are structured topologically.[11]

The subject is finally a Möbius strip. One part crosses over the other part, but both parts face the outside world. One is not under with the other as above. We always imagine the body as a container with what is inside as being contained instead of realizing that from the beginning the baby experiences the world with a sense of bodily fragmentation. The psychotic has a problem with his or her body. The psychotic experiences the body in fragments, not as a totalized image. In neurosis, one reaches the mirror stage and gets out of fragmentation. The psychotic person never mentally gets out of the mirror stage. The person continues to think of their body as something in pieces. The person may become sick with a part of their body whether it may be actually sick or hypochondriacally sick.

I am thinking about the Borromean knot and the paternal function, the name of the father, which ties the rings altogether, but for James Joyce, for instance, the father's name is weak. In Joyce's case, the dimensions of the symbolic, the imaginary, and the Real are not overlapping, as they would be in neurosis. These dimensions are separate in psychosis. In neurosis, the so-called "normal" person is simply somebody who identifies with the Oedipal conventions. We speak about knotting in ordinary psychosis since the three dimensions are not knotted together. We try to work on what it is that the patient is doing as a way to make up for the symptom, which is not held together by the name of the father.

One of my patients, for instance, is reading books all of the time, arcane types of literature. Whenever this person meets me for analysis, he immediately recites from the book he's reading. From memory, he will tell me all about the book. He does not have any social bond. All of the ways we have of being together socially, the social bond, [do] not register in psychosis. The transference does not operate in the same way as in neurosis. The psychotic person speaks to the analyst and can be helped through finding a way to develop a *sinthome*. The work of Willy Apollon, Danielle Bergeron, and Lucie Cantin really lets you see that some patients can begin to live on their own and go to work with support in place.

Now, not every psychotic person is ill. There have been so many psychotics in history who were, for instance, artistic, mathematic, and scientific geniuses. I always used to tell my students in literature that they would have to honor psychosis given that so many of the writers that they were reading were psychotic. The idea that the psychotic is a poor, broken down, pathetic person is not really true. This helps to understand something of ordinary psychosis. The symptoms are so much different from the neurotic. The ability to use language is always there except in cases of totally traumatized autism, where the person does not make it out of the mirror stage at all.

CV: I think of the mirror stage as beginning early in life but also as continuing throughout life as we are constantly taking in discourse from others, identifying and disidentifying with various people, or recognizing and misrecognizing ourselves in various objects. It is as if there is an ongoing process for each individual that begins with the mirror stage.

ER: I would argue that the mirror stage is a structure. I think that if Lacan had only written the paper on the mirror stage this would be enough to submit his reputation to that of the world's geniuses. There is so much about this mirror stage at 18 months of age that pertains to symptoms, ideas, and life. The mirror stage for Lacan is as important as Oedipus was to Freud. Miller says there are no structures in Lacan and that Lacan's myth is like the drives in Freud's myth, but I do not agree. I think there are structures and that the mirror stage is one of them. Miller calls the mirror stage a "logical moment," but this does not preclude the idea that it could be a structure. We keep going back to the mirror stage all the time. It is foundational.

CV: Speaking of the body, you have also written a study of Lacan's theory of sexuation, his formulas of sexual difference derived from symbolic logic. How can we articulate something about the importance of sexuation for readers who may not be familiar with Lacan?

ER: It is hard to articulate, but it is crucial to an understanding of Lacan. In Seminar XX, Lacan puts the final form of the graph of sexuation on the chalkboard (Figure 7.1).[12] It is important to know that on the masculine

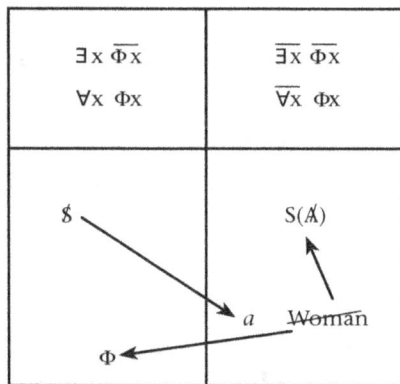

Figure 7.1 Lacan's complete "Graph of Sexuation" from Lacan, Jacques. *The Seminar of Jacques Lacan, Book XX, Encore, 1972-1973: On Feminine Sexuality, The Limits of Love and Knowledge.* 1975. Translated by Bruce Fink. Edited by Jacques-Alain Miller. New York: Norton, 1998.

side it is symbolic and on the feminine side is the Real. The border in the middle of the graph separates the two sides. You do not have biological differences structuring the masculine or the feminine in Lacan, because the masculine side could also be a woman who identifies with that side and the feminine side could also be a man who identifies with that side. When Lacan says that there is "no sexual rapport," he means that there is no sexual rapport of oneness between any two people. We try for this rapport. We believe in it. We think that if we love each other enough it will be there, but each person is so unique in their experience with their own fantasy that this oneness remains a dream. Lacan suggests that it is because there is no sexual rapport that we have sexual relations all of the time looking for such rapport.

On the masculine side of the sexuation graph, there is the barred subject. The phallic function on this masculine side is barred. On the feminine side, there is no final bar. He bars the universal on the masculine side and on the feminine side as well, but in the end the feminine person can go their own way and may not be barred from being able to participate in the symbolic dimension as not-all. In other words, not-all is a function of the sexuation table at the top of the graph. We might say not-all as in not a whole or total person. The masculine side tries to relate to the feminine side by hooking up the phallic signifier to the barred A [Other] on the feminine side. If we return to the mirror stage, there is not any whole woman. We begin to enter into the hysteric's question of "Am I a man or am I a woman?" In Lacan, there is not *the* woman. There is no ideal woman. On the feminine side, the woman is the object that fills the lack for the masculine side. On the masculine side of the graph, there is castration.

Freud and his followers thought more simplistically about castration, believing that it was the woman who was castrated. Lacan does a very different thing where the castrated one is on the masculine side and puts the one who is in contact with the Real on the feminine side. There is an arrow that leads from the barred subject to the *objet petit a*, which is where the masculine meets the feminine in order to complete this trajectory. There is castration on the masculine side and then there is the dependence on the phallus on the feminine side with the barred Other. Even though there is no rapport, the two sides of the graph are an attempt to explain that there are all kinds of efforts going on that try to establish a sexual rapport.

CV: You mentioned Miller's work today. How do you understand his contributions to the Lacanian field, and how have these contributions influenced your own thought?

ER: For me, it has always been about Lacan. I have appreciated many of the early writers like [Jean] Laplanche and [Jean-Bertrand] Pontalis, but Lacan himself has always been most important for me. When I met

Miller, I had no place for him in my thinking because I understood him to be "just the son-in-law," which is how many people tend still think of him who do not really know his work. As I carried on working on Lacan, I began to read Miller's seminars. He began his own seminars on Lacan from when he was very young when Lacan was still living. His interest in Lacan started very young before Lacan was known at all. Miller has now shaped Lacan's seminars. In the office in Paris at *Éditions du Seuil*, the publisher of Lacan's seminars in French, the contract is on display and this contract shows the seminars as co-authored by Lacan and Jacques-Alain Miller. Lacan offered him that place because of how much the dialogue with Miller had influenced him. Of course, Miller refused co-authorship and would never have accepted this position.

Miller is important insofar as he speaks very clearly. Not only does Miller clarify Lacan but he has a great historical link to who Lacan was reading, who influenced Lacan, and who was important to Lacan, but he has the courage to put something forward that cannot be found in Lacan, which is ordinary psychosis. Lacan has the creativity of the symptom but does not really talk about the comprehensive make-believe symbolic father. This is something that comes along with Miller. In the development of the clinic, Miller has been able to understand psychosis much more broadly. Ordinary psychosis has given me a way to think about and work with patients who do not fall into the neurotic category.

Miller has also had a huge influence in Paris on the Lacanian schools and in schools abroad in English. In Russia, Israel, and Poland, for instance, there are New Lacanian Schools that are working in English, not in French. All of these schools are clinical. Miller broadened the scope of what Lacan could do internationally. After Lacan's death, his international influence remained largely in the academy, but Miller has extended this influence further into the clinic.

It was three years after Lacan's death that I stayed with Jacques-Alain and Judith Miller at their country home. He said, "Lacan is gone now. We have to decide where to put our influence. Do we want to go to the law school? Do we want to go to philosophy departments? Or do we want to go to the clinic?" Miller said, "My answer is to go into the clinic." Since then, this has been the effort.

CV: Lacan has been important to my own clinical work, but especially in terms of the *subjet suppose savoir* [the subject supposed to know]. I think that the idea that the analyst is not the one who knows remains a controversial one. Most talks or lectures that one could attend in psychology or psychiatry approach the patient as if it were the clinician who is the expert, the authority, and the one who knows about the patient's symptoms, knows what the patient is thinking and feeling. This is troubling to me for obvious reasons. The ethical position that Lacan takes is so important to me including the whole notion of non-under-standing. It is so easy to think we understand. When I work in the clinic, every time I think I know something about somebody, all it takes is lis-tening for a while longer to realize that I have not understood and that there is so much more to talk about. There is a foreclosure that occurs in most schools of psychology that teach interpretation. I find interpreta-tion can close things down. Lacanian technique, at least for the neurotic, is about opening, opening things up, and then perhaps more opening.

ER: I couldn't agree more. Think about how revolutionary it is to say that the one who knows is the patient and not the analyst. You could take this up in terms of the student and the professor as well, but think about how this idea could completely revolutionize psychoanalysis if more cli-nicians thought that.

CV: It is really a concept that is still ignored or dismissed. I think there are many very experienced psychoanalysts who have not even bothered to encounter Lacanian ideas, out of some fear or resistance of their own.

ER: It is sad. What Miller realized about Lacan's teaching was that Lacan was not just any old psychoanalyst with theories and ideas about the self and other. Lacan was actually changing the field about thinking and changing thinking itself within the realm of philosophy without calling him a philosophy. Miller would say that philosophers speak a master's discourse and do not problematize issues of causality.

CV: You mentioned [Jacques] Derrida earlier. In literature departments, Derrida and Lacan are frequently taught side by side as poststructural-ists, which is not accurate. Even though they may share something in their play with language or their ways of breaking up language, Lacan and Derrida are very different thinkers. Lacan is not a poststructuralist, even though he is sometimes taught as if he were one. I think of Lacan much more as in alignment with structuralists, but with the added no-tion of the Real, which makes him so much different from all of the other structuralists.

ER: Absolutely.

CV: In this respect, I wanted to ask you about the difference between your experience teaching in literature departments for many years and your experience as a clinician. If I understand correctly, you have also com-pleted formation as a Lacanian psychoanalyst with the New Lacanian School. Coming from a background in French studies and language, did you experience any sort of *après-coup* in regard to your thinking and writing about Lacan in beginning to work as an analyst? Is there a shift that one must make from reading to listening?

ER: Working in the clinic shifted me completely. All of these things I thought I understood in Lacan come together in a new way in the context of the clinic when patients are suffering so much and trying to pin things to-gether with what they have. I think I began to understand something much more about the unconscious. We do not talk about the unconscious enough anymore. It has one meaning in Freud and another in Lacan and yet another for those who carry on working with it in the Lacanian field. The unconscious is in the power of speech that can take you somewhere completely different from where you thought you would go. You really cannot know another person until you really listen to them.

More recently, Miller has been talking not just the constitutive aspect of language but the power of words. The Lacanian analyst tends not to interpret very much. Perhaps the analyst will make a noise like, "Mmhmm," because we do not want to intervene in the power of that speech at the moment that the patient is going down a whole other pathway than where I thought they were going to go. The difference between working as a theorist and working as a clinician is amazing.

I spoke with a student yesterday who is getting ready to write his doctoral dissertation. He is working with [Gilles] Deleuze, Derrida, Lacan, [Alain] Badiou, and [Slavoj] Žižek. He has all of these guys in there. He is working with them all at equal levels. He is theorizing these figures as if they were one. For him, Lacan is passé and is referred to historically. This is the university discourse where the knowledge appeals to the desire in the Other. In the university discourse, desire, however, does not produce knowledge of the unconscious, but rather what the unconscious is lacking. It is really hard to even put words to my feelings about psychoanalysis as a clinician as compared to when I was working just as a theorist. It is such a difference. Clinical work opened my eyes, opened my ears.

CV: I found that when I began working with people in psychotherapy and psychoanalysis, all of these concepts in the French school that I had tried to make sense of in the abstract suddenly had a more tangible anchor in the clinical space. Lacan provides an entire language of his own for clinical work that gets at certain nuances that I do not believe anyone else ever has.

ER: In the Lacanian field, clinicians always acknowledge a tremendous debt to Freud and cite Freud.

CV: Can we pick up that thread about the difference between the Freudian unconscious and the Lacanian unconscious? How would you describe this difference?

ER: The Freudian unconscious is always going to be constituted by language and work in the sense of the four discourses. Of course, there is the discourse of the master, the discourse of the university, the discourse of the hysteric, and the discourse of the analyst. The unconscious is somewhere different in each of these discourses and is speaking for the subject in the sense that the subject is barred. The Millerians bring the body much more into the discussion of the speaking subject. There is more attention to questions of the body, *le corps parlant*, the speaking body. Miller has given a wonderful course on the speaking body. Certainly, Lacan talks about the body, but he does not attach the unconscious to the body like psychoanalysts do now since Lacan's death. The body itself has an attachment to language.

CV: Lacan claimed to be rereading Freud, returning to Freud. In this return, he aimed to show what psychoanalysis was not, that is, in reference to movements oriented toward ego psychology and its more recent extensions, including relational or contemporary psychoanalysis. He cautions us, for instance, about the traps of the imaginary and the misrecognition involved in "understanding." He also aimed to reorient analysts toward the symbolic, toward linguistics and language, placing emphasis on the signifier while creating a new discourse and theory for thinking about the clinic. Lacan seems to suggest that his work is an attempt to highlight aspects of Freud's work that Freud himself could not comprehend at the time. In your own return to Lacan's return of Freud, are there aspects of Lacan's system of thought that you have found to be particularly illuminating or generative for thinking and listening in the contemporary clinic? Are there aspects of Lacan's system of thought that he could not comprehend in his own lifetime?

ER: Sometimes when people are trying to understand Lacan, they say, "Well, how can you read this? It's Freud. How can you speak such garbage?" People sometimes say and think such horrible things about Freud. I will suggest that if you read Freud and then you read Lacan, you will see that Lacan essentially overturns Freud. He is totally different from Freud but makes all of these wonderful gestures to Freud with making sense of the unconscious, of images, of affects, and of words. Lacan also brings in linguistics, which Freud did not have access to at the time.

I did not say this earlier when I talked about the sexuation graph, but the one thing that is so clear when Lacan talks about sexuation is that the masculine is located on the side of the all whereas the woman is on the side of the not-all. This is the opposite to historical and mythological notions of castration whereby the feminine would be castrated and deemed thereby subordinate to the masculine. To me, the graph of sexuation conveys something important about interpreting difference itself. There is a difference that is biological between the sexes and this biology has to be accounted for in some way or another in language. Derrida tried to express difference through his notion of *différance*. Derrida would say that this difference makes no difference and is ultimately just another fiction, which is partially why we would consider him a poststructuralist. Lacan would say and I would say this difference makes all the difference in how a person defines themselves in relation to others.

CV: I have always loved Derrida and trying to grapple with his work, but he does offer a critique of Lacan throughout his own writing, accusing him of reproducing what he calls a phallogocentric system of thought. I believe he actually makes the argument that all of Western culture is phallogocentric. Even the notion of castration has the negative connotations that you referred to earlier, but there also is a multiplicity of meaning to this term in psychoanalysis where we also may speak of the first castration as the birth of the child or perhaps the cut of the umbilical cord. Castration appears in psychoanalytic literature in reference to loss, limits, lack, sexual difference, or even the cut at the end of the session. How can we respond to something like Derrida's critique of phallogocentrism?

ER: Derrida was influenced so much by Lacan and was so popular for many years in the United States. One way that you can address the claim of phallogocentrism is to acknowledge that there really is a difference between the two biological sexes. There is a difference. When there is something, a one that is not the same as the other, we begin to use language to account for the difference. We could take the route of Derrida and say that the difference makes no difference, or we could take the route of Lacan and say that the difference makes all the difference. Let me also be clear that the phallus is not the same as the penis. What concerns Lacan is not the biological penis so much as the role the organ plays in the imaginary fantasy of the subject.

It begins with the early effort of the child to understand this difference. This effort to account for difference occurs in all societies and may be different within each society. The effort to establish this difference and understand this difference is the third term that enters the equation beyond the two of the mother and baby into the function of the father's name. The paternal function is also society in some sense or the big Other of the symbolic. The symbol of the difference for the girl does not occur in the same way as it does for the boy. This may upset feminists to hear. There is a lack in being. The lack of castration is a notion that communicates the result of the difference being symbolized as a difference. The difference becomes a lack, a lack in being all, and a lack in having all. Castration means the lack of being all one or totalized as a subject. It is not the lack of an organ. Lacan does a lot with castration anxiety, which was first described in Freud.

CV: Are you currently working on any new projects?

ER: I just finished writing a book called *Lacan and Hysteria: The Logic of Paradox*. I am now finalizing all of my footnotes. I will have it ready in two months for publication. After this, I have a student who is putting together a collection of my most influential essays. I have to get those essays together for him. I am also thinking of putting together a book for feminists on the articles that I have written about women. I'll have to think more about which area of Lacan to delve back into for the next book.

Notes

1 Norman Holland (1927–2017) was a literary critic who studied psychoanalytic criticism and cognitive poetics at the University of Florida.
2 Henry W. Sullivan (1942–) is Middlebush Chair Professor of Romance Languages at the University of Missouri. He is the author of *The Beatles with Lacan: Rock 'n' Roll as Requiem for the Modern Age* (1995).
3 This conference took place at the University of Ottawa, May 10–13, 1984.
4 Schneiderman, Stuart (ed. and trans.). *Returning to Freud: Clinical Psychoanalysis in the School of Lacan*. New Haven: Yale University Press, 1980. Here, Scheiderman edits and translates many works from Lacan's most prominent followers, including Jacques-Alain Miller, Moustafa Safouan, Michèle Montrelay, Serge Leclaire, Charles Melman, and Jean Clavreul.
5 Miller, Jacques-Alain. "How Psychoanalysis Cures According to Lacan." *Newsletter of the Freudian Field*. 1.2 (1987): 4–30.
6 Miller, Jacques-Alain. "Psychose ordinaire et Clinique floue." *Ornicar? Digital*. 1998. Web. https://www.wapol.org/ornicar/articles/mlr0081.htm
7 For Lacan's discussion of the famous case of Daniel Paul Schreber, who believed he transformed into a woman, see Lacan, Jacques. *The Seminar of Jacques Lacan, Book III, 1955-1956: The Psychoses*. 1981. Translated by Russell Grigg. Edited by Jacques-Alain Miller. New York: Norton, 1993.
8 See Jacques-Alain Miller's (2009) paper, "Ordinary Psychosis Revisited."
9 Ragland, Ellie. *Jacques Lacan and the Logic of Structure: Topology and Language in Psychoanalysis*. London: Routledge; Taylor & Francis, 2015.
10 For more on the acquisition of speech and language, see Chomsky and Berwick (2016) and Friederici (2017).
11 Lacan, Jacques. "The Subversion of the Subject and the Dialectic of Desire in the Freudian Unconscious." *Écrits*. Trans. Bruce Fink. New York: Norton, 2006. 671–702.
12 Lacan's complete graph of sexuation can be found in *Encore* in his seminar from March 13, 1973. See Lacan, Jacques. The Seminar of Jacques Lacan: Book XX, *Encore (1972–1973)*. Ed. Jacques-Alain Miller. Trans. Bruce Fink. New York: Norton, 1999. 78.

Bibliography and Further Reading

Chomsky, Noam and Robert C. Berwick. *Why Only Us: Language and Evolution*. Cambridge, MA: The MIT Press, 2016.
Friederici, Angela D. *Language in Our Brain: The Origins of a Uniquely Human Capacity*. Cambridge, MA: The MIT Press, 2017.
Miller, Jacques-Alain. "How Psychoanalysis Cures According to Lacan." *Newsletter of the Freudian Field*. 1.2 (1987): 4–30.
Miller, Jacques-Alain. "Ordinary Psychosis Revisited." *Psychoanalytical Notebooks*. 19 (2009): 139–167.
Ragland, Ellie. *Essays on the Pleasures of Death: From Freud to Lacan*. New York: Routledge, 1995.
Ragland, Ellie. *Jacques Lacan and the Logic of Structure: Topology and Language in Psychoanalysis*. London: Routledge; Taylor & Francis, 2015.
Ragland, Ellie. "Jacques Lacan's Capitalist Discourse." *Psychoanalytical Notebooks*. Spec. issue *Lacanian Politics and the Impasses of Democracy Today*. 32 (2018): 137–150.

Ragland, Ellie. "The Hysteric's Truth." *Jacques Lacan and the Other Side of Psycho-Analysis: Reflections on Seminar XVII*. Eds. Justin Clemens and Russell Grigg. Durham: Duke University Press, 2006. 69–87.

Ragland, Ellie. *The Logic of Sexuation: From Aristotle to Lacan*. Albany: The State University of New York, 2004.

Ragland, Ellie and Dragan Milavanovic (eds). *Lacan: Topologically Speaking*. New York: Other Press, 2004.

Ragland, Mary E. *Rabelais and Panurge: A Psychological Approach to Literary Character*. Amsterdam: Editions Rodopi, 1976.

Ragland-Sullivan, Ellie. *Jacques Lacan and the Philosophy of Psychoanalysis*. Chicago: University of Illinois Press, 1986.

Ragland-Sullivan, Ellie. "The Psychical Nature of Trauma: Freud's Dora, The Young Homosexual Woman, and the Fort! Da! Paradigm." *Post-Modern Culture*. 11.2 (2001): 1–11.

Ragland-Sullivan, Ellie. "The Three Freuds We Have Inherited." *Clinical Studies: International Journal of Psychoanalysis*. 5.1 (1999): 83–107.

Ragland-Sullivan, Ellie and Mark Bracher (eds). *Lacan and the Subject of Language*. New York: Routledge, 1991.

Chapter 8

Lacan in Translation, Interpretation, and the Affiliated Psychoanalytic Workgroups with Dan Collins

Dan Collins, MSW, PhD, of Buffalo, NY, is a psychoanalyst and the founder of Affiliated Psychoanalytic Workgroups (APW), a clinically oriented psychoanalytic organization that puts on annual international conferences, clinical workshops, and study days. He is a member of Lacan Toronto, where he gives seminars in the teaching program, and a guest member of the Toronto Psychoanalytic Society. He is also an associate member of the Association for Psychoanalysis and Psychotherapy in Ireland. Dan translates the works of [Jacques] Lacan, Jacques-Alain Miller, and other psychoanalysts, and he lectures widely on psychoanalysis. This conversation took place at the Toronto Psychoanalytic Society & Institute on 15 December 2019.

CV: You founded the Affiliated Psychoanalytic Workgroups, but what was the initial formation of this organization?[1]

DC: This was back in the 1990s. In the early days, there were not really Lacanian groups in the United States. There was some isolated work on Lacan being done by various people, but it was not like it is today where there are a several Lacanian groups and organizations. What I imagined was similar to what I had with our group in Buffalo, which was a local reading group that I organized. I imagined that APW would become a network of reading groups. I was aware of other reading groups that were around the United States. So, I got together a list of all of the groups that I knew about. First, I sent a paper-and-pencil questionnaire. This was before the internet. I mailed these questionnaires to different groups to find out what was going on. I got a good number of replies back. Based on the replies, the idea followed that APW would be a network of study and reading groups.

It was officially launched in 1999 when we had our first conference, which was held at Boston College. It was successful enough, but I discovered that founding an organization based on graduate student groups wasn't a very stable organizational principle. By their very nature, graduate student reading groups break up when people complete their programs and go onto other things. The idea of a network of reading

DOI: 10.4324/9781003323136-9

groups didn't really work out given the transient nature of graduate studies. After we had a few of our annual conferences, we found that there were people who returned year after year who were committed to the idea. APW became much more of a network of individuals rather than of groups.

CV: You mentioned some of the challenges involved in founding the organization. What have been some of the challenges in keeping the APW going?

DC: The biggest challenge is that APW was not and never has been geographically based. I think the standard model for any psychoanalytic group is to have a base of operations in a specific location. This requires a certain critical mass of people willing to attend and resources. We did not have this. We became a loosely affiliated network of individuals. We needed somebody to host us for each conference. We would rely on friends who had university positions or friends who had access to some free or affordable rooms where we could meet. Local hosts would do a lot of work. We have moved around with conferences all over the place. This has been our model ever since.

For quite a while, I tried to maintain two events per year. We would hold a conference and then there would be a study weekend. The study weekends were meant to be more informal. There were fewer people, a few presentations, and more discussion but not necessarily formal papers. The study weekends would focus on one text. One of the wildest ones we held was a weekend on the signifier in the lack of the Other, which appears in the upper left corner of Lacan's graph. Over the course of the seminar, Lacan frequently apologizes for never bothering to say much about the signifier in the lack of the Other. It is the only thing he apologizes for consistently. For a long time, we maintained this format of two events per year.

CV: Were there others who helped and were involved in the beginning?

DC: Somebody who agreed to work with us at the beginning and continued to work with us over the years was Bruce Fink. We also had Patricia Gherovici host us in Philadelphia. We also held a conference in San Francisco with the Lacanian school there. In recent years, we have held conferences and events in Ireland because we have close ties with the Association for Psychoanalysis and Psychotherapy in Ireland (APPI). We have had events in Toronto since Lacan Toronto is now the local group that I attend.[2] There are many people who have presented at the events over the years and also many people who have simply attended the events year after year, which is also very much appreciated.

CV: What was your first experience with psychoanalysis?

DC: There is some retroaction involved in this because my first experience reading psychoanalysis was when I was young. I was interested in mythology. I remember reading [Sigmund] Freud's *Moses and Monotheism* and *Totem and Taboo*. If I had never gone on to become interested in psychoanalysis, these readings would have been isolated events, but late in college and graduate school, I became more aware of psychoanalysis and Lacan. I remember reading Lacan's *Seminar XI: The Four Fundamental Concepts of Psychoanalysis*. I also recall reading the first chapter about Lacan and how he was excommunicated from the International Psychoanalytic Association. I did not know anything of the history and was confused by it. I began reading more in psychoanalysis from there. Freud's texts were retroactively the first ones I had read.

CV: You had told me that you had worked on a dissertation in the English department about Lacan...

DC: My PhD is in English and during that time I became interested in psychoanalysis and Lacan. As a result of the history that I just outlined, I imagined that I had some grounding in Freud at the time. I was familiar with Freud, but I began to read his work alongside Lacan in earnest during these years. Meanwhile, I was working on a dissertation in English. I went back and forth for a while between whether I was going to write a wholly Shakespearean dissertation because Shakespeare is my specialty or whether I was going to write a wholly theoretical dissertation. I could have written a dissertation just about Lacan, but in the end it was mixed. The dissertation became half theoretical in my drawing upon psychoanalysis and half about Shakespeare.

CV: What was it that had attracted you to the Lacanian texts or this system of thought?

DC: This is a difficult question to answer. As I said, I started reading *The Four Fundamental Concepts of Psychoanalysis* and was confused. I started on the first page. Here was a guy talking about getting excommunicated. I didn't know anything about the history with the International Psychoanalytical Association. I don't know why I didn't just shut the book right then. Like for many people who approach that book, the title is a kind of lure. The title promises an introductory text. I thought if I kept reading maybe I would discover something. There was something in the text that attracted me.

As a student of English and Shakespeare, I am used to dealing with texts. I was aware that these were spoken seminars that had been transcribed. Miller had established this text.[3] I was attracted to the idea of text while trying to figure out what Lacan had said. I found then, and still do, that it is the kind of reading that pays you back. If you put in the effort, you make discoveries and are able to figure out the text. It is fun to start with a page that is a total mystery and if you work hard enough you might get a sense of what Lacan is talking about. There is a sense of accomplishment that goes with that. This reading may be similar to me to reading Shakespeare or [James] Joyce or poetry. I think it is working with text that first attracted me.

CV: You have also done a lot of translation work. You recently presented a series of talks to the Toronto group, which grew out of a new translation of *The Four Fundamental Concepts of Psychoanalysis*. What are some of the difficulties in translating Lacan, and what is your process for translation?

DC: The earliest texts of Lacan's that I translated existed only in French. I had to translate them so that I could read them. This was before the internet. Texts would be passed around. If you were lucky, you would get a paper copy of a seminar. If I really wanted to study and understand a text in French, I would want it in English. I would translate sessions within the larger seminars. The first one that I translated was Seminar XXIV. I was reading it and began to translate it somewhere in the middle because I was interested in a particular passage. The more I did, I realized I was making some progress. Eventually, I went back to the beginning and translated all of Seminar XXIV. The impulse for translating Seminar XI was different. I was dissatisfied with [Alan] Sheridan's translation. I wanted to translate it for myself. The process for translation is very laborious. I can sit down at a desk and begin translating and suddenly eight hours can pass by and I'll have been translating the whole time. It is an activity that I enjoy.

CV: There is so much wordplay and potential for misreading Lacan depending on the passage. As you are translating, are there things that reoccur as a challenge for the work of translation?

DC: To get a piece of wordplay into English is always a challenge, but I don't like to give up on it. I keep working until I get at some English approximation or version of a Lacanian pun. If I really cannot translate something into English, I begin to think about what the English equivalent would be. In French, for instance, the title of Seminar XXIV is *L'insu que sait de l'une-bévue s'aile à mourre*. This is a difficult title. The term that requires some thought is *l'une-bévue*, which Lacan suggests is his own coinage for the unconscious. Now, this is an incredibly elaborate joke. Lacan is imagining Freud's term for the unconscious, *Das Unbewusste*, as having entered the French language and had been worn down into the French language to become *l'une-bévue*, which can be translated as "blunder" or "mistake." At the beginning of Seminar XXIV, Lacan wants to talk about the slip, the mistake, the blunder, or the parapraxis as [James] Strachey translates it in the Standard Edition. *L'une-bévue* becomes Lacan's new word for the unconscious and it is based on his elaborate fantasy that the word had already been in French for a long time. What I had to find in English was a word that meant something like a blunder, a mistake, or a slip, which sounded like Freud's German word, *Das Unbewusste*, if it had entered into English. These were the requirements. What I eventually came up with was the *Unbewoops* since "woops" is what you say when you make a mistake. So, the title that I translated for Seminar XXIV became *Love is the Failure of the Unbe-woops*. This may be successful or may not be, but this is what I like to try to do with these difficult puns and wordplay. I like to find a way to get it into English somehow.

CV: I wanted to go back to Lacan's Seminar XI for a moment. I suppose this was the first seminar that was translated into English in its entirety. Speaking of mistakes or blunders, many academics and clinicians have commented on Alan Sheridan's errors in translation within the text.[4] I'm not sure if we will ever receive an official revised translation of this seminar, as the publisher may not want to set aside the funds for a revised edition. What are some of the major errors in this text? Given that this was the first seminar to be translated, did these errors not lead to a long development of academic work based on these errors? What is your understanding of these errors?

DC: After much time having passed where people have had more experience with other Lacanian texts, I think Sheridan's translation now sounds a little stilted and formal. It does not have the same tone you would expect of Lacan's seminar. There are some choices that he makes that have now become part of the vocabulary but should be looked at again. For example, *le regard* in French is "the look" and Sheridan translated this as "the gaze." As a result, the gaze has become an important concept in film theory. There are now all kinds of secondary texts, books, and articles written about Lacan's theory of the gaze. *Le regard* partially comes from Jean-Paul Sartre, which is the look and can be used more reasonably in sentences. For instance, "the other looks at me." Gaze has a much different set of connotations in English. Simply restoring "the look" would be important.

The section of Seminar XI that Sheridan translates as "The Deconstruction of the Drive" raises some questions. Deconstruction at that point was a translation choice influenced by [Jacques] Derrida, whereas now I do not think this is warranted. There is also the translation of the subject supposed to know [*sujet suppose savoir*] as a concept, which creates a danger in English. The subject supposed to know is the subject posited as knowing or supposed as knowing, but English readers would read it and understand it as the subject who ought to know. In English, "supposed" usually means that there is an obligation to do something. The subject supposed to know suggests something different in English. I have worked for a while on thinking about what to do with this, but it would have been good if Sheridan had tried to avoid this connotation. More generally, Sheridan's text is okay from sentence to sentence, but it does not add up to a good text as a whole. It does not read well in the sense that Sheridan did not really account for Lacan's colloquial tone or for the fact that the Seminar was delivered orally. To be fair, Sheridan was not a Lacanian. He was a translator. He produced translations of

[Michel] Foucault, Sartre, and many other French authors. In the draft translation that I am working on, I am trying to capture much more of Lacan's tone.

CV: As you have said, perhaps it is not as though Sheridan's translations are incorrect, but the connotations of certain choices he made can be misleading.

DC: There are also anomalies in the text where you may come across half a sentence as missing.

CV: Are there other works you have spent time translating or hope to translate?

DC: I have done many translations privately. I have completed a significant amount of work on Miller over the years. I might have translated more of Miller's work than I have of Lacan's. A few of my translations of Miller have been published. With Miller, it is the same thing for me. If I come across a work that I am interested in, I will translate it primarily because I want to read it.

CV: What about this question of the text or the bibliographic work? I gather when people attended Lacan's seminars that they were recording or madly scribbling notes. There was also a hired stenographer.

DC: There was a stenographer who later wrote a book. She was angry with Lacan for never paying attention to her.[5] There is the stenography of the seminars, but from this stenography, typescripts were made. Many of these typescripts are marked up with Lacan's own handwriting. This means at some point – perhaps in the week after he gave the seminar – Lacan would sit down and read over the seminar and write notes on it. I get the impression he was doing this well before there was any prospect of the seminars being published. He took some care with the text. You will hear stories that he would sometimes give out texts of his seminars to friends as gifts. Lacan had all of the seminars and was storing them all. He had some sense of their documentary value. When Miller started publishing the seminars, he worked from the transcripts, turning these transcripts into a text that was intended for readers. Miller made contributions to the extent that Lacan wanted him listed as co-author.

For instance, if you read Cormac Gallagher's translations as opposed to Miller's editions of the seminar, you will see that Gallagher translates directly from the French transcripts. In the French transcripts and in Gallagher's translations – because Gallagher was very faithful to the transcripts – Lacan's discourse will be wandering. Lacan will start a sentence and there will be subordinate clauses and subordinate clauses. He will interrupt these clauses to say something else but then return to the original thoughts from before. Miller actually cleans this up. He turns the text into shorter sentences that are more readable. Lacan was aware of the journey the seminars took on the way to being printed as books. I believe Lacan wanted to list Miller as a co-author and Miller refused.

Later in his career, there were many people who were taping the seminars as if it were a Grateful Dead concert. Lacan would often complain about all of the tape recorders whirring in the front row. In the late seminars, XXII, XXIII, XXIV, and one session of XXV, Miller, who was now the editor of the seminars, produced texts to be published in the journal *Ornicar?* shortly after Lacan delivered them. Although XXII and XXIV have not been published as books, we do have official texts of them because Miller published them as the seminars were being given during that time. When I translated Seminar XXIV, I worked from the *Ornicar?* text, not from the transcripts.

CV: In many ways, the original is quite lost. The seminars have been reconstructed.

DC: There is more documentation than a lot of people would have available. [Ferdinand de] Saussure's course, for instance, was reconstructed from notes. Some of the published seminars of [Martin] Heidegger were reconstructed from students' notes. The Lacanian situation is actually better than some other situations in terms of the text. One of my other interests is in Shakespearian editing. I am interested in what happens to a text in its transmission. As these things go, I think what has happened with Lacan's seminar is pretty transparent. We can find the stenography and read it. If it is an earlier seminar, we can see what was taken down in the transcript. We can see Miller's editing of the transcript and where he cleans things up to make them clearer. We can see where he has broken up sentences and make our own judgments about why and how he did it. I believe what he did was pretty good. If we go on to read a Bruce Fink translation of a Miller text of a Lacanian seminar based on a transcript, it is pretty transparent. Bruce, for instance, provides lots of notes to describe his process.

CV: As a result of the translation and difference between languages, is there something different or distinct that might be communicated when Lacan is translated from French into English? Is there a different way of thinking about Lacan in English?

DC: I think there is a problem here. If one is to think that Lacan is unique to each language, even in French, then you are falling prey to the Sapir–Whorf hypothesis that language channels thought and that you cannot think outside of your own language.[6] I think this is a danger. If we have the words in English "anxiety" and "anguish," and the French have "*angoisse*", and the German have "*angst*", then I think it is a mistake to throw up our hands and say we cannot communicate about that. We also cannot say that language does not matter, because then we are not paying attention to the signifier. We don't want to have a notion of ideal meaning that is only represented in language. So, there are problems with the way we construct any argument about Lacan in English or in French.

My argument would be that no language is a privileged language for understanding Lacan. If one assumes there is a privileged language for understanding Lacan, one would be creating a metalanguage. This is true even in French. I think Lacan can be communicated in English, but there may be certain styles of group organizations, styles of discussion or etiquette, styles of argumentation that may all have an effect on how Lacan is transmitted in a particular language. This falls back on suspect notions on how culture influences transmission. I would prefer to say that language influences transmission. I do not think there are concepts that we cannot get in Lacan because we are English speakers. I also do not think that there are concepts that we may have special access to because English provides us with resources that other languages do not.

CV: Could there be a question about the inadequacy of language no matter what language we are within?

DC: Yes, but on the other hand, there is an adequacy. When I translate a Lacanian text from French to English, I am not concerned with the meaning in French and how to get the French meaning into English. I am not assuming that there is some epiphenomenal, ideal meaning that is hovering above a sentence and that I have to capture that in another language. I am more concerned with French grammar, construction, syntactical patterns, connotations, semantic considerations, and how these things can be put into English. For me, it is a logical and even mechanical process. I take apart a sentence in one language and try to reconstruct it in another language.

I am cautious and careful about the idea that meaning cannot be shared because we don't share language. This is the situation of psychoanalysis. As Miller has put it, psychoanalysis is learning someone else's language. A person comes for psychoanalysis, and initially the psychoanalyst does not know the person's particular language, but over time the analyst may learn more. What is most important is that the analysand will learn his or her own language, too.

There used to be an old saying that you don't know your own language until you know another one. In response to this, I half-jokingly used to say that you don't realize that you don't even know your own language until you realize that you don't know another one. This can be an effect of translation as well. When you begin translating French, you may realize how little you know about English, which can be a good experience. It can be good to not understand too quickly or assume a sentence would be easy to put into English.

CV: There are also multiple prominent translators of Lacan's work. Do you find that there are different voices in these translations as a result?

DC: In terms of a voice, a tone, or a style from different translators, the answer would be yes. Of course, a blind spot for translators is that one may think the decisions made when translating are neutral. One may think it is about translating French into plain English. I have talked to Russell Grigg about this. He finds Bruce's translations to be very American. We might also find various "Australianisms" in Russell's translations. As I mentioned, Sheridan has a stiff formality to his translations that does not sound quite Lacanian to my ears.

There are things that I do to try to capture the colloquial nature of Lacan's discourse. French is a very contracted language. If you look at French written on the page, there are many apostrophes. In English, there is some rule in formal written work that we are not supposed to use contractions. I find that Lacan's sentences, however, translate more fluidly if I use contractions. This is something that is notable in my translations. I try to capture the fluidity of speech by using contractions as an easy device to accomplish this. It sounds more natural to me.

All of this said, I do not think anything on paper, not even in the French, can capture that kind of performance. You have seen Lacan on film, haven't you? He was a very engaging speaker. He was dramatic and slower in his speech than you would think. Lacan delivered his seminars in a kind of oratorical style, which probably served for his listeners as a kind of punctuation. If you listen to the tapes of the seminars or have seen him on film, he is not as hard to follow as you might think he would be. His delivery is actually a kind of punctuation in this sense. This is hard to capture on the page. It is hard to capture the changes in volume. Lacan would speak louder and then more quietly. He would punctuate with that tonic accent, speeding up or slowing down towards the ends of sentences. One cannot capture this in print.

CV: This is what always struck me about films of Lacan delivering the seminar. He appears very slow and deliberate in his speech. It always seemed like a rhetorical style that would leave the audience waiting for the next word. I imagine the audience hanging on to the end of every word.

DC: Nobody can capture that on the page. It is quite remarkable to watch him.

CV: I have also been thinking about the seminars that you gave last year on interpretation. We have recently been looking at Seminar VI, *Desire and its Interpretation*. In Lacanian thinking, interpretation is a notion that is understood much differently than in other forms of analysis. What are your thoughts about the contemporary state of affairs of interpretation?

DC: The full title of the seminar I gave last year was "The Age of Interpretation: From Shakespeare to Lacan." What I was trying to argue in that seminar was that there is an age of interpretation that roughly corresponds with the modern age. Shakespeare and [René] Descartes can be seen as the ones who inaugurate that age of interpretation. I tried to sketch out a history of what interpretation was, leading us up to the twentieth century. This age of interpretation in the title suggests that there is possibly an end date to this time period as well.

People did not always ask interpretive questions the way we do. As we think of it, interpretation is pretty much a phenomenon of the modern age. What I was partially arguing is that psychoanalysis participates in this history and perhaps is very much a product of the age of interpretation. What is remarkable about Lacan's career is that he makes a transition from his early view to his late view of interpretation. I think the question I tried to raise is still an open question: where does interpretation go from here?

When I was studying for my master's of social work, there would be a chapter in textbooks on "interventions" that a social worker would make. There were lists. You would reflect what the person said, encourage the person, and somewhere on the list was that you would interpret. This is a holdover from the days of psychodynamic psychotherapy. In psychoanalysis, there is something similar going on. It is not so simplistic. It would be beneficial to clarify what we mean by the many things that we call interpretation.

CV: Lacanians often will remark that it is the patient or the analysand who is the one doing the interpreting, not the psychoanalyst or psychotherapist. Perhaps what we provide is a construction. You have highlighted the main question already. What is it that we are saying when we talk about interpretation?

DC: Of all the papers I have written over the years, a good number of them are on the question of interpretation. I have been interested in this for a long time. I gave a talk once at an APW conference. I talked about the interpretation anxiety of the analyst. In the old days, it seems to me that analysts were very concerned with the quality of their interpretations and whether or not they could know if these interpretations were "right." This seems to convey something of an interpretation anxiety. We don't usually worry about such questions as much anymore. Today, analysts have an interpretation anxiety that is projected backwards or projected onto other groups. For instance, "Back in the old days we used to interpret that way, but we don't anymore" or "These other groups interpret that way, that's not what we do." There is a funny way in which interpretation becomes what one might suspect someone else is doing "wrong."

[Edward] Glover sent out a survey to a number of analysts and asked them to respond about interpretation.[7] He found that pretty much everybody was doing the same thing. The analysts were interpreting fairly conservatively and in an orthodox way. There was not much of a spread of styles of interpretation. In the state of psychoanalysis at that time, interpretation anxiety would be unwarranted.

CV: I associate interpretation with understanding. In the technique of
Lacan, one might highlight a word or practice scansion of the session.
These are perhaps not even interpretations but function more as punctuations. Such punctuations may not even be about understanding but
might be more about helping a person to produce more speech or to go
further with a signifier. Do you have thoughts about Lacan's emphasis
on interpretation versus punctuation?

DC: This is why I would suggest that we stop calling everything an interpretation. In 1996, Miller announced that the age of interpretation was
over. In English, we read Miller's talk in translation as an essay. His talk
was part of my motivation for giving the seminar last year. I think he
makes a very good argument, but then everyone in the Millerian group
started speaking about a post-interpretive age. I think this also reflects
the sort of interpretation anxiety I was just talking about. "Maybe we
have been doing it wrong" or "Maybe there is some new way to interpret." Miller says it directly in the essay. It is more a commentary than
an edict. He says that Lacan knew this, but that he could not announce
at the time that the age of interpretation is over.

You are right when you mentioned earlier that it is the analysand
who interprets. What is the role of the analyst except to highlight what
the person says, to help the person to listen to the signifier, to listen to
what the person says and not necessarily to what the person means to
say, and to encourage the person to keep speaking. Not every intervention is an interpretation. Meanwhile, it is probably still as it was in
Glover's day, people are probably doing okay with the state of interpretation. The way that interpretation anxiety currently manifests is to
assume that in some other group, some other school, they do old-
fashioned interpretation whereby the analysts would be simply
explaining symptoms to analysands. This was one of Freud's earliest
discoveries. Freud understood that you cannot simply explain someone's symptom to them and hope that it will go away. In the papers on
technique, Freud does explain to people that interpretation is not what
they think it is. Interpretation is not just announcing an explanation
for a symptom, which would be wild analysis. When Miller announces
that the age of interpretation is over, it should not have caused the
anxiety or elation that it caused.

CV: One thing that always stuck with me in regard to interpretation was
from a talk that you gave on the distinction between meaning and meaningfulness. Where do you see the importance of this distinction for analytical work?

DC: I tried to make and work with that distinction for some time. The idea
was that meaning would be the semantic side of the signified, the dictionary definition, or the shared understanding of what a word means.
Meaningfulness would be what the word meant to you. Perhaps

meaningfulness would convey something about the *jouissance* attached to the word. Harry Stack Sullivan has a nice passage where he says "when you promise a five-year-old a pony for their birthday, the word pony will never again have for them the richness that it has as they anticipate that pony as their birthday approaches." There is a meaning for the word pony, a small horse, but when you are promised a pony for your birthday at five years old, there is an incredible *jouissance* attached to it. Lacan has a French term, *signifiance*. Bruce Fink translates this as "signifierness," and Russell Grigg translates this as "meaningfulness."

It was probably the last time that I tried to work with this term because it didn't work out. I could not make the term do what I wanted it to do. Meaningfulness would be what is lost to language. Lacan has a term for it: the phallus is the signifier of all the meaning effects of language. When you enter into language, what you gain is meaning. What you lose is castration. There are already terms for this. We do make this distinction in everyday speech. This is why I found it attractive. If you are teaching a poem, students are concerned with what the poem means. What does this poem mean? They want to know because they might be asked about it on an exam. This is something different from when someone says, "This poem means a lot to me." The poem has some meaningful value to the person.

CV: Could it be a difference between the more objective or dictionary meaning of the word versus the subjective enjoyment of the word?

DC: What I was trying to get at was where Lacan says that metonymy is the proper signifying function of language. When you tell somebody, "Can you stop at the store and pick up a gallon of milk?", you don't want that to be a poem, to be a metaphor, or to be interpreted. You want a gallon of milk. The proper signifying function of language is metonymy. It is on the syntagmatic axis of language where we find that one word moves to the next word and to the next and so on. You get to the end of the sentence and retroactively you know what the whole sentence means. You want the sentence to mean that. You don't want it to be meaningful. Most of the time, we want to use language to communicate, which is why Lacan calls it the properly signifying function of language. What is lost is what is meaningful to the subject.

Notes

1 See the Affiliated Psychoanalytic Workgroups website: http://apwonline.org/
2 See more information about Lacan Toronto at the website: http://lacantoronto.ca. This is a reading and study group offering bi-monthly meetings, teaching, clinical days, as well as courses on Lacan as part of the Toronto Psychoanalytic Society's extension program. Psychoanalyst and psychiatrist Judith Hamilton has led Lacan Toronto since 2012.

3 Jacques-Alain Miller (1944–) is a psychoanalyst and philosopher who married Lacan's daughter Judith in 1966. Miller became the sole editor of Lacan's seminars following his death in 1981.
4 See Russell Grigg's paper in *Ornicar? Digital*, "Lacan in Translation," where he compares Sheridan's translations in English to the original French texts: "In the earliest translations specially, *Ecrits: A Selection* and *Seminar XI*, there are many errors, in fact so many that it is often impossible to work out what Lacan intended, often making the translations unreliable, misleading, or simply inscrutable" (1999).
5 See Marie Pierrakos's *Transcribing Lacan's Seminars: Memoirs of a Disgruntled Keybasher Turned Psychoanalyst* (2006).
6 The Sapir–Whorf hypothesis is named for Edward Sapir (1884–1939) and Benjamin Lee Whorf (1897–1941), American linguists who theorized that the structure of a language influences a person's worldview, cognition, and perception, which are relative to the person's spoken language.
7 Edward Glover (1888–1972) was a British psychoanalyst who undertook the study of questionnaires completed by psychoanalysts, which was meant to target the question of the analyst's role and use of techniques in treatment with analysands. Glover published this study as *An Investigation of the Technique of Psychoanalysis* in 1940 and republished this study as *The Technique of Psychoanalysis* in 1955.

Bibliography and Further Reading

Collins, Dan. "On the Development of Lacan's Graph of Desire." *Studying Lacan's Seminars IV and V: From Lack to Desire*. Ed. Carol Owens and Nadezhda Almqvist. New York: Routledge, 2019a. 153–163.
Collins, Dan. "Psychoanalysis and Education." *Lacunae: APPI International Journal for Lacanian Psychoanalysis*. 17 (2018a): 84–95.
Collins, Dan. "Resistance as a Measure of the Duration of the Psychoanalytic Cure." *Psychoanalytische Perspectieven*. 37.3 (2019b): 787–803.
Collins, Dan. "A Short Digression on the Meaning of Knowledge." *Lacunae: APPI International Journal for Lacanian Psychoanalysis*. 18 (2019c): 79–94.
Collins, Dan. "Stealing Money from Offices." *Lacunae: APPI International Journal for Lacanian Psychoanalysis*. 16 (2018b): 105–125.
Glover, Edward. *An Investigation of the Technique of Psychoanalysis, Research Supplement to the International Journal of Psycho-analysis*. London: Bailliere, Tyndall and Cox, 1940.
Grigg, Russell. "Lacan in Translation." *Ornicar? Digital*, 1999. https://wapol.org/ornicar/articles/ggg0155.htm. Accessed 3 Mar. 2020.
Miller, Jacques-Alain. "The Divine Details." *Lacanian Ink*. Trans. Dan Collins. 34 (2009): 28–51.
Miller, Jacques-Alain. "Matrix." *Lacanian Ink*. Trans. Daniel G. Collins. 12 (1997): 45–51.
Pierrakos, Marie. *Transcribing Lacan's Seminars: Memoirs of a Disgruntled Keybasher Turned Psychoanalyst*. Trans. Angela M. Brewer. London: Free Association Books, 2006.

Chapter 9

Lacanian Psychoanalysis in Mexico with Manuel Hernández

Manuel Hernández is an independent researcher and practices psychoanalysis in Mexico City. He is a former member of the *École lacanienne de psychanalyse* and was its director from 2004 to 2008. He is currently the director of a publishing house, Litoral Editores. He is the author of *El sueño de la inyección a Irma* [*The Dream of Irma's Injection*] (Litoral Editores, 2016), *Lacan en México: México en Lacan – Miller y el mundo* [*Lacan in Mexico. Mexico in Lacan. Miller and the World*] (Ediciones Navarra and Anchomundo, 2016), *Localización del analista: La formación psicoanalítica de Freud a Lacan* [*Location of the Analyst: The Psychoanalytic Training from Freud to Lacan*] (Litoral Editores, 2020), and *El Análisis de Lacan* [*Lacan's Analysis*] (Litoral Editores, Forthcoming). He is also the Spanish translator of Carina Basualdo's *Lacan (Freud) Lévi-Strauss: Chronicle of a failed encounter* (Epeele, 2016) and Francis Hofstein's *El pase de Lacan* (Litoral Editores, 2020). This interview was recorded on 25 April 2021.

Chris Vanderwees: Do you recall the first time you heard about psychoanalysis?

Manuel Hernández: It was very early in my life. I was a child. Psychoanalysis was in popular magazines that I used to read. It was a diluted portrayal of psychoanalysis, but what was in the magazines fascinated me. I asked, "What is psychoanalysis?" I got an answer that came from my mother. She said, "It is a discipline that studies what is the most complex thing in the world: the human mind." This blew me away. As I approached psychoanalysis, little by little, I realized this is what I wanted to do with my life.

DOI: 10.4324/9781003323136-10

CV: When did you hear about Lacanian psychoanalysis? And what was it that caught your ear?

MH: I was a teenager already reading psychoanalysis in 1979. A good friend of mine introduced me to several fields of culture that were alien to me. I was reading quite a bit about psychoanalysis, and I became saddened that I could not find much that was really interesting after [Sigmund] Freud – except [Carl] Jung – I liked Jung. This same friend of mine once asked me, "What do you know about this French psychoanalyst who nobody understands but has the world of psychoanalysis upside down?" I immediately said to myself, "That is exactly what I am looking for." He did not tell me his name since he didn't know. So I snooped around and found that he was [Jacques] Lacan. From that point onwards, I began to search for materials to read because almost nothing was published by 1980 except the *Écrits*, which I did not understand. I found the Anika Rifflet-Lemaire thesis on Lacan, which I bought and tried to read. Namely the preface that Lacan published there.[1] I thought that it must be a bad translation because I could not understand a single word. I decided to learn French and then I realized that this was Lacan's style. It was really hard, but it became a habit to read Lacan after this. At some point after this, I learned that Lacan had just died, which saddened me because I felt I could have met him in person had I known that he was still alive...

CV: How did you come to your formation?

MH: I asked myself with whom I wanted to talk about psychoanalysis. I studied psychology, and it was not with the students, nor the teachers in my faculty, that much I knew, and then I began to realize that I wanted to talk with those who knew Lacan. He was already dead, but I wanted to talk about psychoanalysis with his students, but I realized that did not mean they would want to talk with me, so I began to read Lacan every day, as a habit, early in the mornings. Once I found a group that oddly called itself *École lacanienne de psychanalyse* (which was an anomaly since every Lacanian group was "Freudian" and every IPA [International Psychoanalytic Association] group called itself "Psychoanalytic"), and this group organized a seminar by Jean Allouch. He was teaching the basis of Lacan's work on topology and the symbolic, the imaginary, and the real. My readings had already revealed to me that the symbolic, the imaginary, and the real were the groundings of Lacan work, so I had a path to follow. I already had begun my analysis here in Mexico and I began to work with people here who were related to this school.

   The *École lacanienne de psychanalyse* was founded in France in 1985. I became a member of this school in 1990. At that time, being 26 years old, I was also the youngest member of the school. I later became the first non-French director of the *École lacanienne de psychanalyse*.

Not living in France was a real challenge in many ways. I'm still a member of the school and also the director of *Litoral*, which is a follow-up to the original French journal, but now published in Mexico.[2] In Mexico, we have worked regularly with French analysts, including Jean Allouch, Guy Le Gaufey, Mayette Viltard, Erik Porge, and Francis Hofstein, and analysts from Latin America, such as Raquel Capurro from Uruguay, Gloria Leff from Mexico, and Mario Beira, a Cuban analyst who lives in Miami. In the ELP [Escuela Lacaniana de Psicoanálisis], there are no local groups; we are all part of the same school in Mexico, Argentina, Costa Rica, and Uruguay and in France.

CV: You've done work on the history of the reception of Lacan in Mexico. How would you say he was first received by the psychological or psychoanalytic community in Mexico?

MH: It was not in one direction. The Siglo Veintiuno publishing house in Mexico first published the *Écrits* in Spanish. There was an early translation published in 1972, which was the first part of the *Écrits*, but Juan-David Nasio collaborated with Lacan to edit and publish the whole book in Spanish in 1974. The *Écrits* arrived very early in Mexico along with Buenos Aires, where Oscar Masotta was already introducing Lacan to Argentinians in the 1960s.[3]

The editor that published the Spanish translation of the *Écrits* belonged to a non-Lacanian group, the Círculo Psicoanalítico Mexicano. Nevertheless, Armando Suárez was a bright and cultivated man. He saw the interest in translating Lacan. He asked Tomás Segovia, who was a Spanish poet living in Mexico, to complete the translation. The translation has many problems because translating Lacan is such a challenge, but we have worked with this translation for years and years now. Armando Suárez was head of the CPM [Círculo Psicoanalítico Mexicano], which was in a way close to Igor Caruso and Freudomarxism, so they received many refugees from Argentina who were fleeing military dictatorship, including Néstor Braunstein and Marcelo Pasternac.[4] Braunstein and Pasternac had been working with Lacan's writings in Buenos Aires during the 1960s because they were also reading the texts of Louis Althusser, who published the famous article, "Freud and Lacan."[5] Marcelo Pasternac had also been living in France studying psychiatry at the Sainte-Anne Hospital in Paris. He met Lacan during his talk, "Petit Discours aux Psychiatres" ["Short Speech to Psychiatrists"] in 1967.[6] In 1976 or 1977, Pasternac moved to Mexico as a refugee along with many other refugees from Córdoba, Argentina. Pasternac and other refugee psychoanalysts in Mexico formed a group and began to read Lacan very seriously. They did something very outstanding and remarkable at this time, which was to acquire copies of the French transcriptions of every one of Lacan's Seminars from a Parisian bookshop that sent them to Mexico. These were faulty transcriptions and contained errors, but they were the transcriptions that Lacan had made with a stenographer and his secretary as a record of his seminar, and they read every one of his seminars, something not common even today.

With these copies, this group of four Argentinians in Mexico – Miguel Felipe Sosa, Marcelo Pasterna, Hélyda Peretti, and Estela Maldonado – began to read his seminars every week. By the early 1980s, they had finished their reading of these seminars. One of the members had a friend in France who was in analysis with Argentinian analyst Juan-David Nasio. She was close to the *Littoral* group and she proposed to the group in Mexico that they become a correspondent of the journal. The group rejected this proposal because they did not know much about the publication, but they became subscribers and began to read *Littoral*. This was an interesting journal because it was formed by members who were part of the group that said "no" to the initiative of Lacan to form a new school with Jacques-Alain Miller. This group was formed by Jean Allouch, Guy Le Gaufey, Erik Porge, Philippe Julien, and Mayette Viltard. They had all been members of the *École freudienne de Paris*. Jean Allouch and Philippe Julien had each been named "Analyst of the School" (AE) having done "the pass." They were especially attentive to the difficulties of mixing family and the school, which is why they said "no" to the initiative that Lacan posed at the end of his life for the Millerian school. They separated and began to work in a very original way.

This group [that] formed around *Littoral* was highly surprised to find four subscribers in Mexico. One of the members of the group around Littoral in France had been raised as a child in Mexico; his name was Albert Fontaine. The editors of Litoral were curious to find readers in Mexico, and since he was flying to Mexico to see his family, they told him, "You should go see them and ask them how and why they are subscribers to *Littoral*." He came to meet the group for one hour but stayed for six hours. He was absolutely appalled and surprised to find people here in Mexico who could speak with him about Lacan's late seminars like they had been there. He told them, "You must absolutely meet with Jean Allouch who is in Cancun on vacation right now." Allouch got together with the group on his way back to Paris in Mexico City and this is how this important part story of Lacanianism in Mexico began. The *École lacanienne de psychanalyse* was founded with four Spanish-speaking members as a result. Spanish speakers now make up more than half of the members.

The other way that Lacan's thinking found its way to Mexico was through Uruguayan poet and psychoanalyst Juan Carlos Plá, who came as a refugee as well in 1977. He was very touched by his visit with Octave Mannoni and Serge Leclaire. Juan Carlos already spoke French and had no trouble reading Lacan in the French language to get a grasp of the writing. As a poet, he had no trouble with Lacan's style. He was also a

Training Analyst of the International Psychoanalytic Association when he came to Mexico. This is important because he was immediately taken as a Training Analyst in Mexico but was also working with Lacan, which was absolutely unheard of and impossible to bear at the Mexican Association, so he had to create an independent seminar group outside of the local IPA school, but he remained a Training Analyst within the IPA. He began to talk about the return to Freud, reading Freud with several analysts who were not members of the IPA. He founded his own group, so to speak, which was not a formal group but was an important one. Marcelo Pasternac actually became Juan Carlos Plá's analysand.

CV: What are your thoughts about psychoanalytic formation and transmission today?

MH: This is a difficult question that must be answered in local terms. What is going on in Mexico is different than what happens in Paris, New York, or London. If we speak about Lacanian groups, what appalls me is the careless approach that some groups take in disregarding what Lacan said and did about the problems of formation. What I can see is that the university or academic approach to psychoanalysis has been gaining importance. This is absolutely not what Lacan proposed. My effort is to not only point out what Lacan actually proposed for the formation of the analyst but also to study the history, reasons, and context that explain why Lacan proposed some things that seem rather strange. His proposition of "the pass" in 1967 is strange and does not conform to anything that was usual at that time or now. My view is that he was absolutely correct that this could be a viable option – not an obligation – but an option for someone who has a desire to give an account of the termination of their own analysis and how this relates to his or her desire to practice psychoanalysis. Lacan emphasized the absolute freedom for one to choose their own analyst, not from a list of training analysts as has been the tradition in the International Psychoanalytic Association. He believed that one should choose an analyst only by way of transference. The whole emphasis is then placed upon one's initiative or desire to take into one's own hands the readings and study groups that are necessary to be formed. This is to say that Lacan eliminated every form of curriculum in his school. This is important. Lacan took a different path in structuring his school from anything that was known at that time. I defend and speak up for Lacan's choice. I had the experience of going through "the pass" in the *École lacanienne de psychanalyse*. It was an experience that made a change in my life. I continue to hold this as a possibility for other people who finish an analysis. I can say that people who follow this path are enormously productive because they really want to work moved only by desire. Through this path, one also becomes aware that one can only work from a position of not-knowing. And since there is nobody who can give rapid, quick, or simple answers, one must take into our own hands the work that is necessary to respond to this ignorance.

My point of view is that Lacan really hit the spot. He understood that it is only desire that makes one take action and responsibility in formation. What I can see is that people get engaged and become responsible if there is freedom for them to follow their own path, but we cannot do this alone. We need a community that is critical and demanding in not letting things go without questioning. My community at the *École lacanienne de psychanalyse* is very demanding in this regard. When I publish something, I always am aware that this is going to be read by Jean Allouch or Guy Le Gaufey and they are going to point out things to me. I do the same with them. I can say we are able to speak to each other and criticize each other while respecting each other's point of view. Right now, I work as well with a Comunidad cooperative of about 40 people who are readers of Litoral and mostly not members of the ELP but who have accepted to work following the guiding principles of this school. Many of them are young and very talented, and since every one there knows that this work will not yield financial gains nor any power whatsoever, we are moved only by the desire, *communitas*, to do it, even contributing with a small fee (which helps Litoral to carry on). So, we gather to work only by the desire to do it in a state of loss. This is crucial to be able remove money and power from the center of our activities.

CV: Lacan was working to do away with the university discourse within the school while making an effort to shift formation to be closer to what he called the discourse of the analyst.

MH: Absolutely. He invented what they call in French a *dispositif*, which is a difficult word to translate into English.[7] He created the *dispositif* of the pass, but the school is also a *dispositif*. This is not the *dispositif* of the cure, but rather far from it. The *dispositif* of the cure itself rests upon free association. One cannot work with free association outside of the analyst's office. We work in another way. What commands everything in terms of what Lacan put into place is desire.

CV: You have also spent time researching and writing about Lacan's own analysis with psychoanalyst Rudolph Loewenstein, which took place between 1933 and 1939.[8] What have you discovered in your work on this?

MH: The first thing that I discovered is that Lacanians do not want to know about it. Many Lacanians have taken my research in a very ill fashion. My research on this subject was stigmatized and criticized before anyone had read a single word. What we know or what we think we know about Lacan's analysis largely comes from Élisabeth Roudinesco's books, in particular *Jacques Lacan & Co: A History of Psychoanalysis in France* as well as her biography on Lacan. She has constructed a version of Lacan's analysis that is not supported by the documents that one can find. She has written a novel. One believes this novel because it is an attractive story where Lacan is a hero and Loewenstein is a poor devil. Loewenstein is a sad character in this novel. My finding is that nothing of this version stands at all. When one consults the documents, one finds very different things from what Roudinesco says. It appears to me that Loewenstein was actually a really interesting analyst at that time. After Lacan's analysis was already finished, Loewenstein was drafted for the war in 1939. He went into battle with the French army as a military doctor. He also decided to serve a second tour on his own initiative although he already was a father. He was a brave man and a noble person. The Nazis occupied Paris, and following the Armistice in 1940, Loewenstein had to flee to southern France and then to the United States in 1942. One must realize that ego psychology did not still exist while he was in France, but this is the path that he took only when he arrived in the United States and became close to Heinz Hartmann and Ernst Kris.[9]

Before meeting Hartmann and Kris, ego psychology did not exist in Loewenstein's work. What did exist in his work was a close reading of Freud's papers, a correspondence with Freud where Freud gave him all of his confidence from the beginning of their relationship. One must realize that Sándor Ferenczi was one of Freud's closest colleagues from 1926 to 1933. Ferenczi was like the crown jewel of the movement at that time.[10] Ferenczi was translated into French and often cited by Loewenstein. Largely influenced by Freud and Ferenczi, Loewenstein made it his initial task to come to France to transmit Freud's teaching to the French. Loewenstein's family was Polish, but he learned German and French in his childhood. We have also to take into account that there was antisemitism and Germanophobia in France since the First World War. Many French people did not much like German-speaking people and did not like Jews. As a result, Loewenstein found it quite difficult to teach the writings of an author of German-Jewish descent. He taught to people who did not read German, while the translations of Freud into French were both scarce and faulty.

Loewenstein loved France, and Freud gave him permission to make the translations that he needed to make to continue teaching psychoanalysis there. Although they kept a correspondence, Loewenstein only went to meet Freud for the first time in person near the end of Freud's life. The account of this meeting is really touching. They were both real *mensches*, as Jewish people might say. There is an unpublished interview that someone made with Loewenstein where he describes his way of working with patients and speaks about his relationship with Freud. In Loewenstein, one finds a true analyst who is delicate and subtle.

This was Lacan's analyst, and it was true transference that drove Lacan into Loewenstein's office. There were no restrictions or list in the Paris society at that time. One could go and ask for analysis with anyone in the world. Marie Bonaparte was in analysis with Freud. Sacha Nacht also spent some time in analysis with Freud.[11] At that time, one was able to work with any analyst in the world without restrictions. Lacan chose Loewenstein. When one takes the time to read what Loewenstein wrote and put it into context, one finds an analyst there.

CV: You've said Lacanians don't want to know about Lacan's analysis or perhaps do not want to know about the more dubious aspects of Lacan's life (for instance, his relationship with Catherine Millot). What is this resistance about? And can we reconcile these more troubling aspects of Lacan with his incredible and indispensable system of thought?

MH: Lacan was a human being. He had contradictions just like every one of us. Lacan initially did not want to have psychoanalysis taught in the university. In 1969, Leclaire developed the first Department of Psychoanalysis at the University of Paris VIII (Vincennes), a project that Lacan initially opposed strongly. At the end of his life, however, he gave all of his support to Jacques-Alain Miller's teaching at Vincennes without giving a single explanation at all about why he seemed to change his mind about what he taught and demonstrated previously. Lacan did not give a single explanation for this change in his disposition about psychoanalysis being taught in the university.

What I can say to explain this is that Miller was not an analyst and was hardly analyzed at that time; he was a *normalien*, so his education was in philosophy. On the contrary, Serge Leclaire was a psychoanalyst and had a project of forming analysts at the university, which was not Miller's project at the beginning. Miller was an intellectual who did not begin practicing analysis until after Lacan's death. Lacan died knowing Miller as an intellectual. Prior to his death, Lacan had the confidence to put his work into Miller's hands. Of course, Miller was part of his family as well as a son-in-law. We cannot fail to see that Lacan was seduced by Miller and very much supported Miller's work. Some have claimed that Miller was an opportunist and sought to get close to Lacan through his daughter, but this is absolutely not what happened. Miller was in transference with Lacan and should have become his analysand, but Lacan did not provide this. He practically offered Miller his daughter Judith and took him under his wing and into his family instead. An analyst chooses to accept transference but does not take it as a personal thing as Lacan did with Miller. We are still seeing the huge consequences of this decision now around us.

There are many contradictions with Lacan, such as this example with Miller or with Catherine Millot as well. He taught everything that one must know to not have an affair with an analysand, and he still did it. This does not mean that one has to follow his example. One can follow his teachings without following some of the contradictions that Lacan displayed as a person.

CV: What are your thoughts about the way that Miller has taken up Lacan in his own teaching from the early 1980s onwards? Miller has a very different style than Lacan's discourse. To read Miller often does feel like reading something akin to the university discourse. What are the consequences of this for Lacanianism?

MH: This is complex. On one hand, some psychoanalysts will say that Lacanian psychoanalysis would be dead without Miller. Few people would know about or follow what Lacan taught without him. Miller has been clear about his intention to make Lacan a popular author. Now, Miller has also written publicly that he will not try to provide a transcription of what Lacan has said, but will provide a version of what Lacan wanted to say and did not say. One has to be aware of this twist. One is going to be reading something signed as Lacan, but it will actually be a version of what Miller thinks Lacan would have wanted to say and never said. It is a co-authored affair.

I'm not sure if you are aware of the group Stécriture, which made a transcript of Lacan's Seminar VIII on transference in the early eighties. Miller sued them and took members of the group to court. The result was very interesting. The judge sided with Miller and clearly stated that he had ownership and rights to the material and imposed a penalty to the Stécriture group of only one franc.[12] It was quite a symbolic result. Miller eventually apologized to the Stécriture group for his actions regarding the matter of the transcript. He has said since then that if one wants to work in a critical way with versions of Lacan's seminars as transcripts or recordings, that one is able to do this. He will not pursue any legal actions except if one is meaning to make profit. If someone wants to make a transcription of a recording and study it with a group, this is now possible to do freely.

What I am saying is that there are three ways Lacan is being treated. One way is through Miller where he makes popular versions of the seminars and creates his own versions of what he believes Lacan would have said. He fosters the university discourse in every single way. Miller has made a foundation of many groups, which obviously gives an enormous amount of power to him. It is a pyramid with Miller at the top. Most of these groups distribute power in a descending way so that everyone has a little power to enjoy. In this way, Miller is very wise politically, but I believe all of this is contrary to what Lacan taught and wanted for psychoanalysis. The results have been saddening. I have written about this in my book about Lacan's visit to Mexico. Miller's way is the mainstream.

The second way that Lacan is treated is also through the inheritance of Miller's approach, but those on this path have rejected Miller. It is a rejection of Miller's character but not the forms and structures in place as they have founded groups, distribute power, and frequently use the

Millerian transcriptions. From my point of view, nothing really changes in essence from the first way I have described.

There is a third way of treating Lacan, which is composed mainly of small groups that try to maintain what Lacan proposed for psychoanalysis and are in a position of constantly being critical about what he said in his work. It is a difficult position to hold up because it is not commercial. It is a rather uncertain path. It is not necessarily attractive to many young people searching for certainties and an income that is guaranteed. Obviously, there are far fewer people who are interested in the smaller groups and their ways of doing things. I believe that I belong to this third example.

CV: Depending on the context, calling Lacan into question could result in being ostracized from a group if that group is more dogmatic in its approach.

MH: Absolutely. Some groups do not want to hear anything critical about Lacan. Why? I believe that many Lacanians have taken up Lacan as a guarantee of one's legitimacy as an analyst. If Lacan is put into question, their own legitimacy is put into question. This is why the proposition of the pass is so important. The pass allows the analyst to separate oneself from the family or more precisely to separate from the familial relation to Freud as a founding father. Instead of [suggesting] the family as a model for the transmission of psychoanalysis, Lacan proposed the pass, which allows the analyst to get rid of the debts that the family imposes. One is not indebted to one's own analyst or the analyst of one's analyst. Something is cut out and left out and then one can begin without this debt.

CV: I'm currently writing about Lacan's discourse from the perspective of rhetoric. I'm trying to open up many questions, but especially about persuasion. From an Althusserian perspective, we might ask how is Lacan interpellating his listeners and readers? How does Lacan hail his audience? How did he draw this crowd around him?

MH: Lacan was giving his Seminar during a special time in French culture. He was in dialogue with Jean-Paul Sartre, Simone de Beauvoir, and Claude Lévi-Strauss. He was also in dialogue with Russian-American linguist and theorist Roman Jakobson. This was a lively and rich environment that really put people to work. There was an explosion of production where one could go to hear [Roland] Barthes, Althusser, [Michel] Foucault, or [Jacques] Derrida giving their respective seminars. It was a cultural moment where people were ready to challenge themselves. There was an eagerness to read difficult texts and hear difficult presentations.

If one studies Lacan's own path, we can see that many understood him as an intellectual hero and as a victim of the system. Lacan surrounded himself with fascinating people who grasped the intersections between artistic practice and psychoanalysis. He was friends with avant-garde artists, including the surrealists like André Breton and Salvador Dalí. He was also a friend of Marcel Duchamp and Tristan Tzara of the Dadaist movement.[13] Lacan dined with such artists and learned from the Dadaist and surrealist strategies of his time.[14] Lacan was also able to read Greek and Latin. He studied the classics and rhetoric, which greatly influenced his approach. We can see he uses many of the forms of rhetoric that Quintilian describes.[15] Lacan's style is the style of a good rhetorician or orator who seduces. Philippe Sollers and others who attended the seminars have described them as incredible theatre.

I have proposed a method of reading Lacan's seminar, which is very simple. One takes up one session of the seminar, and those participating in the activity search for all of the texts and articles that Lacan mentions as works consulted in preparation for the particular session of the seminar. Each participant in this activity then reads these works and makes a presentation of this session of the seminar. When we read these texts and one explains their connection to Lacan's discourse, one might find an answer to a very important question: "What is he talking about?" One can start to make links between the sentences in the transcription and the book, article, or play that Lacan is mentioning. This exercise reveals that there is a logic to what Lacan is saying that may have been absent at the beginning of one's reading. It is a rich method that can bring a huge joy to reading Lacan. It is obviously hard work, but one is pointed toward literary and philosophical texts that might bring a lot of joy despite being strange to one's own knowledge. When one begins to make connections between the texts and the seminars, one might be really blown away when reaching a new realization about what Lacan has said.

This is an analogous method to what Freud proposed when interpreting dreams. When one has the book or copies of the seminar, this is the manifest content. One understands nothing even if one thinks to comprehend. Understanding is often misleading, but then one goes to read the book that Lacan read, and this becomes the latent content. But the latent content is not the meaning of the dream. The meaning of the dream is the *connection* between the latent content and the manifest content. When this connection is made, one is surprised because a new sense arises. I had realized years later after studying Lacan in this method that I was actually following Freud's method for interpreting dreams. We carry on with this method, and people are often transformed during their readings when they take up this activity. They begin to practice following Lacan teachings without thinking about it, but only realizing it *après-coup*.

CV: Lacan once said that he did not expect people to understand the *Écrits* but that he expected people to read them …

MH: … and then later he said that they are not to be read. What did he mean by this? I'm writing now about the period where Lacan wrote and prepared the *Écrits*. Lacan says things in the *Écrits* that he never says in the seminars, especially when he speaks about the formation of the analyst. Every problem with the formation of the analyst up to 1966 is outlined in the *Écrits*. I believe one is not to read the *Écrits* but rather is meant to do things with the *Écrits*. One must allow oneself to be led into action from what Lacan says in this text. For instance, this begins with the elimination of the ego for the analyst. One should pause for a moment and think how could Lacan live through this huge and terrible conflict with the IPA that lasted no less than ten years where his authority and legitimacy as an analyst were put into question every single day? How is it that one can find almost no trace in his seminars of his personal struggle with this ordeal? My thesis is that the *Écrits* is the trace that Lacan left about this conflict with the IPA. My interpretation is that this ordeal presented no trauma for him, because he was able to write and publish the *Écrits*.

CV: I suppose Lacan does write a little bit about the legend of this conflict or what he calls his "excommunication" from the IPA at the beginning of Seminar XI. It is as if this conflict is still something of a traumatic break within psychoanalysis itself that continues to have its own repetition compulsions acted out in the tendencies of various groups and within the IPA itself.

MH: Absolutely. I am about to publish a little book about the analytic groups in Mexico. I found that the IPA group in Mexico was closely related to Lacan's partition from the IPA. One of the founders of the Mexican group was trained in Paris between 1951 and 1952. He went to see Lacan as a potential training analyst and this encounter with Lacan scared the hell out of him. He flew from Lacan's office and went to another analyst as a training analyst. This other training analyst was Michel Cenac, clearly on the other side of the border when the partition took place. The analyst from Mexico remained highly affected by this conflict and critical towards Lacan. When he arrived back in Mexico, everything in the Mexican group was tainted by the Parisian conflict. For several years, they could not even pronounce the name of Lacan. It was actually impossible to say "Lacan." They found ways to walk around Lacan's name: "You know who I mean."

CV: How would you describe the situation in Mexico? Is there a strong psychoanalytic following, or has the American cognitive approach to mental health been established in popularity?

MH: Psychoanalysis seems to go through developments from city to city. For a time, obviously Vienna had a huge movement and then there was London and Budapest and Berlin and New York and Buenos Aires. Mexico is now living through a psychoanalytic moment like this. There is a boom of interest in psychoanalysis. And as a matter of fact, common people not only go to the analyst but are approaching psychoanalysis as a way of living. Psychoanalysis has been able to remain apart from the health system. The health system follows its own path based on mainstream psychiatry. The public health service is organized around psychiatry and psychology. Some psychiatrists and psychologists, however, have become very interested in psychoanalysis, but the health system puts them in a subaltern position. Psychiatrists generally give medication, while psychologists give therapy. This therapy is heavily influenced by psychoanalysis, but it is not recognized as such in any form. Nobody in the health system will call themselves a psychoanalyst. People call themselves psychologists or psychiatrists and they are clear about this. In this sense, psychoanalysis exists outside the institution.

CV: It is as if the institution cannot easily absorb psychoanalysis. How can we account for this?

MH: Psychiatrists generally do not want to know anything about psychoanalysis. They are really not interested. They stick to what they do except for some surprising exceptions. A friend of mine who is the director of one of the main public hospitals in Mexico, for instance, has been in analysis for a long time, follows psychoanalysis very closely, and has taken positions in his institution that concern psychoanalysis but has never, ever tried to teach psychoanalysis or say that "this is psychoanalysis." He lets himself be guided by his experience and knowledge in psychiatry and psychoanalysis and may take positions based on what he has experienced for himself as an analysand and as a reader, but he never speaks openly about this. He sticks to psychiatry. He has an ethical position akin to psychoanalysis but does not speak about this. He knows it would cause too many problems and does not get into a mess. He thus practices a very humane psychiatry, but he is a psychiatrist nonetheless.

I believe psychoanalysts have worked hard enough for psychologists to understand that it is very difficult to mix psychoanalysis and the institution. It is not a good mix. The institution has rules and goals of its own that are different from the requirements of the analytic experience. Psychologists here do things in an institutional way, but when a patient arrives, they are guided by psychoanalysis. They listen carefully, take care of transference, and are subtle and delicate with their patients. I have huge respect for the psychologists in Mexico.

CV: I'd like to ask you a final question about the dream of Irma's injection. This is the now famous dream of Freud. I know you have written a book about this dream. What are your thoughts about this particular dream?

MH: It is probably the dream that is the most commented on in all of history. I found that commentators of this dream drift away from Freud's method. There are so many interpretations of this dream in the literature that one can drown oneself in them. In my book, I try to stick to Freud's method. In my writing, I do not take into consideration anything that is not in Freud's texts or directly linked to the dream itself.

There are three texts where Freud speaks directly about the meaning of this dream. The first text is in the interpretation that Freud gives in *The Interpretation of Dreams*, which is incomplete since he only really provides us with his preconscious wish in this book. One wonders, why is this the most paradigmatic dream when the interpretation provided remains incomplete as it does not at all regard the unconscious wish that Freud was aware of? Freud talks about his unconscious wish in the dream in two other texts, which were not meant to be published. The second text is in *The Project for a Scientific Psychology*, where he speaks about the dream in a very enigmatic way. The third text is in a letter that Freud wrote to Karl Abraham where he clearly says what the dream is about, which is that it is a sexual fantasy about having each of his daughter's three godmothers. He says to Abraham that it is the dream of a sexual megalomaniac who wants to have all of them.[16] My challenge was to make sense of the relation between the three places where Freud talks about the meaning of the dream. I believe the book is successful in that sense, something that no other author has even tried, as they usually stick to one or at the most two of the versions Freud produced of this dream.

CV: It sounds as though you tried to stay carefully with the associations and words of the analysand, Freud in this case, rather than offer a myriad of possible interpretations outside these associations.

MH: Exactly. In my reading of the dream, I also drew upon an indication that Lacan gave about the dream of Irma's injection in Seminar II, which is that Freud's signifier of "trimethylamine" is linked to masculine sexuality and sperm.[17] Freud says clearly in a passage of *The Interpretation of Dreams* that trimethylamine points to his relationship with [Wilhelm] Fleiss and his own research about trimethylamine without naming it as such.

While writing this book, I also gave myself the task of trying to find out who Irma really was. A number of scholars thought that she was Emma Eckstein.[18] She is not. Irma was Anna Hammerschlag. She was the daughter of Freud's former Hebrew teacher, who also became his friend. It was in honor of Anna Hammerschlag that Anna Freud got her name. There are hints here and there. When one puts them together, one can be sure it is not Eckstein. It has to be someone else, and there are clues that point directly to Hammerschlag. Ultimately, I knew when I wrote the book that I was going to be confronted with a moment of truth when the manuscript of Freud's *Project* was to be released finally by the Library of Congress. This was a private document and so the name of the patient was not to be concealed. The name or initials of every other participant in the dream whose identity we know for sure can be found in the original manuscript in Germany. The name of the patient is with the initial A. This finding was a great joy for me.

Notes

1 Anika Rifflet-Lemaire is a psychology graduate of the University of Louvain in Belgium. Her book *Jacques Lacan* was first published in French in 1970 and features a preface written by Lacan. The book has since been translated into Spanish, Italian, and Japanese. David Macey translated the book into English in 1977.

2 *Littoral* was founded in Paris in 1981, and contributors were psychoanalysts Jean Allouch, Philippe Julien, Guy Le Gaufey, Erik Porge and Mayette Viltard. Note the spelling variation of *Litoral*, which is a publisher of psychoanalytic texts in Mexico.

3 Oscar Masotta (1930–1979) was an Argentinian writer and psychoanalyst who helped to introduce the work of Lacan to the Spanish-speaking world.

4 See Eliana Rodrigues Pereira Mendes' "Igor Caruso's presence in Brazil," which provides a brief overview of this analyst's work in the *International Forum of Psychoanalysis*. 23 (2014): 101–103. And Fernando González, Igor Caruso: nazismo y euthanasia, Tusquets Editores y Círculo Psicoanalítico Mexicano, Mexico City, 2015.

5 See Althusser, Louis. *Writings on Psychoanalysis: Freud and Lacan*. Trans. Jeffrey Mehlman. Ed. Olivier Corpet and Francois Matheron. New York: Columbia University Press, 1996.

6 Lacan presented this talk to the Cercle Psychiatrique Henri Ey at the Hôpital Sainte-Anne on November 10, 1967. The paper is also known as "La Psychanalyse et la Formation du Psychiatre" ["Psychoanalysis and the Formation of the Psychiatrist"].

7 In different contexts, it is possible to translate *dispositif* into English as "device," "mechanism," "facility," "apparatus," "measure," or "plan."

8 Rudolph Maurice Loewenstein (1898–1976) was an American psychoanalyst who practiced in France, Germany, and the United States. At the request of Freud, Loewenstein arrived in France to train a new generation of psychoanalysts in 1925 but fled the turmoil of World War II for the United States in 1942. He died in New York City in 1976. He is known as one of the most important theorists of ego psychology.

9 Heinz Hartmann (1894–1970) was a psychiatrist and psychoanalyst who is considered a founder of the field of ego psychology as well as theories on adaptation, conflict, and aggression. Ernst Kris (1900–1957) was an Austrian psychoanalyst and scholar of art history. Kris is known as one of the main founders of ego psychology and was interested in early childhood development.

10 Sándor Ferenczi (1873–1933) was a Hungarian psychoanalyst, a major psychoanalytic theorist who developed influential clinical concepts, and also a close colleague of Freud.

11 Marie Bonaparte (1882–1962) was a great-grandniece of Emperor Napoleon I of France. Upon her marriage to Prince George, she was known as Princess George of Greece and Denmark. She was a French author and psychoanalyst. Sacha Nacht (1901–1977) was a Romanian-born French psychiatrist and psychoanalyst who was an influential member of the Paris Psychoanalytic Society.

12 For more on this legal case, see Weber, Samuel. "Psychoanalysis, Literary Criticism, and the Problem of Authority." *Psychoanalysis and....* Ed. Richard Feldstein and Henry Sussman. New York: Routledge, 1990. 21–32.

13 Tristan Tzara (1896–1963) was a Romanian and French poet, performance artist, and writer who was an important figure in the Dadaist movement. Tzara was interested in symbolism and was an early experimenter of automatist techniques while combining humanist, anti-fascist, and communist influences in his work.

14 Hernandez adds here that "if one studies the work of Oscar Masotta, the Argentinian intellectual who opened up the Lacanian field in Buenos Aires, one sees

something very similar. Masotta was not even in analysis, but he was an intellectual who was in close contact with avant-garde artists in Buenos Aires. Masotta introduced Lacan while employing the strategies of a contemporary artist. He was successful at presenting Lacan to Argentinians in a way that no analyst could ever have done."

15 Marcus Fabius Quintilianus (35–100 CE) was a Roman rhetorician and educator. He is known for *Institutio Oratoria* [*Institutes of Oratory*], a 12-volume text on the theory and practice of rhetoric, which was published around 95 CE.

16 See the letter from Sigmund Freud to Karl Abraham dated on January 9, 1908 in Freud, Sigmund and Karl Abraham. *The Complete Correspondence of Sigmund Freud and Karl Abraham (1907–1925)*. London: Karnac, 2002.

17 See Lacan's discussion of Freud's dream of Irma's injection (pages 146–171) in Lacan, Jacques. *The Seminar of Jacques Lacan, Book II: The Ego in Freud's Theory and in the Technique of Psychoanalysis, 1954–1955*. 1978. Ed. Jacques-Alain Miller. Trans. Sylvana Tomaselli. W.W. Norton & Company, 1991.

18 Emma Eckstein (1865–1924) was an analysand of Freud's and became one of the first female psychoanalysts.

Bibliography and Further Reading

Hernández, Manuel. *El sueño de la inyección a "Irma"*. Mexico: Litoral editores, 2016a.

Hernández, Manuel. *Localización del analista: La formación psicoanalítica de Freud a Lacan* [Location of the analyst: The psychoanalytic training from Freud to Lacan] Mexico: Litoral Editores, 2020.

Hernández, Manuel. *Lacan en México: México en Lacan – Miller y el mundo* [Lacan in Mexico. Mexico in Lacan. Miller and the World]. Mexico: Ediciones Navarra and Anchomundo, 2016b.

Chapter 10

On the Philosophical Heritage of Psychoanalysis with Alireza Taheri

Alireza Taheri, PhD, is a psychoanalytic psychotherapist in private practice in Toronto, Canada. He wrote his dissertation for the University of Cambridge on Nietzsche, Freud, and Lacan. He also holds an MA in philosophy from Essex and an MSc in psychoanalytic thought from University College London (UCL). He has practiced psychoanalytic work in London. His recent book is called *Hegelian–Lacanian Variations on Late Modernity: Spectre of Madness* (Routledge, 2020). This conversation took place at Taheri's office in Toronto on 14 March 2020, only a few days prior to the first province-wide state of emergency in Ontario in response to the coronavirus pandemic.

Chris Vanderwees: Do you recall when you first encountered psychoanalysis?

Alireza Taheri: I do. I am not sure which one was the formative encounter, but one of the earliest encounters was when I was 12 or 13. I might have been in class and somebody mentioned Freud at school. Obviously, I knew the name. We all know the name. This happens a lot in life. You hear something and you know that you know it, but you also know you don't know it. I knew he had something to do with psychology in some big way, but what was this guy's idea? At that age, there was a bit of shame in that I may have assumed everybody else must have known so much more about it. Of course, the other 13-year-olds did not know much more about it than I might have at the time.

My mother studied psychology as a bachelor's degree. Sometimes I would hear things about Freud. She particularly liked Freud, but she never pursued a career in this. It also was not something she talked much about except maybe once in a while. So, I had heard of Freud. One day, I got home and there was a university textbook. I have sisters who are much older and who were already in

DOI: 10.4324/9781003323136-11

university at that time. It was a sociology textbook that must have come from their studies. I opened it up and there was a page on Freud like a dictionary type entry. It explained the theory of the id, ego, and superego. I thought it was interesting, though I could not really understand it that well. The distinction between the id and the other two is a bit easier, whereas the distinction between the ego and superego was harder to grasp. Anyway, I must have gotten something out of it.

This leads me to some idea about Jungian synchronicity because somehow it just seems like Freud was in the air. Some days or weeks later, I was in class and the teacher asked if anyone could explain who Freud was. Through this fluke of the textbook, I had this stuff ready in my mind. So, I raised my hand. I said he was a psychologist or psychoanalyst (I would not have known the difference back then), and I explained his theory of the id, ego, and superego almost as verbatim, making myself look very bright. It was like I presented the transcription. At that time, I was more interested in math or philosophy and had some interest in a range of subjects. This first encounter did lead me to read the little Hans case. This was a bit more interesting because it was out of some semi-puerile, infantile, fascination for the sexual. Once in a while, my mom would mention something about a child's *jouissance* in holding the fecal object and refusing to enter into a relation of defiance with the Other or mother in toilet training. I thought these ideas were very interesting in their counterintuitiveness. I was at the age, maybe a little older, 14 or 15, where shocking ideas pertaining to sexuality are of interest. This experience was not particularly formative but it must have had some impact. Regardless, these were the earliest encounters.

The most formative encounter was when I was in my undergraduate degree. At the end of my studies at the University of Toronto, I found out that they had a psychoanalytic studies program called "Psychoanalytic Thought." It was not its own department but was created out of courses cobbled together from other departments. If you took so many of those courses, you could sum them up to make a minor. I majored in philosophy and had a minor in French literature and psychoanalytic thought.

Of all the things I studied, the psychoanalysis courses became the most interesting and this bled into other courses. In my philosophy and literature classes, I would throw in a little bit of psychoanalysis into the coursework. This was a much more defining encounter with psychoanalysis, mostly Freud. I remember using Lacan in a paper that I wrote about [William] Faulkner's *As I Lay Dying*, but I only really was able to engage with his work indirectly or from a few things I'd heard or read.

I recall that I must have read some Jung here and there. I was at the age where I really didn't know much of psychology. It is a very nebulous field to an outsider. Is it psychiatry? Is it psychology? Even prior to really getting interested in Freud in my undergrad, I was a volunteer at what was then the Clarke Institute [which became the Centre for Mental Health and Addiction in 1998]. It was a program where they would pair you with a patient who lived in the hospital or in a boarding house once they were in a slightly more stable condition. I was paired with a man in his late twenties. We would meet once a week for a couple hours and developed an amicable rapport. I did not know if it was psychiatry that I wanted to study. I knew that I didn't really like medicine and that I was never really interested in the life sciences. This was not an option for me. However, I wondered about psychology or the study psychoanalysis as a theory.

The discovery of the "Psychoanalytic Thought" program coincided with a time of my life where personal struggles also existed. We could label it as anxiety. There was some recognition that I was at the end of my teenage years and into my early twenties, struggling with personal or existential questions. My readings of Freud, particularly "Mourning and Melancholia" and "Instincts and their Vicissitudes," overlapped with this time of my life and struck a personal chord. It became inevitable that this would be part of my life whether or not I became a clinician. I decided to do a master's of philosophy at the University of Essex, knowing that there was a center for psychoanalysis there, but there was always some doubt about becoming a clinician. Doubt is maybe not a bad way to approach a type of career that requires a lot of sacrifice.

CV: When did you feel that you might want to pursue a career as a psychoanalyst?

AT: The idea was always in the back of my mind. After the master's degree in Essex, I thought about doing a PhD in France. I moved to Paris to start a doctorate. I did not like the university system there. You had to be very independent as there was very little help provided. It is a publicly funded education, which is commendable, but there is not much holding you together. My French was good enough to do it, but I would have liked some more *encadrement* as the French say, something like a frame or curriculum. I would sit in a classroom and there was no reading list, no assignments, and no instruction on what to do next. For some people, that works. I would fare well with that now, but at 25 years of age, I needed more guidance. I did the master's in psychoanalysis at University College London, but even then, it was always a maybe in regard to becoming a clinician. The only time the "maybe" turned into "very likely" in my mind was when I really discovered Lacan properly and in a much deeper way. This would have been in my second year as a PhD student at Cambridge. My supervisor at Cambridge was John Forrester, who said, "You really need to get into Lacan for the PhD."[1] So, I did but reluctantly because I was aware of how difficult his work can be to read.

Lacan was once asked about the *Écrits*, "Why do you think it sold so many copies, if nobody really understands it, why do people buy it?" His response was that people may not understand them, but that certainly the text does something to them.[2] This was exactly the case with me. It was the *Écrits* that I was reading, as well as *Seminar I*. I could tell it was doing something. I read the Rome discourse, the famous paper on "The Function and the Field of Language and Speech in Psychoanalysis." I probably understood one or two sentences, but surely it did something and had an effect. I'm not sure what the effect is. There is certainly grandiosity to the language and that is perhaps appealing to the uncastrated part of the mind. I was also reading Nietzsche, whose prose is so grandiose. The very title, "The Rome Discourse," or the "The Function and the Field of Language and Speech in Psychoanalysis," or the quotation from Lichtenberg at the beginning, all have this quality or character.[3] It felt like such a breath of fresh air. I was reading a significant amount of poststructuralists at the time, and here is Lacan using words like "truth" and really making it clear what is at stake with Freud. When you first start reading Lacan, you know that you don't really get it, but you don't not get it either. It triggers thoughts in your mind and it is very different from anything else. It started to fascinate me.

I decided to join the Centre for Freudian Analysis and Research (CFAR) in London. I took their introductory course. I entered their training program and went to their lectures, and I began to think that a hybrid career that could combine the clinical and the academic would be a likely outcome, but still not without some apprehensiveness or hesitation.

CV: You mentioned working with John Forrester. Did he have an influence on your writing and thinking?

AT: When I finished my master's at UCL, I was at a juncture that was radical. Did I want to be an academic? Did I want to be a clinician? Did I want either of these things? I had two master's at the time. I did not particularly want to do a PhD, but I did quite well at UCL, and one of the professors there took some time to speak with me and congratulate me. She suggested to me that I might really enjoy doing a PhD at Cambridge with John Forrester since I seemed to have this budding interest in Lacan. I looked into it. I thought, "I'll apply for Cambridge and Forrester – if I get in, I'll think about it." I didn't apply anywhere else. I was too apprehensive of a PhD being another four or five years. It is a big commitment, a life-altering experience for many people. I got in with a full scholarship and so I was able to go and live rather comfortably while studying.

Working with John Forrester was very interesting. He was a historian. He wrote a great work about the beginnings of psychoanalysis, which was called *Language and the Origins of Psychoanalysis*, an important book for me.[4] He always gave helpful suggestions for reading and urged me to pick up Lacan. He said, "This is central." He also had another important influence in that he pulled me out of the Lacanian discourse. He noticed that with the chapters I was submitting, it was becoming more and more Lacanian. My dissertation was about Freud, Nietzsche, and Lacan. The bits I was sending him about Lacan became very Lacanian. I was forgetting about Freud and Nietzsche. He wrote to me to say, I remember his sentence, "It would be very sad if you wrote a PhD just on Lacan." I remember it was almost like a castration, but in a good sense. He separated me from *das Ding*, this object of fascination and *jouissance*, this extreme transference that was more than transference. It became a bit of an erotomanic relation that I developed with Lacan. He said, "You have done good work with Freud and Nietzsche, and the PhD will be more interesting if you include a variety of thinkers." I had a mixture of disappointment and relief in hearing that. Castration is always a mixture like this. It's like a love affair that you are being told needs to be more reasonable. I went back into those texts, made the dissertation more balanced, and finished. This was the gift from John Forrester; he taught me to not let my thinking get monopolized by one author.

If we look at Melanie Klein's thinking, she brings up splitting, idealization. In her language, there is something paranoid/schizoid about that type of one-sidedness. Of course, one-sidedness is a word that constantly reappears in [G.W.F.] Hegel. As a thinker, sometimes one needs to be one-sided, but this cannot be the constant state of mind. You'd be missing half, or in Hegelese, you'd be missing an important moment of the concept. A concept ceases to be a concept when it is one-sided. It becomes akin to paranoia. It has its place, let's say, in the ideological spreading of an idea, when ideas become practical or militant. I do not think that thinking can strive if it is always in this state. This was the lesson I got from John: you cannot have Lacan without Freud or Freud without Nietzsche.

People sometimes get surprised at the link between Lacan and Nietzsche, but this should not be particularly surprising. Lacan credits Freud for discovering *jouissance*, but I think Nietzsche discovered it. The whole point of the third essay of *A Genealogy of Morals* involves a question regarding the meaning of ascetic ideals. For Nietzsche, the answer consists of suffering and joy: *jouissance*. He talks about the lasciviousness of the ascetic and how what seems like an act of renunciation in ascetic ideals actually involves the rapture of *jouissance*. Renouncing the drives is an even deeper immersion into *jouissance*. Nietzsche is an expert of *jouissance*. He can smell the other's *jouissance*. I use the word "smell" purposefully because Nietzsche joked that his genius lies in his nostrils.[5] The idea that *jouissance* could have a smell is a very interesting notion. It could be putrid on one side and delicious on the other.

CV: This reminds me of the "fragrance of the world spirit."

AT: Yes! This is a great quotation from Hegel in the *Philosophy of Right*.[6] Something that I realized over the years is just to what extent Hegel was proto-Lacanian. Of course, this is something that Slavoj Žižek has built the foundation of his teaching and writing upon.

What is interesting for me in Freudian and Lacanian psychoanalysis is the theorization of conflict. Additionally, I have been very interested in the work of Melanie Klein because she is also a theorist of conflict, oppositions, and contradictions. I consider there to be a dual inheritance of psychoanalysis where one side could be seen as Nietzschean and the other side as Hegelian. The Ljubljana school really highlights the Hegelian to the detriment of the Nietzschean.[7] Even Lacan's few remarks about Nietzsche are usually flippant and dismissive. I find this to also be the case in Žižek. Now, Alenka Zupančič wrote a book on Nietzsche, but she makes him out to be far too much of a Lacanian.[8] I would say rather that Nietzsche has a proto-psychoanalytic mind. The notion of the symptom is often credited to Karl Marx. There is truth to that, but one could also look to Hegel and obviously to Freud. There is, however, an incredible passage in Nietzsche's *Beyond Good & Evil* in paragraph 32, where he traces the evolution of morality. It is a fascinating passage. He says that, early on, the worth of an act was judged by its consequence. If a good thing outcome arose, that means you did a good thing. If a bad thing came about, you did a bad thing. Nietzsche says that morality became more sophisticated when the intention was taken into consideration rather than the outcome. A bad outcome may arise but if it was established you were well-meaning, you were pardoned. In the case of a good outcome that accidentally arose from a bad intention, you would not be given credit. He says we have to overcome and go beyond these two ways of basing our moral judgment of valuing or evaluating an action. Nietzsche says that an action or an idea is really a symptom. He actually uses this word: symptom.[9] It is a symptom that is so much more complex and is the outcome of so many different things. You also find the idea of overdetermination in this evolution of morality towards the most sophisticated form where the act is understood as a symptom. This is incredibly proto-psychoanalytic.

Freud also understood this. He had an anxiety of influence, avoiding to read Nietzsche out of fear that he would find his own ideas there. Freud says famously that Nietzsche was a man who knew himself very profoundly or that Nietzsche knew what took him years of clinical practice to discover. In *The Genealogy of Psychoanalysis*, Michel Henry traces a Nietzschean origin to psychoanalysis.[10] Of course, Žižek traces a Hegelian origin. Both of these origins are undeniable. Something that I talk about in my recently completed book is that we need both the Nietzschean and the Hegelian heritage of psychoanalysis – that is, if psychoanalysis is going to help us really kill God. I mean this in the sense of the twilight of the idols that still burden us in modernity. What Giorgio Agamben reminds us is that modernity is still theological. Capitalism, for instance, has many archaic religious remnants. Our modernity is not fully secular.

What makes Nietzsche so essential is his incredible use of profanity. We see such profanations in Nietzsche's *The Antichrist* – what a title! In *Twilight of the Idols*, there is also a critical passage where Nietzsche begins to emphasize the ugliness of Socrates, of whom he says, in Latin, *monstrum in fronte, monstrum in animo*, which means "monster in the face, monster in the soul." The full title of the book is actually *Twilight of the Idols, or, How to Philosophize with a Hammer*. Nietzsche would write these sorts of profanations against Western civilization. There is something in his confidence to write *ad hominem*. If we absolve that and resort only to this Hegelian dialectical thinking, we lose something. Žižek is the great heir to the German dialectical tradition and has rewritten psychoanalysis in a dialectical way. What I admire most about Žižek are his own profanations. He has a Nietzschean side to him at least at the level of form despite his general disdain for Nietzsche. They have very different styles, I know, but it is Žižek's joking and his transgressiveness that remind me of Nietzsche. There is a certain profanation there that is important in order to guarantee our emancipation from the theological remnant of modernity.

Why are we not able to become modern? Why is the regression to the premodern so powerful? I would like to explore these questions. Žižek has said that he "corrupts the youth," but corrupts them into what? I would say that he is corrupting the youth into becoming modern. There is a huge temptation to the premodern today and towards religiousness, spirituality, and Jungianism. Jung has some deep clinical insights, but there is a premodern core to his thinking. Along with other critiques of capitalism, Žižek is a powerful force in reminding us of the importance of the enlightenment project. He reminds us of the importance to not assume we live in a post-secular world. We have established something with the great atheisms of the nineteenth century of which Nietzsche is a huge part. This is where the Ljubljana school has influenced me the most, but this school does not emphasize just how important Nietzsche is as someone who has helped to free us from the clutches of the bad side of Christian morality. Through Nietzsche, we ask, to play with a Brechtian sentence: what is evil against the good in comparison to the evil that is the good.[11] In this sense, Nietzsche taught that the Christian good is an evil. There is a radical dialectical shift here. In *On the Genealogy of Morals*, Nietzsche describes Christian love as just an outgrowth of priestly hate. He calls it Jewish hate, the hate of the romans, or *ressentiment*. There is a form of the good that is dialectically much closer to its opposite than to what it claims to be. We owe something to Nietzsche, who suffered probably more than anybody else from this sort of hypocrisy. Nietzsche said that "[o]ne not only wants to be understood when one writes, but also – quite as certainly – not to be understood" (*The Gay Science* 195).[12] He would hate to think someone understood him, because this would mean that this person would have suffered as he has. This is a saintly sentiment. I do not want to give a hagiography of Nietzsche, but he did truly suffer for what he taught. Those who read Nietzsche and derive something from it may have experienced something of the falsity of the good that is just a mask.

For me, the psychoanalytic heritage of Nietzsche is very important. Nietzsche's profanations carry the work of the death drive. I think we can see that what is essential in the death drive is that it breaks us from the bond of the theological. This is one of the problems that I have with Alain Badiou, one of the great philosophical thinkers of our time. I cannot claim to understand the whole corpus of Badiou's thinking, but I find that in Badiou there is an absence of the appreciation for the death drive. Nietzsche is almost a thinker of the pure culture of the death drive. It is a sacrifice. Nietzsche lived a life of solitude and loneliness. He is not a happy person. Happiness has no place for someone who chooses such a life path.

CV: This heritage of psychoanalysis is very interesting to consider. You have spoken about Nietzsche, but [Arthur] Schopenhauer also comes to mind in respect to the death drive. I also think of the Lacanian analysts who later become fascinated with the work of the Marquis de Sade, who wrote many sorts of texts, including philosophical treatises. If we look at a North American context of psychoanalysis, there appears to be a disconnection from this philosophical heritage. In American psychoanalysis, we have a more medicalized version of the clinic, which is much less philosophical and much less based in the humanities in general. Here, analysis becomes more connected to medical categorization, personality types, and the assessment of symptoms. How does philosophy flow into the clinic for you or perhaps how does the clinic flow back to your philosophical thinking?

AT: The first thought I had was about my psychotic patients. Every psychotic person is a kind of philosopher. Perhaps the psychotic is a person who suffers from philosophy or suffers from life and philosophy becomes the cure. Philosophy is a very ambiguous *sinthome*. It is painful but also a relief. It is a sword that kills and heals. It can be very difficult to know in certain cases which it will be. In the last chapter of my book, I actually discuss philosophy as "the path of despair," which is what Hegel called it. Of course, despair is a reference to Christ carrying the cross towards his own crucifixion.

CV: How to do philosophy with a hammer.

AT: Yes, this is a very interesting connection. I had in mind the more obvious breaking of the idols, but there is also this connection to the crucifixion. Nietzsche also has the *Die fröhliche Wissenschaft* – that is, the "gay science." On the one hand, we have this "joyful wisdom," which is an alternative way to translate Nietzsche's phrase, and on the other hand, we have *Via Dolorosa*, the path or highway of despair, as Hegel calls it. I would argue that the philosophy of despair and the joyful wisdom are two philosophical sides of the same Möbius strip. True philosophical joy is inseparable from philosophical despair. Anything other than this dialectical unity is just tomfoolery or empty happiness. Tomfoolery has its place. Many people choose the path of "happiness." There are a lot of easy recipes for that, and a lot of psychology books are just about that: have good sleep hygiene, eat well, have relationships that are not too passionate and not too sterile, maintain a certain regiment of exercise, make a bit of money, incorporate a bit of love into it, some leisure. This is the contemporary culture of hedonism. I do not think that true joy can be found there, but a person may also not suffer from despair.

More to your question, this really comes into play with the psychotic person since they do not even really have a choice. The life of empty tomfoolery is barred in the psychotic structure. I have not had a psychotic patient who even thinks this is a possibility for them or would even want it. It is a life way too saturated with semblance for a psychotic person to bear the volume of lies that such a life requires. The psychotic does not have to choose. The path of despair or joyful wisdom is already set out for him or her. I work philosophically with my psychotic patients. Of course, the patient is the philosopher and I am the student. This is the reversal or inversion of the transference that Lacan insisted upon. The analyst becomes a secretary to the teacher. I have learned deep philosophical lessons from psychotic patients.

I had a patient once who was a young psychotic man. He was very intelligent and not necessarily interested in the field of philosophy, but he was very philosophical. He made some very interesting remarks and developed his own line of thinking to help himself cope with life and make it bearable, but not at the price of lies. This is the rigor of the psychotic. The psychotic person cannot accept to live a life of lies for the sake of a modicum of happiness. Contrary to popular understanding, this is the great power of the psychotic mind. The psychotic mind has an attunement to philosophy.

The psychotic person can be all too aware of the falsity of the social other, all too aware of the lies and inconsistencies. Of course, as analysts and therapists, we are not there to have people become fools like the rest of humanity. Maybe we can help people suffer less, help people find a way to do something about it, or to live with it. What is really philosophical about psychosis is the attunement to the flaw of language and the social. As soon as I have a psychotic person in treatment, I think that I may have a philosophical partner. It might be a Platonic dialogue over years. I think this can be very curative if one is able to leave the patient in the driver's seat except that we are the ones in transference love and they are not. We must also not take their need to be in the driver's seat as some narcissism that we need to castrate them from. Lacan said very well that for a psychotic person the condition of entering discourse is entering it as master; otherwise, the person may be subject to massive fragmentation. This is something to respect. We must listen to the person. I have found some people can be quite receptive to some helpful suggestions.

The so-called "narcissism of the psychotic" is such a misunderstanding of psychosis. What Lacan always insisted on was respect for the psychotic's knowledge. The person has a knowledge and it is often very interesting. You have to show respect and curiosity. The person will come and benefit from speaking. When working with psychosis, you are the secretary of the alienated. It says much about the clinician's narcissism not to be able to handle the inversion of the transference.

The psychotic is not in transference to the clinician like the neurotic. Of course, the psychotic person is not in transference to the clinician. The person is in transference to the body of knowledge that they have themselves. You are supposed to be in transference to that as well. All you can do is help them solve some of the persecutory elements of that relation to their knowledge that they have. This could simply be some editorial work. They psychotic person is the creator. You are an editor of their work. This can have very good effects.

To return to your question, the clinical work with psychosis resonates very much with philosophy. Often the psychotic person comes with knowledge, thinking, and philosophy while looking for someone to be interested in it rather than dismiss it as insanity. Some people will say to the psychotic person, "Leave that stuff alone, it will make you sick." It could make you sick, but it could also cure you. I think philosophers tread on this Möbius strip. It is a harder life than the hedonistic life. Hedonism and philosophy do not go together. Hedonism is tomfoolery and maybe happiness, but there is no philosophical joy in this path. The psychotic person is impervious to the charms of bourgeois happiness, to put it in a Marxist way.

CV: I also wanted to ask more about your book. How would you describe your premise?

AT: There are a number of premises. It is a book about Lacan and Hegel. I combine these thinkers in a rather personal and different way. Of the contemporary thinkers, Žižek is the most influential here that I draw upon. One of the premises could be this: Hegel treats concepts as people. For Hegel, he writes about a notion and treats it almost as if it were a person. And then I thought of Lacan, who treats people as if they were notions. I saw this parallel where people and notions are somewhat equivalent. Humans are signifiers or are between signifiers. On this basis, I developed a Lacano-Hegelian dialectical theory of my own. What started the book was the realization that all of these contradictions are at work in Lacan. I was reading a French Lacanian, François Balmès, who has passed but wrote some very great books. For every sentence by Lacan, Balmès suggested that one could also find the opposite claim. This is almost true. A lot of Lacan's claims are kind of contradictory. In Hegelian language, we could say these are speculative propositions, meaning propositions that are contradictory.

Here is the ultimate Hegelian idea. [Immanuel] Kant makes a distinction between analytic and synthetic judgments. An analytic judgment is when the subject is included in the predicate and so nothing new is given: "All dogs are animals." This does not tell us anything new about the canine species. The subject is included in the predicate. A synthetic judgment might be something like, "All dogs carry a virus of a certain type." This gives us something new. Hegel's point was that all propositions, no matter how much they sound analytic, are synthetic because of the inner split of the thing. This is what makes Hegel proto-psychoanalytic or proto-Freudian. Nothing you can say about a thing is ever included in itself, because it is itself always already a divided thing. With this idea mixed with Balmès, I started realizing that psychoanalysis finds all these interesting paradoxes. Let us take an example from Hegel: "Atheism is best achieved by Christianity." Here, we have a bit of a paradox where Christianity gives us atheism. True faith, for instance, is also embedded in doubt.

In psychoanalysis, we find that a lie is much more a truth than just some factually true statement. A lie tells much more about the intimate truth of a person. What are they lying about? Why are they lying? Lacan says that truth only comes out in the structure of fiction. Truth and fiction as well as truth and lies are in a dialectical relation. There is also life and death. In a chapter of my book where I am critically engaged with Badiou, I suggest that you can only truly be living life when you are conscious of mortality. It is only at the moment that you realize, "Whoa, this is a transient, short, ending thing." Badiou keeps talking about death as external to life and says that we do not have a representation of it. Of course, we already know this from Freud. Death is something that hits life from the outside. It is not something intrinsic to life in the way [Martin] Heidegger thought of the notion of being towards death. All of this may be true, but it is only when you encounter it in some form in its externality that your life starts to have meaning. "Oh my god, people die. I always kind of knew it, but now I know it." With the coronavirus, this might be an important moment in human history. Mortality is not something that happens to some people somewhere else, but it happens to everybody. We all die. It is only through the recognition of the radical finitude of life that life becomes infinite. Badiou is wrapped up, and I commend him for this, in infinity and the infinite potential of the subject, but he does not assert enough or at all how that finitude is in a dialectical relation to finitude. Only the death drive opens the way to immortality. It is only the moment when you put something above life, when you deny life, that life becomes of infinite importance. Perhaps it is the moment you decide to be a Marxist activist. Maybe it is more than an act of sacrifice where you make this idea of justice or equality higher than your own life. It is at this point that your life becomes of infinite importance. There is the old Latin saying, *fiat iustitia, et pereat mundus*, "let justice be done, though the world perish." This expression only works if the immortal or eternal idea of justice hinges on the notion of perishability of life.

Throughout the book, I am constantly looking at different paradoxes that the mind is, as Hegel said, incapable of appreciating. The common mind in its everydayness is incapable of appreciating the dialectical unity of truth and lies, life and death, faith and atheism, reason and irrationality. One of the central ideas for the book is that the symptom is not a form of irrationality. The symptom is the height of rationality. If a person has a symptom, the person may see or others may see it through their common understanding as a normative craziness. "Why does that person avoid stepping on cracks in the street?" When you look at this, perhaps it is the person's way of keeping ego boundaries, of creating the function of the law. Like the delusion, the symptom could be understood as a form of hyperrationality.

In the book, I am finding these dialectical pairs to reveal paradoxes. What I show is that when these paradoxes are not recognized, when we split or keep to the stringent opposition to truth and lie where a truth is a truth and a lie is a lie, for instance, this splitting is what I call "diremption." Diremption is a word that means to separate. I oppose diremption to notions of sublation or speculation or self-reflection, which are Hegelian terms for when a notion is united with its opposite, and in uniting with its opposite, the notion becomes what it truly is. Truth is only truly truth when it is wedded with fiction. When a child asks you how babies are made, you could tell the scientific truth of it, but if you tell a story that may be more fictitious, such a story may be more alive and may get at the kernel of the real curiosity that the child has, which may be something to do with the coupling of the parents. The splitting of opposites, the inability to fathom their dialectical unity, I call this the work of diremption. I look at what happens when we dirempt, what happens when we sever notions from their opposite. I look at the vicissitudes of diremption. When a diremption occurs, it may lead to greater impasses and contradictions rather than being fruitful. If we dirempt the dialectical opposite of life and death, for instance, life that is not wedded to the death drive becomes a meaningless happiness. It is only when death is a part of life that there is meaning.

Truths that are effective analytically are often ones that have a fictitious structure. Maybe truth arrives in the form of a play on the signifier or through a little humor. Truth does not arrive through teaching the patient about psychoanalytic theory, even though what might be taught may be "accurate" or "scientific." Such teaching has no bearing in terms of what is intimate for the subject.

Why does this severing or diremption occur? Well, I develop a type of dialectical theory in the spirit of Hegel and Lacan. It is a rather simple theory. I apply my theory to various different cases and reflect on philosophy and what it is at the end of the book. The theory becomes a kind of tool to analyze the oppositions. The book has many variations where I begin to develop this theory. I like music, which was what inspired the format of the book. I consider the way in which diremption is so much a part of our contemporary situation and the types of consequences it has today.

I also look at the dialectic between sanity and insanity, which is not really appreciated well enough by non-psychoanalytic thinkers. With psychoanalysis, we are all mad and caught between this dialectical pair. American psychiatry does not see this and understands insanity as a kind of irrationality that should be abolished. I think that psychoanalysis looks at the symptom as the most rational, the hyperrational. The symptom becomes our guide toward the truth of the subject. In pathologizing the symptom in such a way, one is robbing the subject of what could be most special.

CV: American psychologists and psychiatrists are operating at the level of a fiction of normality.

AT: In fact, normality is precisely the irrational part for us. What is a greater assault to sanity than sanity itself? It is an insane idea, wanting to be sane.

CV: From what you have said, I am also reminded of Lacan's insistence on the statement, "I'm lying to you." There is a paradox contained in such a statement. Is the person telling the truth about the lie in the moment of the utterance? Or is the person telling a new lie about the truth? Also, there is a statement that Lacan makes: "You're right to believe you will die. It sustains you. If you didn't believe it, could you bear the life that you have?"[13]

AT: This is a beautiful statement. Again, the fact that we cannot represent death is what gives life its meaning. In philosophy, there is an opposition between Kant's philosophy of finitude and Hegel's speculative philosophy of infinitude. Badiou perhaps makes too much of this opposition, but this opposition fails to appreciate that the infinite can only be recognized through appreciation of the finitude of life. This leads to another topic of my book. I suggest that the true opposition between Kant and Hegel is not really an opposition. Hegel takes Kant one step further toward a slight parallax shift. Hegel does not abolish Kant's philosophy of finitude, but simply draws a conclusion from it. I believe this is how Žižek conceptualizes the relationship between Kant and Hegel. Žižek relies on both thinkers for his own philosophy. Badiou, however, opposes Kant and Hegel. He dirempts Kant and Hegel, their philosophies, as if a radical abyss separates the philosopher of finitude and the philosopher of infinitude. You cannot have Hegel without Kant. To quip [Isaac] Newton, if Hegel saw anything, it is because he sat on the shoulder of a giant, which was Kant. Hegel is no less of a giant, but this is a shift, not an opposite. Kant posited a noumenal and a phenomenal realm, keeping the dualism. All Hegel suggested, to put it in Lacanese, was that the noumenal and phenomenal are two sides of the same Möbius strip. There is no need to hypostasize them as separate realms.

My references to the Möbius strip may also give you a sense that I am speaking about topology in the book. Topologies of Lacan are highly paradoxical objects. A surface with one side is totally paradoxical. The Klein bottle is also a surface with a torsion that does not have another side that is opposed to it. These surfaces only have another side that is the same side. This is what makes these surfaces very Hegelian, as they embody the paradox of being. Lacan was adamant that these objects were not metaphors but rather the thing itself. Hegel made very similar claims. After Hegel, what became most interesting to thinkers was his anthropological work while they ignored something of his ontological works. Žižek has asserted that Hegel's ontology is very important and has aligned Hegel's ontology and paradoxes with quantum mechanics. Žižek shows that Hegel was a forerunner of the quantum mechanics revolution. Hegel with his speculative philosophy and Lacan with his topology both view these things as attributes of the Real, not just human anthropomorphisms. The finite natural world is plagued by contradiction.

CV: Just a little bit earlier, you mentioned music. I wondered if you had any thoughts about music in the clinic. What I am thinking about is the sound of speech. There are pauses, silences. Do you have thoughts about the significance of the musicality of the clinic?

AT: What is very interesting for me here is the idea of *lalangue*, where language and sonority are indistinguishable. Words are enmeshed with one another. Mozart said that the most important notes are the silences. There is one beautiful fantasy that Mozart wrote, one of the fewer pieces he wrote in a minor key. His work is mostly written in a major key. This piece starts with an arpeggio and goes for a few seconds and then there is silence for a few seconds, depending on the pace at which you play. There is a silence. I find this silence to be one of the most beautiful silences in the history of music. It is an incredible silence without which that next note is just not at all what it is. It is almost like an interpretation that allows you to understand what the next note is and what the previous note was about. The silence links these notes together so well.

I wrote a paper on Ingmar Bergman's *Persona* (1966) called "Serpentine Conceptual Autophagia." It refers to a snake eating its own tail. I explore how the concept eats itself up. The reference is partly to counterpointal music in the Baroque era. The unconscious has a counterpoint form where various voices strive for expression. There is a manic, primary process feel to the unconscious. Counterpoint has a maddening quality. Where is the melody? Patients will say, "I just say whatever? I do not know where to start – there are so many voices." This is the counterpoint. The voices are vying for expression. Ingmar Bergman actually studied Bach. It would be very interesting to study in what way *Persona* is like a fugue. His other film, *The Silence*, makes explicit references to Bach. For Schopenhauer, who you brought up, music was the prime expression of what he called "will" beyond representation. It is an interesting idea: music as a non-representational form of art.

CV: Did Nietzsche not also have a close relationship with [Richard] Wagner?

AT: They were very close friends. Nietzsche's first book was written for Wagner, which is called *The Birth of Tragedy Out of the Spirit of Music*. This is the full title. It was written as a celebration of the Wagnerian opera as heir to the Greek tragedy. This book was extremely influenced by Schopenhauer's idea that music has a privileged place. Wagner was also Schopenhauerian. Some say Wagner wrote more philosophy than music. Nietzsche was very interested early on in both Wagner and Schopenhauer but moves away from both of them. One of the last books Nietzsche wrote, for instance, was called *Nietzsche Contra Wagner*. He gave up the metaphysical idea of the will and gave up the privileged place that music had. Nietzsche was a pianist, a composer, and wrote great music. His music is very nice, harmonic, and melodious. He eventually mocks Schopenhauer for thinking that the musician is the ventriloquist of God.

CV: I wonder where Freud would have found music in analysis. [Jean-Martin] Charcot, for instance, objectifies the patients in the Salpêtrière hospital with all of the photography, all of the looking at the hysterics. Basically, Freud makes a shift from this looking at the patient to listening to the patient.

AT: This is like going from representation to will. For psychoanalysis, the question revolves around a speech that is closer to the will. As Lacan mentions in *Seminar XI*, perhaps this is because we can close our eyes but not our ears. He says that the invocatory drive is much closer to the experience of the unconscious than the experience of the scopic. This is why Freud blocks the scopic with the couch. The gaze of the analyst is still there, but the patient cannot control it. I really like your point about this shift from images to listening. I think this is where [Michel] Foucault errs in his history of madness where he argues that Western philosophy closed its ears to the sovereign speech of the madman. He enlists Freud among those who, like [René] Descartes, throw out the madman's speech. Freud, however, read [Daniel Paul] Schreber's memoir and took it seriously. Eric Santner wrote a wonderful book, *My Own Private Germany* (1996), where he takes Schreber's memoir as a testament to the decline of the symbolic order. I thought that it is so interesting to take the madman's speech seriously. Freud often said that Schreber's book is identical to his own libido theory. Lacan completes this and shows us that the madman develops a system of knowledge, a great theory. Eric Santner takes it further and asks, "What is Schreber really telling us here?" For Santner, Schreber provides us with insight concerning the decline of trust in authority in the modern world. In Santner's words, Schreber warns us of the modern decline in symbolic investiture.

Where is the capacity to listen? Freud was a genius in this regard. He took seriously all that people considered to be nonsense at the time. You are going to pay attention to dreams? You are going to pay attention to jokes, to slips of the tongue? What a gamble! He could have been remembered in his time as the guy who was preoccupied with stupidity. He realized that the hyper-rational parts of a person are the stupidities:

dreams, symptoms, unconscious formations, slips of the tongue. You are a famed neurologist, well known at the time, but you are going to leave that all aside and write a book about everyday errors. How daring? It is remarkable. This is the Hegelian moment where the inane and the everyday become the greatest form of insight. A remarkable and hitherto unexpected identity of opposites.

Badiou, for instance, always sees the subject in grand things like art, science, love, and politics. However, subjectivity is in the seemingly stupid things. What I think Badiou is not capable of achieving is finding the symptom in the everyday. The event is everywhere and nowhere at the same time. The symptom is the moment in which the organism is derailed and goes crazy. Every human being is a subject. Badiou has a horrible distinction where the "individual" is outside of the "event" and therefore lives a life of simplicity and the "subject" is tied to the four events. My view is that every human is a subject who struggles with this ethos of trying to be human. If you allow me the tautology, I would say that *the essence of the human is the human.* The subject and predicate here are very different. One is grand and one is everyday. Something as thin as the eyelid separates a common man from the great film director. Once your eyelids fall, there is the possibility of a great invention, something pregnant with meaning, which may even summarize the agony and destiny of a life. This is the primary process. Badiou betrays his own laudable and commendable project of universalism when he splits humans into those who are and are not participants of subjectivity. We are all similar in the fact that we are singular and stuck with a destiny that is entirely our own.

Notes

1 John Forrester (1949–2015) was a British historian and philosopher of psychoanalysis who wrote many influential books and translated Lacan's first two seminars into English.
2 Lacan expresses a similar remark in *The Triumph of Religion preceded by The Discourse to the Catholics*: "What I have noticed, however, is that, even if people don't understand my *Écrits*, the latter do something to people. I have often observed this. People don't understand anything, that is perfectly true, for a while, but the writings do something to them. And this is why I would be inclined to believe that – as opposed to what one imagines when one peers in from the outside – people do read them. One imagines that people buy my Écrits but never open them. That is false. They open them and they even work on them. They even wear themselves out working on them. Obviously, when one begins my Écrits, the best thing one can do is to try to understand them. And since one does not understand them, one keeps trying. I didn't deliberately try to make them such that people don't understand them – that was a consequence of circumstance. I spoke, I gave classes that were very coherent and comprehensible, but, as I turned them into articles only once a year, that led to writings which, compared to the mass of things I had said, were incredibly concentrated and that must be placed in water,

like Japanese flowers, in order to unfold. The comparison is worth whatever it's worth" (69–70).

3 Georg Christoph Lichtenberg (1742–1799) was a German physicist and satirist whose many witticisms and paradoxes were an inspiration to both Freud and Lacan.

4 See Forrester (1980).

5 Nietzsche (1844–1900) writes in *Ecce Homo*, "*Revaluation of all Values*: that is my formula for an act of supreme self-examination on the part of humanity, become flesh and genius in me. It is my fate that I have to be the first *decent* human being; that I know myself to stand in opposition to the mendaciousness of millennia – I was the first to discover the truth by being the first to experience lies as lies – smelling them out – My genius is in my nostrils" (326).

6 G.W.F. Hegel writes in *The Philosophy of Right*, "even if the youth have to be educated in solitude, it is still useless to hope that the fragrance of the world of spirit will not ultimately waft into the solitude or that the might of world spirit is too weak to take power in those outlying regions" (153).

7 The Ljubljana School of Psychoanalysis was founded in the 1970s by Slovenian followers of Lacan's work in what was Yugoslavia at the time. The school brings together thinking from the traditions of German idealism, Marxism, and psychoanalysis in order to analyze social, political, cultural phenomena and to draw upon Lacan's work in order to produce critiques of contemporary structures of ideology and power.

8 Zupančič, Alenka. *The Shortest Shadow: Nietzsche's Philosophy of the Two*. Cambridge, MA: MIT Press, 2003.

9 Nietzsche writes: "In short, we believe that the intention is only a sign and symptom that first needs to be interpreted, and that, moreover, it is a sign that means too many things and consequently means almost nothing by itself" (*Beyond* 33).

10 Henry, Michel. *The Genealogy of Psychoanalysis*. Stanford: Stanford University Press, 1993.

11 Brecht famously asked, "what is the robbing of a bank compared to the founding of a bank". While the former is the small crime of an amateur, the latter is the work of professionals.

12 Taheri raises the question of Nietzsche's rhetorical style, which is perhaps also interesting to consider in the context of Lacan's style during his seminars: "One not only wants to be understood when one writes, but also – quite as certainly – not to be understood. It is by no means an objection to a book when someone finds it unintelligible: perhaps this might just have been the intention of its author – perhaps he did not want to be understood by 'anyone.' A distinguished intellect and taste, when it wants to communicate its thoughts, always selects its hearers; by selecting them, it at the same time closes its barriers against 'the others.' It is there that all the more refined laws of style have their origin: they at the same time keep off, they create distance, they prevent 'access'" (*The Gay Science* 195).

13 See Lacan, Jacques. "*Conférence de Louvain suivie d'un entretien avec* Françoise Wolff." *Jacques Lacan parle* (October 13, 1972).

Bibliography and Further Reading

Costas, Jane and Alireza Taheri. "'The Return of the Primal Father' in Postmodernity? A Lacanian Analysis of Authentic Leadership." *Organization Studies*. 33.9 (2012): 1195–1216.

Forrester, John. *Language and the Origins of Psychoanalysis*. London: MacMillan, 1980.

Hegel, G.W.F. *The Philosophy of Right*. Trans. Alan White. Indianapolis: Hackett, 2002.

Lacan, Jacques. *The Triumph of Religion preceded by The Discourse to the Catholics*. Trans. Bruce Fink. Cambridge, UK: Polity Press, 2013.

Nietzsche, Friedrich. *Beyond Good and Evil*. Ed. Rolf-Peter Horstmann and Judith Norman. Trans. Judith Norman. Cambridge, UK: Cambridge University Press, 2002.

Nietzsche, Friedrich. "Ecce Homo." *On the Genealogy of Morals and Ecce Homo*. Ed. and Trans. Walter Kaufmann. New York: Vintage Books, 1967.

Nietzsche, Friedrich. *The Gay Science*. Trans. Thomas Common. New York: Dover, 2006.

Taheri, Alireza. (2019). "Breaking the Spell of the Slave Revolt in Morality: From the Subreption of Identity-in-Difference to the Repetition of the Paraconsistent." *On Psychoanalysis and Violence: Contemporary Lacanian Perspectives*. Ed. Vanessa Sinclair and Manya Steinkoler. New York: Routledge, 183–199.

Appendix I

Transmission, Affiliation, and the Psychoanalytic Institution

Meeting with François Peraldi*

Conversation by Marie Hazan (Translation by Chris Vanderwees)

> "It's like a love story that ends. You go your way and I go mine."
>
> François Peraldi, February 24, 1993

I François Peraldi

Spring 1992. We had lunch at his place. François Peraldi had prepared a hearty and nourishing meal "which holds to the body," in a word, maternal... He liked to receive, to invite, to share good food and to offer it, at home and in a restaurant. We were talking about the family history he was writing, and I told him about my run-ins with the "counter-transference" of a Parisian analyst. He listened intently and, with his big laugh, said to me: "It gives you an idea of the transference you are creating," adding that I reminded him in a way of [Françoise] Dolto – "her good side!" – and that he himself had sometimes been tempted to talk to me. That day, for the first time, I felt great ease, and the inhibition that still came over me sometimes in his presence – though rarely – flew away. His response, very gratifying, sounded like a recognition, the promise of a different relationship, barely veiling something of his request, of a word in pain about his withdrawal from the Montréal, but also American and Parisian, psychoanalytic scene, but he did not say more. I thought we had some time ahead of us... He was still full of life, his big laugh echoed in his dining room, and a sort of detachment from his situation and his body seemed to give him a certain lightness...

Faithful to this word, I will therefore speak first of the transference he sparked in me. The first time I heard about François Peraldi was shortly after my arrival in Québec in 1979 at a conference organized at UQAM [Université du Québec à Montréal] by the Department of Literary Studies. He spoke up, intervening in a flamboyant and lampoonist manner, a style that would become familiar to me.

---

* Translated from the original with permission: Hazan, Marie. "Transmission, filiation et institution psychanalytique: recontre avec François Peraldi." *Filigrane*. 3 (1994): 135–161.

He then elicited immediate transference reactions in me. In trying to untangle them in the aftermath, it seems to me that they contained the germ of the elements that would constitute the web of the relational fabric that was built between us over the years that followed:

- A fascination for his thinking and for this momentum, this strength, this power of investment in his work, in his speeches. A certain complicity and a pleasant familiarity – though limited by an impassable border – developed over the years, despite our multiple differences.
- An inhibition in the face of what in his mind seemed both so seductive and so categorical. I began to follow his seminar shortly after, and I frequented this place for several years, though with moments of withdrawal linked to this difficulty in speaking there as well as my inability to speak as well as listen to him on certain themes. Despite this consistency over the years, I was not the only one to feel this paralysis, which sometimes engendered heavy silences to which many can testify, and which made him miserable.
- The need to put a distance, safeguards between him and me, and I immediately said to myself that I would never be his analysand. I imagine that it is in such an immediate movement that some people could decide, upon hearing him, to make a request for analysis.
- He had been the analyst for several years for a relative of mine, which we never talked about. He knew that I knew he was the analyst for several friends, buddies, or acquaintances, including people with whom I worked closely. This situation troubled me, and I periodically raised the question of the effects of this interference to him, but he said he had no answer to this question.

In this context, I more or less acted as a messenger between him and the cartels, which was not without pain, until in February 1992, when I withdrew from the *Cartel Network*.

Before writing this text,[1] I promised myself not to praise Francis Peraldi: highlighting his beautiful features with very vivid colors and erasing his flaws to arrive at a standardized portrait. He was too little conformist but also too lively, flamboyant, and… cheerful for that!

I will say, finally, that he could be unfairly ferocious and provocative and that despite his denials he had a formidable ability to silence his supposed opponents…

September 1992. The terrace of *Chez Gautier*, where he was a regular, one of the last beautiful days of summer. Of those that make you nostalgic. The idea for the interview came to me as rumors were circulating about his departure for France as well as his "health problems," as he liked to put it modestly. He was to go live in France around Christmas, or rather die there… I proposed my project to François, which he enthusiastically accepted. It was the last time I saw him alive. Thin and happy, light and euphoric.

Finally, the meeting took place on February 24, 1993. Perhaps I had let things drag on, refusing for a long time to accept the urgency of the situation.

The meeting was postponed a few times by him, which was not unusual in our relationship. But I still wonder why he agreed to see me so shortly before his death, and I was very touched by the trust he showed me. I would add that it was a difficult burden to carry.

I was going to see him with questions that were my preoccupations with psychoanalysis at the time; they had already been discussed between us over the years. It is a question of the paradoxical transmission, of the unanalyzed remainder of the analyst and its effects, of "primitive communication," of psychoanalytical incest, and of the identity of the "margin" in relation to the institution.

I must say a few words about this meeting and the impression it left on me. The first effect was a shock. Shock to see him in the state of physical disrepair I found him in. But above all, what was most difficult for me to integrate was his deep bitterness. And it was only in the aftermath, thanks to Josette Garon with whom I spoke about it, that I was able to identify what was most distressing and made the meeting imbued with a disturbing strangeness: what made me wonder if it was really him was that his smile and, of course, his beautiful laugh had disappeared, not to mention his friendliness.

Subsequently, I thought that François Peraldi had formed a romantic idea of death and perhaps also of his own, which is illustrated in the beautiful text he wrote on the death of Franco.[2] But as he approached his own death, he was in extreme anger, in bitter rage. This bitterness can be read throughout the text of the interview. Moreover, from the outset, when I arrived, apart from having to deal with his great fatigue, his great physical weakness, I had to face the first words of welcome he uttered:

> "What do you want me to talk to you about? Of psychoanalysis? I have nothing to say about it, psychoanalysis disgusts me."

Finally, a dream that I had a few days after his death. He was at my house, in my kitchen, and he was drinking milk. I looked at the box, the date had passed – of course, since he was already dead! – and I told him: "But François, you shouldn't drink this milk, it's no longer good, you're going to hurt yourself."

It's hard to help but think that the illness and death of a loved one could have been avoided...

And how can you protect yourself against contamination? Does psychoanalysis represent the plague as Lacan made Freud say of the boat docking the American continent, a modern plague?...

II Questions and Method[3]

The transcript of the interview contained gross errors and required careful editing. I have listened to the tapes in their entirety seven times, only one of which I compared to the text of the transcription.

For over a year, I struggled with various anxieties, including that of guilt. I found my interruptions and my questions about affiliation and transmission unbearable. I had to give up trying to erase myself and "repair" by reorganizing the text to leave even more room for François Peraldi.

So I ended up making the following decisions:

- The text, a transcription of oral speech, included many sentences left in pains, repetitions, "So," "Um" and other onomatopoeias. I did a minimal "cleansing" of the text to make it more readable, hoping not to distort it too much. But it was not easy for me to assume a subjective position and to decide between the absolutely faithful and unpublishable transcription because it was too tedious and a compromise, which could sometimes appear to me as compromised.
- Indeed, if François Peraldi were still alive, I could have given him a series of modifications, which he would have had at his disposal. It was therefore necessary to agree to talk about him while taking note of his absence...
- Nothing was cut from the text except for very brief questions or comments from me, which served as a stimulus and were often spoken while he was speaking...
- The structure of the text has also not been changed. It is transcribed as it has been spoken. In this way, I thought I would respect its internal logic as well as that of our exchanges, and I had to resist the temptation to move, following his early development, what François Peraldi says about his training below. I had to come to terms with my interruptions...
- What might affect some people, after much thought, was not cut. In fact, there too I was plagued with painful dilemmas, but it was ethically difficult to claim to preserve – who and in the name of what? – some passages and not others, as it was impossible to foresee the effects of his comments and omissions. The idea of exercising censorship struck me as absurd and unbearable.

Moreover, François Peraldi very clearly refuses, throughout the interview, to deliver anything "personal" or "intimate." For example, he doesn't give the name of his analyst, and when he names people, paradoxically, he doesn't seem to be talking about private relationships or settling personal scores. Most importantly, three weeks before his death, he never names his illness or even talks about it. And it was very confusing and worrying for me, even though we both knew we would never see each other again, that he was going to die soon, that I had before my eyes a picture of him that he himself found unbearable, to see him attribute his distance from the psychoanalytic world to all other causes. It seemed to me afterwards that the unbinding of the death drive was indeed at work, and this manifested itself in a lot of bitterness and anger.

But it was reading *The Experience of Silence*[4] from the summer of 1990 that allayed my concern. I understood then that his decision to keep silent about his illness was being carefully weighed and that it gave meaning to what appears to me today as a position taken before or simultaneously with the first signs of his illness. I also understood that the coherence of his attitude was linked to the question of silence both from a clinical point of view and in relation to

[Martin] Heidegger; the question of horror and the Holocaust is not the least troubling aspect in this regard...

That official aspect of his speaking in the interview, the fact that he doesn't open up, at least not directly, as well as his great bitterness could make this text difficult and perhaps distressing. I will end by saying that this decision was his by accepting this meeting and that his invitation to read his articles could clarify his words and his silence; thus, on the question of primitive communication, he spoke in *La transaction*.[5] Did the words of François Peraldi in this interview not essentially concern transmission and affiliation, in the end?

III Meeting with François Peraldi

Marie Hazan: I have many things to ask you, but you'll tell me what you want to talk about. I would like you to talk to me about the question of training, yours, your arrival in Montréal, psychoanalysis here, but also the question of transmission in general and communication as you presented it in *Filigrane*.[6] In fact, what gave me the idea for this meeting was the interview with Dolto that you and Chantal Maillet published in *Études Freudiennes*.[7]

François Peraldi: So go ahead and ask questions, I will answer you.

MH: First, what made you become an analyst?

FP: I always wanted to work with mad people, as we used to say when I was young, when I was doing medicine. But at the time, I believed in medicine, psychiatry, and psychoanalysis at the end of the road. I started medicine, I really did not like it, I realized that psychoanalysts had little to do with psychiatrists-doctors. After a period of hesitation, I left medicine and went back to analysis.

I found a job in a center for psychotic children and continued my analysis with the idea of becoming a child psychotherapist. I don't know where I got it from, but anyway... It was during the Thirteenth, 1968 with [Serge] Lebovici. [See footnote #9.]

So I did a first analysis with someone whose name does not matter but who was part of the Paris Psychoanalytic Society, the International. I left the International, where I was a student, when they refused to approve the controls I asked to do. I went to the Freudian School, where I knew people, where I went to do some supervisions as a supervisee and I went to attend seminars, including that of Lacan.

Now to say deeply, deeply, why I became an analyst would be both too long and too intimate, in a way. I don't know why one becomes a psychoanalyst.

MH: You said that psychoanalysis interested you less or did not interest you anymore. Does this shed a different light on what first hooked you, attracted you?

FP: No. What disgusted me with psychoanalysis was, in the first place, the psychoanalytical milieu, which I found particularly vile, and as a result, all the investment I could have put into psychoanalysis as a mode of theoretical reflection was invalidated by my growing lack of confidence in the milieu. So, as a result, I disinvested, withdrew, from all that.

Of course, it's a complex set of things that makes one become an analyst: why I was interested in crazy children, why I was fascinated by madness, when there are no crazy people in the family... I don't know all this, I probably had to work on this question in my analysis, but I don't think it's of interest. Maybe what's more interesting is how you become one.

At the time, in France, there were two ways[8]: either one joined the Psychoanalytic Society of Paris – that is to say, the International Society – then one made the request, or we went to the very recent Freudian School founded in 1964. I started seriously because I was convinced that the more serious it was, the more painful it must have been and the people of the [The Mental Health Association] of the Thirteenth [district of Paris] impressed me a lot, that was a guarantee for me. Lebovici, [Evelyne] Kestenberg, [René] Diatkine worked together there for years, and they are also the first to have truly founded a psychoanalytic child psychiatry.[9] They were great figures of Parisian psychoanalysis at that time; Lacan was a little separate.

In fact, these were not well-thought-out choices, but rather chance choices, so I entered the International and left. I didn't get along well with the autocratic and hierarchical side of the Society's people. I realized that there was the Freudian School of Paris, something I didn't know about previously, so I went to see them and then I started to work with them. What I was looking for at the beginning was work groups, especially since I was continuing my analysis. It was work groups, seminars, that's what I found, that's what I did; then we made a cartel with [Juan-David] Nasio, Chantal Maillet and two or three other people, it lasted two or three years. I went to Lacan's seminar and to [Jean] Clavreul's seminar, I went to do more or less bizarre supervisions with [Serge] Leclaire. You know, things lead into each other, there's no plan, you don't make a plan for yourself or your career when you enter analysis. It was also, we must not forget, the whole period of the great political upheavals of 1968–69. I was very busy, it was the discovery for me of the political world, I was rather tempted by alliances with very politicized psychoanalysts, very left-wing, on the Trotskyist side.

MH: I have a question, on this very matter, on training and transmission. If you switched from one system to another, did you feel any big differences? This is a question that I personally ask myself about co-op-tation.[10] What makes one become analyst: are there more phenomena of the order of co-optation, of cronyism on the side where the institution is less strongly organized? But is this perhaps a very naïve question?

FP: This is mostly a question that has absolutely no answer. The people of the International have been trying for 40 years to codify transmission extremely strictly, but they really haven't come up with any model of transmission, they don't know what it is. On the side of the Freudian School, one should not believe that one could enter as one wanted, as in a mill: before I became a known and recognized member as an analyst, it was also difficult and it was necessary to climb as many echelons as the IPA, except that it was perhaps more pernicious because more occult. At the International, you knew if you were a student or if you were a member, there was a whole gradation and denominations each time. Neither school, no one, has ever been able to say why and what they recognize as an analyst. We do not know. In fact, we don't know what an analyst is.

MH: And, you, what do you think?

FP: Oh me, I think that's fine, the more you try to codify, the more you get a bunch of idiots, I can see it here. On the one hand, at the Canadian Psychoanalytic Society, they have managed to free themselves from these formal requirements, and that results in much more lively, much more curious analysts. On the other hand, it is not without distress that I see the margin forming into groups (…)[11] with something always reminiscent of psychology, and what do they transmit in these small groups? Did they ask themselves what psychoanalysis is, what the unconscious is, what the hell they are doing there? What do they hope to get from calling themselves psychoanalysts? Do you know? In this kind of vagueness, a sort of therapeutic function is maintained with ill-defined outlines, the transmission of which is most often done through reading, through encounters with others…

MH: What struck me about this interview with Dolto was that, for example, she advocates for the diversity of controls.

FP: I think, indeed, if you want to try to come to some vague agreement and build a consensus on what psychoanalysis is, you have to work together enormously. So, for sure, someone who's been in clinical practice for 25 years might have a little more to say and hear than someone who's just starting out, in a way. In that sense, if you will, controls, that's a simple name to indicate going out and talking about what you're doing with other analysts. The problem is, analysts are often cowards and dare not say to someone, "You are not made to be an analyst, do something else." There are hundreds of people, whom I see in Montréal, who are as much psycho-analysts as I am a butcher.

It's incredible! They even have a sofa at home, they talk at confer-ences, obviously they do everything except analysis. So, of course, for training, I would be tempted to think, like Dolto, that one is born a psychoanalyst.

I think that we are indeed born with a predisposition to hear the unconscious of the other, or not, we may be deprived of it for the rest of our lives, but it is not something that can be learned, it is something that is refined. I believe that a guy like [Clifford] Scott was born with this possibility of hearing in the other, the Other, that is, hearing the unconscious of the other. So, he has refined that over decades of practice, yes. That it has also been refined through continuous work with people who have this same gift, yes. But I would say that if it doesn't start from this initial gift, I don't think we can accept the idea that there are good little psychoanalysts who would do their work well. Either they have the gift or they don't. It's like classical musicians: either they know how to make this gift work or they lose it.

MH: Yes, yes, of course. And this is where I wondered about the transmission and the links between analysts, between elders and younger people, but not necessarily within institutions. How did it happen?

FP: When I came here, there was no connection between the older and the younger, there was nothing. There was just a small group which was 20 years old and which then functioned in an extremely coded way, with international rules, in a very bourgeois, medical environment. (…)

When I arrived in 1974, there were already Mireille Lafortune and Samuel Pereg, who did not call themselves psychoanalysts. We knew their interest in psychoanalysis, we even knew that their therapies had the psychoanalytic form, but they did not call themselves analysts, so I said to myself: this is ridiculous. Doing psychoanalysis on the sly, like that, behind the cover of psychotherapy, is dishonest, and for the people who come to see you, and in relation to the engagement in psychoanalysis.

At that time, I opened a seminar, I said to myself: I'm going to see who, here, is working in a way that would be familiar to me, and it's quite funny because all these people are at the Montréal Society now. I worked with Lise Monette, Josette Léonard, Pat Mahoney, and five or six others, there were about 15 people, and we worked for two years on Lacan's seminar on the psychoses[12]; at the same time, we were working on transmission. It is certain that we knew very well that we still had to know the Freudian texts, that the texts of Lacan had a considerable importance in reworking the reading that we could make of the Freudian texts. We indulged in this work of reading, which continued until two, three years ago, in all kinds of forms. It's quite funny because, as they were accepted, Marie-Claire Lanctôt-Bélanger also came, as they were accepted to the Canadian Psychoanalytic Society, they stopped coming to my seminar. They came when they weren't admitted yet, when they were students, that's funny! Long after, they came back, once they were well established.

Here, I'm talking mainly about what my presence triggered as fantasies that I was going to create a new *École freudienne de Paris*. Julien Bigras's game was extremely ambiguous in relation to the Canadian Society. The only thing I can say is that 10, 12 years later, the constant presence of this interrogation of what analysis is, of what Lacan is, has profoundly transformed both the psychoanalytical milieu as a whole and the Canadian Psychoanalytic Society in its corner. As a whole, I believe that it was a seminar that opened up an immense curiosity, not only about what psychoanalysis is but about what, it seems to me, must surround psychoanalysis – that is to say, the cultural context in which psychoanalysis is possible, a context of philosophical knowledge, of scientific knowledge, I believe that we fiddled with all of that. It was in the wake of Lacan; I didn't invent anything. The great merit of Lacan in France, in Europe, is to have shown that there was no question of being an analyst without plunging one's investigation, one's curiosity, into all sorts of domains: philosophy, anthropology, to do what Freud recommended doing, finally, and that no one has ever done. I believe that my seminar produced this. Did it produce much more than the conditions of curiosity that allow the cultivation of psychoanalytic thought? I don't know.

MH: Are you wondering?

FP: No. To be honest, I don't care, I ask myself because I get asked sometimes. What happened was that in the meantime there were personal tragedies.

When I started working on the seminar: "Lacan's Teaching," four, five years ago, I decided at that time to immerse myself, really, completely, in Lacan's text. To stop scribbling, like everyone else, to read a little thing here, a little bit there, and indeed, I had gathered all of Lacan's written traces, and there I plunged into it for several years. And so I reread everything, I reworked the texts on the *Phenomenology of the Spirit*, it was crazy work!

And there, but this is a very personal reaction, the more I read, the more Lacan seemed to me a forger. He seemed to me an emotional forger, an intellectual forger. At the same time, in this field, I'm not even sure it could be otherwise. But for me, it made me think: I don't want to be a part of this. First, I stopped my seminar, then I turned to something else, to writing, to completely idiosyncratic stuff that has nothing to do with psychoanalysis anymore, at least not directly.

But, fundamentally, moreover, if you will, what is at the same time paradoxical in this situation is that I therefore found myself in this kind of disinvestment in relation to psychoanalytic discourse, in relation to psychoanalysts, but not for a moment did I get bored in my clinical practice. I have always maintained a listening that I sense is there, I sense it from the effects it produces. On the other hand, if I leave this, and I'm going to have to stop soon, I have a feeling that I will be missing something, that there will be a huge loss. I've been listening to people for 25 years, though – I started in 1969 – it starts to add up.

To come back to the question of transmission, indeed, the people I have in supervision who start to listen, it is very fascinating to see how they are already hearing; then I wonder why they come to talk to me about it! But they have to talk to me about it so that the certainty that they are hearing, in the psychoanalytical sense, settles in little by little, and it has nothing to do with their culture or anything else.

I think of a woman who comes to talk to me and who is a nurse. She has an acute sense, quite extraordinary, of the unconscious, but it is like a kind of wild knowledge. So, what she is trying to do at the moment is to tame all that a little. It's interesting to work with her; she has taught me a lot of things, and she showed me moments of analysis that she saw as particularly unsuccessful and where precisely things were unraveling in a very surprising way. She was doing analysis without knowing it and that is what is interesting.

MH: But in an analytical framework? In therapy?

FP: She had patients, she had one or two private patients. She had taken them in to do supportive psychotherapy, the analytic kind, and it turned out that she was actually listening to them as an analyst. Of course, afterwards, there were a certain number of habits that she had to get rid of, such as the concern to help the patient, which was absolutely harmful, the concern to go quickly, the concern to cure them, but cure them of what? I am embarrassed to say. Still talking about transmission, indeed, perhaps the first role of the control serves to scrape off, to eliminate all these kinds of ideological representations, you see. And then, not to mention the ideological cleaning of the image one has of oneself when one is an analyst, because, you know, people are weird. "I'm a psychoanalyst," they declare. Imagine the most aberrant things that go on under there.

MH: Could you clarify what you mean?

FP: For example, both in their therapies and in their professional lives, they refuse to engage in a discussion which, paradoxically, would allow the unconscious to appear too much. They want to speak about the unconscious, but they don't want to let their unconscious speak. This is one of the most common things. Then there are the motivations for which people become analysts. A lot of young analysts imagine that there's a fortune to be made, you know, that all they have to do is sit on their asses in their chairs with their hands outstretched at the end of the session and the money will fall into it, like into the church treasury. They're quickly disappointed, mind you. So, it doesn't last! And they decide to go and do, I don't know, psychology or anything else. So, to come back to the transmission which is at the center of your concerns...

MH: What you are saying is that one is born an analyst, but what is it that from the outside, in relations with one's analyst or with one's supervisors or with other analysts, makes one "co-opted"? I think it plays out like that, in institutions or elsewhere...

FP: Yes. But I believe in co-optation without believing in it, given that I have imposed myself in Montréal. There was no one there to co-opt me, there was no one!

MH: But were you already an analyst?

FP: Yes, I was in Paris. When I decided to do a seminar in 1975, there was no question of co-option, although in a way, they co-opted me because they came. But co-optation is not a very good term, because it makes for little buddies, little cronies, little cliques, and, on the other hand, I believe that what is absolutely essential to transmission is that a group of people try to identify a common object, which is called the unconscious and psychoanalysis, that they work on this object and that they try to write something about it.

   That's about it. Co-option is like the historical phrase, "Kill them. The Lord knows those that are his own." Let them do what they want to do, psychoanalysis, Freud will recognize his own! Freud was very wise about this, he didn't care how the analysis was transmitted. He said that in any case, when one is faced with neurotic problems, one either has a sense of the unconscious problem that causes it or not. The rest is of no importance. He was not at all in favor of a coded transmission à la Karl Abraham, even for didactic analysis. He had once said: "Abraham claims that it is necessary to have done an analysis, it is not useless, but what I would say to you rather is to start listening to someone on the couch, you will very quickly encounter difficulties, and then you will come to see me and we will talk about it again." This, to me, is the essence of co-option: because there is no way to control it, it is essential in the training process to only do certain things if you feel they are absolutely necessary.

MH: Yes. What do you think of the unconscious transmission in the sense of a remnant, of something that is unanalyzed, I even thought of family secrets...

FP: I am not sure that something unanalyzed is transmitted. On the other hand, what would be important is that in the transmission, there are no barriers between the unconscious of someone who speaks psychoanalysis and that of the people who listen to him. For example, it's presumptuous what I'm going to say, but it's nevertheless her who told me, there is this kind of transmission between Dolto and me, when we meet and we feel very well that at the level of the unconscious there is no barrier. But that cannot be put in place, one cannot provoke that.

MH: I was talking about phenomena that are unconscious.

FP: At this moment, it is not the phenomena that count. At this moment, it is the presence of the unconscious, as a place that is there, whether there are paternal or oedipal stories that play out, that's not what is transmitted, it doesn't matter; what matters is that in this place we can be attuned in such a way that we will hear this but also hear something else. But I don't think we pass on unconscious knowledge...

MH: No, it was more in the failures that I finally heard that something could perhaps be spotted, for instance, I became interested in the question of "psychoanalytical incest," in regards to the analysts who analyzed their children, like Freud and Melanie Klein and about the side of the unknown in the transmission. I finally wondered how analysts chose their successors...

FP: I believe that they will be all the more likely to designate their successors, if they don't designate successors, and if they enjoy working with them. Analysts will be all the more likely to have pleasure in working with other analysts, as their relationship to the field of the unconscious will be the same.

MH: How could you clarify, for example, what happened between Dolto and you?

FP: It's hard to say. I think of someone I see from time to time, who I've seen in supervision for many years, who is one of those people who I consider an analyst. But I couldn't say why... What I can say is that his way of listening to the unconscious, on the one hand, is familiar to me – note, it is true that he did his analysis with me – but on the other hand, there is nothing that shocks me in his listening to the unconscious, there is nothing that evokes psychology. On the other hand, there is the speed with which he grasps problems, he dissects them; his curiosity is immense, his culture is very different from mine, but it is enough to point something out to him for him to immediately start working madly in that field. Can I say much more than that? No. It remains very intuitive, if you want, in any case, there is one thing that is certain, it is that in my eyes, there is no code, no criterion that would allow me to evaluate this and that would be external to the situation itself.

MH: My question is more about unknown things.

FP: Yes, but each time these are unique things that cannot be taken in a more generalized discourse. The question is whether we hear them or if we let these things pass.[13] Is this what is transmitted? How can the fact that it is transmitted have an impact on training? I do not know. If you want, for me what is most important is not what is transmitted from the unconscious, which would come from my unconscious universe or from yours; it is the modalities according to which we can start listening to that, the fact of having to live with the unknown, with the unsaid. It is more in the modalities that the psychoanalyst deals with that something can show itself.

MH: What could you say, if you want to continue what you were saying earlier, on your arrival here, on your ambiguous relationship with Julien Bigras? I was wondering if it was not worth clarifying.

FP: There was talk of writing an article for Françoise Bessis's journal.[14] Here, I will not talk about it because it is more about the relationships between men than the relationships between analysts. And, in a way, it's irrelevant. Julien would have been a justice of the peace or whatever, it would have been the same. So, it is certain that he made it difficult for me, because he first suggested – he himself already had extremely conflicting relations with the Montréal Psychoanalytic Society – that I was going to become one of his dolphins. That, people quickly realized that it was not possible, it must be said. And he still wanted to monopolize the field of theory, he took a very bad view that I wanted to do a few things on my own. But at the same time, he tried, he succeeded, to put me in a very embarrassing situation. At the beginning, I got along well with the people of the Canadian [Psychoanalytic] Society, [André] Lussier was president, he received me when there were guests and we could have worked together very quickly, and Julien made sure that it fell apart, probably because he didn't want to see me appear as part of the Society. As a result of dark stories about the coming, as usual, of Conrad Stein, Julien succeeded in creating a myth about me, by making the people of the Society, who are very timid people, believe that I was going to shatter the Psychoanalytic Society. After that, it's my personal relationship with Julien, which analytically doesn't represent anything very interesting for me. He as a man, yes of course, he was a fascinating man; I find that Elisabeth Bigras, moreover, is infinitely more subtle as an analyst than Julien was. Julien's interest is that with his journal, with his megalomania, with his heightened narcissism, he has maintained something of psychoanalysis in Montréal. He maintained a curiosity, he maintained a living interest in all kinds of sciences (...).[15] And, in that sense, his presence, his activity, especially in the 1970s, was extremely important.

So, from the moment we managed, as best we could, to divide up an area where we did not piss off the other, it settled down...

MH: So, in the evolution of your relationship with the people of the Society, was there a cut at some point?

FP: No, the relationship started to change when they started coming back to work at the seminar: they were members and we didn't have to forbid them anything; that was six, seven years ago. People like [Jacques] Mauger, [Jean] Imbeault, Josette Léonard came. At first, the people in their Society didn't like it very much, but eventually they found satisfaction in all this curiosity. At that moment, the people of the Society became much more flexible, they saw that I did not intend to build a team, another Freudian School; at the same time, they said to each other, but after all, what is Lacan? They realized that reading it was not enough to say something about it. And they came back to attend the seminar, so you can see how things are easing. The old seminar pundits who pretended I didn't exist started to greet me.

But what matters is to show that maybe something can circulate. What symbolically was very important for me was the day the Montréal Psychoanalytic Society decided to invite me to make a clinical presentation during their meeting called the "Scientific Day" because it was the first time that they were inviting someone who was not from the International. Throughout this whole story, it was, if you will, a sign of the symbolic openness of the Canadian Society. So, are they going to be able to maintain this? There is a current of orthodox stiffening within the International Society, which is very problematic. Will it have been only a small spring? It is rather difficult to know. Above all, what I am totally unable to know is what all these little groups that are born out of the seminar's life and death are going to give. First of all, I don't know what's going on there, you'll tell me, I'm not doing anything to find out!

MH: But you are in contact with people who are part of it...

FP: I would have to go to conferences. Will it be the same as in Paris, the mess? Relatively similar theoretical orientations and fierce interpersonal struggles, the impossibility of complying with a minimum of consensus in order to be able to work together...

MH: One of the questions I ask myself is how it is that here, in the end, there are either small groups that have been broken up or people who work alone.

FP: Because we are faced with the fact of completely different laws than the laws of analysis, we are faced with the fact that in order for a group to be formed and to really work, it needs a leader. I hate that because by maintaining the seminar as I did, I may have fostered the illusion. I gave the illusion of a leader that I was not, that I could not be.

MH: There was something paradoxical there...

FP: Yes, there was something paradoxical that I was very keen to maintain, so as not to be in the position of the one who will be expected to found. I always refused to do so, and in my opinion, as long as I was able to maintain this paradoxical position, which perhaps went with my own unconscious positions, I have the impression that things worked, that people worked together; but they separated as soon as the seminar stopped. I have the impression that there was a whole stirring going on, but at the same time an enormous pressure for me to decide to found something.

MH: What is your position today with regard to that, with regard to the question of the foundation?

FP: I am hostile towards the foundation for whatever reason, that's for sure. But on the other hand, I know very, very well that this place that I held was only possible for personal reasons.

MH: It couldn't be so personal, by the way, since it took hold of a lot of people. Something held that way, we talked about it several times, because you maintained the seminar and from the seminar, there were the Cartels.

FP: I'm like a founder who founded nothing. I was there first, but I was there like many others. I held the seminar, but I had no position of authority, I didn't decide anything about it, after I founded the Cartels[16] and that's where things got more difficult for me, because I realized that people in the Cartels expected a lot more from me than in the seminar, that if I had presented myself to the Cartels, I would have had to take a leadership position. One more fact was added to this – and which was not simple – that, among all these new arrivals, there were several who had been in analysis with me. That wasn't helping matters either.

MH: What effect does it have?

FP: It's hard to say. On me, an extreme distancing effect, meaning that I always managed not to be where they were. But what effect did it have on them? We should ask them.

MH: I don't know if you said everything you wanted to say about your debut in Paris? What made you leave, come here, what did that mean to you?

FP: Very personal reasons, reasons of private life, but among the reasons which would not be of private life, it was the suffocation in Paris which was becoming unbearable, the impossibility of thinking other than like groups of people, which you were affiliated with, and as I had already left medicine because of that, when I found myself in kinds of theoretical groups like that... The Trotskyists are very good at that...[17] I had the feeling that I wasn't thinking like them. It was a dark feeling, because they kept telling you not to think otherwise, the feeling that I couldn't think what I wanted. I remember once, it was in 1965 or in '66, I was already in analysis and then I spoke with Allouch,[18] who was a good friend at the time, I told him something and he told me:

> – "But Francois, how can you say such a thing? That's Hegelian!"
> – So what? Then after?
> I realized that everything was like this!
> – "But François, how can you say such a thing, it's Lebovici who says things like that!"
> So, that's when I had the feeling of not having a free hand, of being intellectually stifled.

And, yes, when I first came here in 1974, I can't say that I fell into a hyper-refined cultural milieu, but still it was a largely virgin milieu, actually. Cultural stereotypes are very fragile and easily shattered in Canada, and curiosity finds much more room to develop. And, because I didn't give a damn about Canada, Québec, and all that, the possibility of returning from outside to France was offered to me. And when I went back to speak in France, two or three years ago, then I can tell you that the story was no longer the same, and I knew how to put back in place those who didn't like it.

Anyway, if you want, that's one of the things I came for. In fact, what I needed to do was to leave France, but I was very close to getting a position at Harvard. The one at the University of Montréal was the first one that came open and I took it, but it wasn't my first or my second choice. It came at a time when a whole situation in my private life was at a turning point that allowed me to consider leaving France.

I already had an abundant practice of five, six years of analysis. I had done this great work of institutional analysis in centers for psychotic children. I felt it was coming to an end as far as I was concerned, it had to become something else, I had to go.

But it is true that I had friends in Canada. Of course, at the unconscious level, there were signifiers, in my childhood, which indexed[19] Canada... Here we are in a register of speculation which is interesting but nothing more!

MH: Is there something of solitude all the same, compared to psychoanalysis here?

FP: Yes, everywhere, even in France. It's an art of solitude, you're right, but at the same time, you can't practice alone.

MH: The paradox here is that even though people go through these moments of solitude, it's the working together that is problematic: too stuffy, too closed, or too fragmented. Are you saying that it is a lack of a leader that is the cause?

FP: I won't talk about it as a member, it would take a leader to make it not like that. But does it have to be that way? No, I don't think so. I think that what would be catastrophic is if small theoretical or political leaders were to be installed. We should be able to prevent that because it is so singular, like all these people who meet every week, who read, who make colloquiums, who go to great lengths. It's funny, isn't it? You don't do that in history or geography.

There is a great stir that takes place, but here I cannot say anything, I know them all, having had them in supervision or in analysis, but what they do as work between them, what they say between them, I don't know. And to maintain this position of non-leader, I don't want to know, it's just as well that I'm not part of it. It's not that I have contempt; on the contrary, I have an immense curiosity about what's going on, but I believe that it has to develop according to a movement internal to each person.

I will not say groupings, because they are not that, but let us say that at each of these nebulae of analysis, it is necessary that this movement is found around the vacuum left by my absence. Besides, it is amusing to see how one strives to erase even this absence. How there are psychologists, where Mireille Lafortune had screamed, saying: "You are forgetting François Peraldi...." But deep down, I find that very, very good, rather than setting myself up as a dead God.

They all came to my seminar. All of them, and they know it very well, have had these formative years. I think it's great that it created this kind of whirlwind of ideas and that I'm not one of them. I find that very, very good, it's the only thing, if I had any advice to give, or if I had remained in a more militant way, I would have tried to maintain this kind of structure, where instead of the leader there is no leader, there is a lack, but neither are there any horizontal identification structures, small leaders with a totem to take the central place. It's quite complex, first of all, it never happened; I'm not sure it can last long as a thought. I think it happened around Freud in the beginning, but Freud had such a leadership position...

MH: Do you think it couldn't last long, and what could happen?

FP: Oh, right away, a leader who would think he could hold everyone together, or what is in place here, a multiplicity of small totalities, small groupings that function at the same level, with interpersonal conflicts, like in Paris. The paradox of Lacan is that he held a place of leadership for a long time, although I'm not sure he really wanted to. But we saw what happened at the time of his death: his idolization, on the one hand, and the scattering in power conflicts of incredible ferocity, on the other.

MH: When I went to the Inter-Associative conference,[20] I found it really awful! It really made me take a great distance from the Lacanian groups and from Lacan himself.

FP: I believe that these are things that analysis cannot say anything about, that does not concern it. It does not know these institutional phenomena that should be approached otherwise. It would take some kind of science of analytical institutions, but it doesn't exist. It would require thinking about institutional structures, which we feel would be possible.

I think I felt that something was possible with the seminar but that it would clash with the rest of the social institutions in an extremely violent way.

This is kind of what was created in this center in the Jura. They were a kind of nebulae of questioning without a leader, some analysts managed not to be in a leadership position. I took care of autistic children, I did institutional analysis. But the government agencies that subsidized us did not support this at all. They wanted leaders, leaders, a hierarchy, to know who made decisions, for example, about Mimi, a child with autism under care.[21]

This poses some extremely interesting questions; it may not have been what you wanted to discuss, but I will address it for the *Trans* journal.[22] For the moment, there is no political thought properly marked by psychoanalysis: either politics comes from elsewhere and tries to structure the modes of intervention of psychoanalysis, or psychoanalysis gives explanations of world policy that has neither head nor tail. It is around this question that we could approach the question of psychoanalytic politics. We should still thwart the forces of alienation from our knowledge, in the same way we try to thwart the perfecting of the forces of misrecognition of the ego. What could you call it? Institutions or the representations they make of themselves?

When people are in a group, psychoanalysis is invaded by forces, which structure its institution, which have nothing to do with the unconscious. How to thwart this so that there are still forces that invest the psychoanalytic field by giving it an internal dynamic, but without requiring the position of a leader, of a leader, of vertical identifying structures, of hierarchical relationships? In short, of all the relationships that found politics? How can we have different relations, a different policy? Since it never existed, it does not exist; indeed, it remains very blurry, very vague. I have the experience of it, if you will, through the negative – that is, to say through what I especially did not want, where I especially did not want to be caught.

MH: Here?

FP: Here or anywhere, that's why I left France. I left medicine because I didn't want to be the favorite little student or assistant to Professor so-and-so[23] and caught up in this whole hierarchy. I couldn't stand it and yet I was not unhappy: all the doors were open to me. My older brother is a very, very great doctor, very bright, and he opened all doors to me. I would have become a big boss at record speed, I would have been running a service very quickly. It's not jealousy, it's not envy: "Ha! I'll never get to be a department head." I didn't think I could think or work in a context like that. In psychoanalysis, it's the same.

MH: So yes, exactly, how did you experience that? For example, when you started your training, did you find similar phenomena?

FP: Yes. What is interesting is that I left the Psychoanalytic Society of Paris very quickly, after five years; it was very hierarchical, very formal. In fact, one of the didacticians I had seen at the time told me: "You will never adapt here, your structure is different. You will be very unhappy, ultimately your entire training will suffer." He was the one who told me: "Why don't you go and look at the Lacanians, there are some remarkable people in there." And so, the advantage at the time, in 1964–65 among the Lacanians, is that there was no apparent institutional structure, no apparent hierarchy, and the passage from a pseudo-hierarchical level to another was apparently based on psychoanalytic motives. On the one hand, one entered, one became an analyst member of this group, by doing the pass, for example, which was a psychoanalytical means not so much of co-opting as of giving someone the opportunity to show where he or she was in this process, in this relationship to the unconscious that we were talking about earlier. And there were no hierarchical relationships, apparently, but that was a false pretense; in fact, there were hierarchical relationships as rigorous as elsewhere, but they were less apparent.

MH: What do you think about the pass?

FP: I don't think anything, I didn't. I don't know anyone who did it. I do not see very well how that would solve anything, but what interested me with the question of the pass is that it required the question, "How do you recognize someone who became an analyst?" As for the way they answer it, that...

So, this is where we see how, suddenly, hierarchical structures take over. When the pass was functioning and Lacan was there, we didn't have so many criteria, we had these criteria to say that so-and-so is an analyst, because we feel that way, or that such-and-such is not an analyst. As [name inaudible] said: "That one, psychoanalysis fits him like a rabbit's gaiters," which I find sublime, as a remark. Once you've done that, how do you feel? What is it that makes me feel in Dolto and that she feels in me immediately, people in a position to listen to others in a certain way? Neither of us learned it in a school. We perfected it in a school, we polished it in a school. And then, the pass, it was an attempt to take into account what makes one pass from a mode of "normal" psychological distance to this possibility of listening to the unconscious and to make sure, above all, that it does not close up.

But when it becomes like [in some schools] a terrorist mode of ruling over people, it reverts to what all the cooptation procedures are in all the other institutions, whatever they may be as they exist on the face of this planet. From this point of view, the [*École de la*] *Cause freudienne* works exactly like the Proletarian Left![24]

Because it allows a control of who is who in the phase when we want to ensure the right way of thinking or if we want to ensure a pure and hard, fidelity. For the *Cause*, of course, it appears that they increasingly make sure that they have people who will follow the line of orthodoxy. But everything I'm telling you here does not make the idea of setting up a transmission any easier. In my opinion, everyone's choice must remain vague, indeterminate.... On the other hand, it is up to analysts not to pretend to consider people who are not analysts as analysts.

MH: Yes, but how?

FP: Well, telling them or not keeping them in a group.... There are people who are in supervision with me, and I tell them, "What you're doing, the way you're doing it, doesn't seem analytical to me." I can't do more, I can't denounce them and say, "Caution!" On the other hand, there are groups where we feel that the people in them have nothing analytical, we tell them. And that, precisely, is very hard, it's as if hearing everything had to be a law, where everyone has to be heard. That's not it at all.

MH: It's hard when you're in such a small world...

FP: Do you think there were more of them in Vienna?

MH: Or in Paris. In Paris, they are very numerous, but ultimately they function in small chapels!

FP: In addition, they have been very numerous for only 30 to 40 years. Even when I started at the *Société Psychanalytique de Paris*, it was a small company; there were perhaps 180 to 200 people altogether. We only became more numerous afterwards.

MH: Did you all know each other more or less?

FP: Well no, precisely, because at the *Société Psychanalytique de Paris*, the hierarchical mechanisms meant that you only knew people from the moment you reached another hierarchical level, as in medicine.

MH: As in the Communist Party [CP]...

FP: As in the CP, absolutely. So that there was the illusion, at the time, that among the Lacanians, it was more open, that there weren't all these partitions.

MH: But are you saying it's an illusion?

FP: Yes, because it's like here where you're on first-name terms with your boss, but when he kicks you out, he still does it with incredible violence. So this is the illusion of liberalization. The *École freudienne* was a bit like that. But Lacan was not easy to get to know.

But as soon as I got to know Leclaire, that was one of the signs of recognition from another analyst, he got to know me. I remember he was familiar to me from the moment I presented something in New York that he really liked. He was familiar with me from that point on. These are intra-institutional signs of recognition, it's a lot of fun!

MH: I would like to ask you what you think you are doing in relation to this work that you have developed in the seminar?

FP: I gathered all my notes from the seminar, and the problem is I ended up with almost 6,000 pages. Before doing seminars on Lacan's teaching, I had done three seminars on death, two seminars on the Other, one seminar on the subject. For the moment, I am already putting the seminar on death back in good French, so there is something that would eventually be readable. But, I think it's actually better to keep it oral. It would have to be rewritten, but it's absolutely... not worth a job. Basically, you see, if I stay true to my thinking, I think everything that I've done during these years, that I've done orally, has to stay oral. What had to be written, I published in the articles. So, getting those seminar notes back for publication would be a real recovery. There is nothing in there! People can find it all elsewhere. When I was formulating the ideas, it was having effects, but there is not the substance of a transferable teaching, like a course in philosophy. I was rereading what I did on Lacan's teaching and it has no interest. So, I think I'll throw it away.

MH: And what did you get out of it?

FP: Enormously, it forced me to do a job that I would never have done otherwise, because I am lazy by nature. I learned a lot about the way psychoanalytic discourse works, the construction of theory, the links between psychoanalysis and its discourse, and with philosophy. I learned a lot doing this seminar. In fact, it served me in the same way as Lacan's seminar did as a stimulus to curiosity and reading.

MH: And why couldn't it be used that way?

FP: Because it can only be used for that when it is spoken, only when it is in the movement of the word.

MH: What worries you, is it some kind of fetishization?

FP: On the one hand. On the other hand, it will never be read as intended, and then it would be a bit like predigesting things that must be discovered alone or in groups. There is all the difference between what can be transmitted through the text, the book, and what can be transmitted in the speech of a seminar; speech is quite another thing, although it was apparently partly read. I think we have to put the emphasis on speaking, on transmission through the art of speaking.

MH: There is very little that is said about it. I speak of it precisely in relation to what Scott[25] was saying. There is something very particular that is transmitted orally, in speech, and which is ultimately overlooked in writing.

FP: And which for me constitutes the essence of what is kept alive in the fabric of psychoanalytic thought.

MH: Which is precisely in this exchange you're talking about, which comes from the depths of the unconscious.

FP: Yes. That's why all this fuss about journals... Yes, why not have fun writing journal articles, but what is most essential happens in circumstances of speech.

MH: And so, your distance from psychoanalysis, from Lacan?

FP: Well, it's like a love story that ends, you go your way, I go mine, and what I'm dealing with now is uninteresting in a way and has nothing to do with psychoanalysis. I'm working on a biography, on other things.

MH: Could you date that moment or was it progressive?

FP: No. It was gradual, but I can date it, it was in May 1990, when I stopped my seminar.

MH: May 1990 or 1991?

FP: 1990. I had a kind of *break down*, I had gone on a lecture tour in Denmark and I suffered, along the way, a phenomenon of total collapse, I was exhausted, I no longer knew who I was and what I was doing there, well, not at this point... And there I said to myself: "I cannot continue." Then, when I got home, I had to cancel some patients because I had too many. There, that was when, there was a point of extreme saturation.

MH: Was it at the Lacanian Forum?[26] It's true that you looked exhausted...

FP: Yes. I went to Denmark immediately afterwards. You also have to take into account, in all of this, the absolutely phenomenal amount of work that I have put in, and that is being done without realizing it, until the moment when I could no longer do it. Then after that, it just happened, I thought to myself: "This is madness!" And since you can't measure your effort as small economies, as soon as you don't have the psychic and physical strength to sustain it, you might as well do something else. I also feel that I have done what I had to do. I don't feel like I could have done much more. There you have it!

Notes

1 [All following footnotes are included here from Marie Hazan's original French text and translated by Chris Vanderwees.] A draft of the first part of this text was the subject of a presentation at the meeting of the Lacanian Forum, a clinical group bringing together analysts from several cities of North America, of which François Peraldi, with John Muller, was the founder. The Lacanian Forum meets twice a year. The meeting of October 30–31, 1993 took place in Montréal in homage to François Peraldi.

2 François Peraldi, 1991: Franco et sa mort, *Trois*, vol. 6, nos. 3–4, 212–216.

3 I thank Anne-Marie Arrial-Duhau for her listening and her involvement at various points in the process of this long and difficult elaboration, for her careful reading of the text of the interview, for her fruitful advice, and for her participation in this work. I thank all those – and there are a few – who have supported me with their friendship, listening, and words, throughout this work of elaboration and mourning.

4 François Peraldi, 1990: «L'expérience du silence», Textes, numéro «Écriture et psychanalyse», Éd. Paratexte, Toronto.

5 François Peraldi, 1992: La transaction. *Filigrane*, 1, 37–52.

6 La transaction, op. cit.

7 Questions de transfert. Entretiens avec Françoise Dolto. Propos recueillis par François Peraldi et Chantal Maillet. *Études Freudiennes* Nos 23 et 24. Avril et octobre 1984, 95–113 et 115–133.

8 He actually said, "There were two ways, not one way, not two ways."

9 "In 1958, psychoanalysis entered the public sector (…) with Philippe Paumelle who created a mental health clinic in the Thirteenth district of Paris. The experience multiplies (…). The child psychiatry sector will be entrusted to Serge Lebovici." Élisabeth Roudinesco, 1986: *History of psychoanalysis*, volume II, p. 205, Seuil, Paris. Diatkine, Jean and Évelyne Kestemberg will join Lebovici. Among other things, a Center for Psychoanalysis and Psychotherapy will be created and will publish the journal *Les Cahiers du center de psychanalyse et de psychothérapie*.

10 1639: Admission by exception, by privilege. "End of the 19th century: appointment of a new member, in an assembly, by the members who are already part of it." Le Petit Robert, 1983.

11 Here, two unidentified words.

12 This seminar has since been published. Jacques Lacan, 1991: *The Seminar Book III. Psychoses*. Seuil, Paris.

13 He is actually saying, "The question is not whether we hear them or not, whether the question is whether we hear them or if we let these things pass."

14 This is the journal *Nervures*, tome V, vol. 8, November 1992.

15 Here, an unidentified qualifier.

16 Founded in 1986, the Network of Cartels brings together a few people from François Peraldi's seminar (and some others) grouped into "cartels." A Day was

organized in June 1988 around presentations made by members of each cartel and a colloquium was held on January 22, 1993 on the theme of otherness.

17 François Peraldi is saying here something which cuts short on the Trotskyist practice of "entropy", a term which is defined as follows: "Systematic introduction into a party, into a trade union, of new militants from another organization, with a view to modify its objectives in line with those of this organization." *Le petit Larousse*, Paris 1980.

18 This is Jean Allouch, member of the Freudian School, then co-founder of the Constituent Cartels, which he left to found with Philippe Julien and others the journal *Littoral* and the *Lacanian School of Psychoanalysis*. Source: Élisabeth Roudinesco, 1986: *History of psychoanalysis in France*, volume 2, page 677, Seuil, Paris.

19 He might say "indicated," but more likely "indexed."

20 This is the first colloquium organized by the Inter-Associatif, a group founded in January 1991, of mostly Lacanian groups. Some members sometimes met ten years after the dissolution by Lacan of the Freudian School. Six psychoanalysts from the psychoanalytic "fringes" of Montréal attended.

21 He adds humor: "We called him: 'Mimi,' he came." So you can imagine yourself with the children of the DDASS! (DDASS: the Departmental Directorates of Health and Social Action in France come under a central ministry and take care of all centers for abandoned children or children placed in foster care).

22 François Peraldi had planned to give two interviews for the two Montréal psychoanalytic magazines *Filigrane* and *Trans*. He was to talk about the report of psychoanalysis and politics to the journal *Trans* for his number three on *Le politique*. In the end, this second interview could not take place.

23 He cites a name I haven't identified: Professor Diogenes? or Eugene?

24 *La Gauche Prolétarienne*: a "spontaneous" Maoist movement founded among others by Alain Geismar after "May 68." Banned in 1970 by the Pompidou government, his newspaper was illegally distributed by personalities in French intellectual life including Jean-Paul Sartre and Simone de Beauvoir.

25 When I met François Peraldi for this interview, I had just finished writing an article with Clifford Scott and had sent it to him a few days before (Marie Hazan, 1993: Detours around the transference. Meeting with Clifford Scott, *Filigrane*, 2, 190–199).

26 In May 1991, François Peraldi appeared publicly in a great state of exhaustion, in particular during the meeting of the Lacanian Forum in Montréal.

On Heidegger to Lacan

An Interview with William J. Richardson, SJ, PhD

Mario L. Beira, PhD and Sara E. Hassan, MD
(with notes by Beira)

The interview with William J. Richardson, SJ, PhD (1920–2016) which follows, an initiative of Sara E. Hassan, was conducted by her and Mario L. Beira on 21 June 2005 in Dublin (Ireland) following an international conference on James Joyce and Jacques Lacan. The text was initially published in the online psychoanalytic journal *Acheronta*, vol. 22 (December 2005), where Hassan serves as a member of the editorial board; it was reviewed and approved by Professor Richardson prior to its publication in 2005. All explanatory notes appearing at the end of the text are by Beira, who transcribed and edited the text and shared it with Professor Richardson for feedback and final approval. The original endnotes have been revised and expanded since the text was first published in light of new information and publications on Martin Heidegger.

Sara Hassan:	Mario, would you like to introduce Dr. Richardson?
Mario Beira:	It's my pleasure to do so. William Richardson was born in 1920 and raised in the United States, in the borough of Brooklyn in New York, as I recall. He traveled to Europe, to Belgium, for his doctoral training in philosophy at the Catholic University of Louvain. He was already an internationally known Heidegger scholar in the decade of the '70s, when after training as a psychoanalyst in New York City, he began to interest himself with Jacques Lacan and his return to [Sigmund] Freud. Dr Richardson is today a Professor of Philosophy at Boston College as well as a practicing psychoanalyst in Boston, where he lives. I will also add that Professor Richardson is a Catholic priest who has been a member of the Society of Jesus for many years.

My first question concerns his philosophical formation. I've always been curious why it was that he decided to travel to Europe, and Louvain in particular, for his training in philosophy. Secondly, I am wondering if he would be willing to share with us how it was that he decided to do his doctoral dissertation on Heidegger, under the guidance and supervision of Alphonse De Waelhens in particular.

William Richardson: I originally had hoped to study theology in order to teach theology at an American University. I was then told by my superiors that they needed someone to teach philosophy. So when I went to graduate studies, it was with the intention of studying theology. I had done four years of theology at Louvain, at the Faculty of Theology at the Jesuit Seminary, and was told that it would be a good idea to study philosophy in Rome. The Jesuit faculty of theology there had no connection with the university as such, so that the university vouched for me in unknown quantity.

I was told by my superiors that I had to be prepared to teach metaphysics in a new seminary being built at that time in the United States. They needed a fresh faculty to teach there, and I had to be prepared to teach metaphysics. It seemed to me that I could therefore not study theology and that philosophy had then to be studied in a contemporary setting. I learned, almost by accident, that the leading figure and thinker in the area of metaphysics, in whatever sense one may take that, was Martin Heidegger. So I developed at first a casual and indirect interest in Heidegger as a possible subject for research.

At that time, the leading specialist in Heidegger studies, in the French language at least, was Alphonse De Waelhens. Professor De Waelhens had published his doctoral dissertation by then. It was an interpretation of *Being and Time* and, at that moment, the fullest and most articulate presentation of Heidegger's *Being and Time* that existed in the French language. Since it was possible to perhaps study with him, under his supervision, I therefore began developing a more intensive interest in Heidegger. I visited De Waelhens before I left Louvain at the end of my theological studies with the intention of returning there. I grew convinced that there were good reasons for continuing to study in Louvain and with De Waelhens.[1]

During that year that followed, the year of Ascetical Theology, which is a form of spiritual formation that the Jesuits required at the end of a formation period, I spent much time reflecting on what precisely it was that I was interested in doing.

Another subject that interested me was the philosophical background of Karl Rahner, a German theologian who had been influenced by Heidegger. So during the summer of that year, I visited Karl Rahner and spoke to him about working on some philosophical aspect of his work. I told him that I was interested in the problem of death, and he was gracious enough to say: "Here behind me are all my notes on the philosophy and theology of death. If you want them they're all yours. I am too old and too stupid to work on them any further". This was typical of Rahner, a profound and deeply humble man.[2]

At that moment, that seemed very attractive but I discovered that Heidegger, who was at Freiburg, was going to teach the following semester; this was in the fall of 1955. I felt that if it were possible to receive permission from the University to do the first term of my graduate studies in philosophy at Freiburg, rather than in Louvain, and with Heidegger himself, this would be a valid reason for studying Heidegger rather than Karl Rahner. It was an opportunity to see a major figure actually functioning at the height of his form. It was, I think, the last course Heidegger planned to give before fully retiring at Freiburg. The course he was giving then was on the "Principle of Reason".[3]

The University of Louvain and its Higher Institute of Philosophy gave me permission to spend that first semester in Freiburg and so that's what I did. And so it was by serendipity that I came to study Heidegger. All things being equal, I might well have chosen to study with Karl Rahner, who had been influenced by Heidegger. His *Spirit in the World*, one of his major works, was basically a Heideggerian view of the world as presented in *Being and Time*.[4]

These are some of the reasons for why I decided to work on Heidegger and with Professor De Waelhens, who agreed to direct my work if I decided to continue at Louvain.

MB: How interesting. So it was, if I heard correctly, it was because your Jesuit Superiors ordered you to study philosophy that you ended up studying philosophy and ultimately Heidegger. You had at first wanted to study theology?

WR: Yes. Ordered, that's a harsh word for it, Mario. But that is what they wanted me to do and that's what I signed up for.

MB: I see.

WR: I would have preferred to study theology but that was not to be.[5]

MB: So let us thank the Jesuits! Your doctoral dissertation on Heidegger was first published in 1963, under the title "Heidegger: Through Phenomenology to Thought". I have always been deeply impressed by that work because, despite the fact that it was written during the early days of Heidegger scholarship, it is still, in my view, the first and only book that really provides a comprehensive, overall understanding of the trajectory of Heidegger's project. You managed this even before Heidegger had passed away. I find that truly amazing and a testimony to the rigor of your work.[6]

How was it that you were able to produce such a manuscript so early on in the history of Heidegger scholarship? How did you manage such a comprehensive view? Was it the help of Heidegger himself?

WR: Through serendipity, if you wish. I had no idea of what I would work on in Heidegger. I knew that I would have a chance to hear him, possibly to meet him, at least to see him and to work with people who were experienced students of his. I found a place to live in Freiburg. It was in an old people's home, and mostly women lived there. I was there as chaplain, and I was succeeding another Jesuit, who had been chaplain there the previous year and who had finished his work but was still living there during the summer. He had been invited, because of his own work on Heidegger, to join a seminar led by Heidegger on [G.W.F.] Hegel's Logic.

I met this man in the summertime, and he was to be there the following year and so we spent some time together. I really got to know him. He was a really enthusiastic person who was very ebullient and loved philosophy and loved to talk.

MB: His name?

WR: Cannot remember..... He would attend the seminar, this was in the fall of 1955, and would come back from his meetings with Heidegger and other members of the faculty who had been invited to attend the seminar in Heidegger's home in Freiburg. There were maybe 10, 12 to 15 maximum, who attended the seminar. He came home just full of Heidegger, full of what he said and the interpretations of Hegel. He was the first one to tell me that what De Waelhens had written about Heidegger was now *depasée* and that Heidegger would insist upon his actual thought at the time, the academic year of 1955/1956.

So I heard from ... Virgilio Fagone – I think that was his name – Fagone, who subsequently worked on the staff of the Università Cattolica in Rome.

At that time, Fagone had finished his degree and was in Freiburg because he had been invited to take part in the seminar. He was a very, very brilliant guy, like a child exploring his *Brave New World*. So I began to hear about Heidegger from Virgilio. He was very generous and would tell me about what happened that day in the seminar and the differences about an earlier Heidegger as interpreted by De Waelhens and the actual Heidegger who corrected the question of whether Heidegger was an existentialist, which was De Waelhens's assertion.

De Waelhens was basically a phenomenologist. He was a very competent reader of [Maurice] Merleau-Ponty, of *Being and Time*, and certainly of [Jean-Paul] Sartre. It was therefore a more Sartrean, or at least a more existentialistic, approach to Heidegger than Heidegger would accept. So, from the very beginning, I was introduced to a later Heidegger, one that corrected, if not the earlier Heidegger, the interpretations of Heidegger available at that time.

So it was the fact that I was suddenly in a world where there were at least two periods, or at least two ways of reading Heidegger: one, the French one, which was basically an existentialist interpretation under the leadership of De Waelhens, and the second, a more philosophical and more practical interpretation of Heidegger in terms of the problem of Being as such. So it was in that sense that I began to take note, in my reading, of what Heidegger says when you read him, because there is a difference [between the two periods].

My first impression of Heidegger was of a thinker who had gone through at least two periods and that none had been maintained until a certain and clear coherence developed in [and between] the two periods. I decided that the most useful way that I could put to use the opportunity that was given me was to try and decide on what to give who in Heidegger in view of the period one was working on.

I went to see Eugen Fink, who was an assistant of [Edmund] Husserl and had become a student of Heidegger in the late '20s when he first arrived at Freiburg. I spoke to him about the idea of maybe working on a study of Heidegger that would compare Husserl's notion of phenomenology with Heidegger's notion of phenomenology. And Fink said: "No, no. That's too big".[7]

Then I thought about working on the notion of thought in Heidegger. Actually it was Fagone who suggested it to me when he invited me to supper one night. The notion of thought in Heidegger certainly appeared in Heidegger after the late period, so it would be interesting to see if it appeared and how it appeared in the early period. So I noted that as a possible study. That turned out to be decisive. So I talked with Fink and also with Bernard Welte, who was professor of what they call "*Grenzfrage*", a borderline subject between philosophy and Catholic theology.[8]

I also talked to others, such as the assistants of the professors, and asked the question of what they thought would be worthwhile exploring. These assistants were individuals who had already finished their doctorates and were then working on their habilitation theses. So I talked to all of these people as the end of the semester approached.

Heidegger would lecture every Friday, I think it was at 5 o'clock, and he was giving his course on the "Principle of Reason". I saw that outside of his door there were no lines and I figured: "Well, what can I lose? He can't resent my naiveté". He could feel sorry for it or he could dismiss it. But at least, what would I lose if I met the lion at his den, so to speak. So I screwed on my courage to go speak to him and decided to go in and see him with my broken German.

And he was very gracious to me. He could have just dismissed me but didn't. He really treated me like a *Mensch,* so to speak. I told him what I was interested in doing and that I was interested in working on his work. I told him then that three things appealed to me as a student [of his] and that I would be grateful if he would just react [to them].

One was a comparison of his conception of phenomenology and that of Husserl. I told him that Professor Fink suggested that that would be too large. And he said: "Oh yeah, that's much too large." I also told him that I was interested in his essay "The Essence of Ground", where he speaks of the ontological difference, and asked him whether he had written anything else on the ontological difference.[9]

He sort of rolled his eyes. All of the later work, for probably the last ten years, was around the notion of the ontological difference. And he said that, yes, he had written other things that had not been published in that area. So I said: "Then we better wait until they are published". "Yeah, I think so", he said.

MB: And the third topic was...?

WR: was the question of Thought [*Denken*]. I found traces of the notion of thought from *Being and Time* through the later work as I worked to find out what he meant by it. And he said: "Yes!" So I said: "Do you think that is really feasible?" And he said: "Yeah." And so I went and told De Waelhens of my conversation with Heidegger

MB: and he said...?

WR: He looked at me as if I was out of my mind and said: "Are you serious?" And I said: "Yes!" He also said that the later Heidegger was no longer philosophy but just poetry. In his own work, he had established his reputation by articulating his conception of Heidegger's philosophy based on the earlier period, and I was interested in doing something that related to the later period, which for him was just sheer poetry.

So he fell deep in thought and shook his head and said: "Well, it's your decision. Are you really serious? Do you realize what you're saying?". And I was, of course, going by what Heidegger said, so it wasn't my word against De Waelhens; it was Heidegger against De Waelhens about Heidegger. "Yes, that's what I would like to work on!"

And he again shook his head and said: "Well, good luck. I'll try to direct you the best way I can but I have to tell you now that I don't think it's a viable subject". And I came to realize later that maybe he saw, better than I did, well I don't think he did, I think he really believed that the later Heidegger was just poetry and no longer philosophy.

It was only when I began to give him chapters to read that he saw the value of the research. By the time I had finished the earlier period, leading up through 1929, and saw that what I was doing was really headed in a direction that completely sabotaged his reading [of Heidegger].

To his credit, De Waelhens never mentioned the fact. He was supportive and encouraged me all the time and gave me very carefully analyzed reactions to my chapters with rigor and courtesy and kindness. Again, he did this despite the fact that he saw, better than I did, that I was really sabotaging his position. There was a decisive moment in Heidegger's development when Heidegger himself realized that the subject of *Being and Time* did not and could not work.

Eventually, I did not realize this until much later; I saw that what I was doing was really undercutting the entire conception that De Waelhens had. And, to his credit, he honored his task of being a critic and a patron and saw the value of the work.

As a matter of fact, at one point, after I had finished the so-called early period up until 1929, I was getting tired and just wanted to get back to the [United] States to teach and to just finish what had to be done from home. He told me at that point that I had sufficient work for a doctoral thesis and that all I had to do was to give him a month to process it. "But", he said, "you have developed a method that is satisfactory from my point of view. The earlier period has been worked through. You have worked through it and you have come up with something different. The earlier essays have been discussed, but now it is time for the later period".

He added that if I really wanted to do something that would be a real contribution, then I should keep using the same method and continue on to the later period to at least clarify what happened, how the notion of thought developed and so on.

MB: On the question of thought, I now see more clearly how it is that you have come from Heidegger and the question of thought in Heidegger to Freud. Having read most of your published work, it now seems to me that what ties together your movement from Heidegger to psychoanalysis is the problem or question of thought.

It's interesting that in your Heidegger book you decided to not treat the question of theology, the question of God in Heidegger. Not because there is nothing to say but rather, as you mention early on in your text, because there was, in fact, so much to say. You had wanted to study theology, but yet the question of God was not treated there.

I am recalling that you quoted a few lines from a poem by Dylan Thomas, "Vision and Prayer", in your book and that you decided to leave out the words "and prayer" from its title, citing it as "Vision …", with an ellipsis in place of the words "and Prayer". Later on in your career, you, of course, did broach the question of theology in Heidegger as well as the God question as it relates to Freud and psychoanalysis in light of Lacan.[10]

Sara, would you like to pose a question?

SH: Perhaps we ought to start addressing the question of psychoanalysis. Maybe it can be done through the question of thought.

MB: I agree. What are we to make of your passage from Heideggerian thought to psychoanalytic thought, and, in particular, the question of the unconscious? The question of the unconscious has preoccupied you for the last quarter century.

WR: I traced the first mention of thought, as distinct from phenomenology, as something that began to be given [in Heidegger] in 1930. It was not published until 1943. During this time, the change that took place in Heidegger, whatever it was, was called "the Turn". Heidegger's word is "*Kehre*." It involves a turn from the phenomenology that De Waelhens had developed to this notion of thought or the thinking of Being which characterized the later period in Heidegger.

That change, as I've said, took place between 1930 and 1943, and it could be depicted in this one essay called "On the Essence of Truth". Given the various forms of redaction, there was no way for me to know what changes had been made between the 1930 text and the 1943 text [which was] finally published. All I had was the published text that was available. There were no pirated editions floating around – or at least not available to me. So I decided at that point that I would restrict myself to what had been published rather than trying to check out all possible manuscripts of the essay.[11]

There was no talk at that time of Heidegger publishing all his unpublished texts. In fact, when I met with him in 1959, he pointed behind him to an entire bookcase filled with the courses he had given. He said something like: "People want me to publish all that stuff. I can do that when I am an old man", he said, "right now I feel fresh and I'll just move forward."

So there was no thought in anyone's mind, as far as I knew and as far as the *cognoscenti* knew, of it ever being published. So I figured it was a good risk to limit myself to what had been published at that time. I began reading the essay "On the Essence of Truth" and worked through everything chronologically that had been published or was available or was soon to be published.

Heidegger had been suspended from the University in 1945 because of his involvement with the Nazis. He gave a course in 1952 after having been denazified or having gone through the denazification process.[12]

So, in 1952, he returned to teaching after having been suspended since 1945. The course he gave in 1952 was called "*Was heist Denken?*" or "What is called or meant by thinking" or "thought." And there was all of the ambiguity about the calling. "Who does the calling?" "What is the calling?" And so forth …[13]

Anyway, I eventually had a manuscript of around 1,100 pages containing about 5,000 notes, so I figured I had to stop sometime and to limit myself to what was explicitly contained there.

When I came home to the States, I had therefore already met Heidegger. I was actually introduced to Heidegger by Professor Max Müller. Max Müller had become a good friend of Virgilio Fagone and he in turn introduced me to Max Müller. Max Müller became a sort of second mentor to the dissertation. Anyway, it was Max Müller who helped me to meet with Heidegger. He wrote him a letter of introduction, telling him about my work and that it was worth paying attention to.[14]

So through the good offices of Max Müller, just before I began to edit the text for presentation of the doctorate, in the spring of 1960, I [again] went to see Heidegger. He apparently liked my work and responded favorably to it. I had sent him a summary of 25 pages of my large manuscript. He pulled it out of his [desk] draw, and I saw that it was marked red and blue, like an American flag, every page, and with circles around it. And I immediately thought, "Good Lord. Here we go."

He accepted it and actually only made two suggestions, both of which I considered minor.

Firstly, he said that I had used the word *subjektivité* and that that pertained to [René] Descartes. He said that when you talk about [Gottfried Wilhelm] Leibniz, in the German tradition, the word should no longer be "*subjektivite*" but "*subjectite*". So it is no longer subjectivity but subjectness. At least that's what I understood at the time. That was the only serious criticism he had, which was fair enough. I was grateful to him and glad that there was nothing more serious than that.

At any rate, by reason of his suggestions, I presented my dissertation defense as soon as possible, at the end of the exam period in the spring of 1960. I was then invited to do what they call in Louvain the "*aggregation*". It was a way of becoming an honorary member of the Faculty. It required a publication of a book such as the "*habilitationsschrift*". So it was a sort of second degree or second level of a doctorate. That was by invitation only, and it was by the invitation of the faculty. At any rate, I was invited to the aggregation, called at that time *agregé*, and was committed to come back and finish up the "aggregation".

The next two years were basically devoted to preparing the aggregation and to editing the text. I presented the first part of it alone as my doctoral thesis and then the second part became the book as I began expansion of the thesis into the book.

When I came home, having finished the book and the book having been published, or about to be published, I began to be interrogated about the relevance of Heidegger. I was questioned, in particular, by the members of the world of what was then called "Existential Psychoanalysis". Rollo May and Leslie Farber were the two major figures in America at that time. They asked me to explain what Heidegger meant by his work.[15]

Rollo had done work on [Ludwig] Binswanger, a big presentation on existential psychoanalysis. Binswanger, for all intents and purposes, introduced the notion of *Dasein* into the field of psychiatry and psychology and developed a form of psychotherapy that was basically Husserlian. His formation was largely in Husserl. He was a fine and admirable person, and his work was fine work but based on the phenomenology of Husserl.[16]

Rollo May had published his own book based on Binswanger by then and asked me to join a seminar dealing with Heidegger. I did and that got me involved with the field of scholars dealing with existential psychoanalysis.[17]

Then I was asked to teach seminarians. This was in 1963, when the seminarians and students all over the United States were caught up in the sweep leading up to 1968 and that exploded in America in '68, in Berkeley. But 1963 was the year that [John F.] Kennedy was shot; shortly after that [in 1968], Martin Luther King was killed. The Beatles came to America then [in 1964], and Bob Dylan began to sing. This was the world in which I was asked to teach.

The seminarians were, of course, part of that world, and they felt the restlessness of the time. I had a good Jesuit friend who was an enormously intelligent man and a very wise man, but his health made it impossible to be an academic, to go through graduate studies, and he was the spiritual father of the seminarians. I was sent there extensively to do research but was told upon arrival that they had just lost two professors and I was their only replacement. So I was committed and caught up in teaching.

And I got along with the students. To this day, some of my closest friends were my students, who were troubled late teenagers or in their early twenties then and who were feeling the pulse of their times with lots of early-twenties problems.

MB: And you were teaching them what?

WR: I was teaching them philosophy. I was told that I was the replacement for the professor in the history of philosophy and for the professor that taught them natural theology as well.

MB: When exactly did you turn to Freud?

WR: Late in the sixties. I had to devote time to counseling students. It was very weary physically. I was helping them deal with their academic problems and was using a mixture of psychotherapy with theology. So I decided, in 1970, that if I could be accepted for psychoanalytic training, it would be helpful. I then went to the William Alanson White Institute in New York for my training. I made all the necessary moves and cut all ties to philosophy.[18]

I later went to work at Austen Riggs [Center] in Massachusetts, just north of New York.[19]

At the end of 1974–1975 [while at Austen Riggs], I was introduced to the name of Lacan. It was by Ed Podvoll, [who was] the grandson of a surgeon and who had studied medicine at [New York University College of Medicine]. Podvoll had spent 10 years at Chestnut Lodge and was intrigued by the difficulties of Lacan and the practical implications and the application of Lacan.[20]

In the meantime, a former student of mine, John Muller, came aboard [at Austen Riggs]. He was a child of the sixties and had spent three years at an Indian reservation. He had been interested in Indian folklore and Indian imagery and was even made an honorary Indian, of all things.[21]

MB: What year was this?

WR: This was 1975. That's when I began to hear about Lacan, this "impossible man". I was told "Lacan is a big name. He is impossible to understand but he is the big name".

But let me finish with Podvoll, who first introduced me to Lacan. He was so enthusiastic about Lacan that right now I would be suspicious of him. This was the end of 1974, start of 1975. He, as director of education [at Austen Riggs], had the freedom to decide on how the fellows – these were all postdoctoral students, postgraduate people in psychiatry and psychology – should train during their four years of research and clinical work.[22]

Ed Podvoll was so convinced [about Lacan] that he wanted to rearrange the entire training program at Austen Riggs. This was in 1975. Austen Riggs was a place that was traditionally ego psychology. David Rapaport and Erik Erikson were the two chief figures there.

Anyway, Podvoll became more and more extreme in his lifetime. So much so that he set up this entire program for training the fellows, and by the time we began to teach it, just before the academic year began, Ed Podvoll got involved with a former patient, [something] which was [of course] forbidden, and he was dismissed.

So there we were, John and I, stuck, so to speak, with a new training program for the fellows, although we knew nothing, basically, about Lacan. John knew less than I [did]. Anyway, that's how it began for us. I was also committed to teach graduate courses at Fordham University in New York. So John and I began to co-teach a course on the "function and field of speech and language in psychoanalysis".[23]

MB: So how were you able to begin to think of the work of Lacan in light of your previous training in theology and Heidegger? Was there a clash? An epiphany or experience?

SH: This might perhaps be the last question because I would also like to ask a question about the current situation in psychoanalysis in the United States.

MB: Well, perhaps one or two additional questions. This material seems interesting and important, at least to me.

WR: John and I began to teach together. We would prepare our courses together for both Fordham University and the fellows [at Austen Riggs].

And it was in this way that we went through those essays of the *Écrits* that were then published.[24]

MB: In 1977.

WR: Yes. And, at the same time, we got to know Claudia, one of Lacan's former students and analysands, who had learned about our work. So we met with Claudia and began to think that if we wanted to really do this, what we ought to do is go through a Lacanian analysis. So this brings us up to 1978. Lacan, around that time, came to America to give a series of lectures.[25]

Podvoll and I, this was just before John Muller arrived at Austen Riggs, went down to hear him at Yale [University]. Podvoll was completely enthusiastic. At the end of the lecture, which had started with the Law School auditorium filled with 500 people and was left, at the end of an hour, with about 25, including Podvoll and myself, I turned to Ed and asked: "Well, what do you think, Ed?" And he answered: "Well, the man is either a genius or a charlatan or he is mad". That was Podvoll's impression of Lacan's lecture.

But, by this time, we were committed to teaching Lacan. It was soon after that that Ed left us and that John came aboard. So we had to make do and to prepare introductory courses on Lacan's *Écrits*. And we decided that if we wanted to continue this, we would have to get ourselves analyzed [by a Lacanian] so we could give it a go.

In that year, there was a *Petites Journées* on transmission, maybe some remember, and Claudia was there. She came and introduced us to Lacan, although I had already met him on a previous occasion. So she arrived at the *Journées*, at the opening session, and we came over to her when we saw her. She introduced us to Lacan and told him that we would like to meet [with] him. And he said: "OK, Monday morning at 11 o'clock". This was now Friday evening, and we said that we would be there. He came [to the meeting] wearing a bathrobe and in his in slippers.

MB: This was at his home?

WR: Yes, which was also his office... And he came in and said: "*Alô, de quoi s'agit il?*" So we told him and he said: "OK, come back Thursday at 1." So that was it. John was with his wife, and he had planned to travel with her, and she was already unhappy with the idea of spending time away from traveling.

I was planning to travel to Rome. John and I both changed our plans to have lunch with Lacan. Sylvia was there, and we also met Judith, his daughter. Jacques-Alain Miller was supposed to have been there and Lacan himself. So we had a private lunch with Lacan. He offered us a shot of Jack Daniel's [Tennessee Whiskey] during lunch. It was very gracious and very generous of him.

It was at that point that I was invited to lecture at Oxford [University] the following year, in the fall of 1979.[26]

I decided that this was my chance, you know. I had to break obligations with patients. So I was scheduled to lecture in Oxford and to also come to Paris and thus had a year and a half off before going back to teaching in the [United] States. This was around the time that the *École freudienne de Paris* collapsed, so that was my second exposure to Lacan.

But, by this time, because of the involvement with John, we decided that we could make a book out of the collaboration we had done on the nine essays of the *Écrits*, which we did. Our book has since been translated into French.[27]

So, by that time, I was into Lacan. I did not get into analysis with Lacan but with someone whom Lacan did not suggest but of whom he did approve. After this, I returned to America and to teaching and to seeing patients and so on.

SH: Who, then, was Heidegger for Lacan?

WR: Heidegger was for Lacan an important person. He published in 1956, in *La Psychanalyse*, a very good translation of Heidegger's *Logos* essay. The essay, of course, deals with the notion of language – that is, the late Heidegger.[28]

Jean Beaufret had published "On Humanism" and was a patient that Lacan took into psychoanalysis. Lacan found Heidegger's notion of "speaking language" very appealing and used Heidegger as a propaedeutic; he says so [early on] in Seminar XI, which took place in 1964. Heidegger himself, however, was not sympathetic to psychoanalysis.[29]

In '64, Lacan got into topology and went his way alone. In 1959, he worked on *das Ding* or *La Chose*.[30]

MB: Do you think Heidegger understood or even appreciated the unconscious?

WR: Heidegger was not sympathetic to Lacan's understanding of the unconscious. He did not know much about Freud. He did work on clinical cases and had some [idea of] clinical experience. His knowledge [in this area] came mainly from Medard Boss. The relationship between Boss and Heidegger became a friendship, rare in that age.[31]

Boss found Heidegger's analysis of *Dasein* very attractive. He got to know Heidegger 's thought around 1940, and they began to take trips together after they got to know each other. Heidegger was near Saint Moritz and regularly traveled to Switzerland to teach there at Boss's request.[32]

As for Heidegger's understanding of Freud, it was pathetical. Heidegger criticized Freud's inability to pose the term of possibility and felt that Freud failed to understand what Being or "to be" meant. Heidegger, of course, can't account for certain phenomena related to the unconscious.[33]

MB: Obviously – Sara wanted to pose a question about the status and future of psychoanalysis in the United States.

SH: Yes, how do you see psychoanalysis in your country? What is the current situation, and what do you see as its future there?

WR: Psychoanalysis is moribund and has lost its hold on the American audience. While the work of Lacan appears as a possible source of new life for it, the fact remains that Lacanianism has not caught on with the American psychoanalytic community. It has had and continues to have an impact in our universities, in the field of literature and literary studies in particular. Lacan's return to Freud as such remains an open question in the United States.

Note*: William John Richardson died in New England on December 10, 2016, at the age of 96. On several occasions, he shared additional information with me on his encounters with Heidegger and Lacan. He first met Lacan, he once told me, when the French analyst attended the international conference at Johns Hopkins University in Baltimore on "The Languages of Criticism and the Sciences of Man" in October 1966. Lacan told Richardson then that he was no longer as interested in Heidegger's philosophy as he had been in the past.

Richardson also once shared being worried when he met with Heidegger for the second time, this time at his home, to discuss the project of his dissertation. The philosopher's wife, he noted, was known for being hostile to Catholics and disliked members of the clergy in particular. Concerned she might not allow him to enter her house if she learned he was a priest, Richardson decided to take active measures to conceal his Catholic background from her when he visited Heidegger at their home.

Mrs. Heidegger, a fervent supporter of Hitler and the Nazis, never learned of Richardson's religious affiliation and went on to serve tea and cookies to her husband and his guest during the visit. Richardson added that Heidegger phoned Max Müller after this second visit to say that he felt astonished that an American had grasped the meaning of his philosophy as deeply and correctly as Richardson had.

For his training analysis at the William Alanson White Institute in New York (1969–1974), Richardson chose to analyze with Alberta Szalita (1910–2010), a Jewish medical doctor who trained in medicine at the University of Warsaw in Poland. Szalita saw most of her family murdered by the Nazis before migrating to the United States, where she trained in analysis with Frieda Fromm-Reichmann at Chestnut Lodge, where Szalita worked from 1949 to 1953. Considered a gifted and talented psychoanalyst and an expert on the treatment of psychotic states by those who knew, trained, and supervised with her, Szalita moved to New York, where she spent five decades teaching at both the White and Columbia University Institutes.

For his training in Lacanian analysis, Richardson chose to analyze not with Lacan, as he noted in the interview, but with an analyst that Lacan knew and approved of, namely Jean Clavreul (1923–2006), a psychiatrist who analyzed and trained with Lacan but eventually broke from him. Supervision, and perhaps an additional slice of analysis, was undertaken with Joël Dor (1946–1999), a second-generation Lacanian who published widely on Lacan, was the editor of various psychoanalytic journals, and was associated with the University of Paris VII and the *Espace analytique* organization in Paris.

Finally, I note that one of Richardson's principal interests in Lacan was with his conception and theorization of an ethics for psychoanalysis. Lacan's view of ethics, as Richardson saw it, derived from the Marquis de Sade via George Bataille. Siding with Sade rather than Kant, Lacan took Sade as a guide to propose an ethics for psychoanalysis. Richardson maintained that such a model excluded the dimension of respect and responsibility for the basic humanity of the other in light of the Judeo-Christian tradition.

It was Richardson's own personal "misencounter" with Lacan when they met in Paris which most likely contributed to the interest that he eventually developed in the framework and ideas that the French analyst proposed for an ethics of psychoanalysis. For Richardson's publications on this subject, see the following three essays: "Ethics and Desire," in *The American Journal of Psychoanalysis*, 47(4): 296–301 (1987); "The Stakes of Psychoanalysis: An Ethics of the Subject," in *Psychoanalysis and Contemporary Thought*, 12: 663–686 (1989; written with Jean Clavreul); and "The Subject of Ethics," in *The Psychoanalytic Review*, 86: 547–567 (1999).

Along with John Muller, Richardson appears to have been the first to have pondered the possible relevance for clinical treatment of Lacan's ideas for the benefit of an English-reading audience. He was the first to have introduced Heidegger's complex philosophy in their overall totality to English-speaking philosophers in the United States and beyond, hence a double pioneer, introducing the ideas of two of the leading intellectuals of the 20th century to members of the English-speaking intellectual world.

For a comprehensive bibliography of Richardson's publications, see M. Beira "William J. Richardson SJ [PhD], Bibliography of Published Works (1962–2011), in *William J. Richardson, SJ [PhD]: Reflections in Memoriam*, edited by Babette Babich. New York: NNS Press (2017), pp. 97–111; https://fordham.bepress.com/phil_babich/89.

* This "Note" and all of the endnotes in this appendix were provided by Mario L. Beira.

Notes

1 Richardson's reference is to *Le Philosophie de Martin Heidegger*, published by Alphonse De Waelhens (1910–1981) in 1942. Professor De Waelhens later developed an interest in psychoanalysis, publishing a book on Lacan's interpretation of the psychoses in 1972. See *Schizophrenia: A Philosophical Reflection on Lacan's Structuralist Interpretation*, translated by W. ver Eecke. Pittsburgh: Duquesne University Press (1978).
2 Karl Rahner (1904–1984) was a German Jesuit who is considered one of the most important Catholic theologians of the 20th century. His voluminous publications

reveal the influence of diverse theological and philosophical sources, Thomas Aquinas and Heidegger in particular. On the philosophical foundations of Rahner's theology, see T. Sheehan's *Karl Rahner: The Philosophical Foundations*. Athens: Ohio University Press (1987).

3 *Der Satz vom Grund*, Heidegger's 1955–1956 lecture course at Freiburg University. The text, edited by Petra Jaeger, appears in volume 10 of Heidegger's *Gesemtausgabe*, the official edition of his collected works, edited by Hermann Heidegger and published by the Vittorio Klostermann publishing firm in Frankfurt am Main; Heidegger's *Gesemtausgabe* (hereafter GA) totals 102 volumes. His entire oeuvre is, however, larger, some 120 volumes, as a number of Heidegger's texts have been published outside the GA. For a critique of the editorial practices for establishing Heidegger's GA, see T. Kisiel's essay "Heidegger's *Gesamtausgabe*: An International Scandal of Scholarship", in *Philosophy Today* 39:3–15 (1995).

4 Richardson is referring to Rahner's doctoral dissertation, *Geist in Welt*, published in 1939, available as volume 2 of his Collected Works (*Sämtliche Werke*), in 32 volumes; for an English translation, see *Spirit in the World*, translated by William Dych. New York: Herder and Herder (1968). For an essay on Rahner's study, see T. Sheehan's "Metaphysics and Bivalence: On Karl Rahner's *Geist in Welt*, in *The Modern Schoolman*, 63(1):21–43 (1985).

5 I used the word "ordered" in light of my understanding of the precepts which have informed the Society of Jesus since its founding. Jesuits are required to undergo a long period of training, 12 as opposed to the 4 or 5 years that secular priests typically experience. They are, moreover, often described as "soldiers of Christ", partly because of Ignacio de Loyola's military training and soldiering activities prior to his founding the Jesuit order in 1540. Affirming the spiritual leadership of Loyola, the Patron Saint of soldiers, Jesuits are keen to emphasize discipline and required to take vows of poverty, chastity, and obedience (to their direct superiors and the Pope in particular), hence the reason for why they are often described as the Pope's "secret Army".

Heidegger was briefly educated by Jesuits during his student days at the Catholic Archdioceses Gymnasium Seminary from 1903 to 1909, when he prepared to enter the Jesuit Novitiate near Feldkirch (Austria), which he did on September 30, 1909. He was, however, dismissed as a candidate after two weeks, when various physical (perhaps psychosomatic) symptoms began afflicting him. Lacan was likewise educated by Jesuits, known for their role in education, during his early years. On the early history of the Jesuits, see J. Broderick's *The Origins of the Jesuits*, published in 1940 to mark the 400th anniversary of the founding of the Jesuit order by Loyola.

6 *Heidegger: Through Phenomenology to Thought*, preface by Martin Heidegger. The Hague: Martinus Nijhoff (1963), a thick tome of 768 pages.

7 Eugen Fink (1905–1975), an associate and aide to Edmund Husserl (1859–1939), was appointed Husserl's private assistant in 1929. He remained close to the Jewish-born Galician philosopher until the end of Husserl's life in 1939. Widely recognized as the philosopher's best authorized interpreter during his lifetime, Fink began criticizing aspects of Husserlian phenomenology during the 1950s, eventually moving closer to Heidegger's "ontological method".

Fink co-taught a seminar on Heraclitus with Heidegger at Freiburg University during the winter semester of 1966/67 which Lacan highly praised and recommended to his students in 1973, during the Sixth Congress of the *École freudienne de Paris* in Grande Motte, near Montpelier, on November 2, 1973 (see volume 15 of the *Lettres de l'École freudienne de Paris*). The Heidegger/Fink Seminar on Heraclitus was published as volume 15 of Heidegger's *GA* (pp. 9–263); for an English translation, see *Heraclitus Seminar*, 1966/67 with Eugen Fink, translated by Charles H. Seibert. Tuscaloosa: University of Alabama Press (1979).

8 Benhard Welte (1906–1983) was a Jesuit priest and religious philosopher. Born in Heidegger's home town of Messkirch, he was appointed to the philosophy chair in Christian Religion at Freiburg University in 1954. A talented and faithful follower of Heidegger, Welte is best known for delivering the eulogy at Heidegger's funeral. For an English translation of Welte's words at Heidegger grave, see "Seeking and Finding: The Speech at Heidegger's Burial", in *Heidegger: The Man and the Thinker*, edited by T. Sheehan. Chicago: Precedent Publishing, pp. 106–109 (1981).

Vigilio Fagone, a Jesuit priest, was born in Sicily in 1925 and died in Rome on January 7, 1981, at age 56. He received a doctorate degree from Gregorian University in Rome in 1956 and later taught at its Institute of Religious Study. Fagone spent a year studying with Heidegger in Freiburg and published a number of books. He became an authority in the field of aesthetics and art, particularly in relation to religion. Fagone worked for years at *La Civiltà Cattolica*, a controversial Jesuit bi-weekly periodical in circulation since 1850. Its chief editor from 1915 to 1931, Father Enrico Rosa, published a number of anti-Semitic pieces in the journal.

9 Richardson is likely referring to *"Vom Wesens des Grundes"*, an essay he produced in 1928 and published a year later as a contribution to a *Festschrift* for Edmund Husserl. See volume 9 of Heidegger's *GA*, pp. 123–165. An English translation is available in *Pathmarks*. New York: Cambridge University Press (1998), pp. 97–135.

10 To quote the introduction Richardson wrote for his study on Heidegger:

> The altogether central place of foundational thought in Heidegger's endeavor forces us to treat in one way or another almost all of his principal themes. There is one problem, however, that we resolutely avoid: the problem of God. This is not because there is nothing to say about God in Heidegger's thinking. On the contrary, it is because there is too much to say for it to be said merely by indirection. Besides, any study of this problem presupposes, if it is going to be serious, the very analysis that we are attempting here. We reserve the matter, then, for another day...
> (p. xxviii)

While Richardson cites from Dylan Thomas's poem in his study, he decided to leave out the phrase "and Prayer" when providing the title of the poem on page 25 of his book. Richardson tackled the God question in Heidegger, and in psychoanalysis, in a number of essays, including "Heidegger and God – and Professor Jonas" in *Thought*, 40:13–40 (1965); "Psychoanalysis and the God-Question" in *Thought* (1986), 61:68–83; and, finally, "'Like Straw': Religion and Psychoanalysis" in *Eros and Eris: Contributions to a Hermeneutic Phenomenology*. The Hague: Kluwer Academic Publishers (1992), pp. 93–104.

11 *Vom Wesen der Wahrheit*, a lecture that Heidegger initially delivered in Bremen in 1930. Heidegger appears to have revised the text of his lecture at different junctures, delivering it under the same title and different contexts. The final version of the lecture was published in 1943; see volume 9 of his *GA*, pp. 177–202. Heidegger's lecture is not to be confused with *Vom Wesen der Wahrheit. Zu Platon's Hohlengleichnis und Theatet*, his winter semester course at Freiburg University for the 1931–1932 academic year; the text of that particular lecture course was published in volume 34 of his *GA*. For an English translation, see *The Essence of Truth: On Plato's Cave Allegory and the Theaetetus*, translated by T Sadler. London: Bloomsbury (Continuum), 2002.

12 For Richardson's take on Heidegger's involvement with the Nazi movement, see "Heidegger's Truth and Politics", in *Ethics and Danger: Essays in Heidegger and Continental Thought*, edited by A Dallery and C. Scott. Albany (NY): SUNY Press

(1992), pp. 11–24; see also "Heidegger's Fall", in *From Phenomenology to Thought: Essays in Honor of William J. Richardson S.J.*, edited by B. Babich. Dordrecht: Kluwer Academic Publishers (1995), pp. 619–629.

13 *Was heist Denken?* – What is Called Thinking? – is a text based on lectures that Heidegger presented at the University of Freiburg during the 1951 winter and 1952 summer semesters. The text was published two years later, in 1954; see volume 8 of his *GA*; for an English translation, by Fred D. Wieck and J. Glenn Gray, see *What Is Called Thinking?*, New York: Harper and Row (1968). Heidegger's text is known as being exemplary of his late philosophy; see B. D. Robbins 'Joyful Thinking-Thanking: A Reading of Heidegger's What is Called Thinking?', in *Janus Head*, 13(12):13–21 (2014).

14 Max Müller (1906–1994) was a German Catholic philosopher who studied with Heidegger from 1928 to 1933. Müller was fired by Heidegger from his position as leader of the student union at Freiburg University in December 1933, after becoming Rector of the University. Müller apparently expressed disappointment with Heidegger's decision to join the Nazi party on May 1, 1933 and stopped attending his lectures in response. Sheehan (1988) reports that Heidegger then took action to derail Müller's academic career, writing a letter to Nazi officials to inform them that Müller did not support [Adolf] Hitler and should, as such, not be allowed to teach at a German university.

Information I found suggests that Müller joined the *Sturmabteilung*, a paramilitary unit affiliated with the Nazis, shortly after, in November 1933, and that he joined the *Waffen-Schutzstaffel*, another Nazi party organization, three years later, in the fall of 1936, reaching the rank of *Rottenführer*, a non-commissioned position equivalent to a corporal in the US Army. Müller eventually completed his *Habilitation* thesis under Heidegger and Martin Honecker in 1936 and applied to join the Nazi party a year later, in May 1937. He was, however, denied membership, apparently because of the letter that Heidegger had sent to party officials in 1933. Unable to secure an academic position or to join the party, Müller decided to visit Heidegger in an effort to persuade him to retract his damaging letter.

Heidegger responded that he had only told the truth and that Müller, as a Catholic, should stop trying to talk him into reporting falsehoods and lies. Müller apparently kept trying to join the party after meeting with Heidegger, for he was accepted and welcomed as a member in 1940. In 1942, he then began to work as department head of the employment office in Ulm, a Nazi party position, where he remained for a year before becoming director of personnel for an industrial firm in Germany, a position that he kept until 1945, when Hitler was defeated.

In 1946, despite his Nazi involvement, Müller assumed the Concordat Chair of Catholic Philosophy at the University of Freiburg, a position that stood vacant since 1941, when Heidegger abolished it following the unexpected death of Martin Honecker, Karl Rahner's former doctoral thesis advisor, at age 53.

Heidegger and Müller exchanged a total of 89 letters from 1930 to 1979. A. Denker (2013) notes that the letters they wrote each other after the war are of "utmost importance" as they provide crucial information and insight "into the Denazification process, university politics, and Heidegger's role" during the years when the Nazis were in power (p. 68).

The two men stopped writing each other in 1937, when a break between them occurred. They, however, resumed exchanging letters two years after the war, in September 1947, when Müller wrote a long communication to Heidegger on the 19th to thank him for the time he and Bernhard Welte had recently spent together with him at his hut in Todtnauberg, apparently to renew their friendship. The two men continued writing each other for another 27 years, until 1974, two years before Heidegger died.

Müller, for his part, noted the following about Heidegger's endorsement of Hitler and the Nazi regime as early as 1953: "We encounter here the limits of his concrete political judgment – limits which, in the end, do not jeopardize his philosophical stature and the integrity of his endeavors" (p. 205). In other words, despite his faulty political judgment and Nazi past, Heidegger remained, for Müller, a gifted philosopher and important thinker.

On Müller's 1953 statement, see Fred Dallmayr's "Ontology of Freedom: Heidegger and Political Philosophy", in *Political Theory*, 12(2):204–234 (1984). For further information on Müller's position and view of Heidegger, see the interview he gave 32 years later, on May 1, 1985, as well as "Martin Heidegger: a philosopher and politics: a conversation [with Max Müller]", in *Martin Heidegger and National Socialism: Questions and Answers*, edited by G. Neske and E. Kettering, translated by L. Harries. NY: Paragon House; pp. 175–195 (1990). On Müller's activities after he was fired by Heidegger from his position as student leader at the university, see G. Leaman's 1991 unpublished doctoral dissertation "Contextual Misreadings: The US Reception of Heidegger's Political Thought", University of Massachusetts (Proquest AAI9132878), pp. 81–82 in particular.

On Heidegger's correspondence, including his exchanges with Müller, see A. Denker's 'Heidegger's Correspondence', in *The Bloomsbury Companion to Heidegger*, edited by F. Raffoul and E.S. Nelson. London: Bloomsbury (2013); pp. 67–73. On Heidegger's campaign against Müller and other colleagues and students at the university, see Thomas Sheehan's "Heidegger and the Nazis", *New York Review of Books*, vol. 35, no. 10 (June 16, 1988) as well as 'Everyone has to tell the Truth': Heidegger and the Jews, in *Continuum*, vol. 1(1):30–44 (autumn issue, 1990). For the Heidegger-Müller correspondence, see *Martin Heidegger: Briefe an Max Müller und andere Dokumente*. Karl Alber Verlag (2003)

15 Rollo May (1909–1994) was an American psychologist and psychoanalyst who served as the leading spokesman for an existential-phenomenological interpretation of Freudian psychoanalysis during the decade of the '50s and '60s. Leslie H. Farber, who died in 1981, was an American psychologist and former Chairman of the Washington D.C. School of Psychiatry who served as Director of Therapy at the Austen Riggs Center in Massachusetts. His book *The Ways of the Will*, published in 1966, received high praise from both the American and international psychoanalytic communities.

16 Ludwig Binswanger (1881–1966), who came from a Jewish family in Osterberg (Bavaria), served for 45 years as the medical director of the Bellevue sanitarium, a psychiatric hospital in Kreuzlingen (Switzerland) which his grandfather founded. Binswanger studied under [Carl] Jung and [Eugen] Bleuler at the famed Burgholzli Mental Hospital in Zurich in 1907 and, in March of that year, accompanied Jung on his visit to Vienna to meet with Freud for the first time. Freud and Binswanger became lifelong friends, as the Freud-Binswanger correspondence, published in 1992, confirms.

Binswanger is considered the father of *Daseinanalyse*, a term that he coined during the 1940s. His attempt to ground psychiatry within a phenomenological and anthropological framework reveals the influence of both Husserl and Heidegger. Heidegger, however, openly disagreed with Binswanger's interpretation of his philosophy, and Binswanger in turn responded by speaking of his "productive misunderstanding" of Heidegger. On Heidegger and Binswanger, see Francesca Brecio "Heidegger and Binswanger: Just a Misunderstanding?", in *The Humanistic Psychologist*, vol. 43: 278–296.

As Richardson notes, Binswanger was more deeply influenced by Husserl than by Heidegger. This held particularly true during the early and final phases of his career. The theoretical impact that Freud exercised over Binswanger is a complex and difficult matter to assess. Binswanger not only served as President of the Zurich Psychoanalytic Society in 1910 but, in response to a pointed question that he received from Freud in a letter on August 20, 1917, claimed that while his turn to phenomenology helped him to "conceive of the unconscious in a different way" than Freud, he found himself in the end unable to "manage without the unconscious", either in his "psychotherapeutic practice" or "in theory". For an article which treats the question that Freud posed to Binswanger, see R. Frie, "Formulating unconscious experience: From Freud to Binswanger and Sullivan, in *Psychoanalysis at the Limit*, edited by J. Mills. Albany (NY): SUNY Press (2012); pp. 31–48.

17 Richardson's reference is to *Existence: A New Dimension in Psychiatry and Psychology*. New York: Basic Books (1958), the first book to provide English language readers with a representative selection of the work of European thinkers in the area of "Existential Psychoanalysis". The book, edited by Rollo May, featured the work of Binswanger in particular.

18 The William Alanson White Institute of Psychiatry, Psychoanalysis, and Psychology, where Richardson trained as an analyst and graduated in 1974, was founded in New York City in 1946 by Clara Thompson, Harry Stack Sullivan, and Erich Fromm. The institute was not allowed to join the American Psychoanalytic Association after being established as it allowed non-medical doctors, psychologists, to receive psychoanalytic training. It continues to operate as a psychoanalytic training center in New York City today and has been affiliated with the American Psychoanalytic Association since 2016.

19 The Austen Riggs Center is a small open psychiatric hospital in Stockbridge (Massachusetts) which has retained a strong psychoanalytic orientation since it was founded in 1919.

20 Chestnut Lodge is a psychiatric hospital in Rockville (Maryland). Founded in 1910, it has a long tradition of offering intensive and psychoanalytically based treatment to individuals diagnosed with psychosis and other serious mental disorders.

21 John P. Muller received his doctorate in psychology from Harvard University and is a graduate of the Boston Psychoanalytic Institute. He is the author of *Beyond the Psychoanalytic Dyad: Developmental Semiotics in Freud, Pierce and Lacan*. New York: Routledge (1996). For many years, Muller was associated with the Austen Riggs Center, where he served as Director of Training. Along with Richardson, he was a founding member of the Lacanian Clinical Forum at Austen Riggs. For a book that presents the history of the group and features essays by its members, see *Penser La Clinique Psychanalytique: Le Lacanian Clinical Forum*, edited by Gilles Chignon, Marie Hazan, and Michael Peterson. Montréal: Liber (2010).

22 Born in 1936, Edward M. Podvoll graduated from New York University Medical School. He went on to train as a psychiatrist at Bellevue Hospital in New York City and as a psychoanalyst at the Washington Psychoanalytic Institute, where he became a member of the faculty. A former staff member of Chestnut Lodge Hospital and a Director of Training and Education at Austen Riggs, Podvoll became a Buddhist monk and went on to direct the "contemplative psychotherapy department" at the East–West psychology program at Naropa University in Boulder (Colorado).

His meditative experiences led him to found the "Windhorse Project" (in Boulder), which offered a new treatment model for individuals suffering from psychosis and a new framework of care which was based largely on Buddhist principles and insights. Podvoll explained this new treatment approach to psychosis in his book

The Seductions of Madness: Revolutionary Insights into the World of Psychosis and a Compassionate Approach to Recovery at Home, published by HarperCollins in 1990.

Podvoll left the United States for Europe after his book was published, completing an 11-year meditative retreat in a Buddhist monastery in France before returning to Colorado in 2002. An updated and expanded edition of his book was reissued in 2003 by Shambhala Publication under a new title: *Recovering Sanity: A Comprehensive Approach to Understanding and Treating Psychosis*. Described by its new publisher as "an underground classic", the book received positive reviews, including from members of the American psychoanalytic establishment. Podvoll died of cancer in Boulder (Colorado) in December 2003, at age 67.

23 American intellectuals were first exposed to Lacan's work precisely through this essay, his famous 'Rome Discourse' of 1953. The text was first published in English in 1968, with extensive notes and commentary by Anthony Wilden (its translator). See *The Language of the Self: The Function of Language in Psychoanalysis*. Baltimore: The Johns Hopkins University Press (1968). Lacan's 1953 presentation in Rome reveals strong traces of Heidegger's influence, particularly when arguing on behalf of the symbolic constitution of human subjectivity.

24 Nine of the essays in Lacan's *Écrits* were translated to English by Alan Sheridan and published in 1977. The texts chosen for translation and publication then were a partial selection of the 29 major texts and six introductions and appendices which constitute the complete text of Lacan's *Écrits*, published in France in 1966. The first complete English language translation of Lacan's *Magnum Opus*, by Bruce Fink, was published in January 2006.

25 Richardson is referring to a series of lectures that Lacan delivered in some of the more prestigious universities in the American northeast in the winter of 1975. Lacan lectured at Yale University (New Haven, Connecticut) on November 24 (Kanzer Seminar) and spoke at its Law School Auditorium the next day. He lectured at Columbia University in New York City a week later, on December 1, and at the Massachusetts Institute of Technology in Boston on December 2. See "*Conferences et entretiens dans le universities nord-americaines*" in *Scilicet*, vol. 6/7 (1975), pp. 7–45.

Lacan's North American lectures were delivered just after he presented the opening lecture of his seminar on Joyce in Paris on November 8, 1975; the second lecture of the seminar took place a month later, on December 9, soon after Lacan returned to Paris. Lacan delivered his lectures in the United States mostly in French, as he spoke little English. When he did attempt to address his audience in the language of Shakespeare, as he did during his initial lecture at Yale, he quipped that he had been working on improving his English by reading Joyce, a statement that led his audience to break out into laughter.

26 Richardson served as Martin D'arcy Lecturer at Oxford University in England in 1979.

27 Besides jointly editing *Lacan and Language: A Reader's Guide to the Ecrits*. New York: International Universities Press (1982), Muller and Richardson jointly edited *The Purloined Poe: Lacan, Derrida, and Psychoanalytic Reading*. Baltimore: Johns Hopkins University Press (1988).

28 See Martin Heidegger, "*Logos* (Heraklit, Fragment 50)", translated by Jacques Lacan, published in *La Psychanalyse*, vol. I (1956): 59–79. The original German text was published in volume 7 of Heidegger's *GA*, pp. 213–234. It was translated to English by David F. Krell and F. Capuzzi; see "Logos (Heraclitus, Fragment B 50)" in *Early Greek Thinking*. New York: Harper and Row (1985), pp. 59–78.

29 Heidegger's "Letter on 'Humanism'" was written to Jean Beaufret in the fall of 1946 in response to a communication that he received from Beaufret which asked:

"Comment redonner un sens au mot 'Humanisme?'" (How can we restore meaning to the word 'humanism'?) Heidegger's response was published in 1947; see volume 9 of his *GA*, pp. 313–364, English translation by Frank A. Capuzzi in *Pathmarks*. New York: Cambridge University Press (1998), pp. 239–276. Heidegger's well-known statement *"die Sprache spricht"* (Language speaks) is found in his lecture of October 7, 1950, *"Die Sprache"* (Language), available in volume 12 of his *GA*, pp. 7–30. For a related pronouncement by Heidegger *"Die Sprache ist das Haus des Seins"* (Language is the House of Being), see his "Letter on 'Humanism'", reference in the previous note.

30 *Das Ding* (The Thing) was first presented by Heidegger in the form of a lecture at the *Bayerischen Akademie der Schonen Kunste* on June 6, 1950. The text of Heidegger's presentation was published a year later; see volume 7 of his *GA*, pp. 167–187. For an English translation, see "The Thing" in *Poetry, Language, Thought*, translated by A. Hofstadter. New York: Harper and Row (1975); pp. 165–186.

Lacan appealed to and made use of Heidegger's essay on *Das Ding* in his seminar on the ethics of psychoanalysis (1959–1960). Leaning on the philosopher's phenomenological analysis, Lacan attempted to provide Freud's conception of *Das Ding* with a new twist in an effort to retrieve the concept for psychoanalytic theory; see *The Seminar of Jacques Lacan, Book VII: The Ethics of Psychoanalysis* (edited by Jacques-Alain Miller), translated with notes by D. Porter. New York: Norton (1992); consult his lectures of December 16, 1959 and January 27, 1960 in particular. For an article which treats Freud's conception of *Das Ding* in light of a possible ethics for psychoanalysis, see Helen Sheehan's "A Reading of an Ethics of Psychoanalysis from Freud's Formulation of *Das Ding* in the *Project for a Scientific Psychology*", in *The Pre-Psychoanalytic Writings of Sigmund Freud*, edited by Gertrudis van de Vijver and Filip Geerardyn. London: Karnac (2002), pp. 181–189.

Like Heidegger, Lacan affirmed that the French word for Thing (*Chose*) derived from the Latin *"Causa"*, a fact which determined the title that Lacan presented in the lecture that he delivered in Vienna on November 7, 1955: *"La chose freudienne ou Sens de retour a Freud en psychanalyse"*, published in his *Écrits*. Appealing to the philosopher's celebrated analysis of a pitcher or vase as "Thing", Lacan circled back to Heidegger's essay in the penultimate lecture of his unpublished ninth seminar in 1961–1962. In it, we find Lacan appealing to Heidegger's doctrine of *"das Geviert"* (Four Fold) to treat the question of space (*latum, longum et profundum*), categories alone open to man, the Shepherd of Being. All of this hints at the powerful role that Heidegger's philosophy played in Lacan's return to Freud, an influence that even informed Lacan's theorization of clinical praxis.

The title that Lacan provided his 1958 presentation at Royaumont on the "direction of the cure" (*la direction de la cure*), for instance, confirms the impact that Heidegger's philosophy exercised on his thinking. There we find Lacan turning to the word *"cure"* to offer his essay on his conception and vision of psychoanalytic "treatment" with a title which appealed to the word *"cure"* rather than *"traitement"*, the latter term being selected by Lacan to present his essay on the possible "treatment" of psychosis with its title.

Lacan's decision to appeal to the word *"cure"* in that essay points back to section 42 of Heidegger's *Being and Time*, where Heidegger appealed to the Graeco-Roman myth of "Cura" to argue on behalf of the basic structure of man as *Sorge* (Care). Heidegger's influence, in fact, appears throughout Lacan's entire essay, up to and including its final paragraph. There we see Lacan pondering "the final *Spaltung* [splitting] by which the subject is linked to the *Logos*, and about which Freud was beginning to write, giving us, at the final point of an *oeuvre* that has the dimension of [B]eing, the solution to 'infinite' analysis, when his death applied to it the word 'Nothing'".

Logos and Being are, of course, terms that are directly associated with Heidegger's philosophy, as is the case with the word 'Nothing' when capitalized. Let us recall that it was in his essay on *Das Ding* that Heidegger was led to describe death as "the shrine of Nothing, as that which in every respect is never something that merely exists, but which nevertheless presences, even as the mystery of Being itself". Finally, with regard to Lacan's incursions into topology late in his career and his supposedly no longer being interested in Heidegger, let us note the fact not only that Lacan endorsed Heidegger on Heraclitus as late as 1973 but that Heidegger himself grew interested in the topology of Dasein himself.

31 Medard Boss (1903–1990) was a Swiss psychiatrist who founded the *daseinanalytic* method of psychotherapy. He received his psychiatric training at the Zurich Burgholzli under Bleuler and studied with Jung during a ten-year period as well. Boss reportedly experienced a few psychoanalytic sessions with Freud in 1925 before undertaking a formal analysis with Karen Horney in Berlin. He reportedly received clinical supervision from Hans Sachs, Otto Fenichel, Theodor Reik, and Ernest Jones, among others. Boss appears to have first heard of Heidegger from Binswanger. After reading *Being and Time*, he decided to contact the philosopher in 1947. The two men began writing each other and met for the first time two years later, in 1949. They soon became friends, vacationing together with their wives in Greece in the summer of 1962. In an interview that Hermann Heidegger granted Ángel Yáñez in September 2006, the philosopher's stepson reported that Heidegger decided to sever all relations with Medard Boss after realizing that Boss published material from Heidegger without crediting him. For Yáñez's interview with Hermann Heidegger, see http://www.olimon.org/uan/hermann_heidegger_2.htm. Heidegger entered psychological treatment with Baron Victor Emil von Gebsattel (1883–1976) in mid-February 1946, when he experienced a mental breakdown after being interrogated by the denazification commission in December 1945 on his involvement and support of the Nazi regime. Treatment with von Gebsattel, a psychiatrist who also trained as a psychoanalyst, took place at the Schloss Haus Baden Sanatorium in Badenweiler, some 25 miles south of Freiberg near the French border. It lasted until mid-May (three months rather than the three weeks often cited) and consisted, said Heidegger, mostly of walks in the woods that he took with his doctor. The two men apparently discussed theoretical issues during their talks and walks together, including the "philosophical foundations" of psychotherapy. I cite from Heidegger's description to Heinrich Petzet of his treatment; this was in November 1947, a year and a half after returning home from Badenweiler:

> When in December 1945 I was brought totally unprepared before the 'settlement committee' and was confronted with the twenty-three questions of the inquisitorial hearing, and when I subsequently collapsed, the dean of the medical school, Beringer (who saw through the whole farce and the intentions of the accusers), came to me and simply drove me away to [Dr von] Gebsattel in Badenweiler. And what did he do? He just started walking randomly with me through the snow-covered winter forest. *He did not do anything else.* But as a human being he helped me, so that three weeks [sic] later I was again healthy and returned home
>
> (my emphasis, p. 46)

In an article published in 2016, Andrew Mitchell examines Heidegger's treatment experience with von Gebsattel by way of the philosopher's comments to Petzet. Offering his own translation of Heidegger's words, Mitchell has Heidegger saying that von Gebsattel "hiked for the first time with me through the snow-covered winter forest upon the Blauen [a mountain near Badenweiler which, at 3,800 feet, provides stunning views of the German Black Forest (*Schwarzwald*)]." He renders the key sentence in Heidegger's statement as "Other than that, he did nothing (*Sonst tat er nicht*)", a more accurate translation of Heidegger's words in my view. Mitchell, however, claims that von Gebsattel did more than "nothing" as he showed deep care and concern for Heidegger and indeed continued treating him even after the philosopher returned home from Badenweiler in May, prescribing him glucose injections which, says Mitchell, led to Heidegger's healing and to his overcoming his depression (p. 85).

While Heidegger has by now been exposed as a habitual liar, particularly on matters related to his involvement with the Nazis, what he confided to Petzet on his treatment experience with von Gebsattel reveals him placing his finger on a basic and fundamental truth. Dr von Gebsattel indeed showed deep concern for Heidegger and, just as Mitchell notes, helped him regain his emotional balance as a result of the care provided. His interventions, however, in no way helped Heidegger to examine the underlying dynamics which led him to endorse and promote Hitler after reading *Mein Kampf* and indeed to campaign against some of his colleagues who opposed the Nazis.

The mere fact that Heidegger continued to lie about the depth of his previous support and endorsement of Hitler and the Nazis, even after his treatment with von Gebsattel had ended, and never expressed remorse for his behavior and choices during the Nazi period suggests, at least to me, that he never examined the sources informing his lamentable behavior toward some of his colleagues and Jewish students or indeed the reason for his anti-Semitism and support of Hitler's violence during the war.

Gebsattel indeed did "nothing" *(nicht)* – at least nothing analytically meaningful – to help Heidegger face the roots of his malaise to arrive at a deeper healing. A "*traubenzucker* (glucose) cure" (p. 85) is, afterall, never and in no way a psychic cure for such biologically based modes of treatment and never able to reach the heart or soul of a person to heal and transform their being. Heidegger not only never apologized for his endorsement of the Fuhrer but devoted significant time and energy after the war to evading any honest examination of the choices he made during Hitler's reign of terror.

Mitchell approaches the question of Heidegger's healing by exploring the philosopher's views on "what it means to heal [*heil*] and what it means to need help" (p. 72). While Heidegger showed an interest on the topic of health, seeing the "health of a people" as a "determination of the people's relation to the state", Mitchell contends that he eventually came to envision healing as a happening achieved as a product of a process of waiting, a result of Dasein's capacity to be "open to the sudden arriving of what comes" (p. 79). Healing thus "never comes, or is only ever coming" for Heidegger, remaining an "infinite task" that is always present within "the heart of finitude" itself (p. 79).

Be that as it may, Mitchell proposes that Heidegger's treatment with Gebsattel helped the philosopher to achieve psychological healing and a "cure" by 1958 (p. 96). His conclusions on Heidegger's healing strike me as unsound for various reasons. Consider, for instance, what Heidegger confided to his wife in a letter he wrote to her on May 8, 1946, as his treatment with von Gebsattel was nearing its end: "of my authentic things, I speak to no one; even G[ebsattel] knows nothing thereof".

While Mitchell cites this statement from Heidegger, he failed to note that the philosopher was openly admitting to his wife that he had been holding back, not being completely honest with his doctor, not sharing his deepest thoughts or most "authentic things" with him. This alone suggests to me that no true healing ever came to Heidegger as a result of his encounter with von Gebsattel.

A closer look at Heidegger's statement also reveals the presence of the very term that he used six months later, when conversing with Petzel, to describe his treatment experience with von Gebsattel, namely "nothing" (*nicht*). While von Gebsattel "did nothing" meaningful to help his patient achieve genuine healing and a cure, it is crucial to note that Heidegger contributed to his own predicament by actively avoiding exploration of the factors that led him to sink into existential despair after being questioned on his behavior during Hitler's reign. Would Heidegger, I wonder, have fallen into depression and crisis had Hitler won the war?

Heidegger's most intimate and authentic concerns, the reason for his falling into depression, were obviously dodged by him and his doctor during their therapeutic encounter. The three-month dance of avoidance between the two men in Baden-weiler indeed led to nothing analytically meaningful happening. Heidegger not only appears to have kept silent about his Nazi past during his chats with von Gebsattel but failed to address the possible underlying factors that animated his choices and decisions during the Hitler era.

Mitchell explains that Heidegger eventually began to envision the process of healing after his treatment with von Gebsattel as a product and gift of being, even proposing "being itself as that which heals" (p. 87). Mitchell explains that Heidegger now imagined healing as a process requiring "dwelling and dwelling", indeed the "taking up of a habitual residence exposed to beyng. It is the exposure to beyng that heals, for awaiting or dwelling before beyng allows one to surpass the narrow confines of the ego" (p. 88).

This conception of the healing, needless to say, requires the emotionally distressed individual to do nothing other than wait for "being/beyng" itself to magically perform the healing. It also demands no intervention from the doctor conducting the treatment other than to provide the patient with caring support so they can safely wait for the storm to pass. This not only breeds forgetting but tries to actively cover over the deeper underlying cause(s) of the patient's malaise, personal suffering, and symptoms.

Affirming Heideggerian principles, Mitchell proposes that darkness is endemic to thinking and, as such, itself part of the process of healing (*Heilen*) and unhealing (*unheil*). Freudian psychoanalysis, however, affirms that genuine healing emerges from treatment in light of the patient's existential determination and commitment to confront his or her past and, however ugly, to analyze, in honest open fashion, past mistakes, conflicts, and traumas in that history.

Heidegger was, as we know, highly critical of psychoanalysis and indeed particularly hostile to Freud's conception of the unconscious. He not only was not cordial to psychoanalysis but, as a 1941 entry in one of his *Black Notebooks* confirms, was led to describe the father of psychoanalysis as "the Jew Freud" (p. 218; *GA* vol. 96).

All of this suggests to me that Heidegger was never cured of the dark forces which led him to bring his 1933 Rectoral address to a close with a heart-felt "*Heil Hitler*". His report of his experience in treatment confirms that von Gebsattel never intervened to help Heidegger pinpoint, articulate, or examine the origins of his bigotry and hate and of his endorsement of Hitler. All signs instead point to von Gebsattel's failing to present Heidegger with an analytic framework which would help him analyze the roots of his support of Hitler and his anti-Semitism. Heidegger, as we know, endorsed the Fuhrer even after reading *Mein Kampf*.

Freudian psychoanalysis, as Lacan noted in 1964, not only privileges the truth of the unconscious but requires every analyst to guide his or her patient into an encounter with a truth which liberates and frees. To quote Lacan, from his 11th seminar in Paris:

> The status of the unconscious, which, as I have shown, is so fragile on the ontic plane, is ethical. In his thirst for truth, Freud says, *Whatever it is, I must go there*, because somewhere, this unconscious reveals itself
>
> (pp. 33–34).

Psychoanalysis thus necessarily advocates on behalf of a truth discovery process as a prerequisite to possible healing and cure. To quote Lacan's words in Barcelona in June 1958:

> What is at issue here, however, is truth as such, in so far as both in the realm of its discovery and in the realm in which it operates with curative aims, man's relationship to truth predominates
>
> (p. 15).

Heidegger, whom Lacan obviously admired, was thus never "healed" of his "*Heil Hitler*", his doctor, von Gebsattel, never "haling" his patient (in the double sense of the term) in a direction which might have helped the philosopher achieve ontological and genuine existential healing.

The factors underlying Heidegger's dark behavior during Hitler's reign of terror in Germany and beyond were, as such, evaded. Heidegger's conduct and choices during the Nazi period thus remained as black as the midnight darkness on a moonless night in his beloved Black Forest, as black as the ugly darkness we encounter when reading what he recorded and said about the people of light in his infamous *Black Notebooks*. Those factors, to frame the matter in psychoanalytic terms, continued on as Heidegger's personal "*Das Ding*".

The closest that Heidegger appears to have ever come to addressing the roots of his Nazi past and to possibly achieving genuine healing in relation to his political decisions and endorsement of Hitler was when he met Martin Buber for the first and only time in late spring of 1957. The two men, who came together to discuss a possible conference on language (being planned for the following year), spent two days together, taking regular walks in the local forest near Lake Constance to discuss such themes and topics as blame, atonement, and forgiveness.

While the conference indeed took place the following year, Heidegger presented his text "On the Way to Language" during the event; Buber for his part decided to stay away. He did so not only because his wife had died since he had met with Heidegger the previous year but because he found his meeting with the German philosopher disappointing, indeed a "misencounter". During his two-day conversation with Buber, Heidegger apparently failed to bring up the issue of his support and endorsement of Hitler. Heidegger apparently agreed to meet with the leading Jewish thinker at the time on issues related to morality and ethics, hoping that Buber would somehow or other come to forgive or whitewash his past endorsement of the Fuhrer and collaboration with the Nazis.

The fact that Buber's first name matched Heidegger's own might have played a role in determining why the German philosopher turned to the Jewish Martin to approach the topics of atonement and forgiveness – the only time Heidegger appears to have concerned himself in any meaningful way with such issues. The German philosopher had previously turned to another Martin, Luther, to abandon the religious Catholic tradition of his father, the sexton at Saint Martin's Church in Messkirch, where Heidegger is today buried. Buber apparently saw through Heidegger's machinations, eventually publishing material in which he criticized Heidegger, the man and his philosophy. The dynamics that transpired between the two Martins during their two-day encounter in 1957 have, in my view, not been sufficiently appreciated or understood from a psychoanalytic perspective.

For Heidegger's report to Petzet, see *Encounters and Dialogues with Martin Heidegger 1929–1976*, translated by P. Emad and K. Maly. Chicago: University of Chicago Press (1993). On Heidegger's misencounter with Buber, see Gil Weissblei's text "The German Martin and the Jewish Mordechai: A Meeting between Buber and Heidegger, 1957"; available on the web at http://web.nli.org.il/sites/NLI/English/collections/personalsites/Israel-Germany/Division-of-Germany/Pages/Buber-Heidegger.aspx. See also P. Mendes-Flohr's essay "Martin Buber and Martin Heidegger in Dialogue", published in *The Journal of Religion* in 2014, vol. 94(1): 2–25.

For Mitchell's article on Heidegger's "healing", see 'Heidegger's Breakdown: Health and Healing under the care of Dr V.E. von Gebsattel', in *Research in Phenomenology* (2016), vol. 46: 70–97. On Heidegger's collapse and treatment experiences with von Gebsattel, see also Hugo Otto's *Martin Heidegger: A Political Life*, translated by A Blunden. London: Basic Books (1993), pp. 309–351 in particular.

For Lacan's presentation in Barcelona, see "True Psychoanalysis, and False", translated by B. Khiara-Foxton and A. Price, in *Hurly Burly: The International Lacanian Journal of Psychoanalysis*, vol. 11: 15–26. Victor von Gebsattel, Heidegger's analyst, like Boss, knew Freud personally and, according to Maryse Choisy, attended the meeting which Freud and Jung convened in November 1912 at Munich's Park Hotel, where Freud fainted; see M. Choisy's *Sigmund Freud: A New Appraisal*. New York: Citadel Press (1963); p. 111.

32 Richardson's reference is to the *Zollikon Seminars*, a series of meetings and presentations by Heidegger to psychiatrists in Zollikon (Switzerland) which were arranged by Medard Boss between 1959 and 1969. The text and protocols of those meetings appeared in Germany in 1987 under the title *Zollikoner Seminaire, Protokolle – Gesprache – Briefe Herausgegeben von Medard Boss* (Frankfurt am Main: Vittorio Klostermann); an English translation was published, by Northwestern University Press, in 2001.

The Zollikon lectures reveal Heidegger strongly criticizing Freudian metapsychology and Freud's position on causality and conception of the unconscious in particular. Boss himself had argued as early as 1957 (see his book *Psychoanalyse und Daseinsanalytik*) that the *Daseinanalytic* approach to treatment had no use for the unconscious as theorized by Freud.

Heidegger's critique of Freud's conception of causality is, in my view, superficial and ill conceived. On this question, see the piece that Gerben Meyncn and Jacco Verburgt published in 2009: "Psychopathology and Causal Explanation in Practice. A Critical Note on Heidegger's *Zollikon Seminars*", in *Medical Health Care and Philosophy*, vol. 12: 57–66. See also Gérard Granel's essay "Lacan y Heidegger, reflexiones a partir de los Zollikoner Seminar", in *Lacan con los Filósofos*, published by Siglo XXI (1997).

Richardson offered a powerful response to the *daseinanalytic* critique of the Freudian unconscious in light of Lacan in his essay "Heidegger among the Doctors"; see *Reading Heidegger: Commemorations*, edited by John Sallis, Bloomington: Indiana University Press (1983), pp. 49-63. On this subject, see also R. Boothby's "Heideggerian Psychiatry?: The Freudian Unconscious in Medard Boss and Jacques Lacan", in *Journal of Phenomenological Psychology*, 24(2): 144–160 (1993).

For an article which treats Heidegger's critique of Freud in the Zollikon Seminar, see Charles E. Scott's essay "Heidegger and Psychoanalysis: The Seminars in

Zollikon", in *Heidegger Studies*, vol. 6: 131–141 (1990). Scott wrongly suggests that Heidegger's friendship with Boss "lasted for the rest of Heidegger's life" (p. 132). He ends his essay by noting that Heidegger and Boss found Freud's view of man overly "pessimistic", an ironic statement given the Nazi atrocities that took place in Europe during the war.

33 Richardson examined the notion of the unconscious in light of Heidegger in his groundbreaking article: "The Place of the Unconscious in Heidegger", in the *Review of Existential Psychology and Psychiatry*, vol. 5(3): 265–290 (1965). For an essay which treats what Heidegger could have been to Lacan and what Heideggerian philosophy may still offer Lacanianism, see Richardson's "Truth and Freedom in Psychoanalysis", in *Understanding Experience: Psychotherapy and Modernism*, edited by Roger Frie. London: Routledge (2003), pp. 77–99.

In Memory of William J. Richardson, SJ

Notes Toward a Semiotics of Address*

John Muller

I met Bill Richardson in the late summer of 1963. He had just completed his book on Martin Heidegger[1] and was assigned to teach modern philosophy in the Jesuit seminary at Shrub Oak, New York, where I was a Jesuit in training, majoring in philosophy. I was assigned to be his class beadle for the year. As beadle, I made copies of readings, brought them to class, gathered assignments, made announcements, all as needed. It meant I also spent time with Bill, in his office or talking late into the night in one of the cottages on the grounds. He got to know my family members and eventually presided over their funerals. In later years, a small group of a dozen friends who had all left the Jesuits met annually for a day-long cookout. Bill was a faithful member of this group, and we often joked that he would eventually outlive us all and bury us (as he did for four of us).

In time, I completed graduate work in clinical psychology, and Bill, teaching then at Fordham University in New York City, became known to Rollo May and his colleagues engaged in existential psychiatry. Through them he met Otto Will, MD, who had been at Chestnut Lodge (and was analyzed by Harry Stack Sullivan and Frieda Fromm-Reichmann). Otto was then the Medical Director at the Austen Riggs Center, a small, private psychiatric hospital located in the western Massachusetts village of Stockbridge. Otto encouraged Bill to pursue psychoanalytic training at the William Alanson White Institute in New York City and afterwards to come to Riggs as Director of Research. It was in this context that Bill invited me to join him at Riggs. He came in 1974 and I arrived a year later. My job was to treat two patients (meeting four times weekly) and to work half-time with Bill on the texts of Jacques Lacan, whose work Bill had heard of while at Louvain and whose name I had never heard before.

We began to read Lacan together and taught seminars for the fellows and staff at Riggs. In 1978, we went to Paris to attend the *École freudienne*'s Congress on Transmission. While at the welcoming party, we were introduced to Lacan and he graciously invited us to meet with him in his office later in the week. During our meeting, we asked him about his conclusion at the conference, that psychoanalysis was not transmissible. If psychoanalysis was not

* Originally published in *The Letter: Irish Journal for Lacanian Psychoanalysis*. 65 (2017): 27–32.

transmissible, what then, we asked, would be the function of the Écrits and specifically of the Alan Sheridan translation which had appeared in 1977. He responded: '*Pour forcer la transmission,*' gesturing as he spoke by twisting his outstretched hand with thumb and forefinger extended, as if unlocking a door or cutting through a barrier. I shall come back to this.

In 1982, Bill and I published *Lacan and Language: A Reader's Guide to Écrits.*[2] A commentary on Sheridan's translation of a portion of the *Écrits*, we intended it to have a teaching function, with summaries of each of the nine pieces, outlines, notes, etc. This was followed in 1988 by *The Purloined Poe: Lacan, Derrida, and Psychoanalytic Reading.*[3] It included the texts of [Edgar Allan] Poe's short story, *The Purloined Letter*, Lacan's Seminar on *The Purloined Letter*, translated by Jeffrey Mehlman, [Jacques] Derrida's critique of Lacan's Seminar, with excerpts from *The Purveyor of Truth*, translated by Alan Bass, our commentary on Lacan's Seminar, with overview, outline, and notes to the text of Lacan, and more than a dozen commentaries on the texts. This was also intended to be a tool for teachers and students.

In 1986, the Lacanian Clinical Forum began to meet for two weekends each year. It consisted of a group of 25 or so core members, all clinicians, who came together (one weekend at Riggs, one weekend in Québec) to present cases and discuss the relevance of Lacan's ideas to the clinical material. Bill was a founding member. He attended his last meeting in person in 2014, making a two-hour presentation at Riggs, without notes, on Heidegger's notion of truth. He participated briefly by telephone in our 30th anniversary meeting in late October of 2016.

In the spring semester of 2012, Bill and I taught a weekly graduate philosophy course at Boston College [BC], titled 'Addressivity in Freud and Heidegger'. Among other things, we read Freud's case of Katharina, selections from *The Interpretation of Dreams*, and other texts of Freud. We explored how Freud positioned himself to be addressed by his dreams as well as how he used the present tense in addressing his reader. Heidegger's *A Dialogue on Language*[4] showed how we might position ourselves to receive 'the message from the two-fold,' the experience of beings and their Being. This was, I believe, the last course Bill taught at BC, and it was a pleasure to teach with him and to think with him about the question of 'address'. He considered the possibility of address to be fundamental. For example, in a 1992 paper, drawing on Lacan's notion of the Real, he offered the following perspective on religious experience:

My own hypothesis is that the Real, which remains inaccessible to representation of any kind, whether by the language of the Symbolic or the images of the Imaginary, is not absolutely nothing, an inarticulable Void. Nor is it just sheer destructive power like an untamed Moby Dick. The Real is also the still unexplored reaches of science, hidden behind the stars. The Real is the Unknown and Unknowable, the Unimaginable and Ineffable. Why might it not also be the region where we encounter that Mysterious Power that refuses to be named, that we cannot look upon and live, and 'that many call God'? If that were the case, there would be some way to understand why the God of those who believe is so often a 'hidden,' or 'silent,' or 'absent' God, a God that can be affirmed, at base, only by a leap of faith.

I shall not belabor the point, but it seems to me that only if we accept this dimension of the analytic experience can we avoid a sheer reductionism and leave room for the transcendence of God. Whether, and how, such a God might reveal himself/herself to an individual or collectivity is not our business. Our task is to allow it to be possible, and to try to understand how the human psyche responds to such an address with whatever categories we find make most sense.[5]

If we use the categories of the American philosopher Charles Sanders Peirce, we can attempt to make sense of how we are addressed, addressed by signs, especially by the signs we are for one another. Peirce's terms are not Bill's terms, and he (and others) might argue they have little to do with Freud, Lacan, or Heidegger – for Heidegger, at best they may be an ontic classification; and as for Lacan, doesn't he show disdain for the sign versus the signifier? And yet there may be useful links here to be explored as we try to 'make most sense.'

Peirce considered his work to be a phenomenology of experience – his term was 'phaneroscopy', from the Greek root 'to appear'. He had read Kant and Hegel and used a triadic framework based on what he called a 'logic of relations'. His categories were First, Second, and Third. What is First is without boundaries, the undifferentiated, the region of undetermined quality, prior to any subject–object distinction. An example would be the Void of Lucretius. The psychological correlate of Firstness would be unspecified, unthematized consciousness. Second includes any determination of a First; interactions of cause and effect, the 'swerve' in Lucretius that results in the agglomerating collisions of atoms falling in the Void. Thirdness is the realm of law or habit that emerges from the random collisions of force as well as the formulations that allow one to make probabilistic predictions that relate Firsts and Seconds, such as the law of gravity. Feeling is First, the 'outward clash' of forces is Second, and the evolving law is Third.

We are engaged in 'phaneroscopy' through the mediation of signs. A sign is a triadic structure composed of a 'representamen', Peirce's word for the sign-material, the 'stuff' of the sign that catches our attention and stands for something else, its object. The sign is not its object but represents it in some limited respect, which Peirce terms the 'ground' of the representamen. The activity of the sign consists in producing an effect on the sign's receiver. Peirce calls this effect on the receiver the 'interpretant' of the sign. The interpretant brings new knowledge of the sign's object and in turn becomes a new sign producing its own interpretants in an ongoing and largely unconscious process he calls 'semiosis'.

Peirce defines a sign as follows:

A sign, or representamen, is something which stands to somebody for something in some respect or capacity. It addresses somebody, that is, creates in
the mind of that person an equivalent sign, or perhaps a more developed
sign. That sign which it creates I call the interpretant of the first sign. The
sign stands for something, its object. It stands for that object, not in all re-
spects, but in reference to a sort of idea, which I have sometimes called the
ground of the representamen.[6]

Signs address us in different ways. For Peirce, there are three kinds of signs or,
more specifically, sign-activity that serve to 'make sense' of experience by
means of the sign's relationship to its object. Icons are signs that are related to
their objects through resemblance, through a visual or auditory or other sensible quality. A map is an icon, as is a photograph. The second kind of sign is the
index. The index is related to its object through physical contiguity or causality
of fact. Smoke is an index of fire; the pronoun 'I' is an index of the speaker
while speaking. The symbol is the third kind of sign: it stands for its object by
convention, as in language. Words are symbols, as is a nation's flag. Most signs
are an admixture of the three types. A framed photograph hanging on a museum wall is an icon representing its object by resemblance, but it is also an
index of its object by shared spatial-temporal contiguity with the light that fell
on the camera lens, and it is also a symbol, framed and positioned by convention on the museum wall.

The notion of the interpretant is one of Peirce's central contributions, and
in his self-styled 'triadomany', he presents three levels of the interpretant. The
first is the 'feeling interpretant', manifest when the sign produces its effect on
the receiver as an oblique feeling, a mood, or a vague anxiety, without further
elaboration. The second level, the 'dynamic' interpretant, consists of an impulse or an action in response to the sign, an acting-out of the feeling interpretant, or an inner conflict about how to respond to the sign. The 'logical' or
'conceptual' interpretant is the formulation of the sign's meaning and its implications for action, the formulation that joins together the feeling and dynamic
interpretants in a more generalized assertion of what the sign means. The field
of the interpretant is a transitional space, a zone of mediation and translation.
The logical and pragmatic implications of the interpretant constitute its meaning, as manifested in a range of action, from experimental applications in science to moral conduct.

Anything can be an icon of something else – there are numberless ways in
which things resemble each other, most abstractly as 'beings'. But this does not
get us far. Studies of infant development highlight how infants are engaged iconically with their mothers from birth (and even *in utero* through auditory resonance).[7] When mothers and infants engage in mutual gazing games, the facial
features of each have as their effects a replication of the gestures and affect in the

face of the other. These interactions have observable patterns and rules that govern the nature of the interaction, including rules for turn-taking, time outs, and visual-motor coordination. By one month of age, the infant has learned the rules so well that when the mother (in the lab experiments) is asked to keep a still face and not respond to the infant's presentation, the infant appears stunned, makes several more attempts to elicit a response, and then gives up and looks down or away. Mothers reported that it was very difficult to maintain the still-face posture while observing how strenuously the infant worked to address his or her mother and get re-engaged. What we can learn from these studies is the power of the icon to induce its response, to perform its response in the other. Semioticians call this 'enacted iconicity'.[8] Icons induce enactments in dyadic relationships through a kind of emotional contagion or 'coerced mirroring'. Icons generate feeling and dynamic interpretants, largely unconsciously, and bring about the sense that 'we are in this together', even that 'we are the same'. Emotional validation and establishing a common language at the start of treatment rest on the signifying activity of the icon. Iconic displays generate likeness. This has relevance for how patients make the transition from the Real to the Imaginary register. Patients who cannot speak their traumatic experience will show it iconically, through their affective presentation. The analyst's position as addressed in the transference enables him or her to be attuned to the unspoken by means of the feeling interpretants produced by the patient as iconic sign.

The index is a marker of limit, difference, and separation. The index is essential to meaningful discourse, for it defines context through the deictic indicators of 'I-you-here-now'. Psychotic discourse lacks these markers of deixis, making it difficult to establish the proper context for the discourse. The index makes dialogue possible in establishing the boundaries of the field of the utterance, defined by turn-taking. The index makes possible any *après-coup* experience by distinguishing past from present. The index helps to achieve the transition from the Imaginary to the Symbolic register by establishing markers of limit, lack, and facticity.

The symbol generates other symbols; it is the realm of generality, ambiguity, law, and habit. Words evoke unconscious resonances that foster associative processes in an endless production of interpretants. A child named for an ancestor becomes a living sign whose parents become his or her living interpretants in a largely unconscious family dynamic structured by what is said or banished from speech regarding the deceased. The inter-generational transmission of trauma is shaped by such symbolic activity. To make this more concrete, I will now offer a semiotic reading of a published clinical case.

Dr. [Lia] Pistiner de Cortiñas presents the case of a 24-year-old married Argentinean mother, whose father is dead and whose brother is among the disappeared.[9] The case presentation brings for our examination selected elements of the analytic field that demonstrate the early stages of the analytic process. I will examine three such elements: (1) deadness as a living sign, (2) putting on her brother's clothing as a marker, and (3) the spoken word 'cortina', curtain, boundary, limit of safety created by symbols. I will attempt to place these elements in a semiotic framework that supports and grounds the analytic field and also offers us a semiotic line of development that goes from icon to index to symbol.

In Dr. Pistiner's case, the icon works on us by coercive mirroring. She indicates such iconic mirroring when she describes the early stage of the analysis: 'In the analytic relationship I was alerted by my lack of interest in the patient and because if I allowed myself to be taken in by the atmosphere of the session, I was also dragged into 'falling asleep'.' In the transference, she notes a silent absence and lack of vitality. The patient 'had no energy, did not laugh, never smiled, nor did she cry or get angry', nor did she have dreams or fantasies. The patient's deadness is a sign whose object is her mother's deadness and whose interpretant is the analyst's affective response.

The analyst's feeling of deadness corresponds to what the patient is showing. The patient is unable to verbally represent her experience, so she shows it. It is not a representation but a presentation – some would call it an enactment – of her experience as lifeless. Positioned in the transference, the analyst lives her response to this showing: 'In the transference I was a deaf mother who didn't have a mental space for her. When I realised that and could make an interpretation, Ana associated that her mother wanted to abort her'. The patient's showing is producing a transferential iconic effect which the analyst takes: she takes her own experience as a sign of what the patient is showing. Such iconic effects are among the earliest modes of infant–mother communication in what is called primary intersubjectivity. Dr. Pistiner notes that at the beginning such communicational forms are not verbal and that 'Ana's expressions were concrete and imitative.' We see here how iconic signs produce states of relatedness based on similarity.

The next stage introduces the complexity of contiguity and separation by means of the index, a type of sign related to its object not by resemblance but by contiguity in space or time. The patient says: 'In Cañada [in her mother's home] I like to search in the closets' and she takes things 'such as the jacket of her dead brother she wears today.' The jacket of her brother has a history of being contiguously related to his body; it is an index of his body. She wears the jacket: it provides contact with the place of his body, just as she provides embodiment once more for his jacket. The jacket both joins her to him and marks her as separate from him who is not there. The patient has here opened the arena of substitution and displacement, where something can stand for something else, but it is still in the arena of external enactment, of external placement.

Now at this moment, the analyst performs what I think is the crucial intervention – demonstrating the As-structure of the sign. An object or image or word must be taken as a sign of something else for it to serve as a usable sign. The traditional definition of a sign is *Aliquid stat pro aliquo*, something stands for something else. She asks the patient: 'What are you searching for in Cañada's closets? Perhaps a part of Ana, perhaps understanding the relationship with your father, perhaps understanding what happened to your brother?' She gives to the patient these alternative meanings of 'searching' for what is lacking in her by opening up the As-structure of her behavior as a sign of lack and thereby turning her focus inward. The patient hears this in silence, she breathes heavily and she seems tired, and she says:

Friday I had a dream. When I woke up I remembered it and then I forgot it. Sometimes I even don't remember that I dreamed. There was that image of a woman that I knew, then it erased and I didn't know who she was and that woman spoke of something that had disappeared ... (silence) sometimes I think of my brother. I know he is dead, but sometimes I think he will come, that he could be alive ...

This first dream, offered at this very point, confirms the analyst in her effort to show the As-structure of the sign in moving toward symbolization:

Perhaps in those closets you were looking for things that seem to disappear from your mind [like your dreams] ... You are also afraid of the things that can appear in your mind, as your brother. Is he alive or dead? Perhaps I am the woman of your dream that speaks about something that disappeared. But remembering your dream means also that you are beginning to have a place inside, as a closet, where to keep your thoughts, your dreams.

We now have a triad: the subject Ana, the object in the closet, and the object as a sign of a lost part of herself. The closet too is now a sign of her mind as container, a sign of psychic space, of semiotic space, providing differentiation and integration of previously unrelated segments of experience. Without such semiotic or psychic space, 'Ana seems not to be able to differentiate mental problems from body problems, head, hands, back and sex all seem to be the same.'

Differentiated sign function and activity are demonstrated in the symptom of the patient's inflamed hand, where we go from iconic showing to indexical marking to symbolic translation, through the word 'cortina,' 'curtain.' For Peirce, again, words are symbols, and a symbol is the third type of sign that is related to its object not by resemblance, like an icon, nor by contiguity, like an index, but by convention or code, as in the case of words and language. Dr. Pistiner writes:

In her first year of analysis a symptom appeared: her right hand was inflamed, the cracked skin was open, it burned, etc. No medical consultation could give a diagnosis. Ana evoked the sexual relationships of her parents; these experiences overflowed her, since there was no 'door' that separated her from those exciting and frightening stimuli. She remembered a compulsive masturbation without pleasure, which she could not stop, as the only means of 'calming down'. We could link the symptom of the hand with an excess of stimuli that overwhelmed her, now represented by that memory of the sexuality 'doors' of her parents. The patient then said, 'Without at least a curtain',' and this 'was her way of bringing to the transference that excess of stimuli related to the analyst's without name: Cortiñas.

We have here an example of how the symptom joins in the conversation through a progression from the hand as icon, showing inflammation and painful swollen arousal, to the hand as index contiguously marking the site of masturbation, to the need for a curtain as a symbol to establish a boundary and contain painful arousal.

By saying 'without at least a curtain,' the patient is naming its absence as well as naming her desire for the container she lacked. [Wilfred] Bion wrote: 'The thought owes its genesis to the absence of the object'.[10] The word, Lacan tells us, is a presence made of absence: in an iconic sign, the object is present through a shared qualitative resemblance; in the index, the object was co-present by contiguity. But with the symbol no material or existential conjunction with its object is required. In fact, the material link must be negated so that the symbol, Bion's No-thing, can be grounded not in a material relation to the object but rather in a network of mutual desires so that their signifiers, freed from iconic or indexical anchoring, can circulate unconsciously in a network of associations that operate in dreaming. Words then become symbols of great power, ambiguity, complexity, and resonance. Spoken words produce interpretants that consist of other words, unexpected ones, based on unconscious associations. 'Cortina' is such a rich symbol, for it is also an icon of the analyst's name and, as such, also an index marking the identity of the analyst. As a growing symbol, 'cortina' articulates the developing container function by performing it, by creating a new interpretant space. 'Cortina' is not simply a description of a boundary, it performs the boundary by establishing distinctions and gathering to itself a wide range of associations produced unconsciously in the semiotic space of the analytic field. As a result, Ana could now go on to unconsciously use her hand as a symbol, in a parapraxis: she had intended to say, referring to her husband, 'I wanted to speak to him about my hand,' but instead she said, 'I wanted to speak of him with my hand.'

Peirce makes one more important triadic distinction about the interpretant, the third aspect of the sign, the effect produced by the sign in the sign's receiver. This is the new transitional space opened up by the work of the sign, the space for semiosis, what Bion calls 'transformations'.[11] This is what facilitates the analytic process. The first level of the interpretant, as we saw earlier, is what Peirce calls the feeling interpretant. The sign produces an affective state, especially when it is received unconsciously and we have not yet located the sign. We learn as analysts to take seriously these subtle shifts in affective states as a reflection of what the patient is showing us. So, in the case presentation, the analyst reports feeling initially shut down. This deadness is the feeling interpretant of something the patient is showing. The second level of the interpretant is what Peirce calls the dynamic interpretant, and it consists of an impulse or action in response to the sign and the feeling produced by it. The analyst, feeling deadness, experiences a loss of interest in the patient, a distaste to be with her, perhaps an impulse to get away. We are all familiar with this state as we enact the patient's presentation in a painful iconic mirroring. In addition to the feeling and dynamic interpretant, the third level of the interpretant is the conceptual or logical interpretant, disclosing the meaning of the sign. This is the verbal interpretation that links the feeling and the impulse to the sign producing them, in this case the patient as 'disappeared', the patient as living the disappearance of her brother and I think also the emotional disappearance of her mother. But the analyst is likewise living in the transference the interpretation of this disappearance, and we can here see the analyst as the living interpretant of the patient as sign. We live responses to one another before we can make distinctions between feeling and thinking, between types of signs and interpretants. We live and show to one another the sign's impact before we can verbalize and conceptualize the sign's meaning. But what makes us analysts is that we do not simply react, we live our response to the other as sign. We take what is before us and in us as signs; this is our training and our ethical responsibility. Peirce calls this sign activity semiosis: in semiosis, signs operate largely unconsciously to produce interpretants which become new signs producing their interpretants in an endless process.

To summarize briefly, the analytic treatment of this traumatized patient demonstrates the gradual evolution of symbolization. Initially, the patient is caught in the family trauma, living it in an unmediated way, not representing it but rather presenting it to the analyst. The analyst takes the patient's presentation as a sign, allowing it to produce its iconic effects in the analyst. The patient shows to the analyst who has positioned herself in the analytic field, in the transference, to properly take what is shown as a sign of something else – eventually as an iconic sign of the traumatic content (deadness, disappeared, lost brother), or a symbol in the process of being formed, as curtain/boundary/container and safety in space provided by the analyst in the semiotic process.

So how does any of this relate to Heidegger? As I understand it, the early Heidegger offers a phenomenological analysis of how we position ourselves to address beings and their Being, and the later Heidegger presents how Being addresses us.

We can take note of some points of contact between the language of Heidegger and that of Peirce. When Heidegger examines how *Dasein* is 'in' the world, he writes of *Befindlichkeit*, *Dasein's* ontological feature of mood, 'disposition', or attunement, which resonates with Peirce's reference to 'feeling' as a Firstness (and to the field of iconic enactment). When Heidegger emphasizes *Dasein's* ontological 'thrownness', facticity, and spatial-temporal determination, we are in Peirce's Secondness (and the functions of the index). When Heidegger writes of the ontological feature of *Rede* as discourse, language, and logos, we are dealing with Thirdness and the foundations for Peirce's idea of symbol. The icon as conveying qualitative feeling, the index as representing brute fact, and the symbol as inclusive of language and discourse are the ontic vehicles for making sense of experience semiotically.

The index marks facticity. In *Ontology: The Hermeneutics of Facticity*,[12] a lecture course from 1923, Heidegger addresses the conditions for 'gaining access to *factical life*',[13] for 'facticity *is* what is primordial'. We are always in a context of spatiality and temporality as *this* being living at this time: 'Life is concerned about itself and attends to itself and all the while... since care has in each particular case a language ... addresses itself in a worldly manner'.[14] 'Worldly' here means already engaged in the significant network of relationships constituting the world *Dasein* is 'in'. And furthermore: 'The world can be encountered as something distressing only insofar as it is a world which is of significance to us'.[15] And so: 'Something signifies something: lifts it up into a definite context of reference, defines itself from out of beings, it is there'.[16] What is at stake here is how to properly delineate the 'significance' of being-in the world as the ontological basis for a semiotics of experience: 'The character of the being-there of this world can be terminologically designated as "significance." "Significant" means being, being there, in the mode of a signifying which is being encountered in a definite manner. This expression does not refer to a being-which-is-there which, in addition to being there, also signifies something – what constitutes its being is rather precisely its signifying which is being encountered in a definite manner'.[17] My reading: things, people, events in the world are in a signifying manner, and this enables them to ontically address us as signs. We are thereby enabled to take them as signs. Our facticity is mine/ours through and as significance, in semiosis. We are in history semiotically.

A Dialogue on Language develops the notion of appearance as an appearing – as 'the reality of presence in its essential origin': 'For in the source of appearance, something comes toward man that holds the two-fold of presence [Being?] and present beings'.[18] I take the two-fold to mean the ontic/ontological difference, the difference between beings and the Being of beings, precisely that which is not a being. This is what is coming toward us, addressing us. The dialogue continues between the Japanese philosopher ('J') and Heidegger ('I'):

J: That two-fold has already offered itself to man, although its nature remains veiled.

I: Man, to the extent he is man, listens to this message.

J: And that happens even when man gives no particular attention to the fact that he is ever listening already to that message....

I: Man is used for hearing the message ...

J: This message makes the claim on man that he respond to it ...

I: Man is the message-bearer of the message which the two-fold's unconcealment speaks to him ... Then, man, as the message-bearer of the message of the two-fold's unconcealment, would also be he who walks the boundary of the boundless.

J: And on this path he seeks the boundary's mystery ...

I: ....Which cannot be hidden in anything other than the voice that determines and tunes his nature.[19]

This voice resonates in silence.

In Lacanian terms, the notion of address is tied up with the desire of the Other, the unconscious as the Discourse of the Other, as '*Kern unseres Wesens*', 'the kernel of our being', whose utterances in dreams and parapraxes address us enigmatically, provoking the question, 'What does the Other want from me?' This is the basic question our symptoms come to answer. But the question of desire emerges most in the transference, and Lacan uses 'the semiotic triangle' of Peirce to offer some perspective on this. In the Seminars, there are more than a dozen references to Peirce. In his Seminar *Ou Pire*,[20] the session of June 21, 1972, presents a standing right-angle triangle as a schema to indicate the transference. At the bottom is the object, with a straight line going up to the right-angle corner where the analyst is situated as 'representamen'; a line from the analyst extends to the third corner, marked as the 'interpretant', and from there dotted lines go down to the object, but there are several such dotted lines, ever-extending out the line from the analyst to the interpretant. In this diagram, the analyst is the sign of an object that is always being further specified by the analysand who is the interpretant. Lacan states, '*L'analysand, c'est l'interpretant*' – a living interpretant, we can say, of the analyst as sign of an obscure object in the transference: 'it is the couple *representamen-object* which has always to be reinterpreted, this is what is at stake in analysis. The interpretant is the analysand.'

By positioning the analysand as the interpretant (the living Interpretant, I would say), Lacan offers a suggestion about the process of transmission in psychoanalysis. In his 'Conclusions' to the Congress, Lacan stated: 'So now I have come to the idea that psychoanalysis is intransmissible. It's quite annoying. It's quite annoying that each psychoanalyst is forced – since it is necessary that he be forced – to reinvent psychoanalysis.'[21] I do not think Lacan meant that psychoanalysis is a lost process, needing to be re-discovered or re-born from dead. I think we can make sense of his conclusions by considering the living interpretant as the vehicle of transmission. The process of transmission requires that re-invention take place by the analysand in analysis as the living interpretant of the analytic work, embodying the split subject and the known illusion of the *sujet-supposè-savoir*.

I think we can call Bill a living interpretant for us of how being a teacher means being accessible to the address, responding with one's own lack to the address of the text and the address of students as well as to the address of the Mystery. In a series of videos titled "Our dinner with Bill",[22] Tom Sheehan, Professor of Religious Studies at Stanford University and a former student of Bill's, together with two of Bill's colleagues at Boston College (Richard Kearney and Jeffrey Bloechl), speak with Bill about his life and work. Bill concludes one episode in which he was asked, 'and what do you do yourself, Bill?' by responding, 'I teach'. Later in the video, Tom Sheehan says we are all Bill's students. In his funeral homily for Bill, Leo O'Donovan too said: 'For aren't all of us here really his students?'[23]

Leo O'Donovan, SJ, the former president of Georgetown University and currently director of the Jesuit Refugee Service, was asked by Bill to officiate at his funeral mass. In his homily ('Making Sense'), he spoke of Bill's faith: 'His faith was fierce, wrested from the absurdity of life and won, through grace, again and again.'[24] This fierce faith was in the Word, addressing Bill, and Bill's response was to give his word, to live his commitment to and in faith – as a teacher, a living interpretant of the Word as sign of Mystery. Addressed by the Real as Mystery ('the boundless'), Bill responded with a leap of faith to address the Word. In Peirce's categories, the Father is First, the Son is Second, the Spirit is Third.[25] We can take this further and suggest that the Son, the Word, is Sign of the Father ('Philip – he who has seen Me has seen the Father' – John 14, 9). The Word as Sign does not represent an object, however, but rather a non-object that is Mystery, the Father as 'the Unknown and Unknowable, the Unimaginable and Ineffable'. The Interpretant of the Word is the Spirit as the evolving meaning (for us in time) of the Word as Sign. The Spirit as interpretant brings new knowledge of the Sign's non-object – or rather, of the relation between the Word as Sign and its non-object, the Father. We can speculate about grace in this framework as the Spirit operating in the interpretant field, producing effects in the Sign's receiver, always becoming new signs. Interpretants become new signs in the receiver: Bill as teacher produces new effects in us, his students, and we in turn become new signs as living interpretants of Bill's life as sign, a life lived walking the boundary of the boundless.

Notes

1 Richardson, W. *Heidegger: Through Phenomenology to Thought*. Preface by Martin Heidegger. The Hague: M. Nijhoff. 1963.
2 Muller, J. & Richardson, W. *Lacan and Language: A Reader's Guide to Écrits*. New York: International Universities Press, 1982.
3 Muller & Richardson, W. (Eds.) *The Purloined Poe: Lacan, Derrida, and Psychoanalytic Reading*. Baltimore: The Johns Hopkins University Press, 1988.
4 Heidegger, M. 'A Dialogue on Language.' In *On the Way to Language*. Tr. P. Hertz. Harper: San Francisco. 1–54 (originally published 1959). 1982.
5 Richardson, W. 'Love and the Beginning: Psychoanalysis and Religion.' in *Contemporary Psychoanalysis*, 1992. pp. 28–43.
6 Peirce, C. *Philosophical Writings of Peirce*. Ed. Buchler, J. New York: Dover. 1955. p. 99.
7 Muller, J. *Beyond the Psychoanalytic Dyad: Developmental Semiotics in Freud, Peirce, and Lacan*. New York: Routledge. 1996.
8 Johansen, J. *Dialogic Semiosis: An Essay on Signs and Meaning*. Bloomington: Indiana University Press. 1993.
9 Pistiner de Cortiñas, L. *Transformations of emotional experience*. In *International Journal of Psychoanalysis*, 94 (1994): 531–544.

10 Bion, W. (1997). *Taming Wild Thoughts*. F. Bion, Ed. London: Jason Aronson. p. 18.

11 Muller, J. 'Approaches to the Semiotics of Thought and Feeling.' in Bion's work. *Canadian Journal of Psychoanalysis/Revue canadienne de psychanalyse*. 13 (2005): 31–56.

12 Heidegger, M. *Ontology – The Hermeneutics of Facticity*. (1923) Tr. Van Buren, J. Bloomington: Indiana University Press, 2008.

13 ibid, p. 83.

14 ibid, p. 70.

15 ibid, p. 80.

16 ibid, p. 87.

17 ibid, p. 74.

18 ibid, p. 40.

19 ibid, pp. 40–41.

20 Lacan, J. (1972). *Le Seminaire: Ou pire*. Unpublished Manuscript.

21 Lacan, J. (1979). 'Conclusions'. In *Lettres de l'École. IXe Congr's de l'École freudienne*. Paris. Du 6 Au 9 Juillet 1978. Volume I, 25 (II). p. 219. *Bulletin intérieur de l'École freudienne de Paris*. (my translation).

22 Boston College Archives (2009). 'Our Dinner with Bill'.

23 O'Donovan, L. 'Making Sense'. In Babich B., ed., *William J. Richardson, S.J.: Reflections in Memoriam*. 51st meeting of the Heidegger Circle, 30 March–2 April, 2017. p. 1.

24 ibid. p. 1.

25 Brent, J. *Charles Sanders Peirce: A Life*. Bloomington: Indiana University Press. 1993. p. 332.

Index